WARRING

VISIONS

WARRING VISIONS

PHOTOGRAPHY AND VIETNAM

THY PHU

Duke University Press
Durham and London   2022

Designed by Courtney Leigh Richardson
Typeset in Minion Pro by Copperline Book Services

Library of Congress Cataloging-in-Publication Data
Names: Phu, Thy, [date] author.
Title: Warring visions: photography and Vietnam / Thy Phu.
Description: Durham: Duke University Press, 2021. | Includes
bibliographical references and index.
Identifiers: LCCN 2021011955 (print)
LCCN 2021011956 (ebook)
ISBN 9781478010364 (hardcover)
ISBN 9781478010753 (paperback)
ISBN 9781478012917 (ebook)
Subjects: LCSH: War photography—Vietnam. | Documentary
photography—Vietnam. | Vietnam War, 1961-1975—Photography. |
Vietnamese—Attitudes. | Vietnamese diaspora. |
BISAC: PHOTOGRAPHY / Criticism | HISTORY / Asia / Southeast Asia
Classification: LCC TR820.6. P496 2021 (print) | LCC TR820.6 (ebook) |
DDC 779/.909597—dc23
LC record available at https://lccn.loc.gov/2021011955
LC ebook record available at https://lccn.loc.gov/2021011956

Cover art: Courtesy *Vietnam Pictorial.*

I once believed that writing was a lonely, solitary exercise. Writing this book taught me otherwise. For years, I've been inspired, moved, and lifted by the support of friends, mentors, and colleagues. I learned from a special group of friends how to write not just more but also better. For their generosity and unwavering belief in this book and in me, I thank Elizabeth Abel, Sara Blair, Thuy Vo Dang, Deepali Dewan, Erina Duganne, Lan Duong, Nicole Fleetwood, Tak Fujitane, Evyn Lê Espiritu Ghandi, Steven Gin, Jamie Maxtone-Graham, Marianne Hirsch, Dinh Q. Lê, Anthony Lee, Joanne Leow, Ann Marie Leshkowich, Cheryl Neruse, Viet Thanh Nguyen, Doug Niven, Franny Nudelman, Marc Opper, Sarah Parsons, Minh-ha T. Pham, Leigh Raiford, Susan Reid, Sue Schweik, Christina Schwenkel, Sharon Sliwinski, Shawn Michelle Smith, and Alan and Felicity Somerset. I also thank Karen Strassler, Madeleine Thien, S. Trimble, Y-Dang Troeung, Linda Trinh Vo, Laura Wexler, Kelly Wood, Sunny Xiang, Lisa Yoneyama, and Donya Ziaee. In recent years, I have relished the pleasures of writing retreats, walks in the country, and the comfort and warmth of conversation over multicourse meals. In these quiet, soul-sustaining adventures, I have been fortunate to deepen my friendships with Nadine Attewell, Ju Hui Judy Chun, Jennifer Chan, Richard Fung, Tim McCaskell, Malissa Phung, Vinh Nguyen, and Gökbörü Sarp Tanyildiz. Although some habits are hard to shake, I credit the wisdom imparted by the writing workshop coordinated by Eva-Lynn Jagoe and Elspeth Brown with helping me see the form and structure, heart and soul of this book more clearly. My thanks to Diệp Lê, Chau Doan, and Triet Minh Lê, who made me feel at home every time I came to Vietnam and patiently answered my questions, no matter how naive or obvious.

I was able to develop and complete this project because of the support of the Social Sciences and Humanities Research Council of Canada and of Western University, which has provided a wonderfully enriching institutional home for me and where I've benefited from the encouragement of friends, including Nandi Bhatia, Manina Jones, and Jan Plug, and from the resources provided by the Research office. This project also benefited from the assistance and encouragement of graduate students, including Chinelo Ifeyinwa Ezenwa, Julia Huynh, Maral Moradipour, and Zeinab Mcheimech, from whom I learned so much over the years. Archivists at the Associated Press, Swarthmore College, the Hoover Institution, and the Vietnam Center and Archive at Texas Tech University were enormously helpful in providing guidance to their special collections. I was fortunate to share some of my research at institutions including Yale University, where I held a position as visiting associate professor in 2016-17, and the Asia Research Institute at the National University of Singapore, where I spent three wonderful months as senior research fellow. I also presented talks at the University of Tennessee at Knoxville, Mount Holyoke College, the University of Michigan, the University of Toronto, Concordia University, Dartmouth College, Rutgers University/the New York Public Library, the University of Wisconsin at Milwaukee, Colby College, Monash University, Prato Centre, China Academy of Art, Hangzhou, Princeton University, and the University of the Western Cape. For so warmly welcoming me to their intellectual communities, I thank my gracious hosts, including Paul Barrett, Kimberly Juanita Brown, Tina Campt, Gao Chu, Steven Chung, Iyko Day, Kyle Frisina, Richard Grusin, Yi Gu, Patricia Hayes, Eric Harms, Chua Beng Huat, Erin Huang, Jonathan Long, Dan Magilow, Melissa Miles, Joshua Miller, Margaret Noodin, Franz Pritchard, Maureen Ryan, Tanya Sheehan, Lisa Steele, Kim Tomsczak, Ed Welch, and Andrés Mario Zervigón.

I am grateful to my editor, Ken Wissoker, and to my anonymous readers for helping me shape the book more clearly. I thank my brother and parents for sharing their stories and for being part of this project. Any inaccuracies or distortions are, needless to say, mine. My dearest friends, Donald C. Goellnicht and Andrea Noble, always stood by me, lending strength when I needed it most. Their sudden and untimely deaths left me unmoored, but I take comfort in knowing they are still with me in the work they inspired, in the person they helped me become, in the light they shone my way. Not least, I thank Michael, my best friend and partner, for being by my side from first to last.

Because Vietnamese is a tonal language, I have written out names and quotations using diacritics unless they were omitted in original source documents. According to Vietnamese conventions, proper names begin with the surname followed by middle and given names. However, diasporic Vietnamese often adopt Euro-American naming conventions that reverse this order. Instead of imposing a single convention, here, I respect subjects' own naming preferences.

Saigon, April 30, 1975. The last helicopter skitters atop a roof near the American embassy, while below communist tanks advance in slow, inexorable triumph. Press photographers rush forward to capture South Vietnam's chaotic end: desperate mothers, wailing babies, and churning blades. This is what most people see, what they recall, of the day that Saigon fell.

This is what I see: a bus lurching from Sadec, a small town in the Mekong Delta, to Saigon. My mother cradles me with one arm; with the other, she clasps our ticket out. We pitch forward, our driver dodging cracks and craters on a thinning strip of highway until the bus shudders and stills; the road has ended.

We stay behind until another path opens, this time across the high seas, among millions of overseas Vietnamese, refugees, who scatter to the United States, Canada, Australia, and beyond. We leave villages and loved ones, carry what we can, and toss everything else: ornaments useless in lean times, uniforms of a defeated army, photographs betraying doomed allegiances. Wherever we settle, some of us start again; some of us hold losses close to heart; some of us make new images, perhaps to replace those we lost, perhaps to counter the many others that circulate in their stead.

Look here. In 1963 the monk Thích Quang Đức burns, his body shrouded in a horror of licking flame and rising smoke (figure I.1). In 1968 General Nguyễn Ngọc Loan executes Nguyễn Văn Lém, his revolver aimed point-blank at his prisoner's head (figure I.2). In 1972 ten-year-old Phan Thị Kim Phúc flees a napalm attack, her mouth agape in anguish, her burned clothes torn from her body (figure I.3).

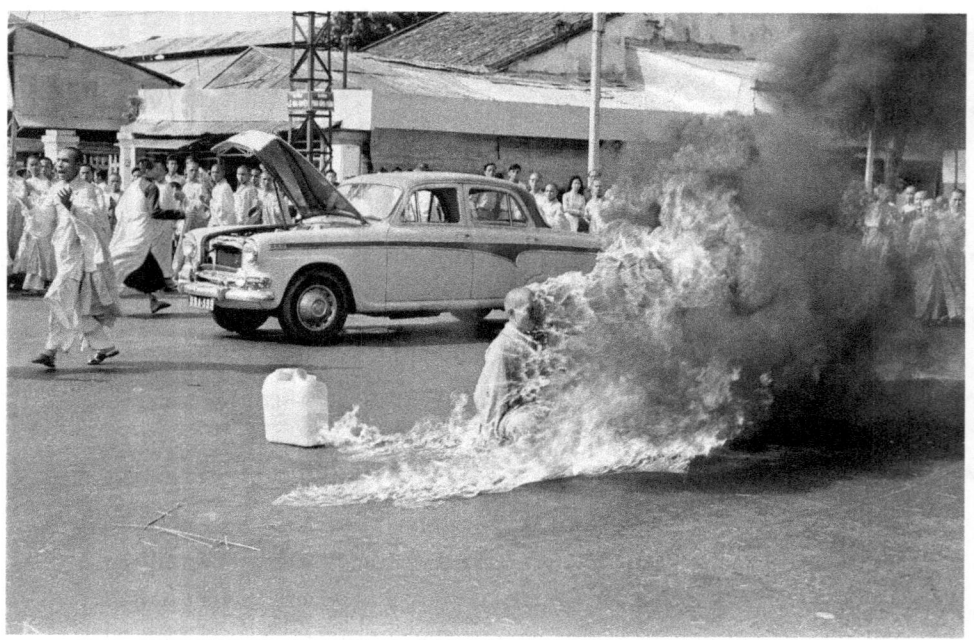

FIGURE I.1 *Vietnam Monk Protest.* The flaming body of a Buddhist monk, the Reverend Thich Quang Duc, is shown as it fell over on the pavement of a main intersection in Saigon, June 11, 1963. The elderly monk set fire to his clothing and burned himself to death in protest of alleged government persecution of Buddhists. Other monks kneel with hands clasped in prayer. Photographer: Malcolm Browne.

Chances are, most viewers of a certain generation do not need a reproduction to see these images; they are so well-known that media critic Sylvia Shin Huey Chong refers to them as the "Vietnam triptych."[1] These three photographs won prestigious awards, including Pulitzer and World Press Photo prizes, and their respective photographers—Malcolm Browne, Eddie Adams, and Công Hùynh Út (who goes by Nick Ut)—catapulted to fame. The photographs are instantly recognized, endlessly reproduced, and tirelessly celebrated by critics for exposing the brutality and injustice of the war in Vietnam. Viewers praise them as icons that transcend this particular conflict to symbolize the atrocity of war in general.

In contrast, picture this: in August 1968, a radiant bride poses in the foreground on a street just outside Saigon while in the background stacked sandbags are sobering signs of the third phase of the ongoing Tet Offensive. (Although I do not reproduce this image for reasons that will become clear shortly, its absence aptly conveys the significance of a broader absence of similar photos from narratives of the war.) In that same year two villagers

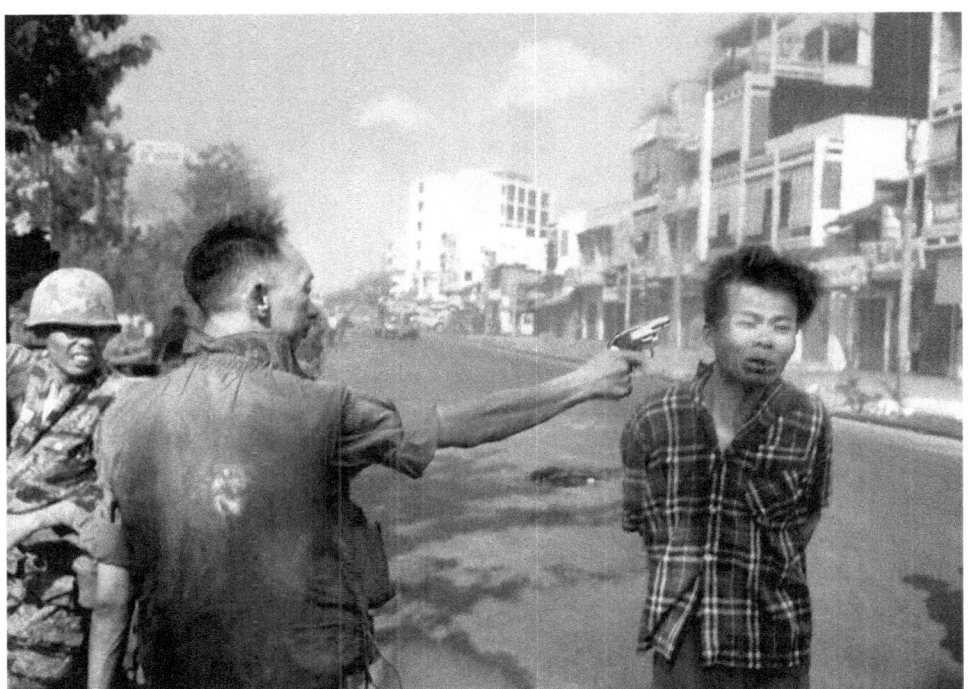

FIGURE 1.2 Vietnam War Saigon execution. South Vietnamese General Nguyen Ngoc Loan, chief of the National Police, fires his pistol into the head of suspected Viet Cong officer Nguyen Van Lem (also known as Bay Lop) on a Saigon street, February 1, 1968, early in the Tet Offensive. Photographer: Eddie Adams.

ferry their boats across the Perfume River in Huế, a picturesque and serene landscape disturbed only by the ripples they make with their paddles. On a beach somewhere in Vietnam, a woman looks through the lens of her camera, seemingly oblivious to her male admirers, the glow of their youthful bodies accentuated with the brush that tints the photograph with vibrant colors.

If these last three images are hard to picture, it is probably because they look unlike those that usually illustrate the war in Vietnam or that exemplify contemporary war photography more generally. A cursory survey reveals contemporary war photography's obsession with battlefield spectacles, its concern with exposing brutality in unflinching close-ups. No surprise, then, that the triptych, which contains the war's most recognizable icons, should be acclaimed. In contrast, the latter images linger in the quietude of daily survival, their ordinariness far removed from war photography's trademark idiom of destroyed bodies and pockmarked landscapes, not to mention

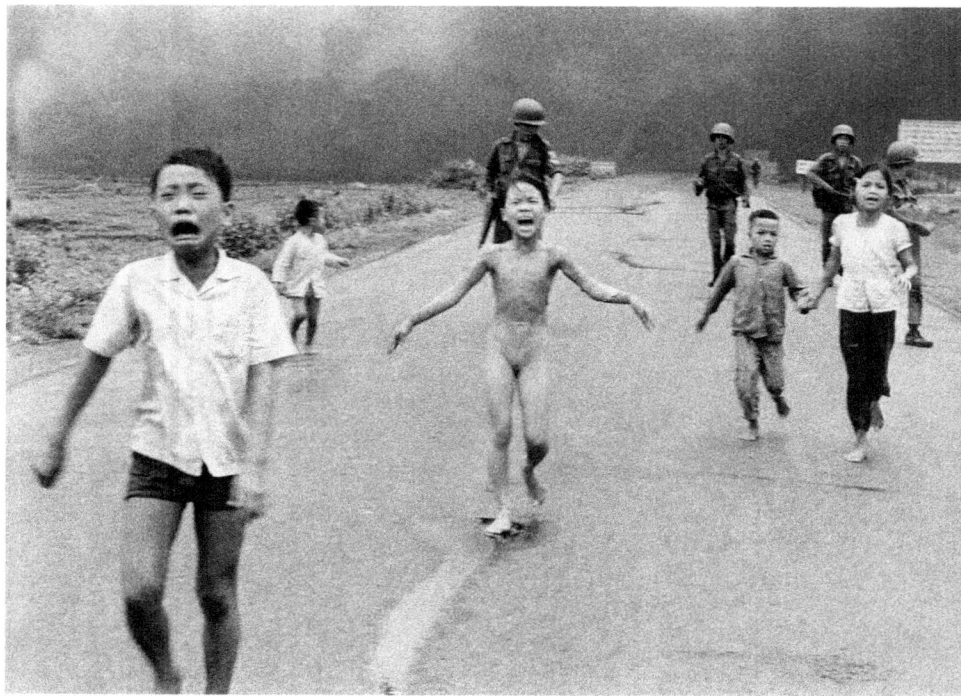

FIGURE I.3 *The Terror of War* (also known as *Napalm Girl*). South Vietnamese forces follow after terrified children, including nine-year-old Kim Phuc, center, as they run down Route 1 near Trang Bang after an aerial napalm attack on suspected Viet Cong hiding places on June 8, 1972. A South Vietnamese plane accidentally dropped its flaming napalm on South Vietnamese troops and civilians. The terrified girl had ripped off her burning clothes while fleeing. The children from left to right are Phan Thanh Tam, younger brother of Kim Phuc, who lost an eye; Phan Thanh Phouc, youngest brother of Kim Phuc; Kim Phuc; and Kim's cousins Ho Van Bon and Ho Thi Ting. Behind them are soldiers of the Vietnam Army 25th Division. 1972. Nick Ut/Associated Press.

its fascination with struggle, pain, sacrifice, and sublime violence. Yet to me they are war photographs even though at first glance they exemplify different genres altogether, such as the quotidian rites of family photography, the sentimentality of landscape, and the glossy slickness of tourism.

As a Vietnamese-born child newly arrived in Toronto in the 1980s, I wrestled with this visual idiom of spectacular violence, its jagged outlines as cutting as the foreign sound of English, which I struggled to learn at the same time. Neither lesson—of English or of seeing Vietnam the way that everyone else appeared to do—was easy. I failed my first test in kindergarten, finding it impossible to match colors to words when I could not grasp the meaning of these words. Similarly, I tried to reconcile my fading memories of Vietnam with documentaries that then played on public television, a seemingly cease-less loop of death and devastation. Although my brother and I were young, even we noticed the repetitious themes: an explosion here, an injury there, death everywhere. We were riveted and repulsed. They were titled *Vietnam: A Television History* and *Vietnam: The Ten Thousand Day War*, the latter directed by Michael Maclear, who was the only North American journalist in North Vietnam when Hô Chí Minh died in 1969.[2] But both might as well have been called "The Never-Ending War," so often did they air and so interminable was their depiction of carnage, or so it struck me then. With its sensational bursts—spectacles forever paused and fixed as still images in my mind's eye—these documentaries first introduced me to Vietnam-as-war. Presented in this way, Vietnam was above all else a war. For Americans, this was a war they entered ostensibly to contain the threat of communism from spreading throughout Southeast Asia, one that four presidents, including Dwight D. Eisenhower, John F. Kennedy, Lyndon B. Johnson, and Richard Nixon, continued despite increasingly vehement public opposition and diminishing hope of success. For Americans, this was a war that continues to haunt the national psyche with the ignominy of defeat. But there was little in this metanarrative that resembled what my family recognized and held close: a country, a home, memories. To be sure, my family's perspectives were bound in many ways to this war and its legacies. But our experiences are not defined exclusively in terms of war, even as they could not be wholly disentangled from war, and certainly not in the way that played before our eyes

Yet these documentaries may as well have been any number of films or books that drew from the same visual idiom and that have appeared in the years since the end of this war. Whether I liked it or not, the idiom I learned—now more familiar and vivid than the fog of my early memories—taught me to look at Vietnam as most of the world did. However, I knew, as do so many Vietnamese, whether in Vietnam or overseas, that there was more to see.

PHOTOGRAPHER JORGE LEWINSKI once marveled wistfully that "so far as photographic coverage is concerned, there never was, and probably will never be, another war like Vietnam. . . . Vietnam was a big production number, a big sell."[2] He was not alone in avowing what is now an article of faith: the war in Vietnam—one of the most visible of the twentieth century's many wars—marked a watershed in visual history, at least as told by Euro-American scholars.

Critics often attribute this distinction to the role that the war between Vietnam and the United States (1955-75) played in transforming moving and still pictures, print and television industries alike. The US involvement in Vietnam began in a limited and unofficial capacity after World War II, with its support of the French effort to regain control of its Indochina colony after the Japanese had been driven out. Although the Viet Minh appealed to the United States to support its cause of independence, one that its leader Hồ Chí Minh explicitly linked to core republican principles of life, liberty, and the pursuit of happiness, its efforts were fruitless because Americans, notwithstanding their disdain of colonialism, supported the French. After the defeat of the French in 1954 by communist patriots, the Geneva Accords split the nation into North and South Vietnam as a temporary measure, with the promise that democratic elections would take place by 1956 and the assurance of peace, self-governance, independence, and reunification. However, the United States began to intervene more directly under the administrations of Dwight D. Eisenhower and John F. Kennedy by backing its own anticommunist pick, Ngô Đinh Diem, as head of South Vietnam; by actively contravening the terms of the Geneva Accords; and by dispatching military advisors to ward off the threat posed by North Vietnam. Although war was never formally declared, tensions escalated with President Lyndon B. Johnson's decision to dispatch ground troops in 1965. Not until 1972, when Richard Nixon signed the Paris Peace Accords, an agreement meant to end the war officially, did American ground troops withdraw. However, this withdrawal served as a pretext for the continued US aerial bombardment of North Vietnam. Not until 1975 did the war in fact end for the Vietnamese.[4]

This war was also important because it was the first to be televised daily, for although US networks sporadically covered the 1950-53 war in Korea, television came of age in Vietnam during the years of American military influence, when newly standardized thirty-minute programs beamed images of faraway violence home to viewers in the United States as they sat eating their suppers.[5] Whereas in 1950, only 9 percent of American households owned television sets, by 1960, that number swelled to 90 percent. By 1968, well into the period of American military escalation in Vietnam, 56.6 million American households owned television sets. Michael J. Arlen stressed the intimacy of this form of transmission when he called the conflict "the living-room war."[6] Moreover, events in Vietnam attracted masses of reporters, as many as 637 in 1968 from North America, Europe, Australia, and even Asia, according to media historian Susan Moeller.[7] These reporters and photographers were drawn to Vietnam largely because the US administration, under the aegis of the Military Assistance Command, actively courted their presence by granting access to reports and to battlefields. Despite this openness, the administration's policy was not wholly uncensored; instead, journalists experienced censorship indirectly in the form of briefings that exaggerated military gains and minimized losses. Journalists also had limited access to North Vietnam and suffered reprisals on the part of the South Vietnamese government under the leadership of Ngô Đình Diệm, who even expelled reporter François Scully in 1962 for writing unflattering stories about his corrupt regime.[8]

Lured by the promise of free accommodation and transportation as well as seemingly unfettered access to information services, journalists and freelancers flocked to Vietnam to make their names. Rookies, including Tim Page, who first flew into Vietnam at age twenty, swelling with ambition but short on cash, cut their teeth chasing stories of struggles in hamlets and jungles. Legendary photographers such as Larry Burrows, Robert Capa, and Bernard Fall sought to burnish reputations earned covering other wars by documenting this one. In their attempts to shoot this war, most photographers risked their lives; many died. Together, photographers produced a voluminous visual record of the war. Although the war marks a turning point in TV, a handful of still images stand out as icons shaping collective memory in the United States. Moreover, photographs crystallized an American experience of Vietnam, one that produced a metanarrative that prevails not just in the United States but also beyond.[9]

Critics also herald this war as a watershed in visual history because images supposedly affected its outcome. Depending on who is talking, pundits and politicians credit or blame images for turning the tide of public opinion in the United States against the war. In an interview, Nick Ut remarked that after taking his 1972 photograph of a napalm attack in Trang Bang, he immediately thought it could well be "the picture that would end the war."[10] Although the US administration hoped to attract favorable coverage through its policy of openness, by the early 1970s, journalists increasingly reported events in such an unflattering light that President Richard Nixon grumbled, "Whatever the intention behind . . . [the] relentless and literal reporting of the war, the result was a serious demoralization of the home front, raising the question whether America would ever again be able to fight an enemy abroad with unity and strength of purpose at home."[11] In 1975 James Reston similarly speculated that "historians will agree that the reporters and the camera were decisive in the end," adding that they "forced the withdrawal of American power from Vietnam."[12]

Even when officials tried to dismiss photographs of the war, their hyperbole betrayed lingering unease about them. Consider, for example, General William Westmoreland's response to Ut's photograph of the horrific aftermath of a napalm attack, which he brushed off as a minor "hibachi accident." His derisive tone echoed the callous sentiments of Madame Nhu, who served as South Vietnam's First Lady (a position she held informally as sister-in-law of Ngô Đình Diệm, the nation's bachelor prime minister from 1950 to 1963). In June 1963 Madame Nhu trivialized the self-immolation of the monk, Thích Quang Đức, as a "barbecue." In response to his protest of the Diệm regime's repression of Buddhist organizations she taunted, "Let them burn and we will clap our hands." Thus, the adherents of two camps fortified their positions, on the one hand praising images for ending the war and on the other hand denying that they had any impact. However, the most important lesson of this impasse is not which side was proved right; media critics show that the truth lies somewhere between these two positions, with images functioning less directly and more equivocally than assumed.[13] Rather, this impasse reveals that despite disagreements about the politics of pictures, the two camps were equally fascinated by images. As much as Westmoreland and Madame Nhu wished to discredit photographs, they could not disregard them. Their contempt belied their studied indifference.

The war in Vietnam was thus a watershed in visual history because it shaped the ways that spectators, located mainly in the global North, look at and think about images. For scholars based in the United States and Europe, where the most influential visual theory developed, looking at images provoked distrust and suspicion. In a series of essays first published in 1973, Susan Sontag captured this quandary when she argued for the necessity of witnessing atrocity, singling out the horrors of the napalm attack depicted in Ut's *Napalm Girl* (also titled *The Terror of War*) for special consideration. Although she conceded the power of this photograph, she still concluded that in a world she bemoaned as "image-choked," the sheer abundance of photographs anaesthetized rather than galvanized ethical action.[14] Sontag was drawn to photos yet worried about the effects of doing so.

This ambivalence stemmed from her experiences in Vietnam, according to critic Franny Nudelman.[15] In 1968 Sontag recorded her impressions of a first visit to Vietnam in a book titled *Trip to Hanoi*, where she confessed early doubts about photography.[16] She had landed in Hanoi, only to realize that photographs had clouded her perspective with preconceptions of Vietnam. To understand how the war truly affected the people in the North, she needed to see beyond photographs. Only a year after her second trip to Vietnam in 1972,

Sontag published the series of essays that first appeared in the *New York Review of Books* and that would be collected in *On Photography,* the landmark book where she expressed her misgivings about the political efficacy of images.

Sontag shared these misgivings with numerous scholars who claimed that images enchant and delude in their guises as agents of ideology, mass entertainments, seductive commodities, and instruments of surveillance. Writing in the 1980s, for example, Victor Burgin and John Tagg considered photography as an apparatus of state surveillance.[17] Likewise, Allan Sekula plunged beneath the depths of the history of bourgeois photographic portraiture to expose a "shadow archive" of surveillance.[18] These critics set out to unmask—and thereby defuse—the tyranny of an image-saturated world. Remarking on this striking repudiation of images, an enduring legacy of this critical moment, Susie Linfield observed that "the postmodern and poststructuralist children of Sontag, Berger, and Barthes transformed their predecessors' skepticism about the photograph into outright venom."[19] Rather than admiring and revering images, the adherents of this critical tradition looked at images only to look away from them.

In short, contemporary visual theorists espoused a hermeneutics of suspicion that mirrored and perpetuated the global Cold War's pervasive mood of fear and paranoia. The foundations of contemporary photography studies were laid during the height of the global Cold War. What's more, photographs of the war in Vietnam—a conflict integrally tied to a broader superpower competition—reinforced these foundations, foregrounding the spectacle that played out in Vietnam. Indeed, the war in Vietnam unfolded in the context and as part of the global Cold War, which conscripted even more players, including Filipino contractors, Australian soldiers, Korean mercenaries, and Laotian allies.[20]

Whether they are casual observers or committed scholars, students of visual culture thus absorb two fundamental lessons: first, the war in Vietnam played a special role in visual history, and, second, an influential thread of studies on photography developed in response to images from this war. Although I studied these lessons, over the years my doubts deepened with the hazy recollection of half-forgotten scenes, though whether witnessed firsthand or described to me I could no longer tell. From this roiling, the blurred edges of one image sharpened into view, a photograph that I remember from my childhood visits to the suburban home just east of Toronto that belonged to my mother's close friend, whom I will call by the pseudonym Hoa.

Compared to our bare apartment, with its makeshift cardboard-box furniture, stuffy summers and drafty winters, and pests skittering beneath floorboards with the flickering of lights, Hoa's modest home seemed luxurious. It even had a fireplace, whose polished mantle she adorned with Wedgwood figurines, crystal candlesticks, and her wedding photo framed in silver. I knew from my time in a Malaysian refugee camp that such knickknacks were unnecessary; food and shelter were all one required, a lesson my thrifty parents never tired of drilling into me. Still, these gleaming ornaments drew me. I returned to the photograph with every visit, moved by different details over the years. For a time, the tiara she wore as an eighteen-year-old bride beckoned; here was a beauty queen awaiting coronation, alluring and resplendent. Then it was the magnificent turquoise Ford near which she posed, a chrome chariot to transport her from the drudgery of the developing world. I looked nothing like this stunning woman. Yet I could not take my eyes away. The photo sparked schoolgirl fantasies of shedding adolescent awkwardness; I wished to smile as she smiled. For years, I lingered on the foreground with its vision of youthful grace, its promise of a felicitous future. I do not know when, exactly, I thought to look, really look, at the background. But then one day, I finally noticed the stacked sandbags, fortification against an unnamed threat, and the photograph's very mood seemed to sink. This family photograph, I realized, was also a war photograph.

My mother's friend was married in a town south of Saigon in 1968, several months after the start of the Tet Offensive on January 10, which had also targeted surrounding southern areas and other regions, particularly in central Vietnam, including Khe Sanh and Huế. The photograph straddles two temporalities, gesturing toward the future while bearing the burdens of the present. The photograph evinces mixed emotions, both a joy to come and an all-too-present fear. To many Vietnamese, this is what war looks like, by turns a hopeful smile and an anguished scream. War improbably straddles battlefield explosions, mundane errands, domestic rituals, and more. For Hoa the photograph suspends the war on the knife edge between expectation and devastation. This is probably why she would refuse to let me include it here, although I know better than to ask. After all, this book shows images from opposing sides, a decision that may unsettle many overseas Vietnamese. For her the war ended in total ruin; like many in this group who fled and whose sense of community coheres around a passionate anticommunism, the very thought of visual reunion with an enemy they cannot put to rest is unfathomable.[21]

The visual record of the war produced by the Western press and described by scholars in conventional histories may be as vast as it is familiar, but it misses such subtleties. According to Moeller, the way photographers shoot war, in some instances guided by their government's objectives, influences how viewers see war. Conversely, the way that viewers expect to see war guides the decisions that photographers make. The process forms a feedback loop of sorts. In the contemporary moment, one of the defining characteristics of war is combat (although, as chapter 3 shows, the banality of war has become an emerging theme).[22] Moeller elaborates: "Combat, no matter how peripheral, how Pyrrhic, how purposeless, is the heart of war. It is what young boys glamorize, old men remember, poets celebrate, governments rally around, women cry about, and soldiers die in. It is also what photographers take pictures of."[23] Yet this was not always the case; historically, war photography encompasses a broad spectrum of war experiences, including not just dramatic action but also the tension and tedium leading up to combat and the stillness of reflection afterward. In the nineteenth century, the wet-plate collodion process posed technical limitations, most notably slow shutter speed, which prevented photographers from shooting battles at all, never mind up close.

The first war photographs, taken during the Mexican-American War (1848), attest to these technical limitations; they feature quiet, contemplative scenes that were staged and most often taken after, not during, battle, as was the case with coverage of the Crimean War (1853–56). During the American Civil War (1861–65), the first war to be photographed widely, Mathew Brady and his associates produced images that were also quiet, contemplative, and staged. Despite this well-documented history, contemporary war photography represses this commonplace practice of staging, a kind of manipulation, and instead idealizes documentary objectivity and privileges the coverage of explosive action made possible with technological developments such as faster film. For a broader perspective on war, we need to expand "war photography" beyond the narrow parameters defined by the Western press. We need to stretch the framework to consider how seemingly domestic images depicting weddings, reunions, and quotidian, apparently frivolous rituals denoting pleasure, survival, and resilience might also be war photographs.

The visual record of war, when considered solely from the perspective of the Western press, overlooks the fuller spectrum of representation. We can attribute this disregard to prejudices concerning what counts as newsworthy, formed because of numerous factors such as personal or political priorities, ignorance, and even indifference. In addition to overlooking unspectacular forms of representation, the Western press, then as now, neglects Vietnamese perspectives, emphasizing instead the American experience of this war, which is understood as a uniform and singular phenomenon. However, recent scholarship in critical ethnic studies and Asian studies has drawn attention to important, long-overlooked sources that document Vietnamese experiences.[24] Indeed, the concept of the universal American experience of war is limited. To grasp the paucity of the focus on the American experience, we need only consider the divisive response to the war in the United States, evident in antiwar movements that mobilized diverse groups across the nation. It would be more accurate to speak of American *experiences* of this war.

Yet this perspective persists thanks to a sophisticated media infrastructure that grants unequal access to the means of production, circulation, and consumption in a process similar to the skewed "visual economy" described by anthropologist Deborah Poole.[25] This infrastructure encourages viewers to see and remember the war in Vietnam in a manner that for some critics constitutes an "American worldview."[26] Because the phrase *American worldview* problematically implies that the United States is a monolith, I draw attention instead to an American framework for viewing the war in Vietnam that foregrounds the heterogeneous political voices of dissent that characterized this tumultuous period. An American framework for seeing became persuasive because of a hegemonic political economy, which exerted a determining influence on the production and global circulation of photography. This American framework, in other words, affected what images are made and which ones are widely seen. To emphasize the American framework for viewing the war in Vietnam does not suggest that there is a uniform US way of seeing; indeed, in the United States responses to the war in Vietnam were contentious, and as I have shown, debates about the impact of press images of this war published in American magazines and newspapers remain unresolved.

Nor does one have to be American to contribute to an American visual framework. Both American and Vietnamese photographers, in their capacity as freelancers or "stringers," shaped this framework. News organizations and wire services hired stringers to contribute photographs and provide information for stories, especially when they lacked resources to engage the services of full-time foreign correspondents. Vietnamese stringers were valuable because of their language fluency, knowledge of the terrain, and local contacts. Horst Faas particularly depended on his network of stringers, known as "Faas's Army," whom he trained and equipped with cameras. Vietnamese stringers were such a fixture at the Associated Press (AP) Saigon office that Faas recalled they were even "living in the darkroom day and night."[27] Despite the importance of Vietnamese photographers, agencies paid them a per-picture rate and seldom credited them for their work.[28] Recently, a *New York Times* obituary confirmed this practice in a story honoring Nguyen Ngoc

Luong, whom reporter Sam Roberts identified as a "guide" for the newspaper during the war. In his tribute, Roberts acknowledged that "hundreds of unheralded guides and translators like Mr. Luong have served in war zones around the world, [and] their contribution to journalism [is] as essential as it is anonymous."[29] In an online eulogy, David K. Shipler reflected that "there are hundreds of people like Luong all over the world, local citizens of countries in conflict, who interpret, arrange, guide, open doors, and protect the foreigners who arrive as journalists or aid workers to observe and assist. Their help is crucial, and is done mostly behind the scenes, where they become invisible heroes."[30] An American visual framework emerged as such—as American—in part by ensuring the anonymity of stringers, such as the men who photographed for the AP, including Dang Van Phuoc, Le Ngoc Cung, Tran Khiem, Huynh Cong La, Ha Thuc Can, and Huynh Cong Thanh My.[31] At its most cynical and self-promoting, then, an American visual framework for the war disavowed the contributions of Vietnamese stringers even as it depended on their labor.

The most well-known of these stringers is Nick Ut, whose brother, Huỳnh Thanh Mỹ, was killed while on assignment for the AP. Ut was just sixteen when Faas hired him in 1965 after his brother's death. Seven years later, newspapers and magazines worldwide selected Ut's 1972 photo *Napalm Girl* as their cover image. At first glance, this iconic photograph would seem to tell us little about the American framework: it was made by a Vietnamese stringer and focuses on Vietnamese suffering. However, Chong reminds us that as was the case with the triptych of iconic photographs that emblematize the war, *Napalm Girl* became especially meaningful as an index of the range of *American* responses to this suffering instead of critical conversations about the significance of Vietnamese perspectives. The iconic photograph became meaningful not just for its representation of the child's pain but even more so, arguably, because it launched an agonized critique about the extent to which the United States might salve this pain or, as Chong puts it, how Americans might save the burning child and thereby realize the white savior fantasy.[32] This is not to say that American and Vietnamese perspectives cannot overlap, but so long as an American framework remains transfixed on the exposure of the Vietnamese child's pain while still perceiving the child as other, they remain distinct. Conversely, the American visual framework for war has fixated on images that attend to the vulnerability of US soldiers.[33] Larry Burrows's raw photographs of mortally wounded Marines in a series of photographs he took for *Life* magazine vividly portray this theme and, along with similar images taken by Eddie Adams and others, helped establish an enduring metanarrative of the war that dwells on the suffering and sainthood of American soldiers (plate 2). Neither monolithic, nor unified, nor essentialist, an American framework for the war nevertheless centers US perspectives in all their messy heterogeneity, hawkish or not. Moreover, an American framework for seeing the war entails overlooking other perspectives.

The global Cold War offered competing frameworks for seeing. Indeed, Chinese and Soviet newspapers took advantage of stories about violence against civil rights protestors, which buttressed their claims about the fundamentally unjust US system.[34] Similarly, the communist Vietnam News Agency (VNA) and Liberation News Agency (LNA) paid careful attention to US and worldwide coverage of antiwar protests, selecting images from the American press to promote their struggle instead of mainstream American perspectives. Among the many US press photos that proved especially potent for socialist purposes were shocking images of the self-immolation of antiwar protestor Norman Morrison in 1965 and the devastating napalm attack on Trang Bang that scarred ten-year-old Phan Thị Kim Phúc. As the former editor of the state-run *Vietnam Pictorial* Nguyễn Thắng remarked, after communists saw the photo of Kim Phúc, "We used it right away."[35] By reframing this photograph, the communist press challenged the American perspective. When we attend to the ways that the Vietnamese press redeployed *Napalm Girl*, we can observe more clearly the contest for meaning: the icon became a warring image and not just an image of war.

Warring—I invoke this gerund deliberately to denote the active deployment of photographs for the ends of war and to suggest the labor and practice of war. Visual struggles are central to the conduct of war and its memory. Elsewhere, I have written about the ways that the socialist Vietnamese state recirculated images of Kim Phúc, especially in the 1980s, to establish its moral authority as the child's protector and as guardian of an emerging nation struggling to recover from the damage wrought by American imperial aggression.[36] The circulation of US press photos in communist contexts further unsettles not only the primacy of an American framework for seeing but also the ostensible singularity of the American experience that this framework secures and legitimates. *Napalm Girl* does not signify an essential American quality; however, the reception of this photograph in the United States underscores the influence of a political economy that shapes ways of seeing the Vietnamese child's pain to foreground the US response.

Accounting for the full range of wartime experiences requires a contrapuntal approach that decenters the United States and considers Vietnamese responses within a broader, international context. Indeed, to discern the complexity of these links, as novelist and scholar Viet Thanh Nguyen reminds us, we need only observe the multiple names by which the war in Vietnam was known.[37] To Americans, it was the Vietnam War. Sometimes it is known as a conflict because the United States never officially declared war on North Vietnam, instead preferring to consider itself merely advisors to the South Vietnamese. To the North Vietnamese, it was the American War. Within South Vietnam, and for numerous overseas Vietnamese or Viet Kieu, it was a bitter civil war—in which the fractured nation served as proxy battleground for the global Cold War. Yet with few exceptions, visual histories of the war in Vietnam have nearly erased Vietnamese perspectives, relegating them to the backdrop of an American obsession with national humiliation and, in the post-1975 period, with moral redemption through militarized humanitarianism, wherein the United States rescued hundreds of thousands of Vietnamese refugees.[38] Even photographs that unequivocally disclose the magnitude of *Vietnamese* suffering attest to the so-called American experience, according to these conventional histories. After all, the triptych of icons, as noted above, documents Vietnamese violence, whether waged in response to Vietnamese injustices (the burning monk), in retaliation (the Saigon execution), and as the result of an accidental bombing run (the napalm attack). Yet scholars persist in imputing to these icons signs of American guilt, grief, and sympathy, and in ascribing to them the ability to fashion an American public sphere. What counternarratives emerge if we reflect on Vietnamese experiences of this war?

This book invokes the concept of "warring visions" to examine these nuances. Warring visions denote how Vietnamese communities actively enlisted images to project aesthetic and ideological positions, the stakes of which were nothing less than legitimizing competing claims to the nation. The concept of warring visions also enlarges the category of war photography, a genre that critics usually consider as consisting of images that illustrate the immediacy of combat. Despite an amply documented history of war photography's varied forms and subjects, many viewers still define this category in narrow terms: authentic illustrations of active combat qualify as war photographs whereas images that are staged or manipulated do not. Warring visions redefine the genre of war photography beyond simply illustrations, to encompass the ways that communities engage images in symbolic combat. This engagement extends beyond the image object, however, for it can also take the form of refusal, as Hoa's protective stance on her wedding portrait reminded me. Warring visions form part of an arsenal of soft power, they serve as a strategy for peaceful reconciliation, and they provide a means of quiet resistance. Warring visions thus necessarily include manipulated images—whether they are produced through seemingly innocuous approaches such as staging or seemingly more deceptive artifices such as enhancement, retouching, colorization, cropping, and reenactment—to explain how these communities crafted their account of the war and imaginatively reckoned with the war's aftermath. Just as importantly, the concept of warring visions reveals how Vietnamese communities deployed images to secure the moral resolve, political allegiance, and cultural memory of viewers. *Warring Visions* thus surveys an expansive range of images, including disparaged and overlooked ones, which communities mobilize for the ends of war. Together, these images enrich our understanding of how war is waged, how it unfolds, and how it is resolved.

Warring Visions traces how Vietnamese photography shaped Vietnamese experiences of the war. It joins a growing body of work that examines the visual record of the "other side," extending this scholarship to consider the diversity of alternative perspectives.[39] The very notion of Vietnamese experiences challenges conventional perspectives that consider the American experience as a singular, uniform phenomenon. However, the notion of Vietnamese experiences does not replace one reductive perspective with another so that a focus on Vietnam simply supplants the dominant concern with the United States. Rather, attending to Vietnamese experiences expands insights in the visual culture of this war, highlights overlaps and discontinuities between multiple perspectives, illuminates how these perspectives converged and diverged, and explains the cultural contexts for the creation, circulation, and remediation of images.

PHOTOGRAPHY IN VIETNAM

It is perhaps fitting that historians should be split on the story of photography's emergence in Vietnam given the ways that the nation has been violently divided. Vietnam has endured the turmoil of war for centuries, including uprisings against Chinese rule (111 BC – 938 AD) and resistance against French colonialism (1887 – 1954) and against American imperialism (1955 – 1975). Following the defeat of the French under the leadership of Hồ Chí Minh, the Geneva Accord split the nation, in an ostensibly temporary arrangement pending elections, into North Vietnam and South Vietnam along the seventeenth parallel at the demilitarized zone.[40] Consider, for example, the historian Nguyễn Đức Hiệp's account, provided by scholar Ellen Takata, which singles out French photographer Alphonse Jules Itier for distinction.[41] Itier had accompanied diplomat Théodore de Lagrené on a mission to negotiate the 1844 Treaty of Whampoa, the first agreement between France and China. That year their travels brought them to Danang, a port city in Vietnam's central region, where Itier took photographs of Vietnamese soldiers. At this moment, travel overlapped with war in a process that underscores photography's amenability to the process of colonization. These photographs, which depicted the militarism of French colonial rule, are rare first images of Vietnam. But it was Émile Gsell who, sometime in the 1860s, set up the first commercial photography studio in Saigon. Nguyễn Đức Hiệp's story about photography's emergence in Vietnam emphasizes photography's status as a French invention and its utility for advancing French colonialism.

Lê Ngọc Minh tells a different story. An amateur photographer based in southern California, Minh penned an unpublished history that credits Đặng Huy Trứ, a mandarin under Emperor Tự Đức, for bringing photography to Vietnam.[42] In 1865 Trứ embarked on a state visit to China, where he bought a camera, developed film he shot there, and persuaded a Chinese photographer to engage in a joint business venture. They returned to Hanoi, where on March 14, 1869, they opened the first Vietnamese-owned commercial studio.[43] This unmistakably nationalistic account of the emergence of Vietnamese photography emphasizes the role of an enterprising Vietnamese photographer. Although he may have acquired his expertise and equipment from China, Vietnam's main rival, Trứ successfully adapted both for local uses. In the talented hands of the Vietnamese photographer and shrewd businessman, Vietnamese photography developed and thrived.

These different tales of photography's path to Vietnam share a concern common to modernizing nations struggling for independence: the problem that this technology posed as a foreign innovation and commodity to national self-fashioning and a nascent anticolonial consciousness. But as Karen Strassler persuasively argues in her study of Indonesian modernity, popular photography is simultaneously national and transnational.[44] Practitioners adapt "foreign" technologies to create idioms to express local desires, to fashion what Strassler describes as "refracted visions," ways of seeing specific to a local context while also inseparable from geopolitical contexts that also shape this nation. A similar framework for how to see developed in Vietnam. The second version of the story thus salves photography's threat by crediting China as a relatively innocuous source of the technology's introduction to the emerging nation, for in the late 1860s, French colonizers were more despised than the Chinese. By contrast, the first version spells out the principal obstacle for Vietnamese patriots. To enlist photography toward the ends of anticolonial resistance, these patriots needed to overcome France's corrupting influence. They had to adapt a French instrument for Vietnamese purposes. From 1865 to the mid-twentieth century, however, commercial studios catered to the desires of a bourgeois class that could afford to commission their likenesses. Salon photography, characterized by its indulgence of decadent bourgeois tastes, flourished. The question of how photography could be marshaled for class warfare—how it could serve revolutionary ends—would not be posed explicitly until well into the twentieth century.

The Vietnamese public began to appreciate photography's political potential in 1945. During this year a disastrous famine struck. Directly caused by the Japanese occupation of French Indochina during World War II and indirectly by decades of inequitable land policy at the behest of French colonial administrators, the famine claimed as many as two million lives in North Vietnam, then known as Tonkin. Photographer Võ An Ninh traveled throughout the region, documenting the catastrophe. His photographs attest to the brutality of Japanese occupation and French colonialism.

With the end of World War II the French sought to reclaim Vietnam as a colony but met fierce resistance from the Viet Minh, the abbreviated name for Việt Nam Độc Lập Đồng Minh Hội, an organization led by Hồ Chí Minh. This clash between French colonizers and Vietnamese nationalists is known as the First Indochina War (1946-54) and culminated in the legendary standoff at Điện Biên Phủ, where French soldiers sought to draw out and crush Viet Minh guerrillas using superior firepower. But they suffered defeat instead, underestimating the guerrillas' resilience and tactical sophistication. The First Indochina War ended with the Viet Minh as victors and saviors of Vietnam. The French were forced to quell their colonial ambitions just as the Americans stepped forward as powers in the region.

Although the Western press covered the First Indochina War with keen interest, particularly on the part of French newspapers and magazines, visual documentation of the conflict on the part of Vietnamese photographers was sparse.[45] A respected Vietnamese photographer from that era is Nguyễn Mạnh Đan, who started out as an apprentice in a Hanoi photo shop. When he was only twenty-two, a French journalist entered the shop asking whether anyone spoke French. Mạnh Đan recalled that "I stood up. The Frenchman looked at me from head to toe and said, 'Come to the editorial office tomorrow for probation.' I was so stunned and happy. There were very few Vietnamese photographers working for the French at the time, so I was paid a lot of respect wherever I went."[46] Recruited to work alongside a French photographer, Mạnh Đan took photographs for *Indochine Sud-Est Asiatique*, an illustrated magazine published in France.

In May 2013, I met ninety-two-year-old Mạnh Đan at the Saigon studio in District 10 at a shop that his grandchildren and great-grandchildren now operate. Though retired, he still presided over the photo studio he had opened more than sixty years ago, an ever-present cigarette burning to the stub between bony fingers. Smoke curling in the dusty air, he reminisced about his adventures photographing the wars in Vietnam. Working alongside the French, he remembered, prepared him for the next war, when he embarked on a project for the Government of Vietnam alongside Nguyễn Ngọc Hạnh (no relation), who was then a young officer with the Army of the Republic of Vietnam (ARVN). By 1968, the year that their project was published in a book titled *Việt Nam Khói Lửa*, Mạnh Đan was an esteemed senior photographer. He invited Hạnh to participate, asking, "Do you want to be famous?"[47]

It was thus not until the Second Indochina War (yet another name for the war in Vietnam) that Vietnamese photographers began testing in earnest the camera's capacity to represent their struggles, to broker their political positions, and to establish solidarities with other organizations. In 1968 Nguyễn Mạnh Đan and Nguyễn Ngọc Hạnh documented the course of the war and its toll on soldiers and civilians in South Vietnam, including their own coverage of the Tet Offensive and its aftermath in a book published by the Government of Vietnam and printed in Hong Kong, a site selected likely because of scarce local resources.[48] To my knowledge, this is the only surviving official visual record of the fallen Saigon regime. The original title, *Việt Nam Khói Lửa* (literally translated in the English edition as *Vietnam in Flames*), is a phrase that refers to the book's overall theme of conflagration. The phrase also stresses the photographers' distinctively Vietnamese perspective insofar as *khói lửa* is the Vietnamese idiom for war. Just as importantly, the South-based Republic of Vietnam projected a vision of war that encompassed more than fire and brimstone; the photographers structured the book loosely into sections that focus on the sites hardest hit during the Tet Offensive, including Saigon, Khe Sanh, and Huế. The book also features photographs that pause to marvel on unexpected beauty, as with the picturesque landscape of the Perfume River ferry ride (figure I.4); to admire the stillness of the countryside, a reminder of the stakes of struggle; and to meditate on the gravity of grief, a photograph that I discuss in detail in chapter 3 (see figure 3.4).

Walter Benjamin famously worried about mass culture's power to entrance the masses and urged that it be harnessed for revolutionary ends. In his oft-cited essay "The Work of Art in the Age of Mechanical Reproduction," he

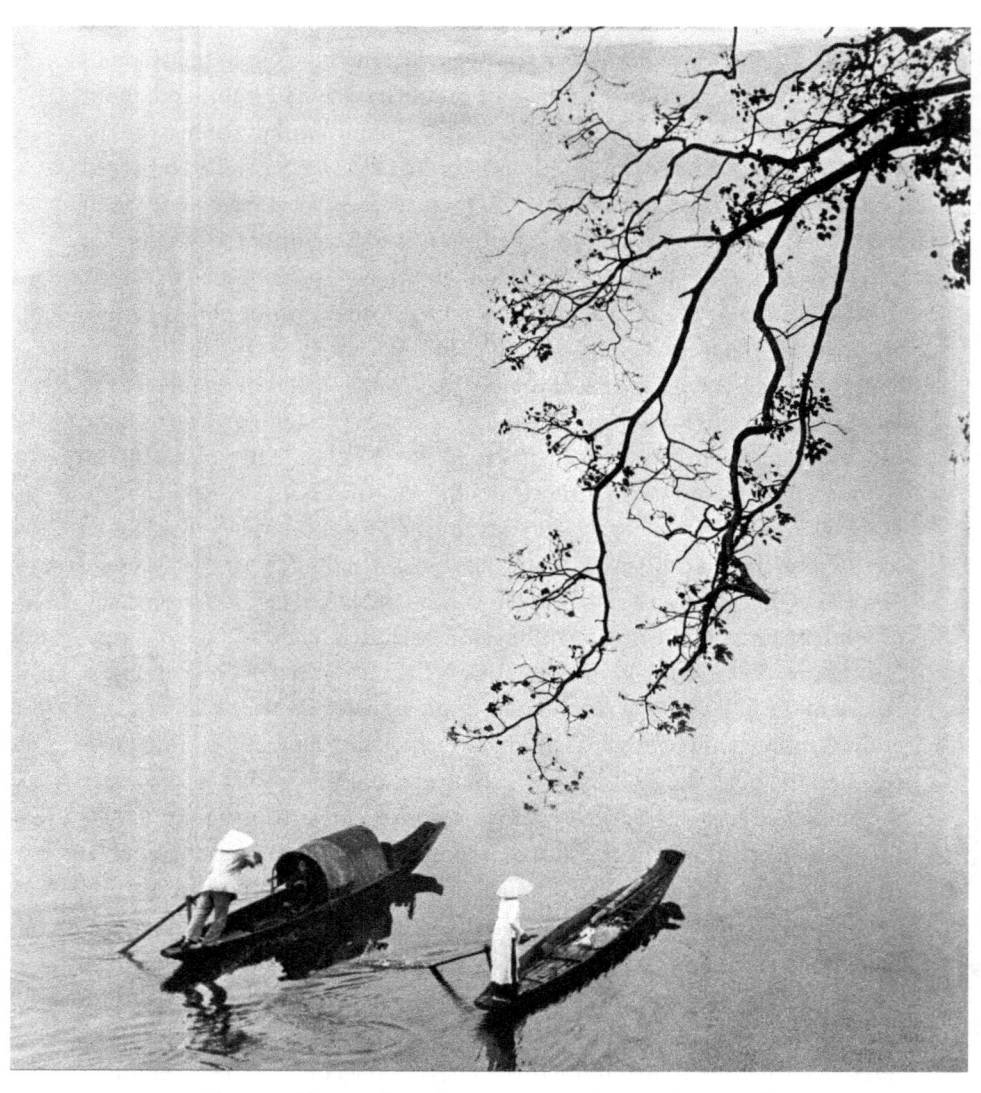

FIGURE 1.4 Villagers paddling on the Perfume River, 1968. Photographer: Nguyễn Mạnh Đan.

argued that mass culture be deployed to mobilize and politicize the masses.[49] Photographers from South Vietnam need not have known about Benjamin to grasp the urgency of this challenge, which they readily took up. During the war, their counterparts in the north, namely the Hanoi-based VNA, likewise dispatched photographers to produce images, also in hopes of reaching the masses. The VNA established training programs for journalists and photographers who went on to produce images and stories that would promote the cause, recruit volunteers, and foster sympathy with antiwar organizations and other decolonizing movements. Despite scarce resources and rudimentary media infrastructure, the communist press sought to project a vision of socialist revolution through photography. At the same time, the proliferation of propaganda posters, which were often displayed to peasants in the jungles where they were made, attests to the magnitude of the technical obstacles that the communist press encountered; posters supplemented and, when needed, substituted for photos. As I explain more fully in chapters 1 and 2, these photographers shaped a socialist way of seeing as a process that entailed purifying the taint of French and bourgeois influence from photography, developing a style amenable to revolutionary ideals in a distinctly unapologetic way. Plate 1, a photograph published in 1957 on the cover of the illustrated magazine *Vietnam Pictorial*, exemplifies the communist stance on propaganda. Depicting children at play in a field of impossibly large and implausibly hued flowers, the photograph seems painted in luminous tones that make plain its fantastical contrivance. This painted photograph makes no effort at naturalism. Rather, the photo overtly conjures a socialist future that had yet to come. Put simply, the National Liberation Front and its People's Liberation Armed Forces of South Vietnam, the North Vietnamese Army, and their supporters published, displayed, and circulated these photos during the war without hiding their status as propaganda.

Not surprisingly, critics, who prefer at least the semblance of objectivity if not neutrality, repudiate such photos as heavy-handed vehicles of ideology, as evidenced in recent controversy in response to reports that work by the VNA had been manipulated (a case that I explore in greater detail in chapter 1). Viewers attuned to the ideals associated with a certain style of photojournalism and to a taste for documentary naturalism associated with a Euro-American tradition of critique are quick to dismiss the relevance of such photographs to visual histories of the war, most likely because of blinders imposed by abiding assumptions about objectivity as a measure of journalistic truth. In this sense, conventional visual histories of the war in Vietnam are incomplete because they offer little guidance for how to understand propaganda, merely judging such material as worthless. This reflex judgment is as clumsy as the material it indicts, enabling groups and states—who are far from disinterested—to dispense with inconveniently competing perspectives on the war. Consequently, the United States could disregard evidence of civilian bombing raids by labeling them as propaganda.

For their part, communist photographers and photo editors were not above such tactics themselves, even though they were open and indeed unashamed about their use of propaganda. At times, communists wielded the very judgment they endured as a damning weapon to dispatch ARVN opponents. During the postwar, late-socialist period the Vietnamese state drew on communist photography to shore up an official narrative of reunification and liberation. Võ An Khánh's touching photograph of embracing matriarchs (see figure E.1) offers a powerful allegory of national reconciliation, one cleared of rancor. At the same time, the state reinforced this official narrative of national reunification by discrediting the only complete set of ARVN images that remain, namely the work of Nguyễn Ngọc Hạnh and Nguyễn Mạnh Đan. *Vietnam in Flames* is fiction rather than journalism, charged Nguyễn Đức Chính in his history of photography in Vietnam, because its photographers staged images instead of presenting scenes as they happened.[50] All sides— whether American, North Vietnamese, or South Vietnamese—volleyed the charge of propaganda as a means of putting their images at war with one another. *Warring Visions* thus names a contest for what can be seen in a way that extends beyond just image objects to include a jostling for power to render invisible subjects and sites deemed ideologically unacceptable. Although critics often perceive propaganda as ham-fisted, it can also be nuanced, operating subtly and heavy-handedly to broadcast information for the ends of political persuasion.

Visual counternarratives require alternative archives, resources that are not easily accessible or interpretable. Consider, for example, the problem of records relating to the ARVN perspective. In contrast to the abundant record left by the VNA and LNA, the visual legacy of the ARVN is sparse. In its time the book *Vietnam in Flames* was well-known, its photographers widely admired. These days, however, few members among the overseas community know of the photographers or have heard of *Vietnam in Flames*. Copies of the English version are rare and expensive (one online auction has even listed it at more than $2,500). Only after months of online digging did I manage to acquire my edition for a more modest price and have yet to come across a copy of the Vietnamese version. In Vietnam, many collectors and photographers know of the eminent Nguyễn Mạnh Đan, but only a few admit they

have heard of Nguyễn Ngọc Hạnh, who, because he served as an ARVN officer, was sentenced to a labor camp, where he spent eight years before a human rights organization secured his release and eventual resettlement in the
United States. (By contrast, his partner, a civilian, received a lighter sentence
of several months in a reeducation camp.) A couple of these collectors cau-
tiously admit they are aware of *Vietnam in Flames*. During one of my research
trips to Vietnam, I spoke with a man whom I will call Khải. After greeting
me warmly, he excused himself and dove into a warren of notes and papers,
emerging after some moments clutching a clandestine copy. Khải never told
me how he found this contraband artifact. The book was in pristine condition, but when I opened it, I realized that a photograph of the flag of South
Vietnam, whose display the state still forbids, was missing from one of the
front pages.

If I had not studied my own copy of the book, I would not have suspected
the surgically precise excision. In this moment, the thrill of my discovery—
proof that a record of an ARVN point of view, however partial, persists in
Vietnam—deflated with dawning awareness that much remained ungrasp-
able. All the questions I had—how *Vietnam in Flames* came to be, why it was
published in Hong Kong, how the photographers selected their images, what
they hoped to accomplish, and more—dissolved at the tip of my tongue when
I met Mạnh Đan, who after an hour of conversation grew impatient. He was
eager to return to his storefront perch so that he could contemplate Saigon's
afternoon traffic while smoking yet another cigarette. As for Nguyễn Ngọc
Hạnh, Mạnh Đan's erstwhile collaborator, he had fallen ill, I learned, and
could not be interviewed.

Confronted by these challenges, I was constantly reminded of the commonplace notion that those who wind up on the losing side of history disappear from official records. Little wonder, then, that scholars are drawn to
iconic images. I count myself among them, having written about the napalm
photo of Kim Phúc, and in chapter 2 I consider how icons function within
Vietnam.[51] By definition, icons are hard to miss and easy to talk about, so
scholars endlessly debate them. Icons also help shape collective memory and
public culture, according to communications studies critics Robert Hariman and John Louis Lucaites.[52] Indeed, icons shore up dominant narratives
through the influence of sophisticated mass media infrastructures that in
many cases outmatch, technologically and logistically, the resources of developing nations. In so doing, icons often erase marginalized stories from collective memory and public culture—as is the case with the Vietnam triptych—
whether deliberately through censorship or tacitly through indifference. Yet

icons can direct attentive viewers to forgotten or forbidden stories when we take them back to their original contexts of production, circulation, and reception, as critic Andrea Noble contended in her study of the Mexican Revolution.[53] We gain much by looking at icons, for they illuminate supposedly universal truths. However, we lose even more if this is all we dwell on, not least a sense of the specificity of struggles and the varied shades of meaning. When we look closely, the general truths that icons impart turn out to have a history, but this history tends to be obscured.

Warring Visions is thus not a book that focuses solely on icons understood in the conventional sense as transhistorical signifiers. However, this book does consider some icons, particularly in chapters 1 and 2, which trace the circulation of socialist images and the potency of the symbol of the revolutionary Vietnamese woman. Nor is this a book about dashing photographers who earned their laurels through derring-do, nor even about conventional approaches to the genre of war photography, which favor the canonical, the icons, and the heroic photographers who produced them.[54] Instead, this book enlarges the category of war photography to account for a full range of visual practices and styles, from studio portraiture to photojournalism to propaganda to domestic images and beyond, which all engage with what war means and what it looks like to those who survived it and must reckon with its legacies.

Official archives provide scant information about the despised and disavowed from South Vietnam. In today's Vietnam, for example, state rites of remembrance take highly visible forms, such as monumental statues that praise the sacrifices of the humble soldier, farmer, and factory worker while denying altogether the existence of an opposing side. What one can ask and say about the war depends on where this discussion takes place. Only in the shelter of the home do family members privately participate in ancestral rites that resurrect the memory of "this" side, rites that subvert official narratives of the war, according to anthropologist Heonik Kwon.[55] In the United States officials reserve rites of commemoration for their own troops; at the most famous monument of this war, the Vietnam War Veterans Memorial in Washington, one finds on its implacable granite surface only the names of American soldiers. Officials are silent on the subject of their fallen ARVN allies, whom they maligned during and even after the war as unworthy and cowardly. This phenomenon persists, as demonstrated in the controversy sparked by *The Vietnam War*, the much-heralded release of the documentary by Ken Burns and Lynn Novick, which serves as a heady remainder of the public's seemingly inexhaustible fascination with this topic. Although the film is nearly eighteen hours long, as I discuss more fully in the epilogue it is hardly an exhaustive account of the conflict and ultimately leans into an American framework for seeing, despite attempts to take account of the viewpoint of ARVN veterans and South Vietnamese survivors.[56]

For a glimpse of the ARVN perspective, I had to look elsewhere. *Vietnam in Flames* was just the start. I scoured vintage shops, where I was told I had the best chance of finding artifacts too incendiary for families to hold on to. With their record of such bourgeois indulgences as holidays abroad, of impolitic friendships with foreigners, and of allegiances to the losing side, such albums were too perilous to keep. Consider, for example, the school album of Thủ Đức Military Academy, which artfully chronicles close male friendships formed through military service (see figure 4.4). How did it end up in a store, tucked away among chipped porcelain, and kept near stacks of orphaned family snaps, an artifact painstakingly assembled yet carelessly left behind?

The shopkeeper, whom I will call Mai, tells me that many families who fled Vietnam as refugees carried with them only a few valuables that could be traded along the way for water, food, or favor. They sold or discarded photo albums. In the hands of strangers, these albums have become orphaned objects, lacking names, dates, and contexts. Personal records often take up subjects that state records dismiss as irrelevant and unimportant, which is why I turned to diasporic Vietnamese communities for insights on images that managed to survive the war and the journey. Chapter 4 details the loose images and albums I found and the war stories they contain.

Oral history interviews with some community members about their family photos helped fill in some of the blanks left by the orphan images. However, the material I stumbled on through luck, serendipity, or sheer stubbornness offers only glimpses of the overall picture of the war in Vietnam. At the same time, such recalcitrance suggested that counternarratives form in unexpected ways. Counternarratives sketch details that occasionally fill in the blanks of official histories. For all that I managed to piece together, a lot remains missing from the overall picture. Still, blanks make up a crucial part of the overall picture. Instead of simply obscuring narratives of Vietnam, the silence and secrecy of these alternative archives, to say nothing of official archives, integrally form *Warring Visions*.

This book surveys both highly visible and less obvious subjects and, to delineate the opposing perspectives, is divided into two parts. Part I addresses the communist perspective, following its production by photographers in the Vietnam News Agency stationed on the Ho Chi Minh Trail and among the National Liberation Front in the Mekong Delta; its exhibition among Vietnamese villagers to promote socialism; and its circulation among international communities to establish moral authority for the joined causes of anticolonialism and national liberation. Chapter 1 explores the development of a socialist way of seeing, a concept that I borrow from art historian Xiaobing Tang's study of visual culture in China, to explain how North Vietnam produced and disseminated ideological perspectives in dialogue with yet distinct from its Communist Bloc allies. This chapter considers how North Vietnamese photographers confronted material, technical, and infrastructural obstacles in the course of shaping a socialist way of seeing specific to local contexts and the cause of national liberation while attuned to and eager for an international audience. This process entailed adapting the French introduction of photography as a resource for Vietnamese liberation, rejecting aesthetics as bourgeois indulgence, while slipping into the picture stylistic flourishes in the form of ideologically suitable subjects and embracing, instead of condemning, contrivance as part of its signature boldness. This chapter also considers the futurity of this socialist way of seeing by focusing on *Vietnam Pictorial*, an illustrated magazine run by the communist state, and its striking use of color in 1954–75, a period bracketed by two wars against the French and Americans. This was also a period of aesthetic innovation in illustrated magazines, according to Moeller, who notes that starting in 1963, *Life* began experimenting with color photography to capture more vividly combat's gritty quality in photo essays that covered developments of the war in Vietnam. At around the same time, *Vietnam Pictorial* began printing sections of the magazine in color but without any attempt at the realism to which *Life* aspired. Instead, communist photo editors rendered color in fantastical ways that imagined a future of national renewal and unity that had yet to come.

Chapter 2 addresses the gendered dimensions of socialist ways of seeing by focusing on the symbol of revolutionary Vietnamese women. This chapter considers the contexts in which communists martialed the symbol of revolutionary Vietnamese women to link two causes, women's emancipation and national liberation. It also explores the remediation and resignification of this symbol at the hands of various actors and groups in Vietnam and abroad. During the war, different organizations within Vietnam and abroad—including the Vietnam Women's Union, the Women's Solidarity of Vietnam (a group founded and led by Madame Nhu), and women's movements in Canada and the United States—projected and reinvented the symbol of revolutionary women to suit their own political aspirations. However, these groups did so in ways that did not necessarily align with one another, even though they deployed this figure in the name of international solidarity. In a process that evokes anthropologist Anna Tsing's concept of "friction," misperception, unwitting and sometimes willful, served as the basis of, not obstacle to, establishing solidarity.[57]

Part II examines the warring visions projected by South Vietnamese photographers. To do so, however, the chapters address a central methodological problem—the lack of archives devoted to the history of South Vietnam—by looking more closely at materials not usually considered part of the canon of war photography: images that have been staged, vernacular artifacts, and personal collections. All of these materials engage with experiences of war in unexpected ways and disclose how the process of constructing "warring visions" is critical to rites of commemoration, acts of recollection, and the constitution of diasporic communities.

Chapter 3 investigates the category of images that critics are loathe to include in the history of photography: those that are manifestly staged or reenacted. This chapter focuses on reenactment as it appears in photographs created during the war and in its aftermath as a way of understanding the war's legacy and considers how reenactment challenges historical interpretation. Chapter 4 turns to personal images, especially family photographs, as a means of understanding the intimate connections between ordinary domestic rites and extraordinary experiences of war. Family photographs reveal a quieter dimension of survival and offer a means of recollecting the full range of what war looks like. *Warring Visions* concludes with an epilogue that considers how the opposing sides of North and South might be reconciled. Visual *reunion* provides the potential of healing the political fractures that the discourse of national *reunification* only deepens, although in considering this issue the chapter also acknowledges the significance of diasporic Vietnamese community members, including my mother's friend, who refused to contemplate this potential. This epilogue also considers the public approach to reunion offered in the *Requiem* exhibition, which was organized by US-based researchers in collaboration with partners in Vietnam, and more recent efforts to broach reconciliation through *The Vietnam War* documentary. By contrasting these forms of visual remembrance, the epilogue assesses the contexts in which photographs might reconcile war's psychic wounds.

Warring Visions explores Vietnamese photographs produced by dispersed communities in North Vietnam, in South Vietnam, and across the diaspora. Vietnamese communities are as disparate as the wars that split them apart, as contradictory as the memories that shape their postwar lives, and as distinct as the photographs they made to prosecute this war and to reflect on its traumas. From 1954, with the end of the First Indochina War, when the Viet Minh defeated the French, through to the end of the Second Indochina War, with the fall of Saigon and the defeat of the Americans, to the Đổi Mới era of economic renovation, and to the present era of market liberalization, Vietnamese photography circulated within the nation and, to a limited extent beyond, as a means of shaping how the war would be seen and ultimately the terms in which it would be remembered and forgotten.

I

SOCIALIST
WAYS OF SEEING
VIETNAM

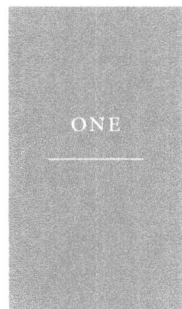

ONE

AESTHETIC FORM,
POLITICAL CONTENT

In 1972 Đoàn Công Tính, a photographer for the communist Vietnam News Agency (VNA), gathered his modest supplies and headed toward the citadel in Quảng Trị, a province in the north central coastal area.[1] He had heard that a great battle would take place there between the National Liberation Front (NLF) and its opponents, the US-backed Army of the Republic of Vietnam (ARVN). He was keen to capture the action, but the journey to the citadel was arduous; first, he hitched a ride with a fisherman for part of the way, and then he swam the remaining distance while holding lens, film, and camera body aloft to keep them dry. Once inside the citadel, he had to contend with poor equipment. Tính's photographs are imperfect, the result of equipment that reveals not the extension of vision, the camera's reputed technical advantage, but instead its limitations (see figure 1.1).

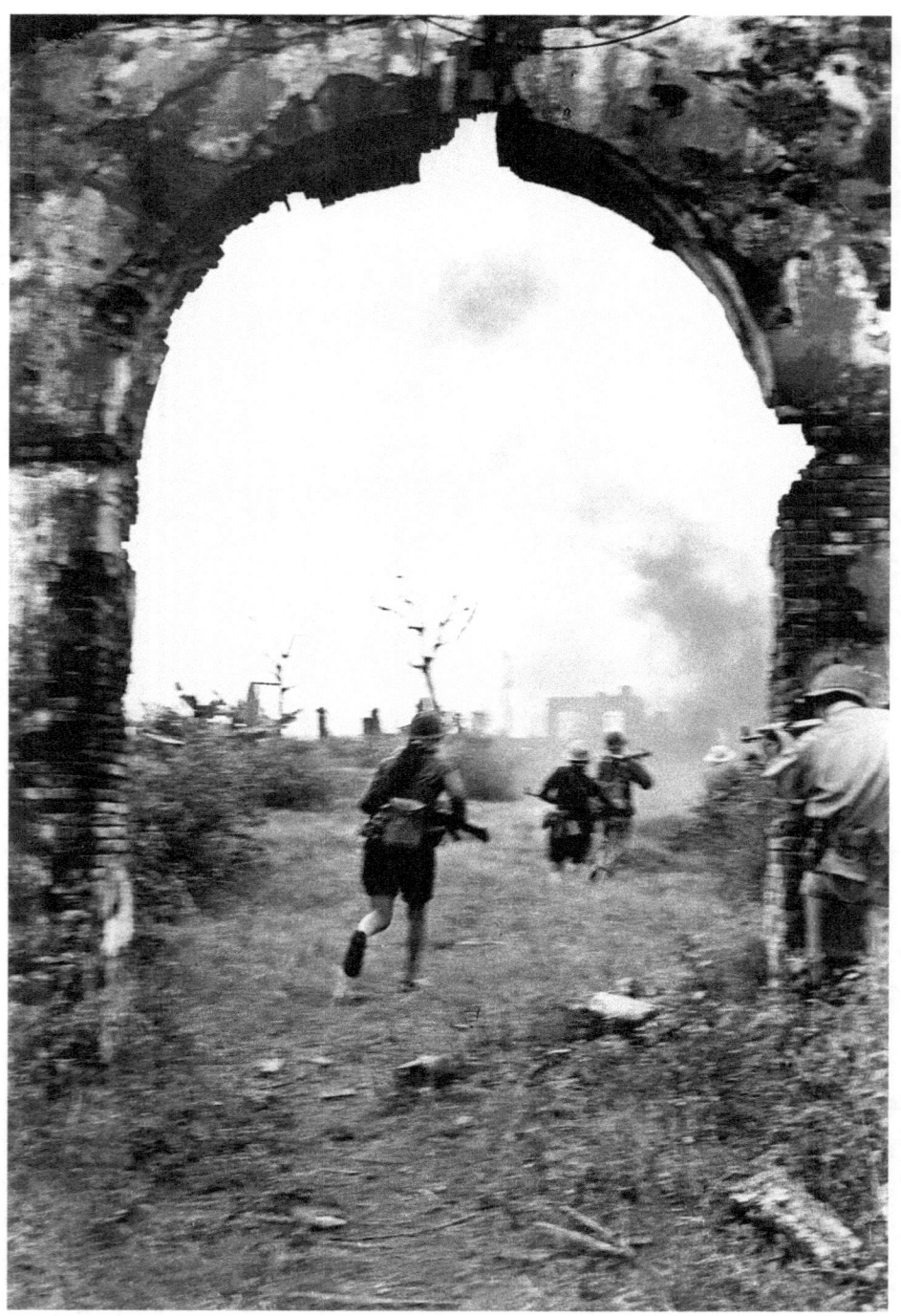

FIGURE 1.1 Battle for Quảng Trị Citadel. Photographer: Đoàn Công Tính.

By depicting the dangers of war in all its grittiness, his photographs offer what today might be described as a shaky-cam documentary look, although he struggled simply to take the picture, not to create an effect. Yet his own story about the making of the photograph glosses over its technical imperfections by emphasizing the themes of heroic physicality. Communist photography is contradictory; it provides a flawed technical perspective at the same time that it exalts a potent physicality as necessary for overcoming material challenges. What accounts for the marred quality of this way of looking? In what contexts does a socialist perspective incorporate ideals of aesthetic beauty? When does it disavow these ideals? What is the significance of this embrace or disavowal? In short, what role does photography play in revolution?

In the nineteenth century, writers were preoccupied with a less overtly political matter—the revolutionary nature of the camera—and focused on explaining how photography might influence the arts and alter faculties of perception. Critics did not emphasize the issue of how photography could transform the structure of social relations until the twentieth century. The tumult of the 1917 October Revolution in Russia ushered forth a new era, according to Sergei Morozov and Valerie Lloyd, who highlight the camera's efficacy for disseminating socialist ideas. In the wake of this momentous historical shift, they contend that artists and journalists strove to produce images "whose form and content were closely related to the ideals of the Revolution and to what were seen as the contemporary tasks of the new Soviet government in the socialist reorganization of society . . . at a time when the new republic had to defend itself against counter-revolutionary attacks and foreign interventions."[2] Soviet state-run cultural organizations and publications, including the proletarian Union of Russian Photographers and Sovetskoe Foto (an agency established in 1932 to distribute Soviet photographs to the United States), emphasized the value of photography for promoting revolution by communicating socialist reality.

However, artists and critics disagreed about the most effective way to represent this reality. Debates, which extended beyond the USSR, centered on the core problem of the most politically suitable form to convey socialist content. Although these debates mainly involved literature, they also touched on photography. On the one hand, "straight photographers" favored sharp focus and detail as more suited to communicating revolutionary reality in an objective manner. On the other hand, avant-garde photographers experimented with skewed perspective, diagonal framing, extreme close-up, and photomontage to bring images together in dialectical tension to expose the fragmentation of modern life. The Stalinist state decisively settled this contest when, in 1934, it declared the official form of revolutionary art to be socialist realism, identifiable in terms of its requisite and defining proletarian, typical, realistic, and partisan qualities. Socialist realism became so prominent that it now signifies as a kind of shorthand for revolutionary forms of expression, even though, within the Soviet context, cultural producers chafed against its dominance. A persistent underlying tension about ideal form suggests that this mandate was taken up equivocally rather than univocally.[3] Moreover, nascent socialist states—including Hồ Chí Minh's Democratic Republic of Vietnam— sought their own ways to represent socialism, a process that is aligned with but cannot simply be subsumed by socialist realism.

Given the rapid ascendence of socialist realism, however, it is no surprise that when Walter Benjamin's landmark essay "The Work of Art in the Age of Mechanical Reproduction" appeared in 1936 (just three years after Maxim Gorky published his famous pamphlet "On Socialist Realism"), he tackled head-on the very question that, by then, had concerned critics for decades: photography's relation to revolution. Although he did so without explicitly invoking socialist realism or its defining qualities, Benjamin's argument "parallels contemporary Marxist polemics in art," according to Esther Leslie.[4] Benjamin emphasized photography's transformative political potential as a medium of mass communication. Because of his canonical status in the field of photography studies, it's worth pausing to reflect on the implications of Benjamin's argument, which has become a touchstone for leftist critique. Although he was characteristically unclear in this essay about the precise nature of this political transformation, Benjamin introduced compelling possibilities through his concept of an "unconscious optics."[5] According to Benjamin, an unconscious optics not only carries a psychoanalytic resonance (the term establishes an analogy between the operation of the camera and that of psychic drives) but also a technical one (it underscores the camera's capacity for visual enhancement). In the introduction to their coedited book *Photography and the Optical Unconscious*, Shawn Michelle Smith and Sharon Sliwinski stress the significance of the "unthought known," that which the camera sees but the mind has yet to grasp.[6] In so doing they politicize the psychic registers of Benjamin's concept of the optical unconscious. Benjamin was also concerned with the technical dimensions of the camera, specifically its capacity to capture reality to illuminate social conditions and everyday people who have not been previously represented.

Like his contemporaries, Benjamin marveled at the image worlds revealed by the camera. For Benjamin, photography could be drawn on as a potent political weapon against fascism and in service of revolution precisely because the camera could capture images that "escape natural vision."[7] He insisted that the camera conferred agency to the masses because its capacity to reproduce images diminished the auratic power of an original image. Accordingly, Benjamin deployed military tropes to stress photography's forcefulness; in the skilled hands of Dadaists, still photos are "an instrument of ballistics" that "hit the spectator like a bullet," and film, as a medium integrally tied to photography, "burst this prison-world [of familiar objects] . . . by the dynamite of the tenth of a second."[8] Viewed thus, the concept of an unconscious optics offers a visual parallel to the literary theory of the political unconscious that Marxist critic Fredric Jameson would develop many decades after Benjamin's untimely death in 1941,[9] piercing through the illusions of workaday life with incisive force. Photography activates its political potential when it enables the masses to penetrate and thereby battle ideology with unprecedented acuity and accelerated speed. In this way, Benjamin's essay introduces unspoken assumptions about the camera's technical capacity to reveal reality. To access an optical unconscious is to ignite political action.

Long after socialist realism fell out of favor by artists and critics alike—the USSR relaxed its official policy in the 1960s, whereas viewers in capitalist states judged this style as bad art—Benjamin's statements about the revolutionary potential of photography have influenced writers from the mid-twentieth century to the present. Yet a crucial difference is that Benjamin was primarily concerned with how the camera could counter the rise of fascism in World War II, but subsequent writers responded, directly or indirectly, to the global Cold War.[10] Arguably, it was a key aspect of the global Cold War, the war in Vietnam in particular—because of this event's reputedly unprecedented visual coverage[11]—that prompted many critics to reconsider Benjamin's optimism about the camera's revolutionary potential. In so doing, however, they adhered to his political vision while adopting a wary stance.[12] This coverage of the war in Vietnam prompted a generation of theorists to amend their views on photography and revolution, even moving well-known writer Susan Sontag to caution against looking at photography.

As the introduction to this book explains, Sontag turned away from photographs after her brief 1968 visit to North Vietnam's capital, a trip that expressed her solidarity with antiwar activists. However, she did so by resisting prevailing assumptions about photography's potential to galvanize activists. Instead, in *Trip to Hanoi* she lamented the fact that myriad press photographs had preformed her perception. "Indeed, the problem was that Vietnam had become so much a fact of my consciousness as an American that I was having enormous difficulty getting it outside my head," she reflected, adding that "[t]he first experience of being there absurdly resembled meeting a favorite movie star, one who for years has played a role in one's fantasy life, and finding the actual person so much smaller, less vivid, less erotically charged, and mainly different."[13] Her distrust of images prefigured her now-famous ambivalence about an "image-choked" world, which she lamented in a series of essays written shortly after visiting Vietnam a second time in 1972. In these essays, which were first published in the *New York Review of Books* and subsequently collected in her book *On Photography* (1978), she expressed doubts about photography's political potential. These doubts typify a hermeneutics of leftist suspicion that persists in a foundational thread of Euro-American critique. In 1967, just a year before Sontag's first visit to Hanoi, Guy Debord summed up a general judgment of visual repudiation when he inveighed against the "society of the spectacle" and its reduction of images to commodities.[14] Scholars struggled to reconcile Benjamin's Marxist legacy with the increasingly capitalist image worlds they confronted. One's faith in the revolutionary potential of photography might understandably be tested by revelations about photography's less-than-revolutionary role in constructing personality cults around the ruthless Stalin, the charismatic Mao Tse-Tung, and the avuncular Hồ Chí Minh.[15] Many luminaries—Roland Barthes, Susan Sontag, Allan Sekula, and John Tagg, to name just a few—worried that rather than exposing ideology, photography perpetuated it.[16] Rather than quickening revolutionary hope, they feared that the camera posed a threat in the form of surveillance, control, and dehumanization.

My point in summarizing critical perspectives on the issue of photography and revolution is to emphasize their contemporaneity with the war in Vietnam. In providing this summary, however, I am not claiming that Euro-American scholarship influenced Vietnamese photography. (Although Euro-American critics responded to the highly visible war in Vietnam, they took account of images made by the Western press while overlooking those made by Vietnamese photographers.)[17] Nor am I suggesting that it provides a ready-made tool kit to explain the significance of Vietnamese photography. Indeed, the work of Vietnamese photographers, with its earnest faith in the camera's revolutionary potential to develop socialist ways of seeing, can be construed as a rejoinder to Euro-American critique and its prevailing mood of skepticism.

I borrow the concept of socialist ways of seeing from Chinese art historian Xiaobing Tang, who conceptualizes a phenomenon he calls socialist visual culture, which he argues is important because it "expressed a critical awareness of the relationship between the visual and social transformation."[18] In his suggestive study, Tang challenges claims about the transcultural basis of visual culture, which he considers problematic for its Euro-American assumptions.[19] At the same time, Tang counters critical commonplaces about Chinese socialism—for that matter, socialism in general—as an undifferentiated monolith. Moreover, socialist visual culture in China did more than merely illustrate socialism. Instead, Tang posits, it *produced* socialism, making values and ideas visible and more easily graspable for China, where much of the target population was illiterate. This process involves not only official policies but also grassroots experimentation, creating artists who self-reflexively sought to express a vision of revolution in tension with the state at the same time that they were required to follow this state's mandate. Socialist visual culture thus raises questions about what a socialist way of seeing entails and the work that it does. Photography, as an integral component of visual culture, prompts similar questions.

Although it would be a mistake to universalize the Chinese example (there are diverse forms of socialism, so a singular socialist way of seeing does not exist), the implications of Tang's argument are worth considering for other contexts, including Vietnam, particularly if we are mindful of his crucial point about attending to local specificities. Following Tang's insights, I posit that there are socialist *ways* of seeing, which emerging states developed in local sites intimately connected to international contexts to give shape and form to their revolutionary visions. Socialist ways of seeing circulate in an intricate and as yet under-studied network of visual exchange—through, for example, circulation of illustrated magazines and other printed materials, cultural exhibitions, and organization of training workshops—that afforded fruitful opportunities for mutual influence. Formulated in response to an international network whose reach and impact are not yet fully understood, socialist ways of seeing align with the more familiar movement known as socialist realism but are not reducible to this movement.

This chapter explores the role of photography in constructing socialist ways of seeing in Vietnam I argue that these ways of seeing develop as a practice that does not explicitly name itself as such, nor do they cohere as a set of guidelines for artists to rally behind. For revolutionary artists in Vietnam, socialist ways of seeing emerged in response to local photographers' nationalist aspirations and to photo editors' ambitions to reach the masses within the embattled nation through this mass cultural medium. Just as importantly, socialist ways of seeing in Vietnam responded to site-specific material conditions, even as its chief architects sought to appeal more broadly to sympathetic antiwar organizations worldwide and depended on Communist Bloc allies for support by importing technical equipment and exporting images. As my interviews with communist photographers reveal, veterans struggled to overcome conditions of scarcity and violence, typical of asymmetric warfare, in order to produce, reproduce, and circulate images. The photographs they made bear the traces of these fraught conditions of production and the demanding contexts of reproduction. As blemished documents, the photographs show how imperfection is a defining characteristic of socialist ways of seeing in Vietnam, at least as socialism unfolded during the war years. In contrast to their counterparts in the Western press, who benefited from access to ample technical, financial, and infrastructural resources, Vietnamese photographers made do with what they had and strove to overcome physical hindrances and material constraints in the form of defective or limited supplies. Whether these photographs are blurry, scratched, torn, or patched together, the flaws visible on their surface (or evident when these flaws make the resulting image hard to see) suggest a "style" that's distinctively imperfect. However, this flawed style is at odds with the ableist content of the photographs, which celebrated idealized forms, especially the healthy bodies of workers and warriors. These sturdy bodies strive toward a utopian socialist future at the same time that they symbolize the vigor and strength of this future.

The fascinating contrast between imperfect style and idealized ideological form acquires further layers of complexity when we consider the display of these photographs in the postwar period of market liberalization. After the Đổi Mới policy of economic renovation and market liberalization was launched in 1986, Vietnam entered an era of late socialism. Socialist ways of seeing have accordingly shifted to reveal this changed approach. Most curiously, these displays reimagine, sometimes by retouching, photographs from the war, all but erasing the harsh material conditions of their making. The last section of this chapter accordingly explores the significance of manipulation for understanding how socialist ways of looking have changed in contemporary Vietnam. Under late socialism, photographers and viewers have begun reckoning with—and reworking—this legacy of looking in a process that has sparked controversy. Notably, another photograph made by Đoàn Công Tính (figure 1.2) provoked controversy in 2015, when it was revealed that the image was manipulated, even though manipulation is the rule rather than the exception in the history of war photography, not to mention the history of photography more generally.[20]

I contextualize this controversy by drawing on the concept of the "beauty regime," anthropologist Nina Hien's term to denote varied practices of photo-

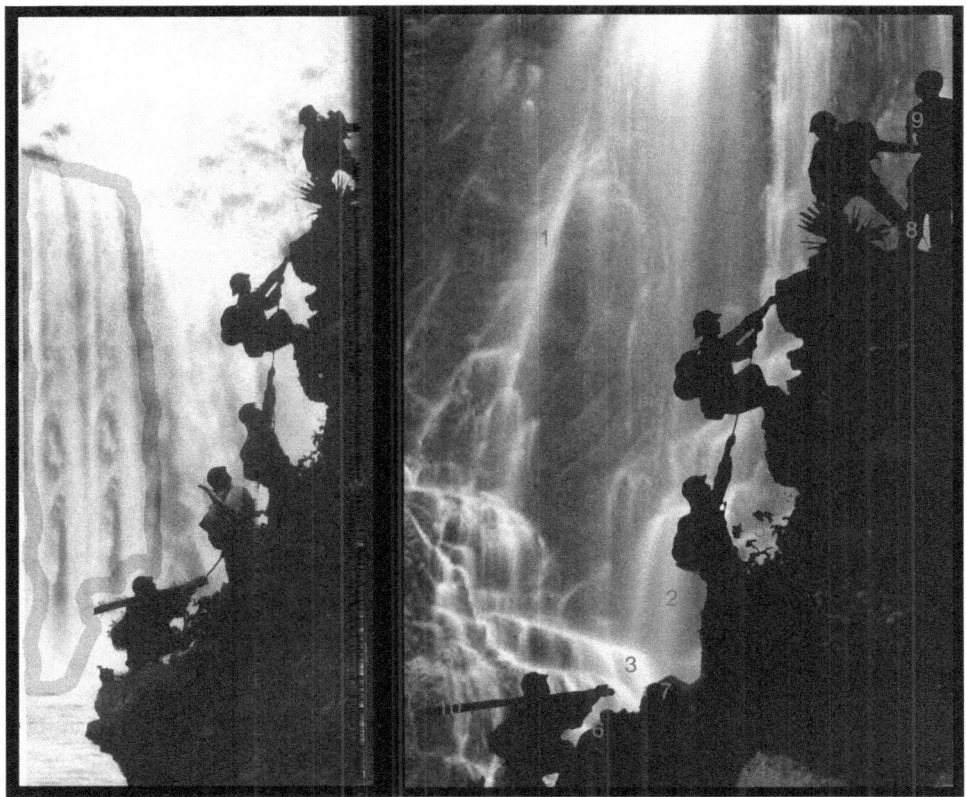

FIGURE 1.2 Trường Sơn waterfall "original" print and retouched version. Photographer: Đoàn Công Tính. Courtesy Jørn Stjerneklar.

graphic manipulation that have become increasingly pervasive since the state announced its Đổi Mới policy.[21] Although I invoke this concept of the beauty regime, I try to avoid the ableist discourse that it denotes. Instead, I argue that the concept enables the state to recalibrate socialist ways of seeing to reconcile the seeming contradictions of late socialism, in which communist values were made to accord, however awkwardly, with market liberalization.

IMPERFECT CONDITIONS, REVOLUTIONARY VISIONS

Mai Nam's living room features a small ancestral shrine, typical of homes in Vietnam, where he and his wife pour tea, offer sweets, and burn incense as a filial rite, which, though once shunned by the state as bourgeois tradition, is

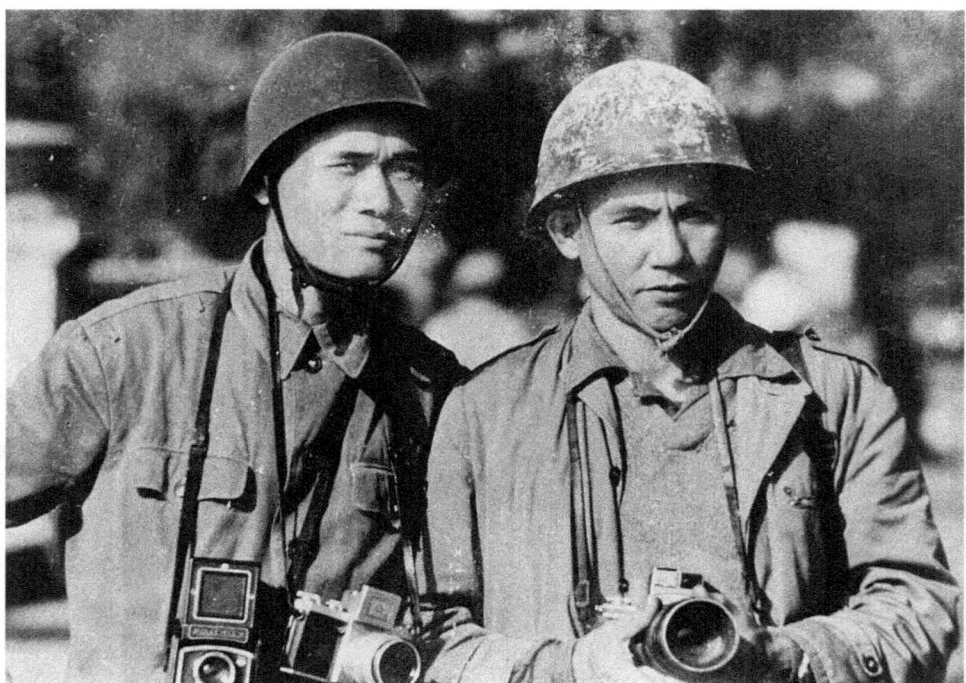

FIGURE 1.3 Portrait of a youthful Mai Nam. Photographer: unknown.

now embraced as part of the new Vietnam.[22] What sets the room apart is the brightest corner of Mai Nam's home, where the ceiling extends to the rooftop instead of receding as it does in the shadowed receiving area. Mounted on the highest wall of this corner is an altar of sorts, although this honors photography instead of the customary ancestors. At the top of weathered plaster ascends his portrait, taken in the 1960s, when he was a handsome photographer for the Young Pioneers, a communist youth organization (figure 1.3).

He worked with the Young Pioneers, tasked with documenting its members' efforts to build roads and cultivate crops in the mountainous region of northern Vietnam. In the photograph he poses with another photographer, who also wears a uniform and helmet. Squinting into the camera, Mai Nam poses with his own camera dangling, like a jewel, from a strap around his neck.

When I ask whether the artifacts hanging on the wall along with this picture are from the war, Mai Nam's face brightens when he sees that I am pointing to one of his most prized treasures, a rifle and camera, which hang just below his portrait. "That's a Praktica I bought in a vintage shop in the 1980s—like the camera I'm holding in my photo but not the same one," he explains.[23] The original East German model, which replaced the Russian Kiev that Mai Nam first used, was not well made and was likely discarded after it could no longer be repaired. On the rare occasions that Mai Nam and his colleagues met with foreign photojournalists, who had traveled to Hanoi to cover press conferences about prisoners of war, they coveted the sophisticated Nikons and Minoltas that their counterparts carried, a striking contrast to their own cameras. Yet acquiring even this inferior equipment, especially during the early years of the conflict, was difficult: "It wasn't easy to have a camera at that time."[24] He did not own the one he used; it was loaned to him by the Young Pioneers, which likely acquired it when its delegation traveled covertly, by way of the northern mountains of Vietnam and China, to Berlin for a youth conference.

Vietnamese photographers who covered the American War relied on equipment made and supplied by communist allies or "liberated" from the enemies they captured. Communist allies provided cameras and lenses that were made in East Germany and the USSR and delivered to Vietnam via Hong Kong or over the northern mountains, presumably along the same routes traveled by Soviet-made weapons. Images were then wired outside the country in a process that was so expensive, time-consuming, and unreliable that photographers held little hope they would be widely seen, and none at all that they would be "news" if they were; wire services during the war were spotty even for the Associated Press, never mind for Hanoi media agencies with limited access to key resources. Still, these northern-based agencies persisted, clinging to the promise that mass culture could enable them to reach the masses.

During the war, three main groups were the ideal audiences for these images. Within Vietnam the North Vietnamese state deployed these images to persuade peasants and fighters of the justice of the revolutionary cause and to embolden those who had already committed to the cause. The images circulated more broadly, within the network of visual exchange described briefly above, particularly in exhibitions organized by Communist Bloc countries.[25] Photographs were also distributed to foreigners beyond the Communist Bloc, especially to members of antiwar organizations, some of whom received copies of *Vietnam Pictorial*, an internationally circulated illustrated magazine whose significance I discuss in greater detail below. Visitors to Hanoi, who represented these antiwar organizations, were also shown copies of these photographs as part of an overall strategy on the part of the image-savvy communist state to win their sympathy and to cultivate international solidarity.

In the 1960s and early 1970s, cameras, accessories, and film were in such short supply that they were not issued to individual photographers but were stored at the headquarters of organizations such as the Young Pioneers, the Army's photographic department, and the VNA. Among these organizations, the VNA, a state-run news organization, remains the most important and influential. Based out of Hanoi, the VNA was founded in September 1945, less than two weeks after Hồ Chí Minh issued his Proclamation of Independence, announcing the sovereignty of the newly formed Democratic Republic of Vietnam (DRV) after the success of the August Revolution. (The Socialist Republic of Vietnam was formed in 1976, when communist victory resulted in reunification and the dissolution of the DRV.) However, one of the agency's first tasks in 1945 was to broadcast news of the Proclamation, which promptly established the VNA as the premier mouthpiece for the DRV.

Subsequently, during the American War the VNA worked alongside other socialist organizations to distribute scarce equipment to photographers. Who received what depended on experience and renown. These photographers had to account for and return cameras once they came home from their assignments at the front. Specialized lenses such as telephotos were in even shorter supply than camera bodies and standard lenses. For this reason, they were seldom issued. One photographer lucky enough to receive this special lens was Văn Bảo, renowned for capturing on film the downing of an American plane. Đoàn Công Tính marvels at the time he found a Minolta from a helicopter that had crashed: "They [Minoltas] were so well made, they survived the wreckage." He regretted having to turn the camera over to the VNA for safekeeping.

Mai Nam's work is now celebrated, but during the war he was treated no differently than his colleagues. A self-trained photographer who learned the craft by reading a French manual he had purchased in a secondhand bookstore in the late 1950s, Nam had access to only one camera and a single lens. When he went out on assignment, he received at most ten rolls of film, although in some cases even fewer rolls were issued. (Legend has it that one photographer had to cover the war with just one roll of film.) However, most of the photographers who worked for the VNA were selected from among Hanoi's university elite. Plucked from their programs, these students enrolled in eighteen-month training courses in journalism, followed by another six-month program on photojournalism, which was led by veteran Vietnamese photographers, some of whom trained in Germany and Russia. Kim Đang remarks that knowledge of both journalism and photojournalism was a benefit: "I think that if I were just a writer, then I would be quite ordinary. I have to use a camera. If I were to see an interesting and good visual story, then I would record that story by photos. But if I cannot shoot or I cannot shoot very well, then I would use my writing, my pen."[26]

Although most of the students enrolled in these courses were men, the VNA director confirmed that as many as four women completed them. One of them, Thu Hoài, is an active photographer today who credits her training in 1973 for introducing her to the craft. Despite the fact that these training courses included women, the profession is still dominated by men, and to my knowledge none of these women were sent to the front as photographers.[27] The photographers I spoke with insisted that women were spared the hardship and danger of covering the war. For her part, Thu Hoài admits that she was not sent to the front to photograph this war, although she subsequently covered the Sino-Vietnamese War (1979). These days, when it comes to honoring contributions to the war effort, women are praised as mothers of revolutionaries, seldom as revolutionaries themselves, although as the next chapter shows, this was not the case during the war. Socialist ways of seeing were gendered, for women were represented as revolutionaries but apparently were not included as producers of images.[28]

Men and a few women were trained in journalism and photography, yet men were the ones dispatched to the field and the front, most of them carrying, as Mai Nam did, a camera, a standard lens, and at most ten rolls of film. In such conditions of scarcity, photographers did not have the luxury afforded to today's digital generation of snapping whatever and whenever they wished; instead, they were forced to shoot sparingly, to compose and stage their images prior to shooting.

The grueling journey required to complete assignments resulted in numerous delays, which meant that the photos that made their way back to VNA head offices accompanied stories that were no longer news. Whereas photojournalists working as freelancers or on assignment for Western press agencies hitched rides on US Air Force helicopters that brought them to the action and back out, communist photographers traveled by bicycle, most often the same Czech-made bikes that volunteers used to clear the Ho Chi Minh Trail. In addition to documenting stories about their struggles, the photographers did double duty, assisting in the tasks of transporting food and conveying communications. Because the trail was more of a clearing in the early years of the war, photographers had to carry their bicycles over otherwise impassable areas and sometimes arrived at their destination only after months of exhausting travel.

Văn Sắc recalls one such adventure, wherein militiamen had to disguise a bridge by day and by night place wooden planks across its bare tracks to be able to move equipment and supplies. He came upon the tracks during the day and, despite the risk of being discovered, resolved to cross quickly, reasoning that the story would not wait for him. Spreading his legs wide across the thin rails, he inched forward with his bicycle awkwardly balanced in his hands and his camera slung on his back. Halfway across, however, he paused: a plane was circling overhead. With a racing heart and shaking legs, he waited for shooting to start and bombs to drop, but after a few breaths the plane drifted away: "I was lucky."[29]

Getting to the story was only the first test. Transporting the images back to headquarters was also tough. Although messengers were tasked with carrying rolls of film to VNA offices, their unreliability prompted some photographers to take matters in their own hands. To ensure that his rolls of film arrived at their destination, Định Quảng Thành took on the responsibility of acting as courier himself. Đoàn Công Tính traveled on the Ho Chi Minh Trail after it was wide enough to let trucks rumble along rocky, uneven roads. Sometimes he carried paperwork that authorized him to hitch along, but the times he did not, he would sneak on board and hope that the vehicle would convey him to headquarters before he was detected.

For Kim Đảng, who was an army photographer, it was unnecessary to move images to distant viewers. His photos were meant for inclusion in the army newspaper to be seen by soldiers. For this reason, the darkroom he used was located within the encampment itself, dug from the earth and adapted from material extracted from the natural surroundings. Fashioned out of a shallow bunker described by the VNA's publication as "the darkest place in the world," much like the shelters in which soldiers sought protection from bombing raids, the darkroom had a small opening for controlled light exposure.[30] Although hidden beneath the earth, the darkroom bunker was too shallow to withstand intense bombing. The water he used to wash the film was scooped from nearby rivers and streams or from the pools collected in surrounding bomb craters. By day, volunteer youth groups labored to fill these craters so that vehicles could pass through wrecked roads more easily; by night, the soldiers used the water gathered there to relieve thirst and wash film.

The jungle offered an array of resources: cover for the transport of supplies, shelter for soldiers' camps, amenities for the construction of darkrooms, and a venue for photo exhibitions. Pieced together out of the physical environment and carved from nature itself, these camouflaged darkrooms were portable, mobile, and adaptable. Drawing on guerrilla warfare tactics, photographers were able to rise to the dual challenges of material deprivation

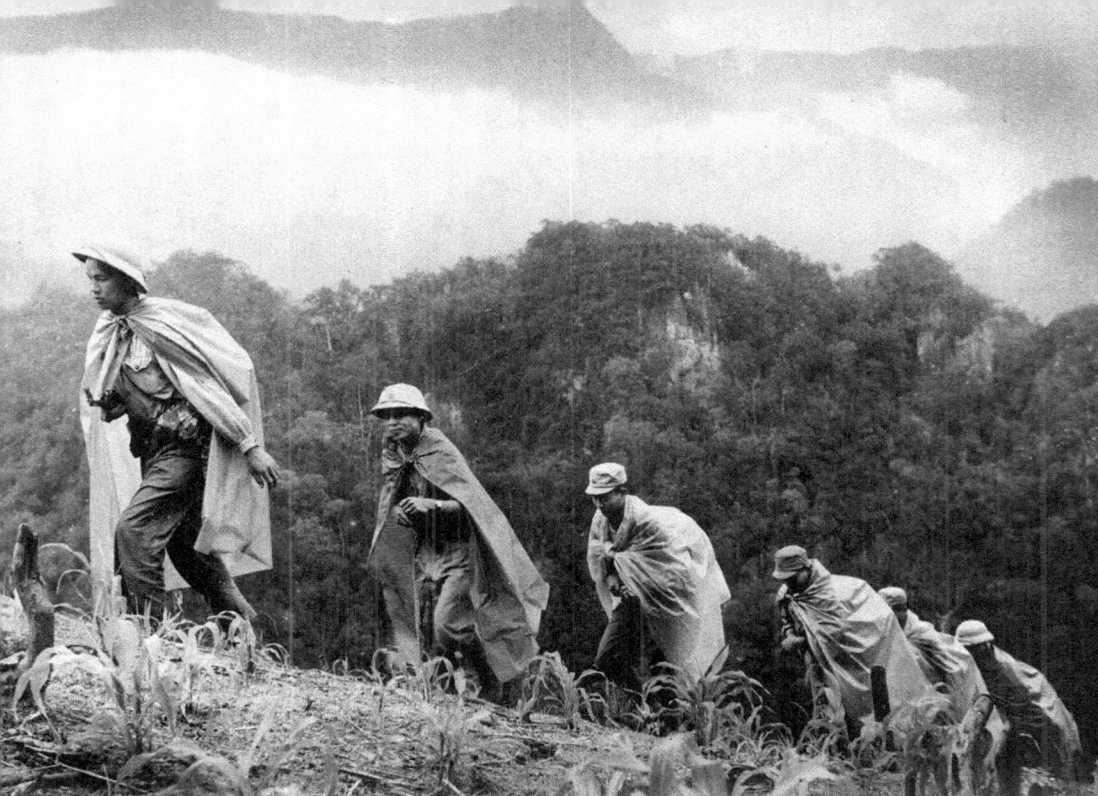

FIGURE 1.4 Vietnamese landscape (Ho Chi Minh Trail). Photographer: Lê Minh Trường.

and arduous conditions. In these contexts, warring visions entailed deploying the instruments of war. Moreover, the landscape often featured as a stunning backdrop to, if not the very subject of, revolutionary photography (figure 1.4). In this way, as I elaborate below, the photographers could reconcile their revolutionary objectives with the corrupt aesthetic sensibility associated with French colonial taste.

   In addition to illustrating stories published in the army newspaper, which were meant to boost the morale of soldiers, Kim Đảng's photos were displayed in makeshift jungle exhibitions assembled from such humble objects as a line of string, which, when tied to trees, provided a surface for photos to be hung with clips. Võ An Khánh also displayed photos in jungle exhibitions in the South, where surrounding villagers would gather to view the images he captured as well as those smuggled from the North (figure 1.5). He describes these events as crowded with curious villagers, who flocked to exhibitions with excitement "because in the countryside, there wasn't TV and the exhibitions were a kind of entertainment."[31] Besides offering a pleasant

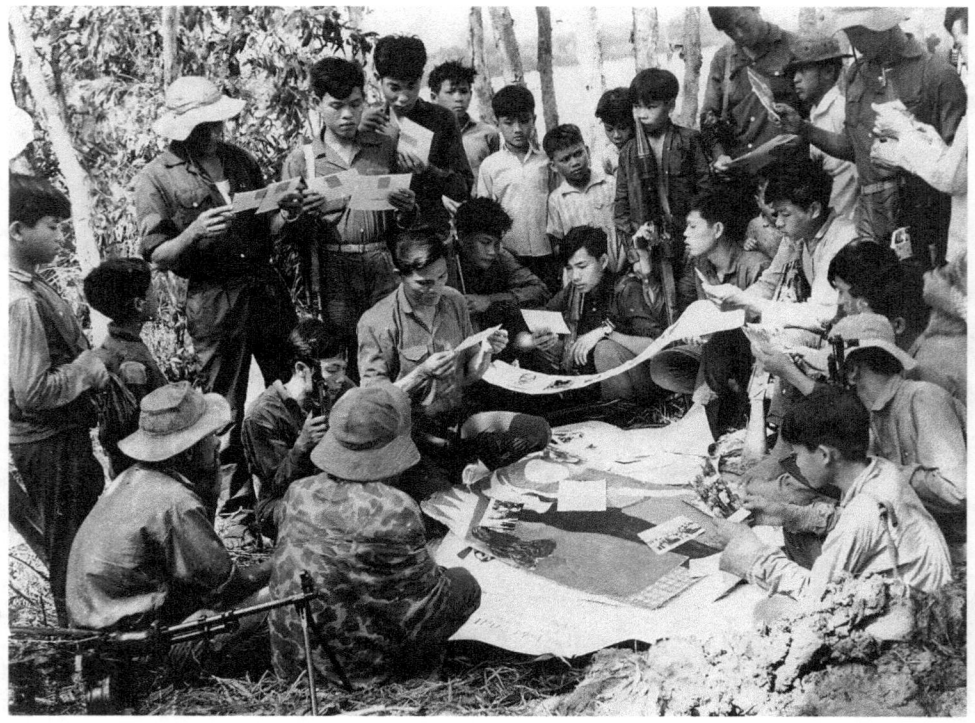

FIGURE 1.5 Jungle exhibition. Photographer: Võ An Khánh.

distraction from the tedium of daily life, such photos updated peasants about the progress of war in the North, information censored by the Saigon-based Government of the Republic of Vietnam. They served an additional purpose of recruiting local peasants.

Võ An Khánh had extensive experience in promoting socialism in South Vietnam during the 1960s and 1970s. However, he got his start by producing propaganda posters. Because these objects were cheaply and easily made, they could be distributed widely, which also explains their prominence at jungle exhibitions. But Khánh's subsequent shift to photography suggests continuities between these two means of visual communication. Propaganda posters and photographs may be different in form (posters are colorfully striking and sometimes fantastical in contrast to the predominantly somber black-and-white tones of supposedly more realistic photography), but their relationship is nevertheless complementary rather than contradictory. They both functioned as visually informative and pleasing ways to express abstract ideas concretely.[32]

Khánh also embraced photography with the enthusiasm and resourceful-ness of the soldiers he celebrated in his images. Like the rebels who crafted pongee traps of bamboo spikes hidden deep in the earth or who improvised long-range weapons by exerting the force of their bodies, Võ An Khánh ap-proached photography as a weapon that could strengthen allies and wound enemies. Although he stops short of invoking an explicit link between the practices of asymmetric warfare and the shooting of pictures with scarce sup-plies and inferior equipment, his approach nevertheless implies an analogy. Like other photographers, he stored his camera and film in sturdy US am-munition containers packed with bags of roasted rice, necessary to protect technical equipment from mold in a humid climate. During the day, the like-liest time for bombing raids, he buried these containers in the ground for safekeeping. At night, he dug them up. Producing warring visions required repurposing the instruments of war, not just invoking the familiar parallel between shooting guns and cameras.

In contrast to Võ An Khánh, Mai Nam explicitly establishes an analogy between asymmetric warfare and photography but goes beyond clichés about shooting to emphasize the resourcefulness of revolutionaries. At his home, it is hard to miss the prominent display of his portrait—and the fact that be-neath this photograph hangs both a camera and a rifle. Although he scoffed at the notion that he used the gun as a weapon during the war, stressing that he armed himself with the camera instead, he also explained that he made the hunting rifle himself out of material he gathered and repurposed. Mai Nam's resourcefulness in producing the gun extends to his work in produc-ing pictures.

This approach of making do is the hardscrabble response of the disadvan-taged, of which the refashioning of discarded enemy equipment to protect film and camera is only one of many tactics. Conditions of scarcity fueled innovation. Further innovations arose in the wake of rationed equipment. For example, the technique of piecing together multiple shots (*ghép*) cre-ated a panoramic view without need of a wide-angle lens (figure 1.6). Editors would later suture these shots, with the seams and repetition of foreground figures intact, as telling indicators of a makeshift but no less artful style of expediency.

Another innovation became a common trick that helped solve the prob-lem of shooting without a flash: rockets firing against a dark sky (figure 1.7). Photographers would sit back with steady hands on the camera's switch, wait-ing for the right moment when the weapons of war would double as accesso-ries to cameras that lacked the flash necessary for nighttime shooting. Getting

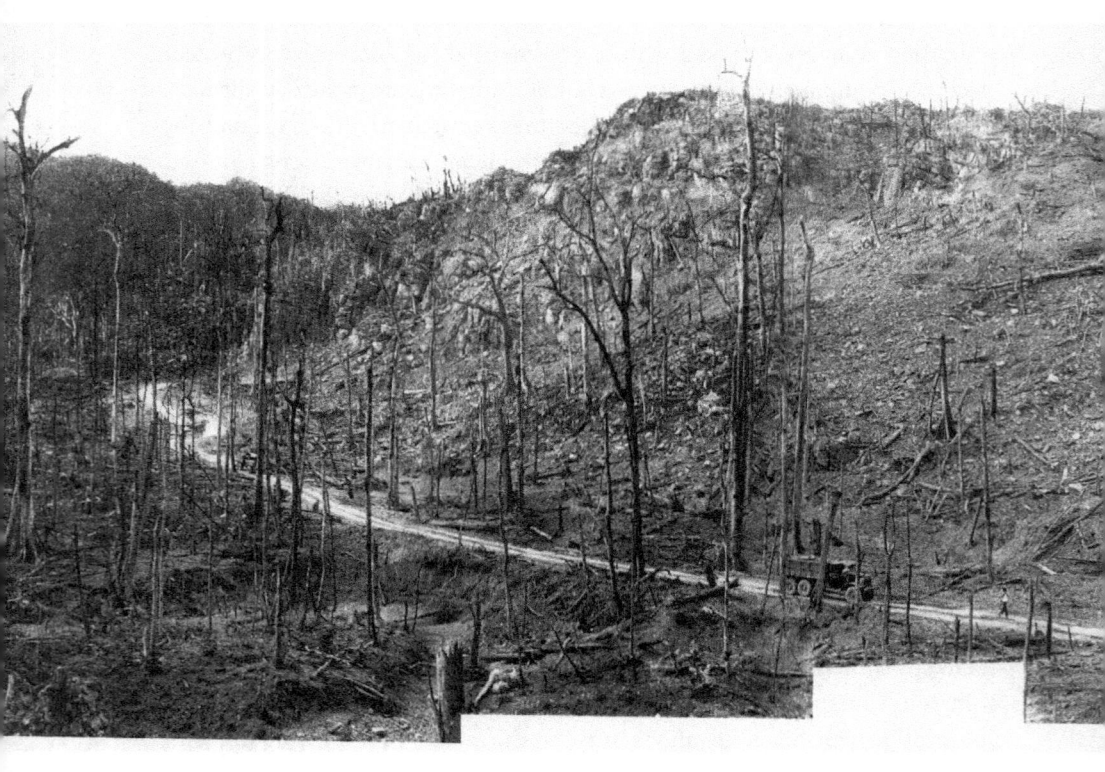

FIGURE 1.6 Improvised panorama, circa
1960s. Photographer: unknown.

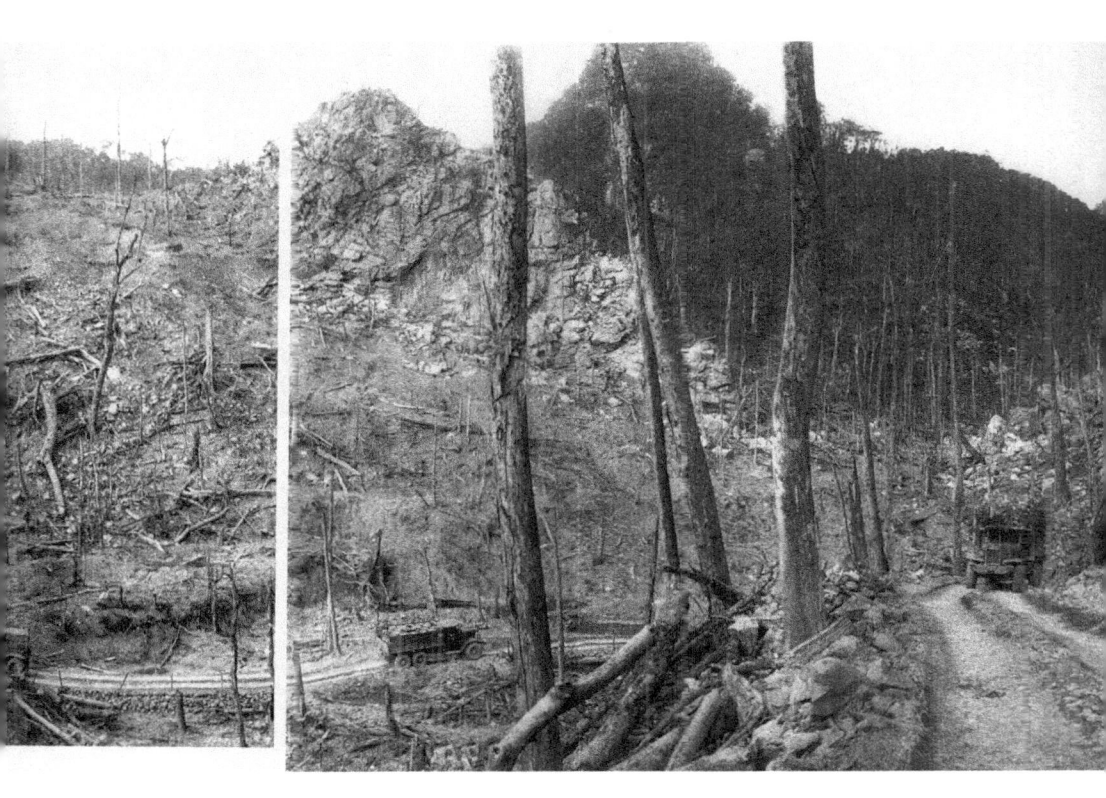

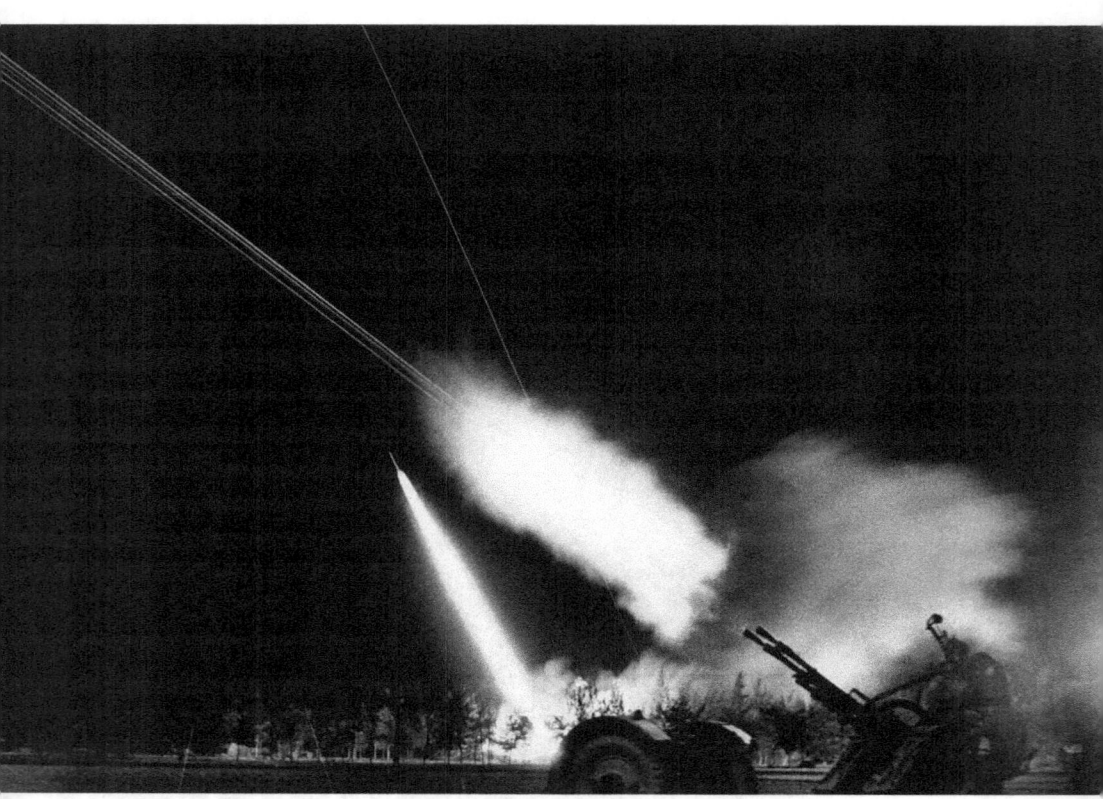

FIGURE 1.7 Rockets fired at nighttime. Photographer: Đoàn Công Tính.

the picture required patience and luck as much as skill. In such photos, flares operate as improvised flashes illuminating the shadows of soldiers under an electric sky.

Although the night sky was challenging, it was still possible to photograph. Beneath the earth, where soldiers and villagers retreated for shelter during bombing raids, it was even harder for photographers to operate. If aboveground rockets lit the way, bullets provided a solution to less than ideal lighting conditions in underground tunnels. Having absorbed principles of chemistry from his French photography textbook, Mai Nam reasoned that gunpowder could substitute for the magnesium powder used for flash photography. First, he composed the scene, then whittled apart a bullet and tapped out the gunpowder. When it was ignited, he was able to capture a vision of life in the tunnels.[33]

Antiwar activists and other radicals participated in a form of tourism, and in their visits to Hanoi and they paused to admire these ingenious improvisations.[34] Akin to the bricolage that cultural anthropologist Claude Lévi-Strauss and others have theorized as a creative method of the impoverished, the primary aim of this response to material deprivation was to make use of the seemingly unusable. Although such a practice is hardly unique to socialist photographers, this recycling ethos is among the revolutionaries' signature style. Out of the scraps of downed warplanes recyclers were able to salvage metal that they then repurposed as fences, flowerpots, and even combs and knives, which they gave as gifts to the radical tourists. Many of these tourists marveled at how little was wasted, in contrast to their own habits of mindless consumption of commodities—a practice, we might add, that extends to photographs that circulate in capitalist image worlds, which are no less mindlessly consumed.

Not surprisingly, the recycled objects were war trophies, everyday reminders of the rewards of cunning and unified effort. Later, these recycled objects became more than just reminders: they served as monuments of tenacity and perseverance. Exhibitions at the Military History Museum (formerly the Army Museum) in Hanoi exemplify this gritty spirit of innovation. Among intact fighter jets, tanks, and helicopters is the wreckage of one of the greatest wartime targets, a B-52 bomber. Pieces of the bomber's rusted shell are massed together and crowned with its broken nose. Firmly buried on the cement grounds devoted to the story of socialist success, the upward thrust of the nose exposes the hubris of American military ambition.[35]

Yet sculpture tells only part of the story of the ideological roots of the recycling ethos. Photography is also indispensable to this display. Beside the twisted metal is an image blown up to an exaggerated scale proportionate to

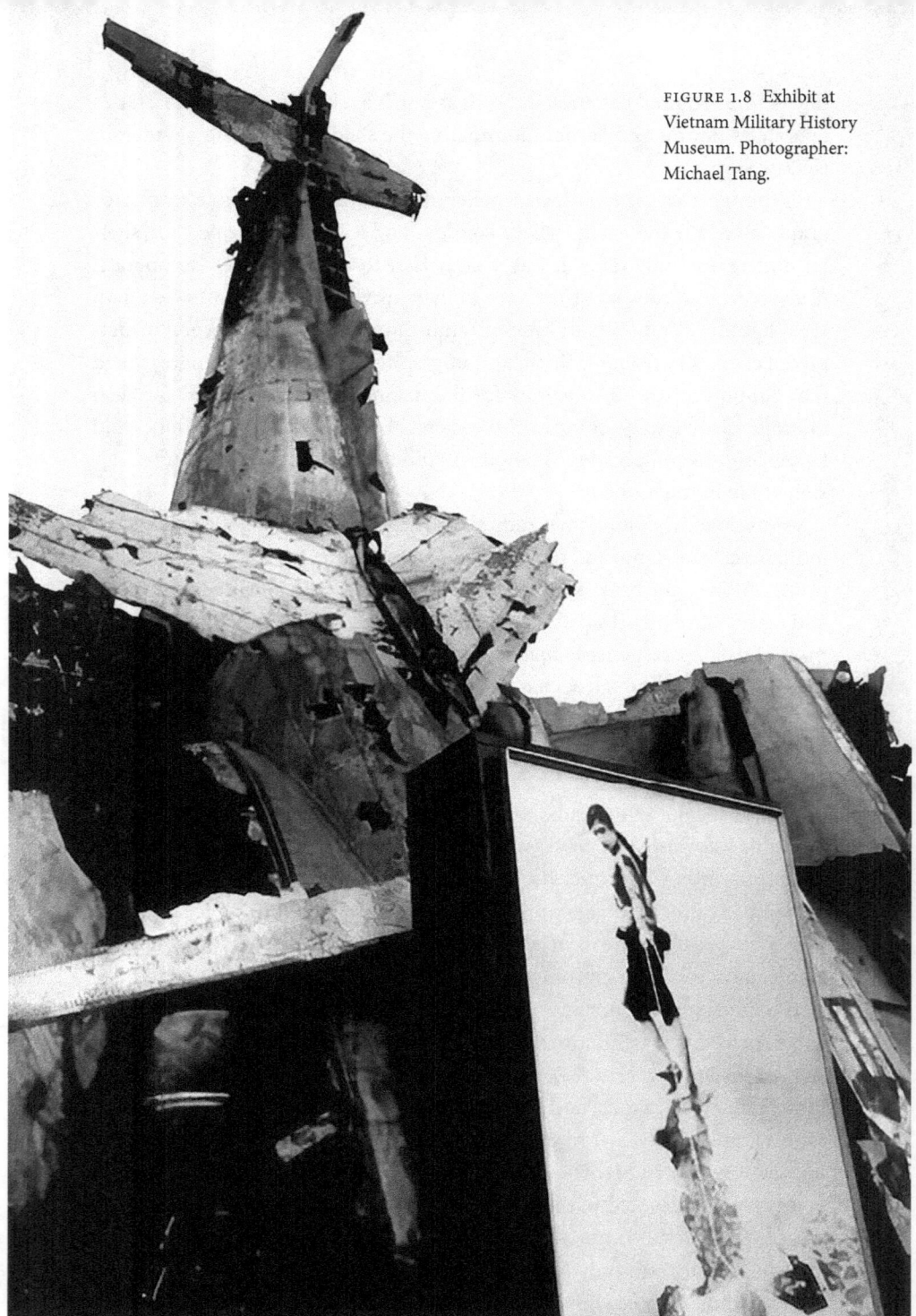

FIGURE 1.8 Exhibit at Vietnam Military History Museum. Photographer: Michael Tang.

the massive sculpture itself (figure 1.8). This famous photo, taken by an un-known photographer of an unnamed woman salvaging wreckage, is not just an illustration of the process of reconstruction; rather, it feminizes and styl-izes the recycling ethos. More than merely the subject of the photo, salvage here becomes a defining feature of Vietnamese photography; salvage forms the material of and lends inspiration to an exultant vision of revolution. In-deed, as framed by the museum, the photograph is visually arresting, accord-ing to the ableist rhetoric of the image, because of the contrast between the beautiful and significantly whole body of the woman and the broken ma-chine parts that she recovers. In this way the state draws on photography to establish socialist ways of seeing, attuned to the healthy body as a metaphor of the state's vigor and calibrated in defiance against the imperial forms of vi-olence responsible for partitioning the nation and, during the war, wounding its people.[36]

Not all photographers affirmed this dominant metaphor of whole-bodied anticolonial nationalism. Instead, some photographs attempt to expose the discourse of prosthesis. Whereas the notion of an unconscious optics as pros-thetic lens assumes that the camera extends the limits of the human eye, some VNA photographers were concerned with contemplating the limits of the camera's vision, subtly undermining the DRV's celebration of whole-bodied strength. Viewers can detect one such limit in the static and posed quality of their images. This perhaps explains why such photographs are not usually included in histories of war photography, so long as enthusiasts of the genre emphasize proximity to battlefield action as a defining feature. For example, the photograph of the battle for Quảng Trị, introduced at the beginnning of this chapter, is unusual because it marks one of the few times that a com-munist photographer managed to be up close to the action (see figure 1.1). However, its blurry quality—the result of slow shutter speed and the limits of equipment, among other factors—makes it technically flawed. The docu-mentary qualities of verisimilitude and immediacy in such photographs attest to material constraints that produce an imperfect picture of revolution, even as discourses of revolution promoted a kind of embodied perfection, empha-sizing resiliency and overall potency through the steadfast resolve of workers and warriors.

Given the DRV's primary and markedly ableist concern with physical strength as a trope for anticolonial resistance and national reunification, the work of Lâm Tấn Tài is all the more extraordinary as a departure from this unspoken rule; his camera reveals the blindness that other photogra-phers overlooked. Although Lâm was blinded in one eye while covering

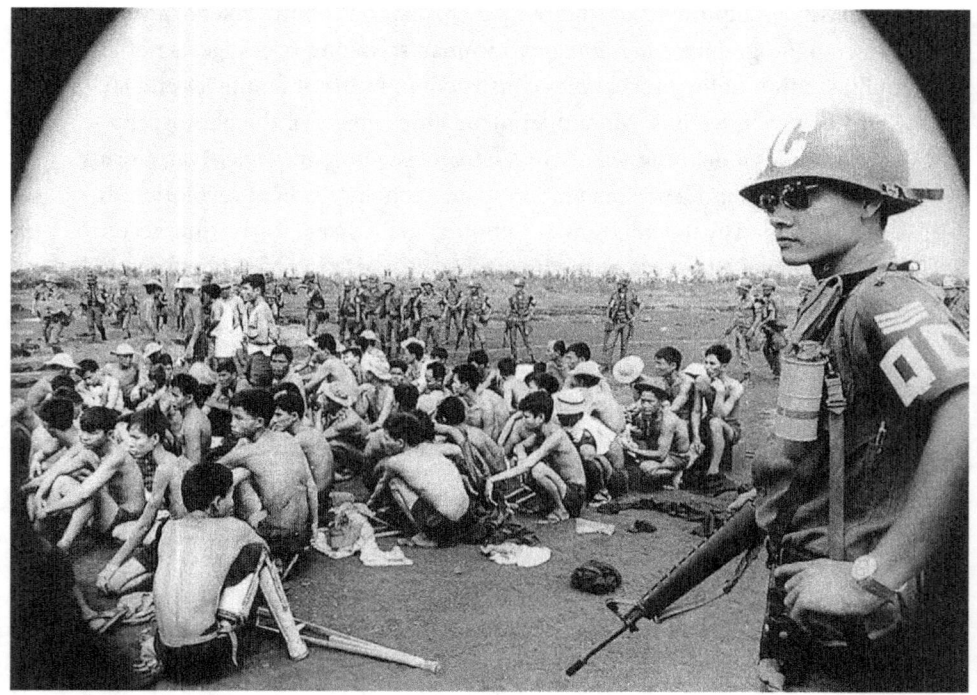

FIGURE 1.9 Prisoner Exchange. Photographer: Lâm Tấn Tài.

the 1968 Tet Offensive, he continued to photograph. In 1973 he was in Lôc Ninh, on the border of Vietnam and Cambodia, to report on an exchange of prisoners. Given the glare of the midday sun, he must have squinted across the baking tarmac where the men awaited their freedom. To correct for the harsh light, he attached a shade to his lens, but it was the wrong one. The resulting photo is framed by inky curved edges (figure 1.9).

More than just a mistake, these black edges are the imprint of the unseeable, transforming Lâm's photograph into a paradoxical display of imperfect vision: this is what it looks like when a blind eye sees. Yet so solid is the blackness of the framed edges, which attests to technical imperfection as a result of compromised peripheral vision, so seldom encountered, more rarely reproduced, that even after many glances it is easy to miss what is squarely captured in the center: most of the prisoners awaiting exchange are themselves injured. They sit on the tarmac cradling their amputated limbs with their crutches and prostheses close by. This is not just a photograph by a disabled photographer; the image hints at the ways that a vision of disability, however partial, might offer an alternative to the discourse of enablement championed by the DRV in its development of socialist ways of seeing. His photograph is remarkable because it exposes what socialist ways of seeing were reluctant to show: injured and dead bodies, censored as dispiriting and thus unsuitable subjects for revolutionary representation.

Glimpses of this alternative perspective can also be found in one of Võ An Khánh's most famous photographs from 1970, which portrays a makeshift surgical operation deep in the midst of the U Minh jungle in the Mekong Delta (figure 1.10). Set as it is against an improbable backdrop of unhygienic slime and sticky heat, it is little wonder that many viewers question its authenticity, reasoning that a scene so surreal as to come with a gauzy scrim must be staged.

These photographs are fascinating because they are part of the socialist state's archives despite the fact that the images, by representing injured bodies, nuance revolutionary ideals of strength and uplift. Even though the state censored photographs that portrayed wounded, suffering, or dead bodies, images show injury obliquely, whether enveloped in a misty and incongruously artful setting, as in Võ Anh Khánh's photographs, which focus on repair of injury, or as in Lâm Tấn Tài's photograph, hidden in the plain sight of blind vision. In their works, Võ Anh Khánh and Lâm Tấn Tài thus provide a subtle rejoinder to the able-bodied workers and soldiers who were the dominant subject of photography and attest to the state's concern with revolution as a project of political enablement. In grappling with subjects at odds with the state's explicit objectives of uplifting spirits, anticolonial resistance, and national reunification, these unusual works suggest that socialist ways of seeing are more complex and less uniform than critics have recognized.

Indeed, socialist photography should not be dismissed as mere propaganda (*tuyên truyền*). As Sabine Kriebel points out, labeling images as propaganda is an unsatisfactory method of visual analysis, foreclosing rather than prompting critical inquiry.[37] In its fixation on, and derision of, obvious techniques of persuasion, pejorative judgments of propaganda risk missing other, no less important, parts of the story—in the case of Vietnamese photography, the parts of the story that touch on themes of suffering that were at odds with the state's promotion of physical strength as a metaphor for political vitality. Although Kriebel's discussion of the aesthetics of information and politics of persuasion focuses on Weimar-era photography, her call to take propaganda seriously opens up a more nuanced approach to apparently simplistic images.[38]

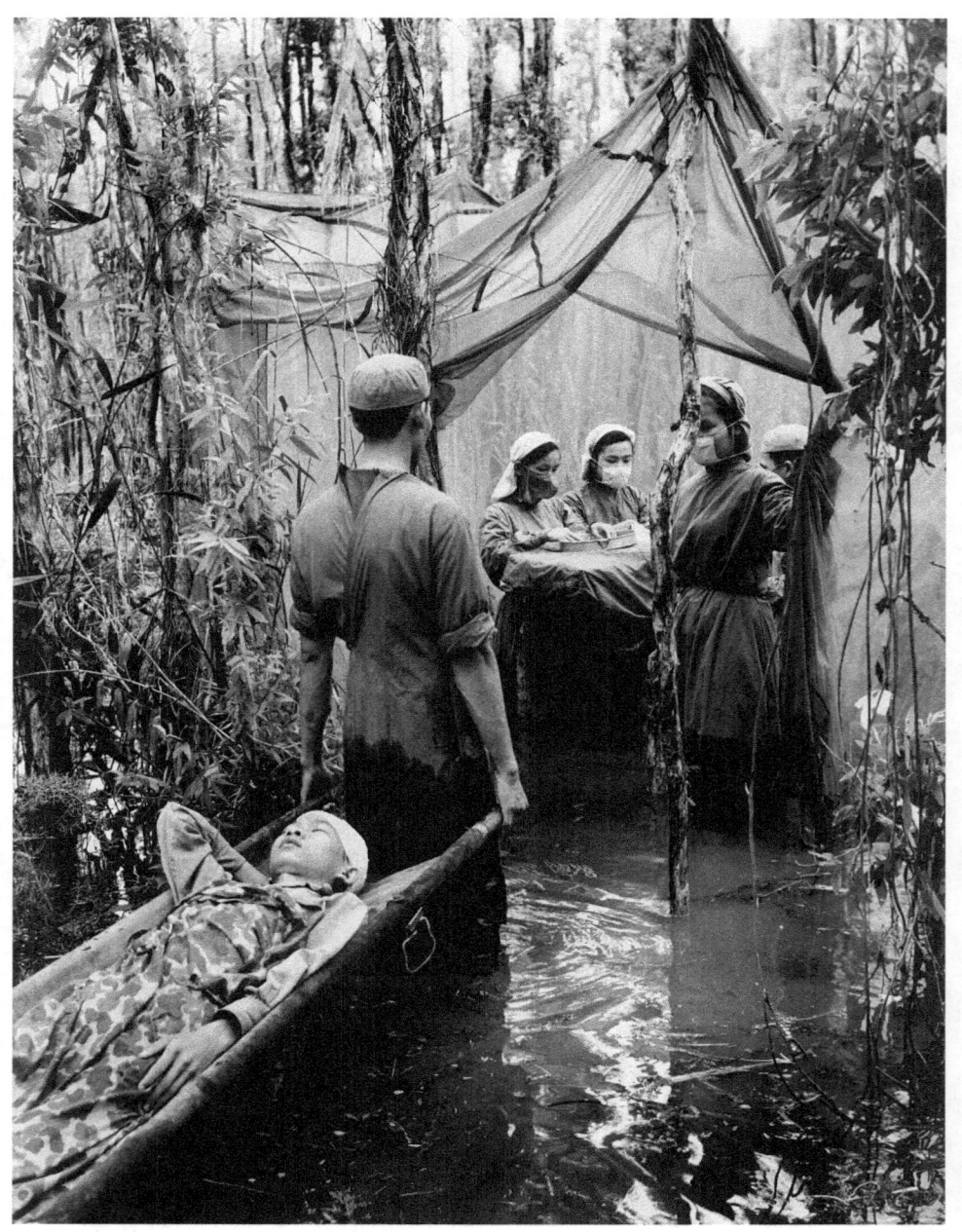

FIGURE 1.10 M.A.S.H. unit. Photographer: Võ Anh Khánh.

According to Pham Tiên Dũng, the now-retired photo editor at the VNA, the state's position was unequivocal: although form mattered, other elements of photography, namely ideological content, took precedence. He explained that the "basic nature of news photography" includes the following five elements: ideology, truthfulness, news currency, mass appeal, and—last of all—aesthetics.[39] The VNA's history of photography outlines an additional five key themes that emerged in the post-1954 era, when the North broke the yoke of French colonial rule and the first photographers' group organized exhibitions as events to reclaim photography from their oppressors. Specifically, these exhibitions stressed the themes of socialist values, expression of clarity, praise of national unity, the honoring of country and people, and the building of friendship and world peace.[40] Accordingly, this new form of photography presented two quintessentially revolutionary subjects: the sacrifice of heroic fighters and the toil of laborers in fields and factories, whose efforts on and off the battlefield were essential to the waging of total war. Taken together, these themes constitute the ideological basis of revolutionary photography in a manner that dovetails, yet should not be conflated, with the familiar tenets of socialist realism, particularly its glorification of proletariats. Ideology informed the subject matter of these photographs and guided practitioners into what to look at, how to represent it, and how to instruct spectators to recognize what counts as revolutionary.[41]

These primary components of ideology and aesthetics seem resolved insofar as the latter followed from the former, but members of this first photography organization acknowledged the difficulty of achieving this resolution. In short, a problem arose when "the pictures that conveyed ideology were dry and lifeless, but beautiful pictures lacked the breath of the new life [of communism]." Although the VNA's explanation of its principles does not account for how, precisely, to balance ideology with aesthetics, a 1969 conference of patriotic photographers provided an answer. At this event, the participants urged photographers to abandon aesthetics in favor of more pressing political subjects: "There are those who have yet to renounce old habits, and fool themselves by looking through distorted lenses in pursuit of beautiful subjects. . . . Saigon, through our clear [communist] lenses, we will produce a new day."[42] In short, socialist photography had to renounce aesthetics—in a manner that parallels the triumph of the Soviet documentarians over their rival avant-garde modernists—so that it could adhere faithfully to ideological principles. Yet if we look closely, we can discern how beauty slips back into the socialist picture.

What, for the DRV, was aesthetically pleasing? A key approach to invoking beauty was highly gendered, through a focus on the representation of women and constructing this figure as a multiform symbol of revolution (the concern of chapter 2). Although women did not serve as battlefield photographers during the war, they entered the visual field, specifically when the theme of feminine beauty served to enliven the otherwise "dry and lifeless" substance of revolutionary ideology (figure 1.11).

Similarly, photographs taken of roadwork and military operations along the Ho Chi Minh Trail, on the formidable Trường Sơn mountain chain, center the sublime landscape as the source and symbol of revolutionary resolve, endurance, and triumph (see figure 1.4). The focus on landscape was acceptable, it seems, so long as photographs established a connection between this setting and collective struggle, as evident in the men and women who are most often portrayed working alongside one another and seldom in isolation. Although Vietnamese critics at early exhibitions decried the stain of French influence as, at best, bourgeois and, at worst, a throwback to colonial ways of seeing, they did not jettison aesthetics outright. Instead, by invoking the acceptable theme of nationalism, rendered through pleasing forms of femininity and landscape, Vietnamese photographers managed to reconcile form with content.

In these varied ways, revolutionary photography sought to correct the ideological distortions of a decadent bourgeois aesthetics and, in so doing, represent unrepresentable subjects deemed antithetical to the building of a new society. That is, by amplifying the message of socialist uplift, photographers resolved the problem of aesthetics. The visual record of revolution uneasily reconciles the contradictions of aesthetics and ideology.

SOCIALISM'S NATIONALIST COLORS

The task of reconciling these contradictions was perhaps most vividly expressed on the covers of *Vietnam Pictorial*. The word *pictorial* denotes a type of print publication devoted to photographs as illustrations and is also often referred to as an illustrated magazine.[43] One of the Communist Party's longest-running magazines, *Vietnam Pictorial* was launched only five months after the Viet Minh defeated French troops on May 7, 1954, at the battle of Điện Biên Phủ, as a way of heralding North Vietnam's newfound independence. Appearing continuously on a monthly and then biweekly basis, the illustrated magazine was, in its first few decades, published on rough, cheap

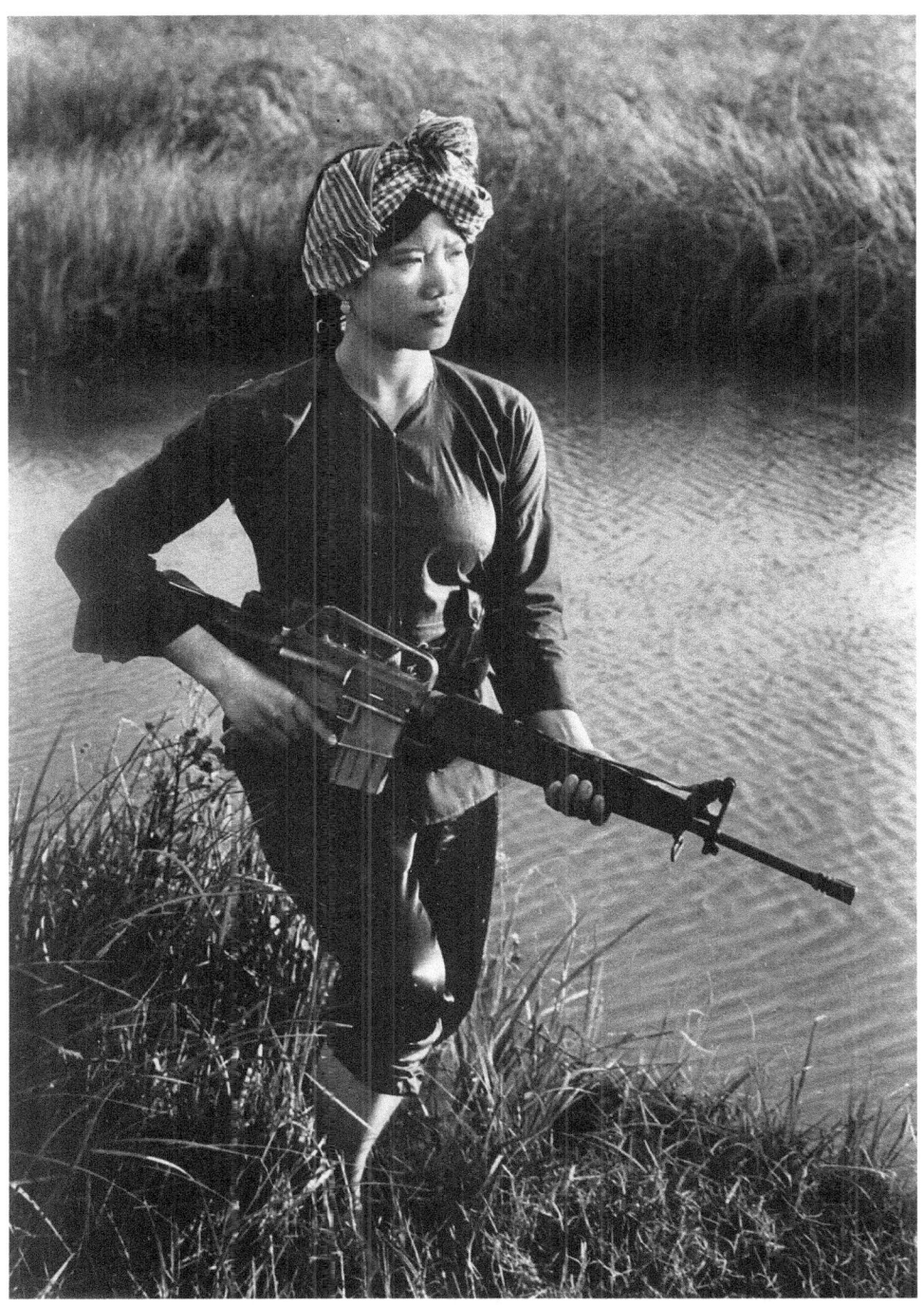

FIGURE 1.11 Militiawoman. Photographer: Lê Minh Trường.

paper. It remains in print to this day and has also expanded to include electronic issues.

From the outset the fledgling state supported the magazine, which first operated under the auspices of the Ministry of Culture and Information Commission, subsequently under the direction of the Central Propaganda Department, and presently as part of the VNA. Although the illustrated magazine reached a domestic audience, its overall mandate was expansive; the VNA sought to project an image of the nation abroad to sympathetic audiences among the Vietnamese diaspora scattered across the world. At the same time, the existence of English-language versions of the illustrated magazine suggests the importance of an international readership, especially among antiwar activists and socialist allies behind the Iron and Bamboo curtains.

In its first few years, *Vietnam Pictorial* reproduced predominantly black-and-white images, even on the cover, and continued to do so well into the 1960s and 1970s. However, color entered the picture from the very beginning: the bright, eye-catching masthead, which was printed alternately in blue, red, and later yellow, showed that color printing was possible though not commonly used in the magazine. That the magazine chose to print in color sparingly attests to financial and technical constraints because of the prohibitive cost of color printing.[44] By 1957, the magazine began printing its cover in vibrant colors, although the inside of the magazine featured only a handful of color images until the late 1970s (plate 1).

This pattern of sporadic color printing arguably departs from the illustrated magazine's international history. In the nineteenth century, this genre emerged, and when color printing was introduced in the early twentieth century, many illustrated magazines began taking advantage of the technology. By the 1930s, color printing became a staple of these magazines. It was taken up enthusiastically by advertisers, which relished the possibilities it afforded for illustrating commodities with lush brilliance, the fashion industry particularly embracing color in markedly gendered ways.

Historians trace the decline of illustrated magazines to the 1970s, when the ascendance of television hastened the failure of major publications such as *Life* and *Look*.[45] As advertisers increased exposure on television, they cut spending on magazines. Just as importantly, the decline of the illustrated magazine coincides with the visual history of the war in Vietnam, which, as I noted in the introduction, marked television's coming of age and photojournalism's last glorious gasp.[46] Significantly, an important innovation on the part of photojournalists, in the Western press at least, was color photography. To compete with television, which usually ran black-and-white footage, *Life* magazine published its first color combat photo essay in 1963, accompanied with an editor's note boasting that "back came this week's pictures showing, as only color can, the blood and mud and savagery of this war."[47] War photographs included in American illustrated magazines claimed a heightened realism to challenge the verisimilitude of televisual reporting.[48] Depicting the setting in the rich greens of the lush jungle setting against a brown palette that captured the muddy terrain with striking vividness, the color spread sought to represent the war in more realistic ways than black-and-white images could convey. Larry Burrows, who died in a helicopter accident, famously experimented with color film with photographs that emblematized the grittiness of the war (plate 2). Not all photojournalists took to color as enthusiastically as Burrows. Notably, famed photojournalist Philip Jones Griffiths remained skeptical. Although he also shot this war using color film (yet included only black-and-white images in his celebrated photo book, *Vietnam, Inc.*), Griffiths attacked color as "the biggest single hindrance to photojournalism the world has ever seen."[49]

However, *Vietnam Pictorial*'s use of color provides an implicit rejoinder to this history of color printing in illustrated magazines and its attention to verisimilitude. We may never know the reasons for *Vietnam Pictorial*'s decisions regarding image selection and color printing—to my knowledge, no records about the editing process exist, although it is possible that the state liberated or took over equipment owned by French colonial magazines.[50] But what is clear is that color is rendered with little, if any, regard for the realistic effect that US advertisers and others sought when they turned to color printing amid an overall prejudice that the inclusion of color trivialized serious matters. According to David Batchelor, this prejudice amounts to an overall "chromophobia."[51] We can attribute this fear and disdain to color photography's association with commercial culture—color photographs were from the outset used in ads—or with gender, as women were often represented in color. Yet as Jennifer Bajorek reminds us, such commonplaces demand further reflection and scrutiny of the "extra-moral" dimensions of color.[52]

Consider, for example, the first cover issue of *Vietnam Pictorial* that appears in color (plate 1). Is it a copy of a painted photograph? Or is it a black-and-white photograph that has been colored through the half-tone process of reproduction? One cannot tell by looking closely at the cover. When I consulted with experts on color printing, they cautioned that viewers cannot discern, just from looking at a copy, whether an image was originally a painted photograph or whether it was black-and-white photography that was subsequently colored. To my knowledge, no original print exists. What

I am sure of, though, is that this cover makes no attempt at the realism that Larry Burrows strove for in his groundbreaking photo-essay for *Life* magazine. Rather, this *Vietnam Pictorial* cover deliberately strives to achieve the *effect* of a painted photograph. This is obvious in the unrealistic colors and the incongruity between the opacity of the blooming flowers and the transparency with which the children's flesh is rendered. In fact, most of the color images in *Vietnam Pictorial* evoke this effect of a painted photograph, at least in publications from 1954 to 1965, the early years of the war against the Americans leading up to the escalation of US military involvement.

This effect is especially noteworthy when one flips ahead to 1973, when color is rendered more "naturally," that is, in a manner consistent with color photography (plate 11). It may be tempting to dismiss this effect of the painted photograph—or what I am calling a colored photograph—as shoddy work, particularly when it comes to the first colored cover. However, the evidence of other finely rendered images demonstrates technical ability. To dismiss this effect of the painted photograph for lack of skill because of its obviousness is to miss the point: color is applied in a conspicuously contrived style, whether to suggest deliberate amateurism, to highlight fantastical qualities, or to achieve a painterly impression reminiscent in mood to propaganda posters (further attesting to the continuities between the two media) and arguably making the bourgeois tastes of pictorialism suitable for socialist uplift. Part of the reason for this contrived quality is easy to explain: bright colors make for more attractive and striking covers. This may also account for why images of beautiful women—portrayed in color—frequently adorn these covers. However, this commonsensical explanation isn't the only way of accounting for why color enters the picture. After all, colored images also appeared *inside* the magazine, though only sporadically. What does the embellished effect of painted photography connote?[53]

A close look at the contents of *Vietnam Pictorial* alongside its covers reveals that it was not just any kind of image that was colored, but instead those that underscore the theme of socialist futurity. Color accords with a fantasy about the future.[54] The magazine drew on photography's indexical qualities, its capacity to capture that-which-is, to render, in other words, this fantasy in a plausible way. In her book about the subjunctive mood of images, Barbie Zelizer contends that photojournalism invokes two temporal registers, the as-is and the as-if.[55] Although Zelizer focuses on a wholly different context, her insights about these two temporalities opens up an intriguing approach to *Vietnam Pictorial*'s use of colored photographs. The brilliance of the magazine's color images likewise suggests multiple temporalities, an as-if or, rather, what-will-be, which establishes its viability through the irrefutability of the indexical as-is of photography.

A range of images illuminated the technical dimensions of the fledgling nation's visual aspirations: factories aglow with transcendent light reflected off polished chrome machines, scientists in lustrous white poring studiously over their instruments in gleaming laboratories, laborers radiant with pride over their skilled work (plates 3–5). *Vietnam Pictorial*'s vision of futurity invokes socialist realism's cherished themes of industrialization and collectivization. Although *Vietnam Pictorial* harnessed the reality effect of photography to project these themes, the undisguised contrivance of colorization enhanced this reality. Color lent definition and vibrancy to a reality that appeared rooted in the present yet was still to come.

Vietnam Pictorial also emphasized the theme of socialist futurity through its focus on children, particularly members of the Young Pioneers, whose scarlet scarves singled them out, in communism's familial discourse, as Uncle Ho's own children. Given the magazine's fondness for children, it is especially significant that the first colored cover features children at play in a meadow of incongruously large, fantastically colored flowers (plate 1). This is a fantasy about the socialist future.

Its playfulness perhaps fancifully evokes Mao Zedong's Hundred Flowers Movement.[56] Initiated by the Communist Party of China in 1956, the Hundred Flowers Movement encouraged citizens to express their candid views of the communist regime. Mao Zedong best captured this spirit of ostensible openness when he stated, "The policy of letting a hundred flowers bloom and a hundred schools of thought contend is designed to promote the flourishing of the arts and progress of science." An anti-rightist crackdown on dissidents quickly ensued, heightening in 1957, with such ruthless imprisonment and punishment that the Hundred Flowers Movement is now widely seen as a ruse to flush out Mao's political opponents.[57] Although the editors of *Vietnam Pictorial* were likely aware of events in China, which was a close communist ally in the late 1950s (a relationship that deteriorated in the 1970s), there is no evidence that they set out to illustrate the Hundred Flowers Movement when they selected this fantastical meadow for the magazine's first colored cover. Still, the harmony between Mao's idealistic expression of desiring to let "a hundred flowers bloom" and the magazine's depiction of countless, impossibly large blooms provocatively suggests how socialist ways of seeing in China and Vietnam may have converged at this moment.

Given the magazine's emphasis on futurity, it may seem strange that the other group of colorized images depicts agrarian scenes. The photographs are awash in the sentimental flush of timelessness, when farm boys ride water buffaloes and peasant women contemplate a golden harvest, rest joyfully, or smile as they ferry an abundant crop to market (plates 6–8); as such, they seem to point nostalgically to a past far removed from the metallic radiance of a triumphal future to come. Stylistically, they resemble brilliantly hued propaganda posters more than the sedate monotones of the documentary photographs that the tints covered over.[58]

If we look more closely, however, we can grasp how agrarian scenes serve as a foundation for socialist futurity. Nostalgia, according to cultural critic Svetlana Boym, looks to the past to discern the future: "Nostalgia can be retrospective but also prospective. Fantasies of the past determined by needs of the present have a direct impact on realities of the future."[59] With an economy that then—as now—depended on agrarian production, such bucolic scenes idealized rural life and glorified peasants and their contribution to revolutionary efforts.

Likewise, images that appear over-colored and merely ornamental turn out to mythologize history in fascinating ways. Take, for example, a striking colored photograph that depicts women picking lotus flowers in an impossibly lush setting; they are rendered with little regard for verisimilitude (plate 9). The lotus flower is a decorative element in Vietnamese art with special meaning, hearkening back to the Ly Dynasty in the first century. At a time when Vietnam was at war with China, Emperor Lý Công Uẩn dreamed of a lotus in the lake and built the famous One Pillar Pagoda, Chùa Một Cột, in Hanoi to symbolize his dream that Vietnam had been blessed by Buddha and was thus able to withstand imperialist invasion and maintain the nation's independence. The magazine presents these decorative colored photographs in a manner consistent with the Communist Party's practice of absorbing—and mythologizing—Vietnam's thousands of years of resistance against foreign invaders as the foundation for its revolutionary mission. The colored photographs feminize the qualities of purity and beauty, assigning to women the responsibility of cultivating a sacred national destiny. As the next chapter details, the Communist Party anchored the contested and unfixed concept of nationhood to the symbol of revolutionary Vietnamese women, which, perhaps aptly, was just as culturally fluid and contested.[60] The colored photograph thus rendered a Buddhist symbol legible to a specifically Vietnamese context. Just as importantly, we can also discern the intricacies of localized renderings through the painterly qualities of the colored photograph, which evoke the tradition of Vietnamese brush painting.

For *Vietnam Pictorial* a socialist way of seeing also entailed surveying the nation in full. In this sense, the magazine's original name, *Hình ảnh Việt Nam*

(*Images of Vietnam*), was quite literal in meaning. But the initial title also had a symbolic meaning. In 1954 the Geneva Conference split the nation in two along the 17th parallel. By invoking "images of Vietnam," the magazine promoted reunification with South Vietnam, particularly as hostilities against the United States escalated with the start of regular aerial bombardment campaigns against the North. Images of Vietnam projected a vision of a reunified nation still to come.

In contrast to the socialist ways of seeing that, say, German and Russian photographers and publications promoted, *Vietnam Pictorial* rarely experimented with composition and form, although why this is the case is difficult to discern given the absence of editorial records. This is not to suggest the absence of stylistic influence. Notably, one cover depicts a sculpture similar to the famous *Worker and Kolkhoz Woman* by Vera Mukhina, which was displayed as part of the Soviet Pavilion at the 1937 World's Fair in Paris (plate 10).[61]

However, a careful survey of the magazine shows the uniformity of layouts, particularly their adherence to a linear structure. A survey of the magazine also reveals how rarely photographers and editors employed photomontage, a common technique, as we have seen, in the Soviet context.[62] Yet when we consider that photomontage is also popular in advertising, *Vietnam Pictorial's* conventional layout can be seen as a rejection of this capitalist co-optation. Instead, the publication was state funded, and notably, from 1954 to the present day, *Vietnam Pictorial* has excluded advertisements altogether.

Vietnam Pictorial included numerous photographs that were sometimes organized into thematic sections. These sections were variously called "Ảnh Đẹp" ("Interesting Pictures"), "Ảnh Việt Nam" ("Pictures of Vietnam"), and "Ảnh Nghệ Thuật" ("Art Photography"). Each of these sections described exhibitions, praised award-winning photographers, and explicitly drew on photography to create a common vision for the nation (figure 1.12). Together, these sections presented a vision of the nation and the Communist Party's dreams of reunification.

Within *Vietnam Pictorial*, editors took pains to assure readers that contributing photographers came from and ranged widely among the far-flung regions. The magazine's photo spreads symbolically sutured the nation together. Given this important function, it is unsurprising that images included in these visual stories were selected for coloring. These colored photo spreads featured picturesque landscapes of fertile valleys, sparkling rivers, and lush gardens. In a similar spirit, images of Vietnam's ethnic minorities, such as the Thái and Dao, many of whom resided in the highlands, are colorfully rendered to emphasize unity in diversity.

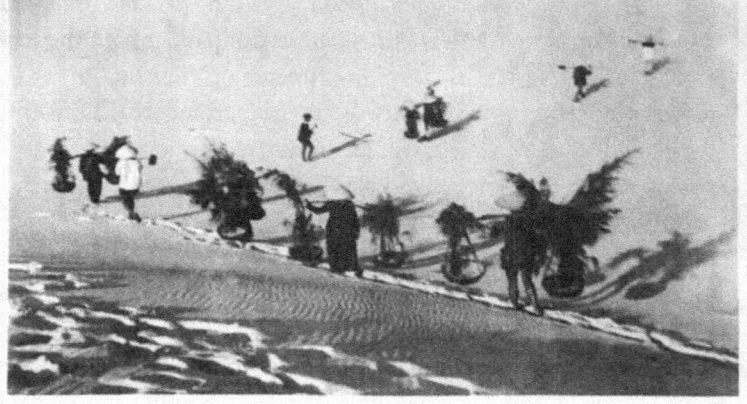

Biển cồn cát thành rừng xanh. *Ảnh: Văn Bảo*

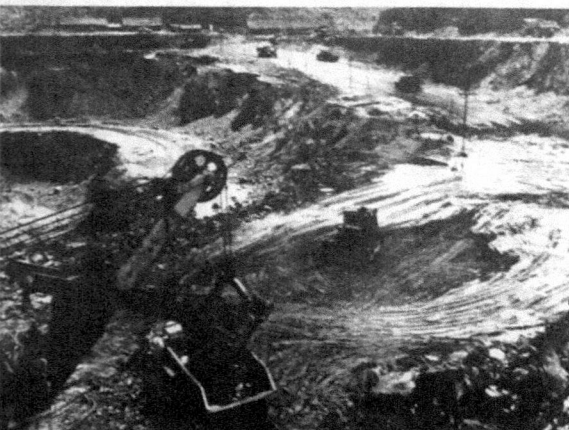

ẢNH ĐẸP

TRIỂN LÃM ẢNH NGHỆ
THUẬT LẦN THỨ IV

y xúc than. *Ảnh: Nguyễn đức Văn*

Chiều hè trên sông Hồng. *Ảnh: Hà kiên Dụei.*

CUỘC triển lãm ảnh nghệ thuật lần thứ tư tổ chức tại thủ đô Hà-nội đã được đông đảo các nghệ sĩ nhiếp ảnh khắp miền Bắc tham gia. 183 tác phẩm của 104 tác giả đã được chọn và trưng bày. Đặc biệt lần này có các tác phẩm của anh chị nhiếp ảnh trong · Mặt trận dân tộc giải phóng miền Nam ra tham dự. Phòng triển lãm ảnh nghệ thuật năm nay đã cho người xem những hình ảnh vui tươi của miền Bắc vươn lên trong cuộc sống mới, phản ánh một cách sinh động những thành tựu to lớn và đầy sáng tạo của nhân dân đang xây dựng chủ nghĩa xã hội và đấu tranh hòa bình thống nhất nước nhà. Trong triển lãm này cũng có những bức Việt-nam đã được giải thưởng trong các cuộc thi ảnh quốc tế năm nay: 5 huy chương vàng, 2 huy chương đồng, 1 bằng khen, 2 phần thưởng bạc và nhiều tặng phẩm khác.

Đông đảo nhân dân đã đến xem triển lãm. Hồ Chủ tịch, đồng chí Trường Chinh, ủy viên Bộ chính trị Trung ương Đảng cũng đến thăm triển lãm.

Triển lãm ảnh nghệ thuật lần thứ IV chứng tỏ sự tiến bộ nhanh chóng của các nghệ sĩ nhiếp ảnh Việt-nam. Anh chị em bộc lộ một nhiệt tình yêu nước, yêu chủ nghĩa xã hội và mạnh dạn đi sâu vào cuộc sống thực tế. Chúng tôi xin giới thiệu một vài ảnh đẹp đã được trưng bày trong triển lãm.

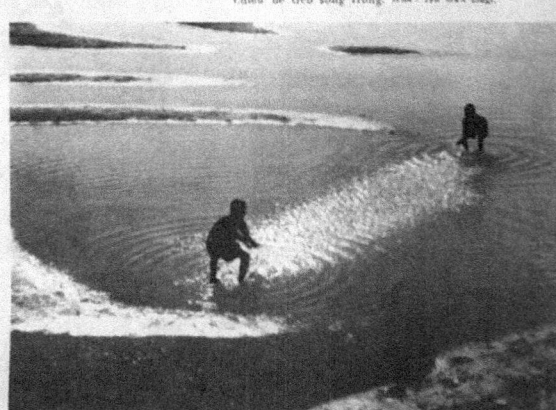

FIGURE 1.12 *Ảnh Đẹp. Vietnam Pictorial.*

Between 1954 and 1965 the illustrated magazine drew on photography to bring into focus a vision of nationhood, on the heels of the victory over French colonial tyranny, and in defiance of the United States and its colonizing aspirations. With the inclusion of color on covers and, occasionally, within the magazine itself, *Vietnam Pictorial* enhanced its cultural mission, projecting a socialist future that could be realized, at least imaginatively, through its illustration and selectively fanciful coloration.

As these covers and selections from within the magazine show, the colored photographs had the effect of painted photographs and seldom attempted, in this period at least, to appear more naturalistic or realistic, although the magazine harnessed the reality effect of photography for the purposes of accessing a socialist utopia that had not yet been realized. This contrived quality of the "painted photograph"—a colored photograph trying to look like a painted photograph—highlights how manipulation is a fundamental characteristic of photography more generally. When it comes to *Vietnam Pictorial*, colored photographs evoke the style of painted photographs as a way of merging two temporalities, an idyllic, mythologized past and an idealized socialist future, and of aligning the realism of photography with the fantastical contrivances of propaganda posters. Images anchor this past and future firmly, if dreamily, within the indexical reality effect of photography. It goes without saying that all of this is in service to propaganda. The undisguised artifice of *Vietnam Pictorial*'s approach to coloring images suggests an unabashed embrace of manipulation in striking contrast to the more common tendency to disavow or dismiss this practice.

Perhaps there is no better way to illustrate the cultural work of visual restoration than an image that both envisions what is left after a battle and fantasizes a flourishing future after the war has ended. It is only fitting that legend holds that *Vietnam Pictorial* enjoyed Hồ Chí Minh's enthusiastic support. Prior to establishing the DRV in 1945, Hồ Chí Minh led a peripatetic life and worked a number of odd jobs; in an intriguing twist, during a stint in Paris sometime in 1915–17, he helped restore images as a photo retoucher. Although Hồ Chí Minh was paid only modest wages, his biographers emphasize that photo retouching was crucial for his revolutionary activities because this work funded the publication of tracts attacking the brutality of the French colonial regime in Indochina.[63] According to legend, this humble experience with visual restoration led him to grasp photography's political potential. As the magazine began to tint and layer, it displayed in full colors a vision of the nation's future.

Now that this future has come and gone—the American War ended in 1975 to be followed by nearly a decade of economic austerity in the wake of devastating trade sanctions—how have socialist ways of seeing altered? In 1986 the state launched the Đổi Mới policy of economic renovation, meant to undo years of austerity. In the Đổi Mới era we can see that Vietnamese official histories of the American War deploy photographs to bolster state-sanctioned metanarratives of national reunification, but in ways that disavow the fraught conditions of the making of these photographs.

By 1994, with US President Bill Clinton's lifting of trade sanctions that kicked off the present, late socialist period of market liberalization, this process of visual correction had become an accepted, everyday practice.[64] Indeed, as I learned in the course of research in Hanoi, recent versions of the national narrative emphasize triumph over adversity and discount if not altogether disavow the distinctively make-do quality of the revolutionary visual record. The communist state has tacitly repudiated imperfection, adopting instead a restorative style as part of an ideologically reparative gesture of historical re-visioning. The state's projection of a postwar vision of seamless renewal glosses over the material flaws that defined revolutionary Vietnamese photography. In so doing, the Đổi Mới perspective entrenches a familiar emphasis on prosthetic visual enhancement while disavowing the marred qualities that had brought a complex picture of socialism into focus in the first place.

Efforts to retouch visual records transform the political purposes of communist photography and recalibrate socialist ways of seeing for contemporary Vietnam. By altering the look of revolution—by making it sharper, brighter, better—recent displays of socialist photographs at state museums and other public venues in Vietnam and abroad offer a corrective re-visioning, one that reimagines revolutionary history as an invigorating process that erases the material and technical imperfections integral to the making of this history. This *corrective* re-visioning remakes the reunified nation as robust, strong, and spectacular. In this regard, socialist ways of seeing in the period of late socialism entail unseeing, obscuring photography's role in constructing and reconstructing state ideology.[65]

In the two metropolises of Hanoi and Ho Chi Minh City, museums memorialize the spirit of revolution by displaying photographs of proud peasants, defiant workers, and smiling soldiers. Đoàn Công Tính's portrayal of the third group, posed during a lull in the fight for Quảng Trị, exemplifies this preference for positive images. Against the backdrop of the ruined citadel the young men's wide grins anticipate a victory that was not yet certain at the time the photograph was taken (figure 1.13). Đoàn explains how he produced this photo op: "I coaxed them from their bunkers and asked them to show me how they felt about the battle so far." He points to the shadowed background: "Look, this one stayed underground. After the rockets started falling, the rest scrambled back to their shelters. I don't know what happened to them after the battle ended."[66]

These strong features and robust bodies, as symbols of the optimistic vision of virile masculinity, are in stark contrast to the broken figures featured in images of atrocity that were the staple offerings of the Western press, of which the celebrated triptych of Pulitzer Prize–winning photographs, taken by Eddie Adams, Nick Ut, and Malcolm Browne, are the most recognizable but hardly unusual. More often than not, a so-called American worldview of the war emphasizes Vietnamese victimhood. Although I am told that similar dispiriting images of mangled, dead bodies exist and are held in a folder at the VNA archives, they were not among the volumes I reviewed during this trip; instead, I was told they have long been strictly censored, and veteran photographers admit they were ordered to refrain from taking such morbid photos.[67] During the war the VNA promoted uplifting images and frowned on, even though it no longer officially censored, dispiriting ones, perhaps to shore up a vision of reunified wholeness that the nation, then partitioned into North and South, had yet to achieve. The whole bodies of workers and warriors are thus a metaphor for the national wholeness they labored to attain.

Yet photographers sometimes recount a different story that dampens this mood of uplift, of what happened after their cameras captured workers and fighters, men and women with the tools of their craft. Kim Đằng recalls with gratitude a soldier who led him high on a mountaintop perch for an unobstructed view of the Ho Chi Minh Trail. "I found out he died the next week," he told me, his voice trailing off.[68]

On a similar stretch of road, Đình Quảng Thành came across a group of a dozen women working to fill an enormous bomb crater as the sun set. The light plays tricks in this photo so that the women's bodies cast an eerily doubled reflection, with shadows on the ground and rippling in the water (figure 1.14). There is thus the illusion of three rows of women, each blending into the others, each becoming less distinct. This visual effect of blending also resembles the bodies' fracturing, lending to the photo a premonitory ambiguity: of the dozen women whom Thành saw that day, ten were killed when a bomb exploded. This premonition is at odds with the photograph's overt concern

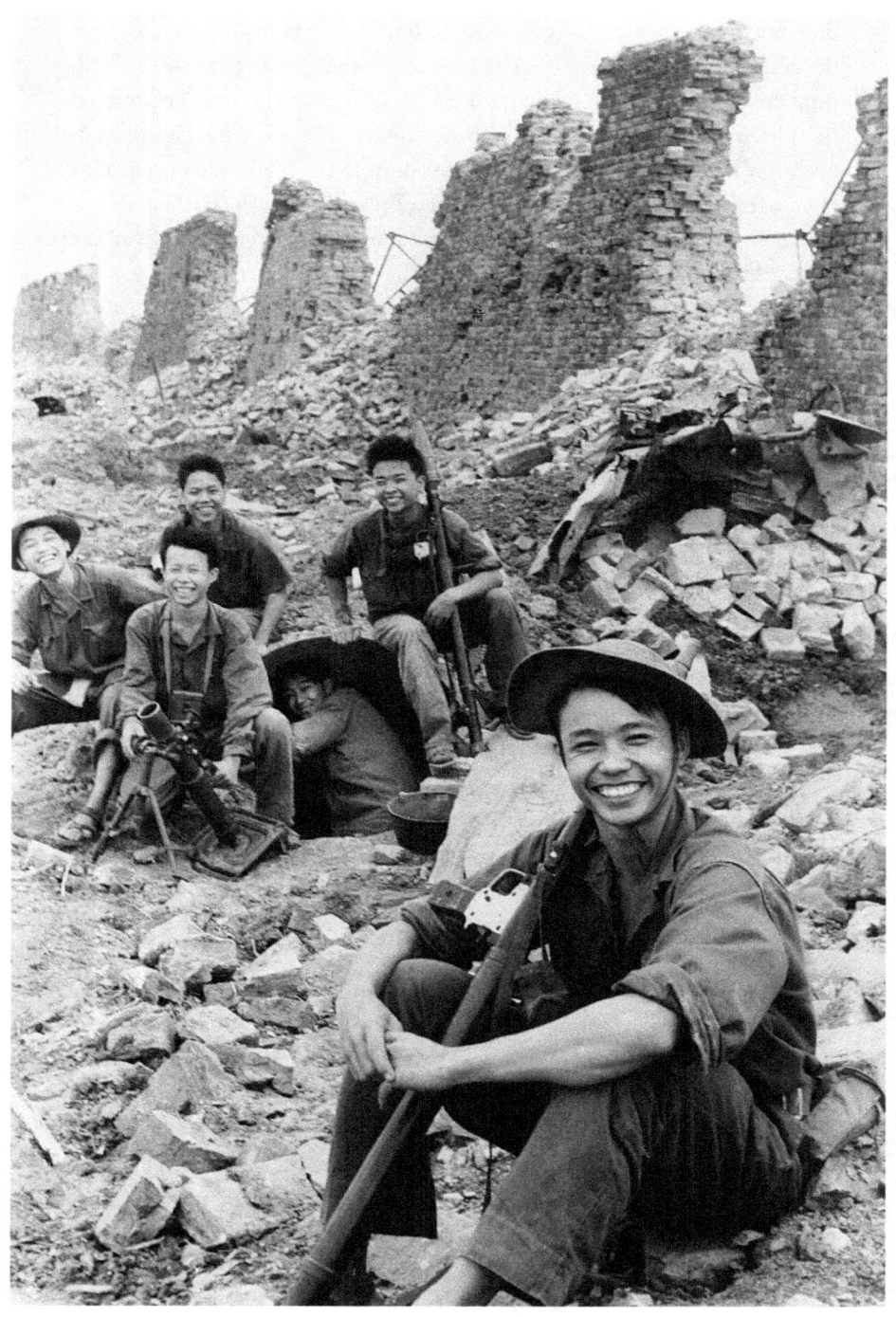

FIGURE 1.13 Smiles at the battle for Quảng Trị. Photographer: Đoàn Công Tính.

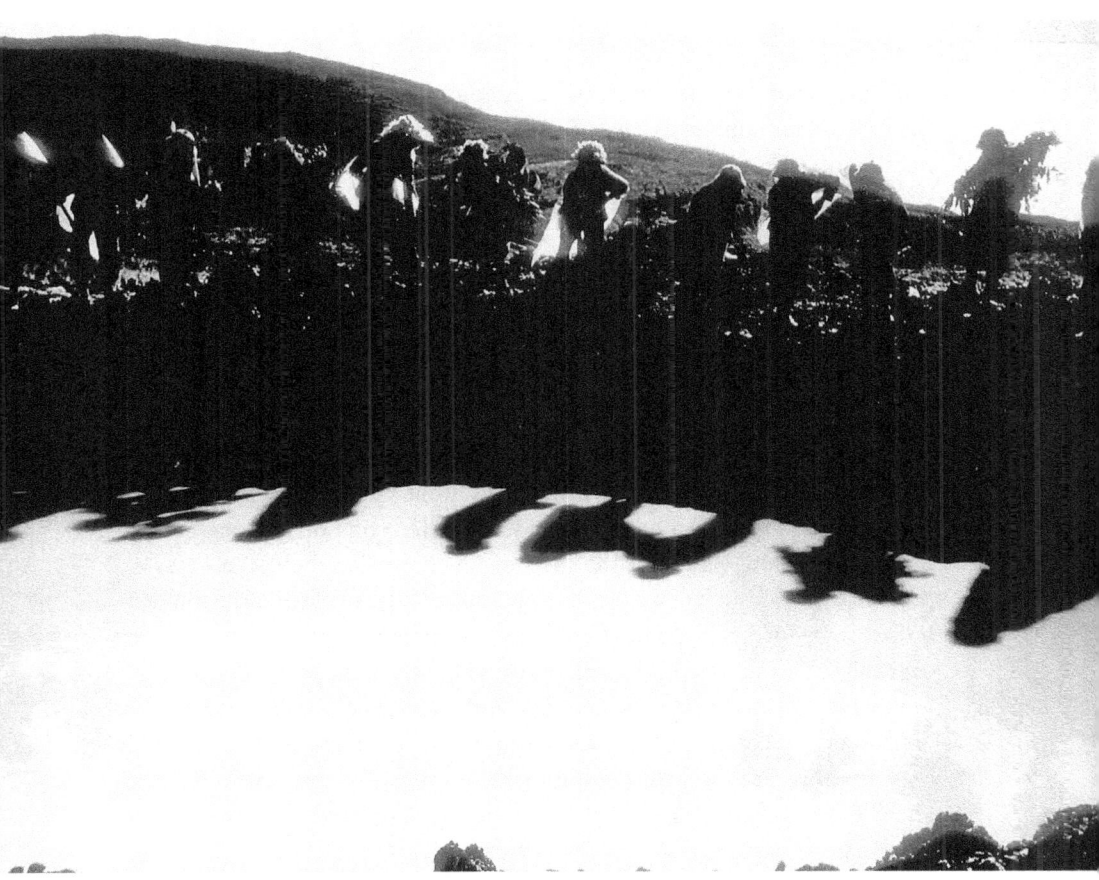

FIGURE 1.14 Women at a bomb crater. Photographer: Đình Quảng Thành.

with linking collective effort with socialist reconstruction; these ostensibly healthy bodies repaired what bombs wrecked. The photograph cannot show what happened afterward to the bodies when more bombs came.

Retouching is also significant because it is a job that requires covering up blemishes, removing imperfections, and producing beauty. Anthropologist Nina Hien observes in her study of the history of Vietnamese photography that photography studios and printing shops throughout Vietnam advertise their skill in restoring old images (*phục hồi ảnh cũ* or *phục chế ảnh cũ*) through retouching, painting, and, in the digital age, Photoshop. The term *chế*, Hien points out, is common in Hanoi and is especially important because it denotes invention: old images are not simply repaired; just as importantly, the process generates new images. At its core, visual restoration is a process of manipulation. Hien also observes that the opening of markets in the Đổi

Mới era introduced a new tolerance for photographic self-representation that the state once shunned as bourgeois decadence, preferring instead the production of images that would accord with the sanctioned vision of political reunification. According to Hien, although this "beauty regime" enables subjects to express individual identities in contrast to, even in resistance to, the state's collective ideology, at times the regime aligns with the state's own political priorities of economic development. That is, the regime offers a style that complements Đổi Mới renovation, a style that recalibrates the revolutionary aspirations of socialist seeing for the market-driven demands of late socialism.[69]

Hien's insight can be extended further: the state has, in effect, refined a way of seeing to tackle the dual tasks of reckoning with the past and heralding a prosperous future that has ostensibly come. Drawing on sentimental aesthetic conventions that favor the soothing over the disturbing, the state's approach to renovation entails producing pleasing instead of wounding images. It does so by further entrenching a discourse of embodied progress, covering over the scars and wounds of war, disavowing their very presence by replacing them with images that for the state and its problematically ableist ideologies are more congenial to official narratives of uplift, rather than reflecting on ways of reckoning with the traumatic aftermath of this war.[70] Although Hien's focus is on the late-socialist era (from 1986 onward), her insights help illuminate an earlier period of Vietnamese revolution.

Against this backdrop, the imperfect qualities of socialist ways of looking during this extended conflict contradict the state's own memorialization practices. In the era of market reform and national renovation that Đổi Mới promotes, today's displays of photography emphasize the camera's enabling capacities. Contemporary rites of remembrance repudiate the imperfect conditions from which this visual record was made, substituting it with a revisionist nationalist narrative of collective unity, altogether overlooking occasional glimpses of injury, not to mention the haphazard qualities that defined the production of socialist photography. The visual history of Vietnam unfolds amid the ideological clash between positive images of future-looking optimism and images that emphasize themes of desolation and despair, which the state censored as displeasing lest they contradict its account of the revolutionary spirit.

I encountered this corrective approach to the past in the archival offices of the VNA's photographic division, where I requested a copy of a "panoramic" view made by Văn Sắc, among many other images. As mentioned above, these panoramas were joined from several developed images, and during the war this piecemeal approach to photographic production betrayed its make-do methods, evident in uneven lengths of paper and repetitive motifs. No longer. When I received my digital print, I found that the VNA had stitched together the shots to form a seamless whole (figure 1.15). It could have been an honest mistake: I had tried to ask for one image made out of three prints that showed signs of suture, but the VNA might have misunderstood. Or possibly it found my preference for the imperfect composition odd given that the alternative—a seamless whole—was now possible. Now that Photoshop is so widespread as to be a verb and not just a trademark, photographic manipulation hardly raises an eyebrow, or so it seems. Digital enhancement offers a means for this official archive to stylistically represent the nation's modernizing aspirations.

Only Nguyễn Minh Lộc, a veteran VNA photographer, at first appears to depart from this fondness for the beautiful, at least in the form of strong bodies. Although his fellow photographers scoffed when I asked about him in Hanoi, telling me that he had few photographs, and no noteworthy ones, I was undeterred, and I resolved to meet him in Ho Chi Minh City after coming across the set depicting a cave M.A.S.H. unit at the archives.

Minh Lộc was responsible for covering the coal industry near Hanoi toward the tail end of the war. His images contrast stalwart workers against a sublime backdrop of yawning pits and massive factories. I had set aside a few for reproduction and kept returning, for some reason, to one image of explosion and smoke in a factory yard. As noted earlier, the communist VNA, for which Minh Lộc worked, emphasized three central subjects in war photography: the heroic struggle of soldiers, the toil of workers, and the sacrifices of revolutionary Vietnamese women. In its simultaneous depiction of two of these three subjects, an attack at a worker's factory, Minh Lộc's photographs were fascinating and unusual. They clearly took up the core subjects that preoccupied the VNA.

There was a problem, however. When I looked closely, it was obvious that the explosions that spread across a number of images turned out to be the same one (figure 1.16). Whether this attack had even occurred under Minh Lộc's watch was unlikely, given these clear signs of manipulation. In short, when he started photographing, these bombardment campaigns had ended. But when I asked him why he pasted explosions in the photos, he did not reply. Instead, he insisted that his images looked good. Images of spectacular violence were aesthetically pleasing, and he seemed indifferent about the fact that by adding explosions he reduced the documentary value of his photographs.

FIGURE 1.15
Altered panorama.
Courtesy VNA.

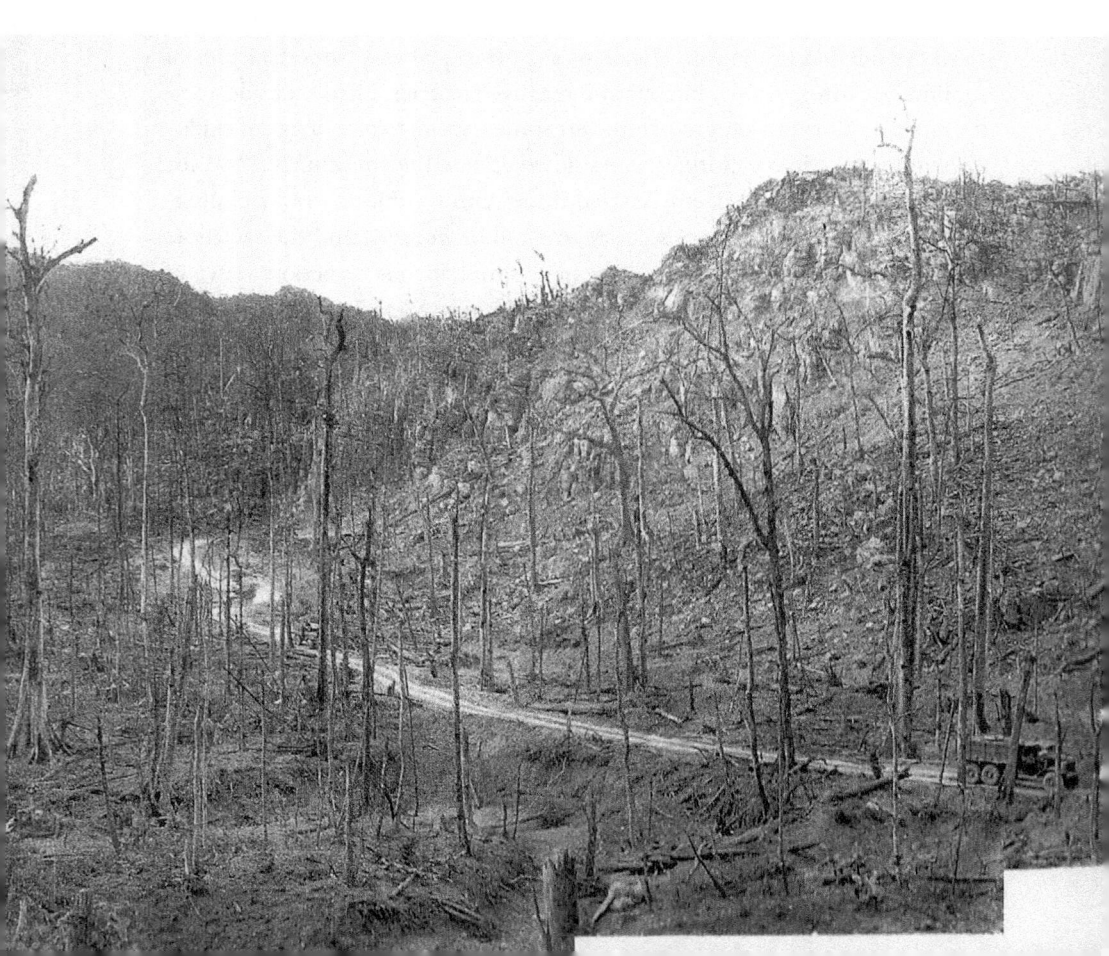

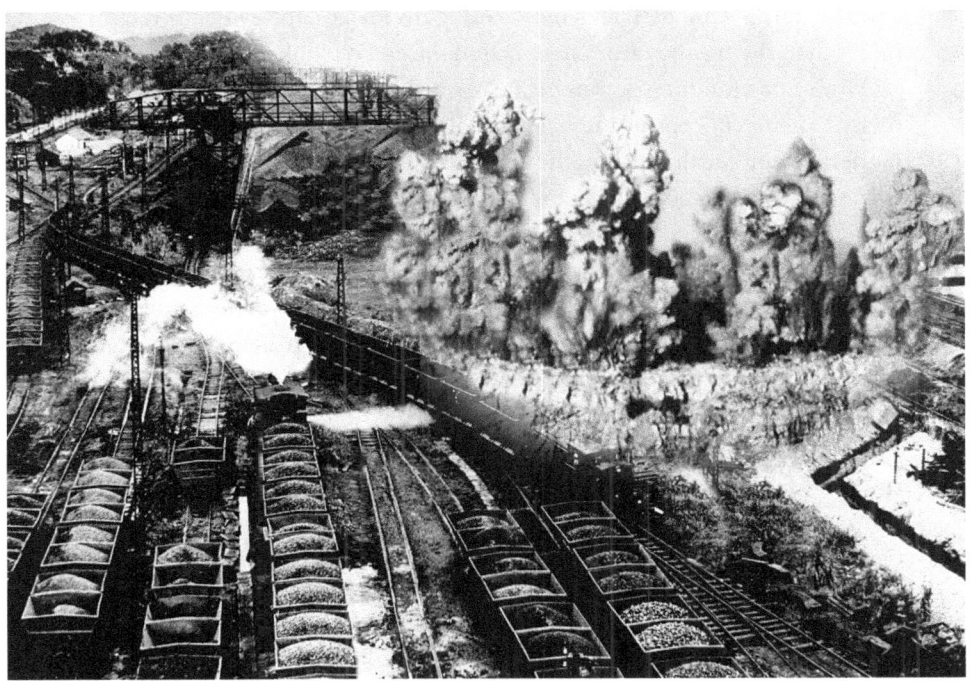

FIGURE 1.16 Attack at a factory, 1973. Photographer: Minh Lộc.

Perhaps, I reflected, he wished to imply that he was witness to spectacular action and not just industrial labor. Although both military and industrial efforts were considered valuable subjects, today it is the spectacles of war, such as the downing of American airplanes and battlefield victories, which the state celebrates most. My puzzlement over the second issue, of why he altered the photos, initially obscured the significance of the first (that doing so obscured, even falsified, historical events) and was not resolved by the photographer's evasive replies. Yet there was no question that Minh Lộc's altered images were arresting, for they challenged the defining divisions of the socialist visual archive—that is, divisions that the state implicitly set up when it determined that only pleasing images would circulate while evidence of injury and death would not, with wholeness befitting the official vision of a revolutionary future to come and injury seen by state censors as threatening this future. Decades after the end of the war, however, physical destruction for Minh Lộc had apparently become the condition for a beautiful image— one that was unlikely to have been acceptable during the war years lest it betray weakness—so much that he would go to great lengths to achieve his aesthetic ideal. Although he denies altering his images, the evidence is clear: rather than shying away from destruction, Minh Lộc took pains to create it.

Minh Lộc's fondness for embellishment simultaneously exemplifies and revises Hien's concept of the beauty regime, in which retouching offers a modern technique that creates the look, to complement the policy, of renovation. On the one hand, such a practice keeps pace with that of contemporary studio photographers who, as Hien documents, heal scarred bodies, lighten dark skin, and unify families with disappeared members. On the other hand, Minh Lộc's idea of "perfection" scrapes rudely away at the wholeness of these idealistic illusions; he conjures picturesque destruction on an industrial scene where there was none, a formal attention that did not always invoke the favored figure of whole bodies featured in photographs produced during the war. Rather, Minh Lộc's idea of beauty centered on the smoke, rubble, and ruin of a factory where there are no bodies to be seen. This is in marked contrast to Đoàn Công Tính's approach. When Tính posed his smiling soldiers against a crumbling citadel, it was to celebrate the strength and perseverance of the surviving men, not to revel in ruin, as Minh Lộc seems to do. Moreover, Minh Lộc worked within the context of late socialism. Aesthetic flourishes such as the ones cleaning up messy seams from a panoramic view made from three joined photographs or placing a spectacular explosion here and there provide an illuminating analogy to the task of reconciling the current era of market liberalization, an economic process that seems fundamentally at odds with the official policy of socialism. Such aesthetic flourishes give visual form to this task of reconciliation. These flourishes also commodify revolution and aestheticize socialism to make it clearer, cleaner, and neater.

Unsurprisingly, his peers among VNA veteran photographers dismiss Minh Lộc's work. But far from breaking ranks with the VNA in this regard, Minh Lộc's work reveals just how central aesthetics is today (and, to a different extent, was even in the 1970s) as the state wrestles with the task of memorializing the war. Thus, although it may be tempting to dismiss retouching as a rare element of Vietnamese war photography, it is more commonly employed than the veteran photographers I spoke with are willing to admit.

Although the issue of retouching is an open secret, it blew up recently in the wake of shocking revelations that one of the most remarkable photographs of the war, by none other than Đoàn Công Tính, had been manipulated. Although manipulation is a more common practice in the history of war photography than many critics are willing to admit, the advent of the digital era having further normalized this practice, nevertheless photojournalists decry images that have been altered.[71] The exposure of Tính's photograph as manipulated ignited a fierce debate. The untitled photograph from 1970 features soldiers climbing a rope against the spectacular backdrop of a waterfall (figure 1.17). This photograph was displayed in 2014, alongside other well-known works by North Vietnamese photographers, at France's International Photojournalism Festival of Perpignan (*Visa Pour L'Image Perpignan*). Exhibition co-organizer Patrick Chauvel, an award-winning photographer who had covered the war for France, timed the event to coincide with the publication of his new book on the subject, *Ceux du Nord* (literally, *Those in the North*).[72] The *New York Times* Lens blog selected Đoàn Công Tính's spectacular waterfall to illustrate its positive coverage of the event. Chauvel followed up on this successful launch with an exhibition at the Institut Français in Hanoi as a companion to the Perpignan show. *Reporters du Guerre* (*War Reporters*) opened during the fortieth anniversary of the end of the war, in April 2015, where once again Đoàn Công Tính's photograph was singled out as the image to grace the poster for the event.

However, a scandal erupted when photojournalist Jørn Stjerneklar pointed out on his blog that this iconic image was doctored.[73] The extent of manipulation is obvious when we compare the two versions, the recent print that appears in the exhibitions and the "original," which was published in Đoàn Công Tính's 2001 book, *Khoảng Khách* (*Moments*). The very details that make the photograph breathtaking—the intricate path of the rushing water, the addition of figures and foliage, and the sharpness of the soldiers' silhouettes, among others—are precisely the ones that have been altered (see figure 1.2). In a follow-up article on his blog, Stjerneklar credits a keen-eyed reader for pointing out that even the "original" had been retouched, as evidenced by the repeating pattern of the water, and was likely a composite of another VNA photograph, which is displayed at the War Remnants Museum in Ho Chi Minh City. Stjerneklar's story was picked up worldwide, and Chauvel as well as Perpignan Festival founder and director Jean François Leroy defensively accused the photo blogger of "spoil[ing] a beautiful event."[74] The two organizers backed down only in the face of overwhelming condemnation. As for Đoàn Công Tính, he initially denied knowledge of the manipulation and, when pressed, speculated that someone else had altered the photograph after the negative had been damaged. He has since apologized.

In quick order, the reputations of all three—Leroy, Chauvel, and Đoàn Công Tính—were tarnished. Critics slammed the festival for its hypocrisy: how could it claim to champion the integrity of documentary photography when the exhibition had so flagrantly relaxed its own standards? Although

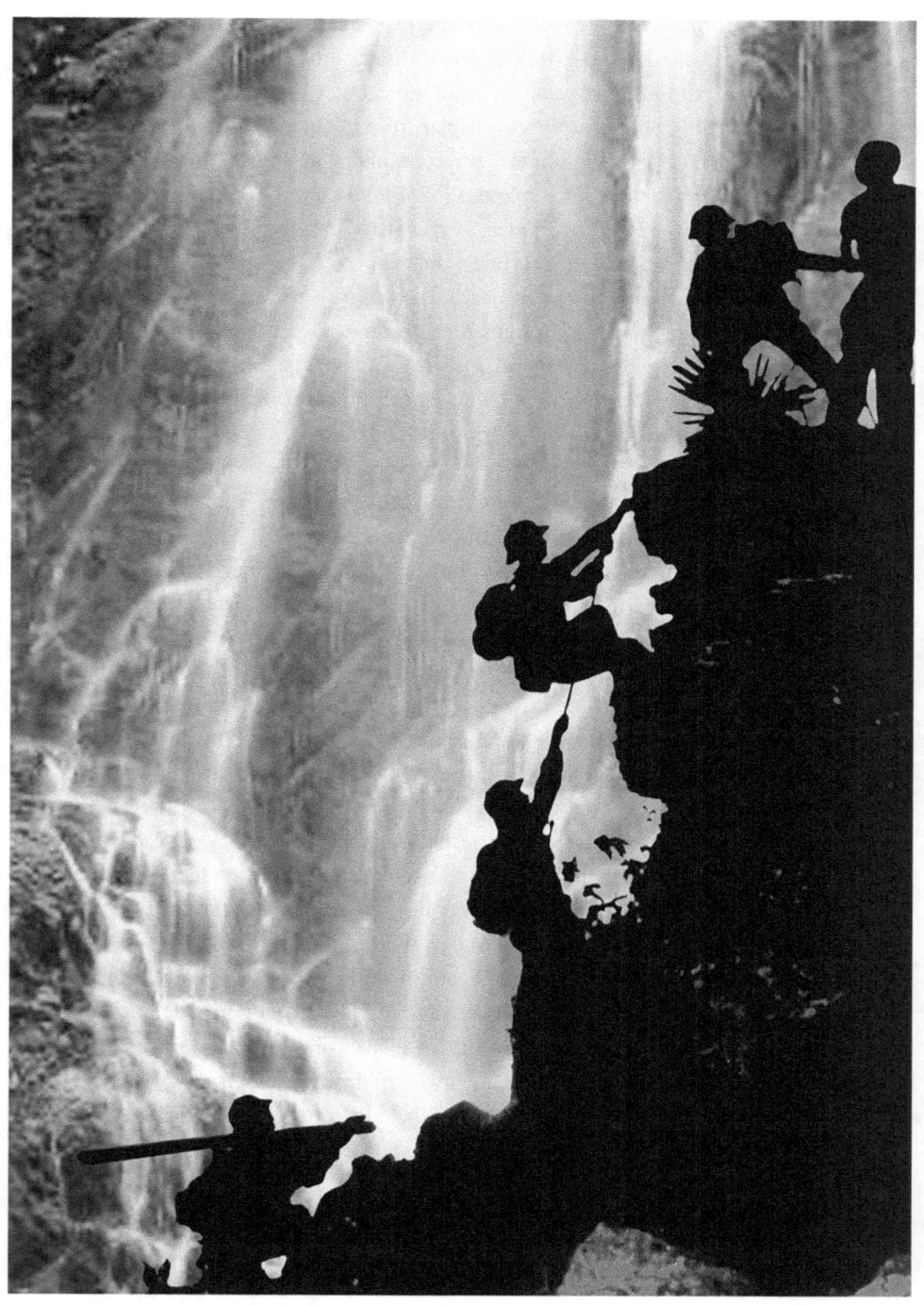

FIGURE 1.17 Waterfall on the Ho Chi Minh Trail. Photographer: Đoàn Công Tính.

Đoàn Công Tính denied altering the waterfall photograph, he was held to account for compromising journalistic ethics.[75] Indeed, the viewers who weighed in on the scandal conflated ideological with technical manipulation; in other words, they dismissed communist photography outright for its propagandistic zeal.

Given the widely accepted belief in the necessity of accurate reporting, these responses are understandable. However, the outpouring of moral outrage focuses only on the question raised by the photographer who broke the story on his blog: "Aber Warum?" In response to the incredulous "but why," the resounding judgment is the admonishment: "don't manipulate," a throwback, of sorts, to the foreclosing judgment of propaganda. Critics seem reluctant to consider the different but no less important question: what might such manipulation mean for the historical record and for the politics of memory? Instead, most viewers are preoccupied with unmasking the signs of propaganda, a task that seems beside the point given the express purpose of these photographs in the first place. As Christina Schwenkel astutely points out, Vietnamese photographers were hardly shy about rejecting "objectivity" as the standard by which photojournalism was to be judged.[76] Yet the outrage expressed by spectators, fellow photographers, and critics in the wake of the scandal involving Chauvel's exhibit stemmed, in part, from their sense of betrayal.

Guarding oneself against trickery thus seems more important than understanding the ends that manipulation serves. Consider, for example, the intriguing case of Bùi Công Tường, who was a Communist Party member for twenty-three years before he defected under the Chiêu Hồi (or Open Arms program). Tường was also a member of the top Province Party Committee for Kiến Hòa. Even more importantly, he served for a decade as chief of Propaganda, Culture, Education, and Training. These top-level roles distinguished him, according to Robert F. Turner, as one of the most senior defectors. When debriefed by Chiêu Hồi agents, Tường explained that he switched sides because "he was tired of telling lies to the people." He went on to work as a Chiêu Hồi interviewer himself, debriefing other defectors.[77] Repenting his deceptions, Tường advised his new allies on how to detect them, how to read images for trickery. Tường supplied three photographs as evidence. One shows so-called American imperialists evicting an old man, but Tường claimed that all the people in this photograph were members of a drama group in Kiến Hòa province who were enacting an orchestrated scene that he photographed with a Leica.

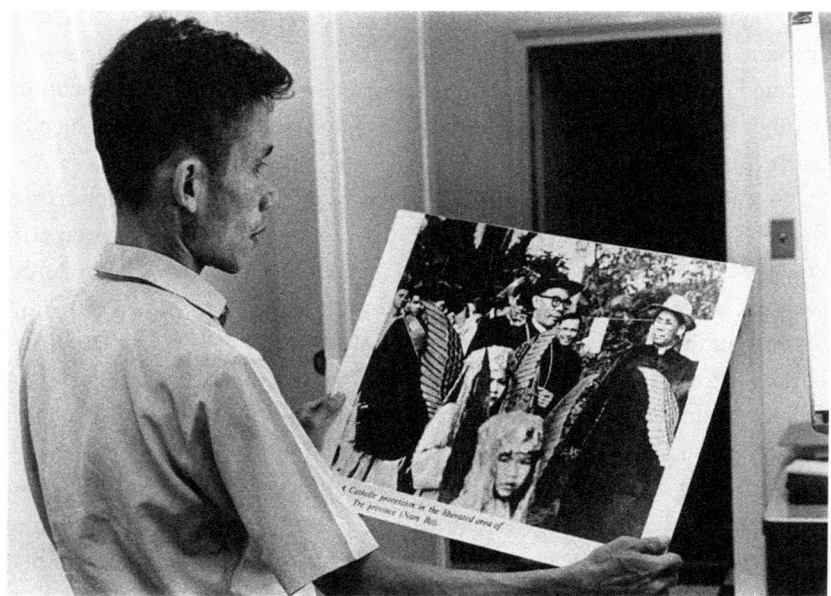

FIGURE 1.18 Bui Cong Tuong contemplates a photograph that he had orchestrated when he served as communist chief of Propaganda, Culture, Education and Training in Ben Tre province, South Vietnam. Photographer: unknown. Robert F. Turner Collection, 74040-10 A–V, 1970, Envelope S, Hoover Institution, Stanford University.

Another photograph that Tường supplied as evidence of manipulation depicts a Catholic procession in Bến Tre province in South Vietnam, which was under communist control (figure 1.18). In the corrected caption, Tường elaborates that this photograph was meant to illustrate communist toleration of religious freedom; however, he cautioned, things were not as they seemed: "the 'Priests' are actually Communist Party members who infiltrated the church system for just purposes as this."[78] His guidance bolstered claims on the part of the United States and South Vietnam that a socialist way of seeing was a manipulation of things as they were. As convenient as Tường's testimony was, the instructions he provided can hardly be considered shocking. As we have seen, communist leaders during the war were candid about their reliance on propaganda as a vehicle for communicating information and swaying opinions. In Tường's case the Chiêu Hồi program acquired further ammunition in the arsenal of what South Vietnamese officers and their American advisors already knew, that the enemy disseminated propaganda (just as *they* did, for example, in the form of leaflets distributed through airdrops through the North). In the battleground of popular opinion, the Government of Vietnam and its American advisors could use this ammunition to neutralize their enemy's images by invalidating them. The charge of propaganda enabled this political expediency.

When we look again at these two images by Đoàn Công Tính, the "original" and its revision, there is no doubt that these are manipulated visions of war. Although the opprobrium directed against him is understandable when we consider long-standing assumptions about the veracity of photojournalism, it is also disingenuous, given that critics acknowledge manipulation has been central rather than peripheral to war photography from its inception.[79] By dismissing images by Tính and others as nothing more than propaganda, the critique spun on its tautological wheels: visual manipulation is ideologically manipulative. The political work of propaganda can be more nuanced than this, however. Considering these images together enables us to perceive how the paired images typify, while also undermining, the state's recent approach to photography and official account of the camera's function during and after the American War. That this impossibly perfect counter-revolutionary picture of socialist struggle has proved seductive, at least for Chauvel and the organizers of the Perpignan Festival, suggests that the process of re-visioning history is not just a state initiative. At times, this process enjoys, even actively solicits, assistance worldwide from photojournalists and photography enthusiasts. This contradiction unsettles the seemingly ideologically cohesive core of socialist ways of seeing.

When we juxtapose this latest scandal of photographic manipulation alongside Minh Lộc's spectacle of ruin, we can discern how both offer a distinct yet illuminating fantasy of the past, reimagined as beautiful and not always in exaltation of gendered, whole-bodied strength. Recent displays of war photographs draw on the visual record of revolution as a resource for uplift, beautifying that record further by reconfiguring and reimagining it as sources of intensified aesthetic pleasure in addition to national reunification. Notably, landscapes, which from the outset were a key way that VNA photographers could reconcile aesthetic form with political content, became even more of a favored subject for beautification and aesthetic contemplation than they were decades earlier. These repurposed photographs offer a renewed vision of revolution, one that draws on and strives to improve the visual tropes of socialism—that is, to reconstruct socialist ways of seeing for a late-socialist era. Yet such repurposing is at odds with the spirit of revolutionary struggle and at times even amounts to a revisionist history of the war in

Vietnam. As I show in my next chapter, one of the central figures in this revisionist history is the symbol of the revolutionary Vietnamese woman. During the Đổi Mới era of late socialism, a politics of visual renovation rewrites the key components of socialist ways of seeing for the ends of ideological renovation.[80]

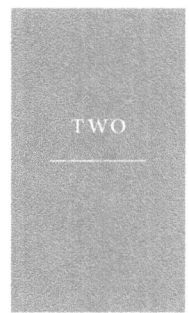

TWO

REVOLUTIONARY VIETNAMESE
WOMEN, SYMBOLS OF
SOLIDARITY

In the main stairwell of the Women's Museum in Hanoi, an elegant silhouette of a militiawoman stretches across four panes of glass (figure 2.1). To see outside the museum, at the shaded courtyard and the boulevard beyond, one must first gaze at this ideal image of the revolutionary Vietnamese woman.

With a rifle slung across her back, she pauses in her forward march, as though awaiting, or rather beckoning, those behind to join her. This silhouette was adapted and reversed from a famous photograph taken in the 1960s by Mai Nam (figure 2.2), one of many made by communist photographers to depict women at war. By adapting Mai Nam's photograph, the Vietnam Women's Union (VWU), the organization that founded the Women's Museum in 1987, offers a prism for understanding the modern nation: to view Vietnam properly one must recognize the role of women in national liberation. How-

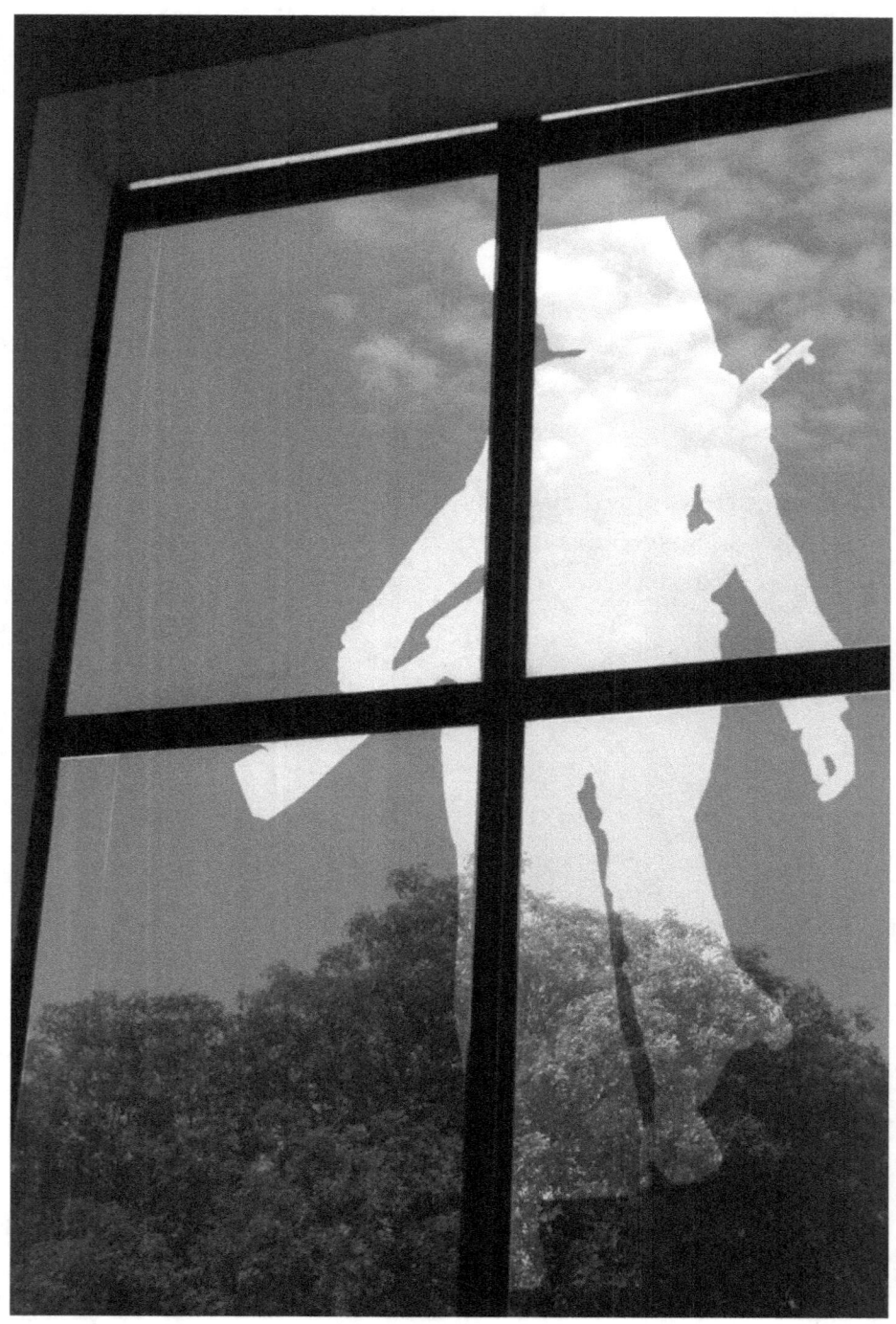

FIGURE 2.1 Hanoi Women's Museum. Author photo.

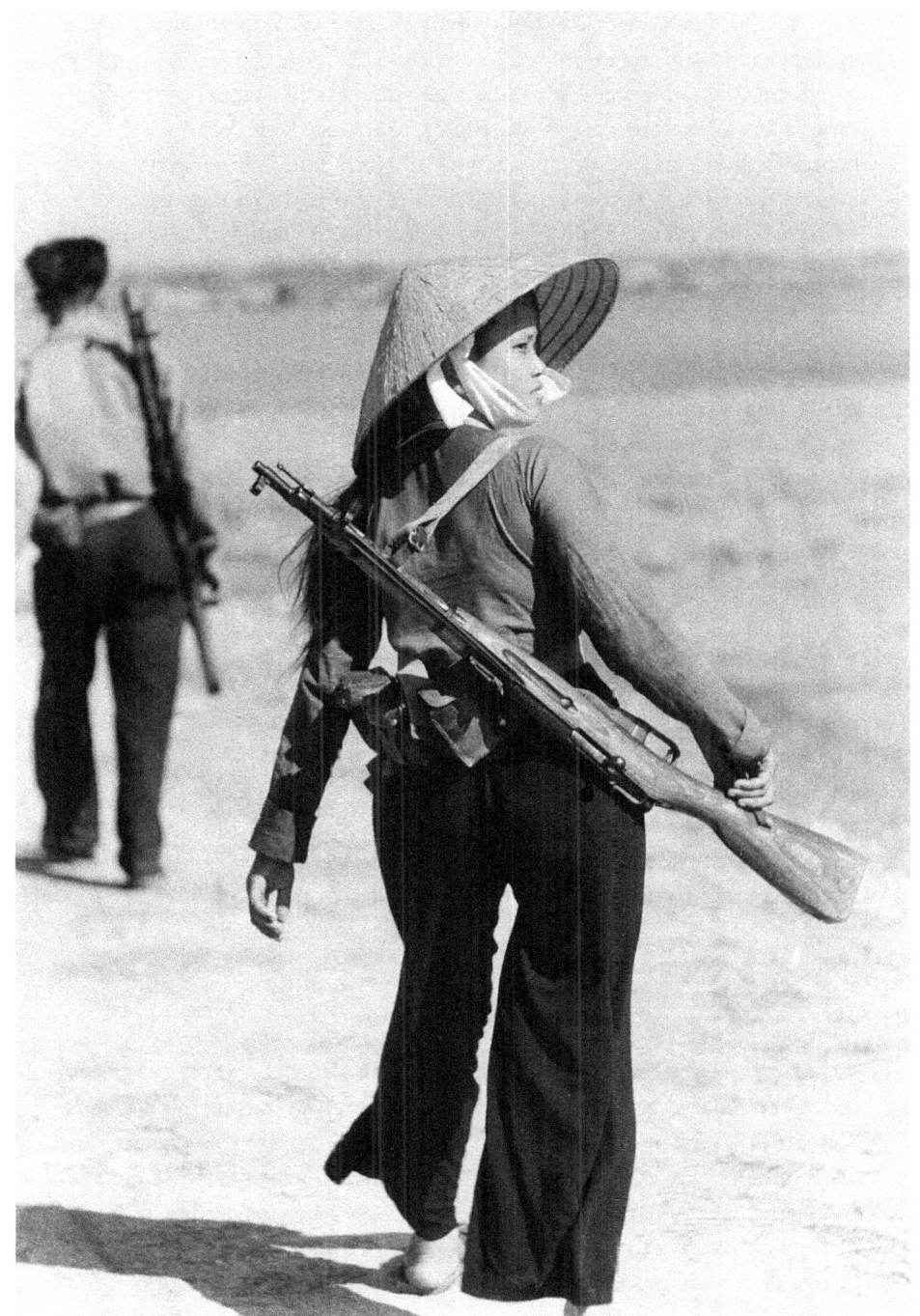

FIGURE 2.2 Militiawoman. Photographer: Mai Nam.

ever, the museum's rhetoric of transparency belies the complex history of the symbol and its shifting meanings.

During Vietnam's war against the United States, the symbol of the revolutionary Vietnamese women was highly contested. Deployed by both the communist and anticommunist factions in North and South Vietnam, this symbol was used to support clashing political ideologies. It then proceeded to capture the interest of diverse viewers beyond the nation. This is not to suggest that the revolutionary woman is universal, for doing so risks reifying problematic claims about the "transhistorical" nature of visual culture.[1] Although this symbol was not unique to Vietnam—as a way of representing women, the symbol was pervasive in Cuba and Nicaragua, among other proxy sites of conflict during the global Cold War—its localized framing requires that we attend to specific contexts.[2]

In North Vietnam, the Young Pioneers, the Vietnam Women's Union, and the Vietnamese People's Army mobilized photographers to document war efforts and shape an overall vision of socialism. The state-run Vietnam News Agency (VNA) served as perhaps the most prolific producer of photographs of Vietnamese women. Under its aegis, photographers emphasized themes of collective struggle, strength, and resilience. Their work set out to glorify women's contributions to the war, in accordance with the VWU's "three responsibilities" movement, which entailed replacing men in their work, freeing them for military service, encourage enlistment, and joining in combat (figures 2.3 and 2.4).[3] Women who served in this last capacity formed the contingent of "long-haired warriors," whom Hồ Chí Minh praised for their tenacity and patriotic fervor.[4] These photographs were printed and circulated among communist fighters to reinforce socialist ideals of unified effort and shared objectives, and among peasants in order to explain the cause and recruit volunteers. Just as importantly, they were broadcast internationally to solicit sympathy and feminist solidarity from a wide array of actors, from antiwar pacifists to freedom fighters.

Meanwhile, in South Vietnam Madame Nhu also claimed the symbol of the revolutionary Vietnamese woman by founding and leading the Women's Solidarity Movement of Vietnam (WSM). She did so by drawing on a similar visual idiom of collectivity and unity, which she connected to a discourse of solidarity that converged with, yet departed from, the version disseminated by her political rivals in the North. Ultimately, however, as will be explained below, the northern version of the revolutionary Vietnamese woman as a symbol of socialism won out, and it was the VWU's version of the symbol that circulated prominently outside Vietnam.

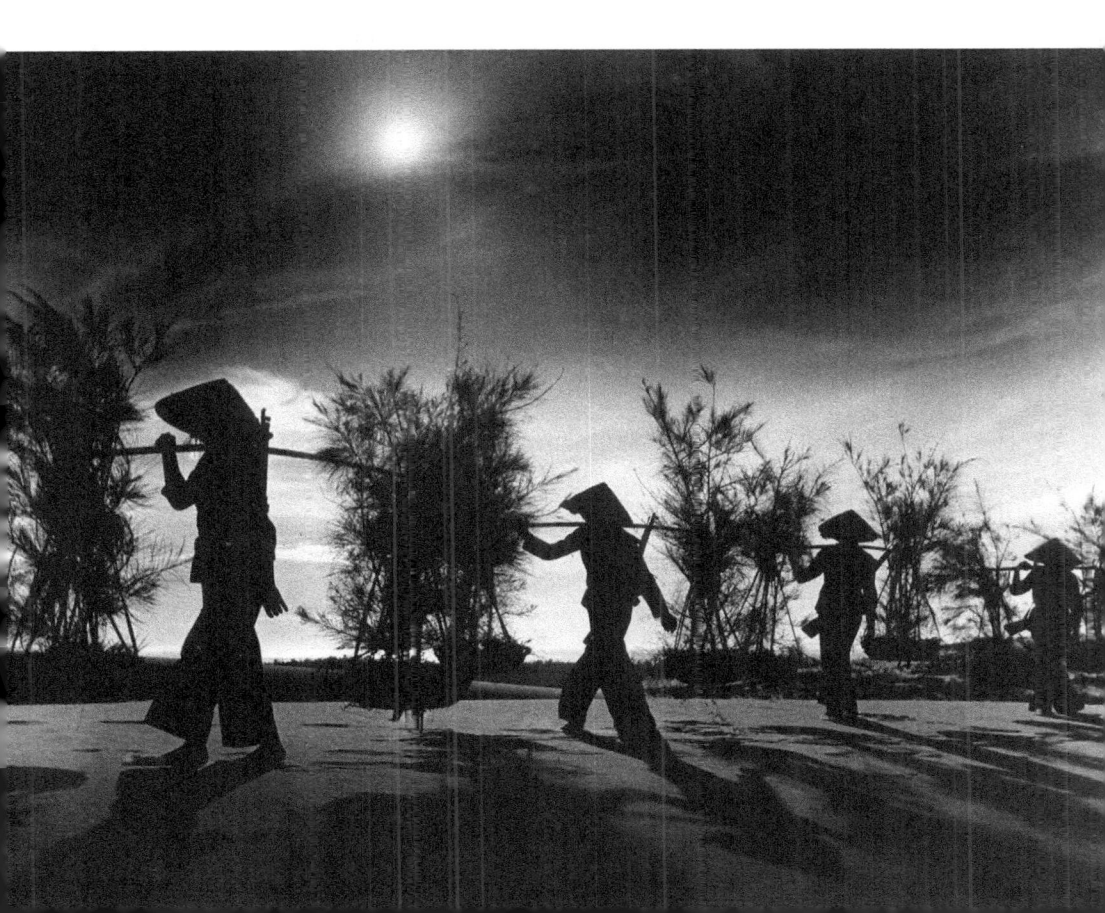

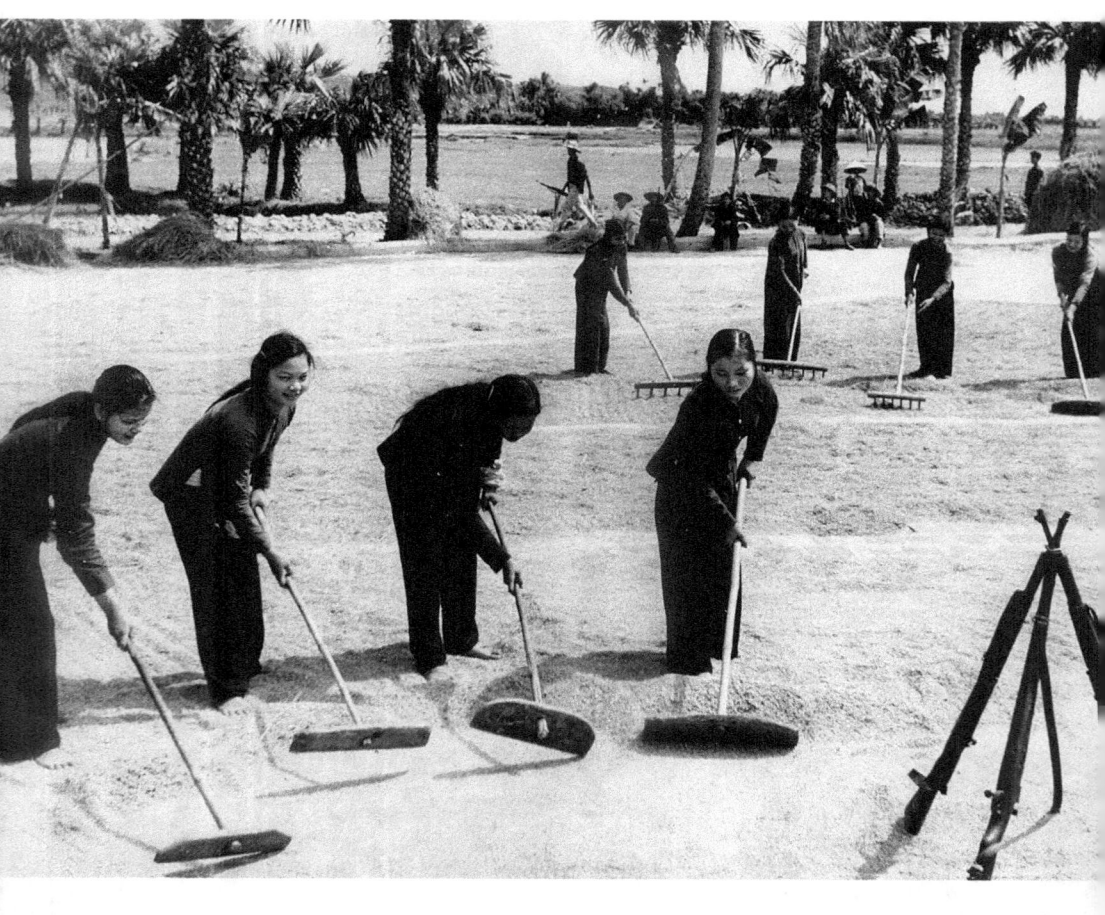

FIGURE 2.4 Women
clearing a road. Photographer:
Lê Minh Trường.

Given how contested this visual rhetoric was and how influential and durable it proved to be, I approach the visual representation of the revolutionary Vietnamese woman as more than just image, in line with theoretical approaches to photography as a cultural practice of geopolitical encounter and a labor of war, which need not result in or even involve an image object and which intersect with textual and other cultural practices. Instead, I explore the Vietnamese revolutionary woman as *symbol*, significant because of the social and cultural consequences that it can bring about. The symbol operates in a manner analogous to the "figure," a concept that political philosopher Thomas Nail develops to expand on notions of personhood.[5] According to Nail, the figure is neither a "fixed identity" nor a "specific person" but can be understood as a "mobile social position" and "social vector." When individuals position themselves in relation to a figure, their sense of selfhood is shaped by it. The symbol of the revolutionary Vietnamese woman is meant to conjure a collective, a sense of solidarity made legible to individuals when they position themselves in relation to, and in ostensible alignment with, the symbol and its associated ideals.

Other scholars have associated symbolization with objectification, depoliticization, and a lack of female agency. For example, Elizabeth Armstrong and Vijay Prashad have lamented the difficulty of pinning down the precise role of Vietnamese women during and after the war, observing that "women in Vietnam, at their most objectified, were rendered as symbols: of revolutionary resistance, of the Third World, and perhaps most commonly, of a separatist force within the larger struggle against US occupation."[6] Mary Ann Tétreault adds that the symbol's flexibility and ambiguity pose challenges to the task of historical interpretation.[7] These critics decry the proliferation of the Vietnamese revolutionary woman as symbol, lamenting that symbolization obscures the active role she played. But symbolization does not necessarily entail depoliticization. During the war a key role for Vietnamese revolutionary women was *as* symbol.

Therefore, emphasizing women as symbols neither diminishes their political potency nor dismisses the extensive contributions and sacrifices of Vietnamese women. Instead, symbolization for these women was a pivotal tactic for asserting cultural influence. Indeed, the "revolutionary Vietnamese woman" was a multiform category, which different groups, including the Vietnamese state and women's movements independent from the state, sought to pin down for their own ends.

This chapter traces the emergence of this symbol and the routes of its transpacific circulation, with a focus on the contest for control over its meaning among opposing groups in Vietnam and its subsequent appeal for members of the North American women's antiwar organizations, namely Women Strike for Peace (wsp), Voice of Women (VoW), and the Women's International League for Peace and Freedom (wilpf). These organizations were especially responsive audiences for vwu outreach activities, despite the contradictions in their positions with respect to war, which few, if any, members of these North American women's activist groups noticed. I contend that this disregard amounts to a form of misrecognition, an unwitting but occasionally willful misunderstanding of the significance of the producer's intended meaning in favor of viewers' sensibilities and priorities. By misrecognition, I do not mean to imply that there is a single "correct" essence of Vietnamese revolutionary womanhood. On the contrary, my aim is to emphasize what Anna Tsing theorizes as "frictions" in her ethnography of postcolonial Indonesia. Tsing's concept of frictions denotes discordances and misunderstandings that may be counterintuitively generative. Here, I examine the potentially productive misunderstandings between a socialist way of seeing in Vietnam and a broadly leftist sensibility that developed in markedly disparate contexts, even as adherents pledged solidarity with the antiwar cause.[8] Through an exploration of the symbol's varied permutations, I explain how the revolutionary Vietnamese woman contributed to socialist ways of seeing, demonstrating how these socialist ways of seeing transform in response to diverse contexts. Charting the transpacific circuits of influence helps reveal the many ways that the symbol of the revolutionary Vietnamese woman was produced and consumed, and how in the course of visual exchange the symbol became a key arsenal in the warring visions of opposing—and allied—sides, which conscripted the cause of women's emancipation for competing political objectives.

The symbol of the revolutionary Vietnamese woman exemplifies "parallax vision," historian Bruce Cumings's term to denote how ways of knowing shift depending on one's viewing position.[9] These dissimilar perspectives produce diverse permutations of this symbol. Notably, photographers, artists, and radical newsletter editors represented the revolutionary Vietnamese woman in varied ways: as girls with guns; as militarized mothers representing a martial maternalism; as, at times, glamorously arrayed but more often than not humbly garbed peasant warriors and diplomatic representatives (in the case of Nguyễn Thị Bình); and finally as mothers who posed simply and conspicuously *without* guns. What accounts for these diverse permutations, and who was responsible for shaping them? What was the cultural politics of the production and circulation of this symbol? To what extent did this process establish solidarities, and how did misunderstandings complicate this objective? I contend that rather than sabotaging solidarity, misrecognition shored up sisterhood, expanded socialist ways of seeing beyond the Vietnamese context, and stretched the concept of "socialism" to accommodate gendered objectives that did not wholly fall within the scope of the Vietnamese photographers who produced this symbol, which subsequently took on forms that diverged from the vwu's designs.

GENDERED VISIONS OF MODERNITY IN A DIVIDED VIETNAM

Despite being deployed abroad as a means of expressing parallels and solidarities, the symbol of the revolutionary Vietnamese woman laid bare ideological differences even within Vietnam, not least of which were tensions between socialism and women's emancipation. In Vietnam, which from 1954 to 1975 was partitioned into North Vietnam and South Vietnam, this very symbol became the means for opposing administrations to vie for the mantle of national liberator and champion of women's rights. As noted above, the Vietnam Women's Union in the North was especially concerned with shaping this symbol to suit its purposes and did so by elaborating on women's collective contributions to revolution. Yet given the significance of collective struggle as a socialist virtue, the composition of some of these photographs might at first appear odd, for they feature a single Vietnamese revolutionary woman removed from the company of her comrades. As we saw earlier, the Hanoi Women's Museum opted to represent this symbol as a singular presence (figure 2.1), adapting Mai Nam's iconic photograph by cropping out the second person who appeared in his original print (figure 2.2).

Despite the isolating effect of this excision, its seeming contradiction can be resolved when we consider that the photograph implies the presence of others. After all, visitors are encouraged to look at and in this process presumably see and sympathize with her accomplishments. The visual idiom of singularity did not necessarily emphasize the individuality of the Vietnamese revolutionary woman. Rather, this visual idiom gestures toward collectivity through an implicitly expansive notion of singularity. Specifically, the decision to frame this symbol in a singular way is consistent with the vwu's broader strategy of exalting select revolutionary women as exemplary fighters in propaganda pamphlets, also called "emulation" tracts, designed to recruit more women in solidarity with the cause of anticolonial struggle.

Perhaps the most visible model of exemplary collectivism, which is to say a singular revolutionary whose contributions laid a path for others to follow, can be seen in the representation of Nguyễn Thị Bình, particularly in her carefully composed performance of femininity while negotiating the Paris Peace Accords on behalf of the Communist-sympathetic Provisional Revolutionary Government–National Liberation Front (PRG-NLF). Although she was nervous about appearing before the press, Nguyễn Thị Bình understood the importance of appearances. "After all," she reminisced, "a gentle, petite woman from a land where war raged had stood before them, speaking with reason and feeling. Indeed, our first steps had created sympathy among the press."[10] Madame Bình presented herself to be seen, playfully responding to clichés about the so-called Orient (as evident when she described herself as "gentle" and "petite"). Significantly, Madame Bình also appeared in public at these talks wearing áo dài, the traditional Vietnamese dress, as a gendered display of nationalism (figure 2.5). In Vietnam, revolutionaries expressed their discipline in plainer style, with the peasants' signature black pajamas and checkered scarves. Madame Bình was well aware that her self-consciously feminine demeanor enabled the delegates of the Provisional Revolutionary Government/Democratic Republic of Vietnam (PRG-DRV) to appear as progressive compared to the exclusively male representatives of the Republic of Vietnam. Her counterparts at the negotiating table failed to realize that by sitting cozily with the all-male delegation of American diplomats, they projected an old-boys-club cronyism.

Although the connection between socialist liberation and female emancipation first emerged in the Soviet and Chinese revolutions, Hồ Chí Minh expressed his commitment to women in several speeches.[11] For example, at a 1959 cadres meeting, convened to debate the merits of a draft law on marriage and the family, Hồ Chí Minh declared that "women make up half of society. If they are not liberated, half of society is not freed. If women are not emancipated only half of socialism is built."[12] The passage of this law in 1960 attested to the Vietnamese Communist Party's protection of women's rights by abolishing concubinage, forced marriage, and child marriage. In a speech for the Vietnam Women's Union on the organization's twentieth anniversary, Hồ Chí Minh expressed how "deeply grateful [our people are] to the mothers in both South and North Vietnam for having given birth to and bringing up the heroic generations of our country." He pointed proudly to a tradition of women and revolution in Vietnam extending two thousand years back to the rebellion led by the legendary Trung sisters against the injustice of

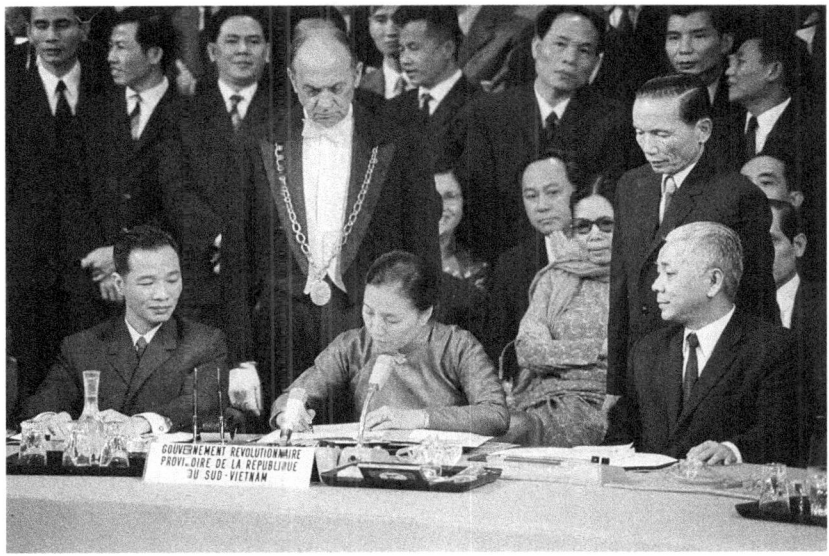

FIGURE 2.5 Mrs. Nguyễn Thị Bình signing Nine Point Plan.
Photographer: Bettmann. Getty Images.

Chinese colonialism.[13] Madame Bình's presence at the talks seemed to bring to fruition this socialist promise of women's emancipation.

By presenting herself as determined yet vulnerable, Nguyễn Thị Bình sought to represent Vietnamese women more generally, as part of an overall "people-to-people" strategy that opened up the diplomatic front to complement the military front. "This new diplomatic front," she declared, "could enhance our influence on international and US public opinion, isolate the forces of aggression, and provide effective support for the battlefield."[14] Such a strategy both affirms and refines the principle of armed propaganda that the Viet Minh resistance introduced during the First Indochina War against the French. In *People's Army, People's War*, general Võ Nguyên Giáp asserts that by armed propaganda, "we had not to attempt to overthrow the enemy, but try to win over and make use of him."[15] With the Second Indochina War (the American War) the communist strategy, adapted from the example set by Chinese advisors, expanded. It became imperative to win over not just enemies but also to attract friends, most notably members of the North American women's movement.

Yet the communists were not the only ones to claim women as allies and to broadcast their vision of the revolutionary woman, which they cast in the mold of the revered Trung sisters. Madame Nhu projected a competing version of this figure within Vietnam, asserting that the Vietnamese women of the Saigon-based Republic of Vietnam could defend the nation against communism and foreign corruption. Specifically, Madame Nhu expressed her commitment to this vision of militarized motherhood by advancing the cause of the WSM, a South Vietnamese paramilitary organization that she founded in 1960 and headed to oppose socialism.

Madame Nhu was a powerful and polarizing leader who performed a version of revolutionary femininity markedly dissimilar from that of Madame Bình. In contrast to Madame Bình's modesty, Madame Nhu favored a more risqué style of áo dài, which Saigon-based intellectuals worried bore the taint of foreign influence (figure 2.6). Yet Madam Nhu was aware that her detractors, whom she labeled "traditionalists," blamed her for the immodesty of Vietnamese fashion. She defended herself by declaring that her intent was hardly "to launch a cosmopolitan fashion, and less to encourage extravagant attire" that was "fanciful" and "alien" but instead to feature designs of "ancient Vietnam . . . which are still common among the tribes of the Highlands."[16] Traditionalists revered áo dài as reflecting a distinct Vietnamese national identity.[17] However, this dress has evolved over the course of the nineteenth and twentieth centuries to incorporate foreign fashions. Despite the disavowal of external influence, the áo dài exemplifies an invented tradition.[18]

In the early nineteenth century, áo dài, worn by both men and women, consisted of a loose-fitting tunic split into two panels and worn over trousers. The way that men and women wore the tunic, whether hung loose or knotted together at the ends, varied according to region. In the early twentieth century, Hanoi artist Nguyễn Cát Tường, also known as Le Mur, made a splash with his version of áo dài for women. Adapted from French fashions, Le Mur's design cut the tunic to fit tightly to bust and torso, thereby showing off feminine frames without exposing much flesh. Indeed, a high collar hid the neckline entirely. Fashionable Vietnamese women embraced this style as a modern version of the áo dài. In their eyes it was no less a national dress for all that it adapted the figure-hugging lines associated with French tailoring. By the 1960s, the increased presence of American advisors and soldiers, particularly in the southern capital of Saigon, brought greater urgency to the issue of foreign influence as the injection of billions of US dollars in aid encouraged corruption, created a market for prostitution, and stimulated a black market of illicit goods, drugs, and services.

One can see signs of this influence in Saigonese fashions; women adopted elements of risqué Western dress, of which the miniskirt was perhaps the

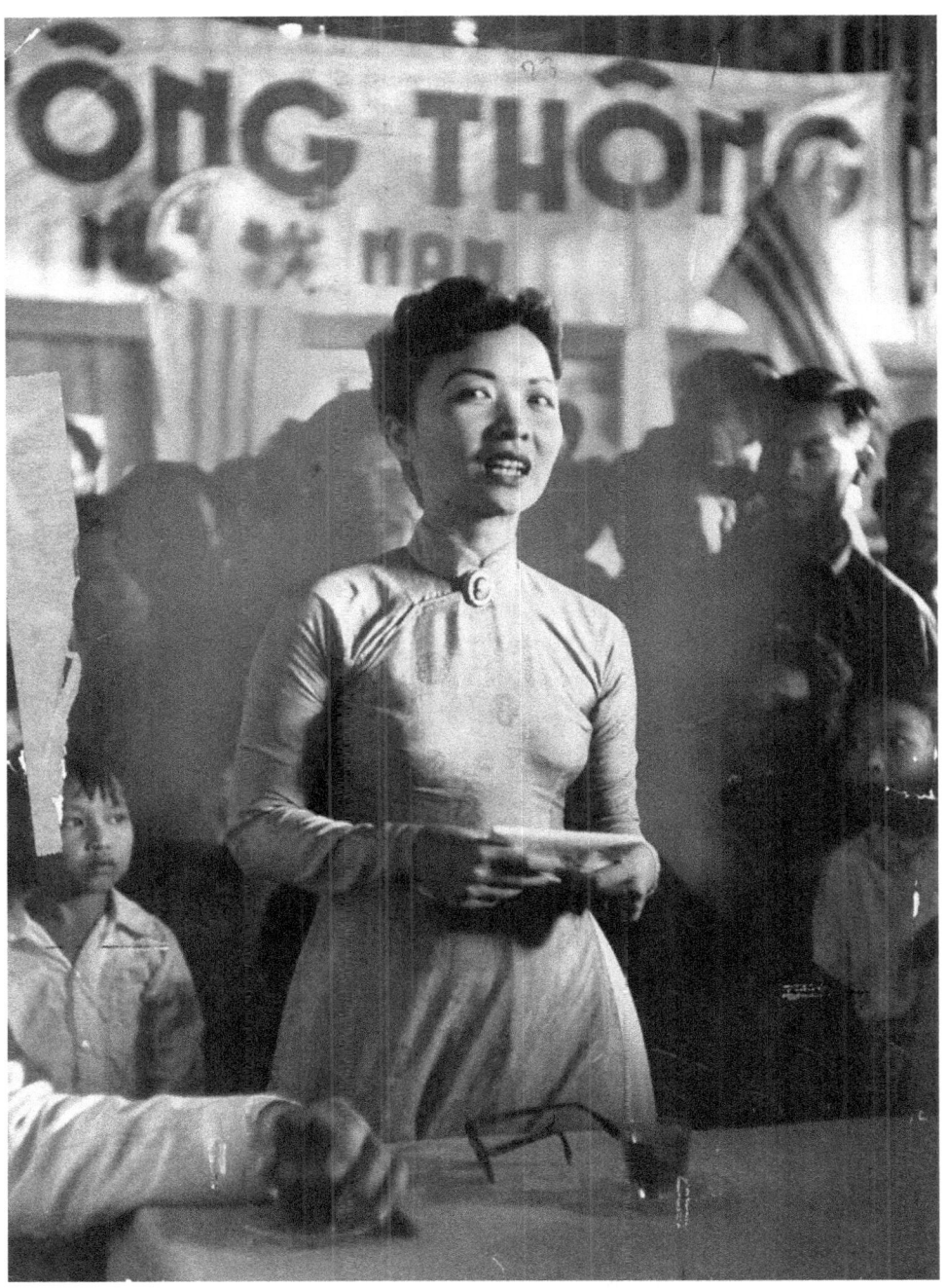

FIGURE 2.6 Madame Ngo Dinh Nhu, acting as official hostess for President Ngo Dinh Diem. Photographer: John Dominis. Getty Images.

most scandalous. (Here, the contrast to the United States, where the miniskirt connoted countercultural values, is striking.) Accordingly, the hemlines of the áo dài inched higher, while stiff mandarin collars that hid the neckline disappeared altogether, with Madame Nhu favoring the new designs. Although the traditionalists gossiped about Madame Nhu's áo dài, their disapproval was hardly a trivial matter; as the First Lady, Madame Nhu symbolized South Vietnam through her comportment and dress. When magazines remarked on her open-necked áo dài, they also embarked on gendered speculation of just how open she, and by extension the Diem regime, was to American influence. When Madame Nhu insisted that the open-neck style harkened to folk traditions, she sought to quell this speculation, deflecting attention by disavowing Western sensibilities and insisting on the local origins of her signature áo dài.

By the time Madame Bình entered the world stage as a prominent revolutionary and political leader at the Paris Peace Talks in 1969, the significance of áo dài was well established. It was a sartorial sign that, for better or for worse, stitched women to nation. Depending on who was looking, the áo dài modeled a modest and dignified socialist statement or a more modern, salacious South Vietnam. Like Madame Nhu, then, Madame Bình deliberately crafted this sign for her purposes and to claim the mantle of modernity; in her more modest rendition, Madame Bình embodied a vision of gendered nationhood—and revolution—whose plainness contrasted starkly with Madame Nhu's grandeur.

Madame Nhu sought visibility in other ways, by taking advantage of the attention afforded by the Western press to project her vision of Vietnamese modernity for local and international spectators. In 1962 *Life* magazine featured a child at play with First Lady Madame Nhu. In this photograph, Madame Nhu and the child point toy pistols at each other. More than her acclaimed beauty, the photograph stands out because of its theme of militarized motherhood—the very theme that would also be forcefully taken up by the VWU and the NLF-PRG, her ideological opponents. Although this photograph is playful, Madame Nhu took her self-presentation of militarized motherhood seriously, even presenting her daughter Lệ Thủy a pistol as a gift on her eighteenth birthday.

Madame Nhu also supported militarized motherhood by backing the WSM (figure 2.7). Established with much fanfare in 1960, the WSM's main objective, outlined in its charter, was to "become a force on which the Nation can count and which the Nation must take into account."[19] To be eligible for the WSM, women had to be between eighteen and fifty years old and willing to under-

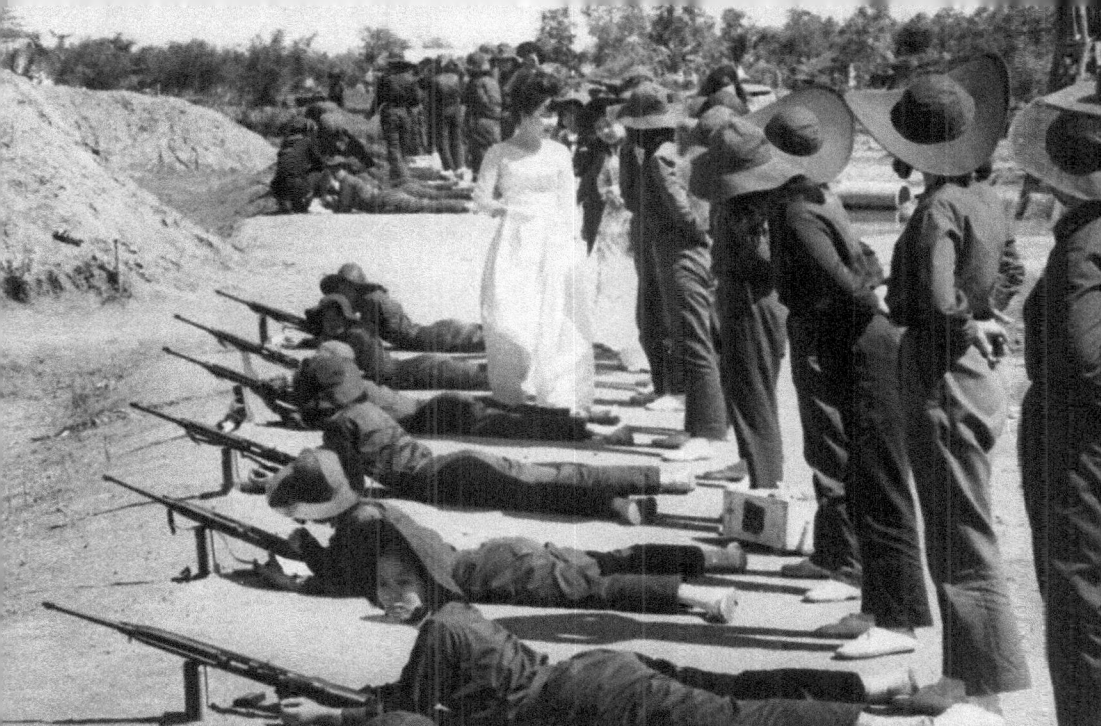

FIGURE 2.7 Mrs. Ngo Dinh Nhu, Vietnam's First Lady, visiting militiawomen. Photographer: Larry Burrows. Getty Images.

take seventy-two-hour training sessions at the Quyết Thắng ("Determination to Win") Training Center, located just outside Saigon. Training for these women consisted of military drills, marches, and some first aid, after which the paramilitary group was dispatched to provide protection and assistance at strategic hamlets, an unpopular program of land removal meant to destabilize communist guerrillas. Madame Nhu believed that peasants in these hamlets would welcome paramilitary women as warmly as they greeted her, but as the US ambassador wryly noted, she overestimated her own popularity. A State Department brief notes that hamlet chiefs coached peasants prior to her visits; moreover, her "cool" and "aloof" manner alienated locals.[20] American observers, who watched the emergence of the WSM carefully, doubted that her paramilitary organization would be any more effective than she was in cultivating warm relationships with locals.[21]

In contrast to the singularity that made up part of the visual rhetoric of collectivism associated with Vietnamese socialism, however, Madame Nhu sought above all to represent the WSM as a tightly unified mass that was part of her vision of republicanism. Accordingly, press photographs of the WSM

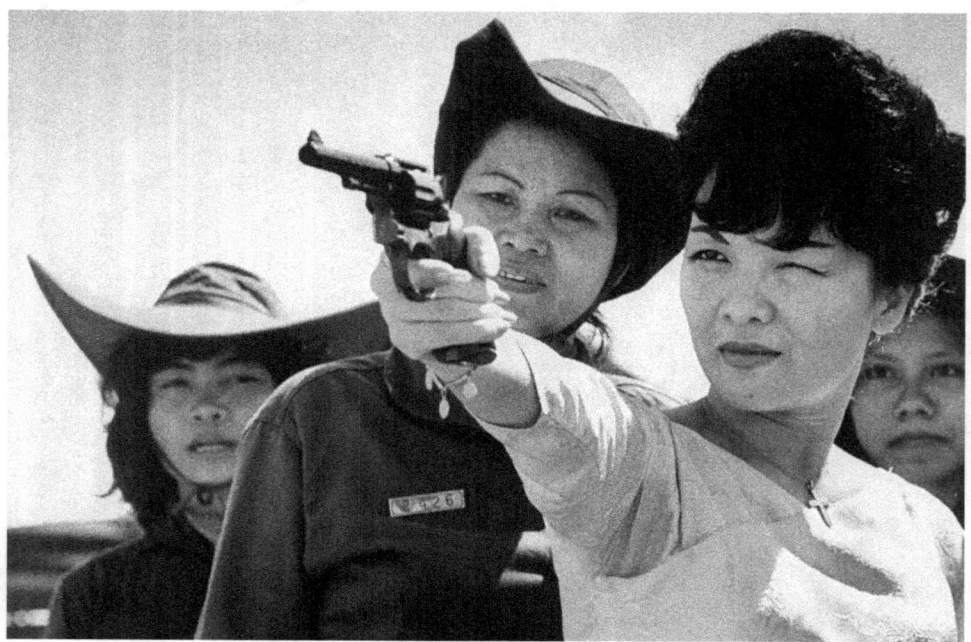

FIGURE 2.8 Mrs. Ngo Dinh Nhu firing .38 pistol. Photographer: Larry Burrows. Getty Images.

captured the women in military formation, in training, and at drills. Align-ing herself with this discipline, Madame Nhu had herself photographed at target practice in a now-famous image (figure 2.8). The image of disciplined military formation marks her understanding of solidarity; through the ap-pearance of women in line in defense of the republic, Madame Nhu projected a sense of firm resolve. The overall picture of the WSM that Madame Nhu sought to orchestrate was a proto-feminist formation in which she strove to wrest the moral authority of women's emancipation from her opponents on behalf of the Government of Vietnam. However, for all that these movements were designed to communicate the unity of its members, their highly coor-dinated and synchronized quality belied the organization's internal divisions.

The WSM accepted volunteers from all classes. One recruit was Thang Thị Út, a member of the Republican Youth, an organization loyal to the Diem re-gime. The twenty-two-year-old was among a group of cadets who gathered together in Phước Tây province to celebrate Hai Ba Trung Day, in honor of the Trung sisters. Participants at this event were attacked, however. After the event, a truck transporting the girls of the Republican Youth struck a land mine. As the damaged vehicle careened toward a nearby military outpost, guerrillas shot at the trapped passengers.[22] Út was one of two people killed. According to a press story about the ambush, the young woman, who was about to marry and start her own family, was cut down on the cusp of womanhood. As narrated by the Diem-controlled South Vietnamese press, the attack on Út and her female companions was nothing less than a betrayal and perversion of the very tradition of revolutionary womanhood that Hai Ba Trung Day was meant to commemorate. In this way, Madame Nhu claimed her WSM as the true inheritor of the Trung sisters' legacy.

A year before unveiling the WSM in 1960, Madame Nhu sought to demonstrate her leadership on women's rights by introducing the Family Code, a set of laws that she pressured the South Vietnam Assembly to pass. Saigon elites found Madame Nhu's stance tough to swallow, gossiping that, at best, the code evinced the Catholic prudery of the Diem regime and, at worst, served as a vehicle for a petty personal vendetta against her brother-in-law, who was about to abandon her sister. (She punished them by blocking their divorce.) In fact, the Family Code was groundbreaking legislation that preceded by a full year the Communist Party's Law on Marriage and Family, offering the very landmark reforms—prohibiting polygamy, outlawing arranged marriages, and curtailing grounds for divorce—that would be lauded in the other law.[23] Nevertheless, Madame Nhu's Family Code proved to be unpopular. Although she hoped to demonstrate the sincerity of her desire to emancipate women through her paramilitary organization, from the outset the WSM required more force to make an impact. Indeed, some of Madame Nhu's policies suggested her commitment to the cause of women's emancipation was, at most, halfhearted. For example, she announced that pregnant WSM members would be granted unpaid maternity leave of two months and reassignment to other, less physically strenuous tasks, her desire to be scrupulous with the budget or at least seen to be so outweighing any consideration of tangible compensation.[24]

The public nevertheless harbored suspicions of incompetence and malfeasance. On August 20, 1962, François Sully sparked controversy with an article he published in *Newsweek* titled "Vietnam: The Unpleasant Truth." The story criticized the Diem regime for its ineffectiveness in the war and included a photograph of WSM volunteers completing the paramilitary training program, captioned "Female Militia in Saigon: The Enemy has more drive and enthusiasm." The article mocked the recruits' patriotism and punctured Madame Nhu's buoyant vision of the WSM as revolutionary women fighting for nation and family. In a letter sent to the editors of *Newsweek* the following day, WSM members protested that "*Newsweek* is supposedly an organ of information and its correspondent in Vietnam must be well aware that day in day out, in uniform or not, arms at hand or not, the women of Vietnam are second to none and especially to the enemy in drive and enthusiasm—above all when the fight for the survival of our nation is concerned."[25] Irate, they demanded Sully's immediate expulsion from Vietnam.

Although Sully appealed, the Diem regime authorized this decision, and he became one among just a handful of journalists to be expelled. Sully was a cautionary example to other correspondents of the costs of criticizing the Government of Vietnam and a reminder of the limits of press freedom during the war in Vietnam. This move to expel Sully—he managed to stay in South Vietnam, where he eventually died while on assignment—nevertheless counters claims about the unrestricted access that journalists had in this supposed golden age of print and televisual media. The symbol of the militarized revolutionary woman, as mobilized by Madame Nhu, may have seemed so innocuous as to be ineffectual, at least for *Newsweek*. Yet this symbol served as a lightning rod for debates on freedom versus censorship, with the freedom granted by the United States peremptorily removed, or so it seemed, by the South Vietnamese government. Behind these deliberations lurked the even more troubling concern about the relationship between the Diem regime and the United States. At this moment the shaky nature of the American alliance with Diem prompted US analysts to chafe under the "uncomfortable predicament" imposed by the "scarcity of acceptable alternatives" for leadership in South Vietnam.[26] This predicament was only exacerbated by Madame Nhu's rhetoric, which a US diplomat sardonically described as "highly readable and frequently vitriolic."[27]

Like her counterparts among the VWU, who cast their net wide for allies around the world, Madame Nhu appealed for support. Although she particularly sought sympathy from among overseas Vietnamese, she also welcomed foreign women as "associate members." This is why the organization's name was changed from the Vietnamese Women's Solidarity Movement to the Women's Solidarity Movement of Vietnam. Nonetheless, a major problem arose from Madame Nhu's very approach to "solidarity." For her there were clear limits to solidarity; significantly, she stopped short of ceding national objectives to larger international organizations. Specifically, the WSM "would count on the broad reciprocity" of allies in other nations who would, she declared, exchange "a community of ideals and objectives, though each organization is able to keep its complete independence and implement the common rules of approach in its own national field of activities." She explained how her approach differed from others who put their energy into a "single international committee," which she dismissed because it "usually serves only to keep international contacts but is in general ignored in the national life of the member countries."[28] She rejected approaches to solidarity that folded national groups under the umbrella of international organizations lest they lose the specificity of struggles for independence. Solidarity could strengthen the movement, she admitted, but only if the organization's objectives remained central. A form of solidarity that lost sight of nationalist concerns might as well not be solidarity, according to Madame Nhu. Photographs of the WSM, in emphasizing the martial choreography and uniformity of women in formation, expressed a vision of solidarity between Vietnamese women in spite of American imperialism, even as the administration that Madame Nhu represented was propped up by American advisors.

On August 3, 1963, Madame Nhu used these rousing words to address a group of cadres who were about to complete their training at the Quyết Thắng Training Center: "Place your confidence in us and I assure you, the women of Vietnam will always inspire respect—at most, envy, but never pity, the less contempt."[29] The press, invited to come along and document the proceedings, duly filed their stories, taking care to illustrate their accounts of the training with the photogenic militarized women. However, Madame Nhu's many detractors claimed that the symbolism she so carefully crafted lacked substance. According to Nguyễn Thị Tuyết Mai, a member of Saigon's elite, women joined the league lest their husbands, who were bureaucrats in Diệm's administration, lose their jobs.[30] For Mai, fear and intimidation stitched the movement not into a durable bond of solidarity but rather into a frayed semblance of cohesion that was quickly unraveling.

In November 1963 a CIA-backed coup, led by General Dương Văn Minh, resulted in Madame Nhu's exile to Europe after the assassinations of her husband and brother-in-law. Madame Nhu boasted that in its heyday her WSM included more than a million members and claimed that its training center had to turn away volunteers for lack of space.[31] By 1964, South Vietnam shook as one administration after another toppled in the violence of successive coups. By then, whatever semblance of cohesion the WSM had established through the force of Madame Nhu's personality had thoroughly dissolved. When other movements abroad invoked the symbol of the revolutionary Vietnamese woman, they did so by taking up the VWU—that is, the communist—version of this symbol, not the splashy parades and training exercises staged by Madame Nhu and her paramilitary women's organization. Today, hardly anyone remembers the existence of the WSM.

The competing versions of the symbol of revolutionary women within the divided Vietnam lays bare the contested terms in which women and revolution came into visibility. Ironically, this symbol signified—depending on which group in Vietnam invoked it—socialism and its opposing ideology, republicanism. In Vietnam the category of woman is disorderly, according to anthropologist Ann Marie Leshkowich, who contends that the invocation of "woman" sparks fierce debates on nationhood and modernity—and, we might add, solidarity.[32] Given this context, in which the production of the symbol of revolutionary Vietnamese women exposed competing visions of modernity, whether socialist or republican, it is hardly surprising that its meanings acquired further complexity through the circulation, remediation, and reinterpretation of this symbol or, more accurately, the North Vietnamese iteration of the revolutionary woman, the version that triumphed with the collapse of the Diem regime.

On October 14-17, 1967, four years after the dissolution of the WSM, the Council for the International Democratic Federation of Women adopted a "Resolution on the Vietnam Problem" at a conference in Prague, where the idea for the first North American conference involving Vietnamese women as delegates was hatched. This resolution called on all women "to show the greatest material and moral solidarity with the Vietnamese people and, in particular, with the women of Vietnam"[33]—by which was meant North Vietnam. If the absence of any references to the WSM in antiwar archives tells us anything, it is that the North American women's organization pledged solidarity, not with Madame Nhu and her movement, but instead with her opponents among the VWU.

TRANSPACIFIC ALLIES: MOTHERHOOD AND MILITARISM, 1965-1975

As early as 1965, when the US military involvement in Vietnam escalated with Operation Rolling Thunder, the symbol of Vietnamese women struck a resounding chord among prominent US activists from organizations within the women's movement. Representatives from antiwar organizations, most prominently WSP and VoW, traveled to Vietnam at Hanoi's invitation to see the impact of the war firsthand. During these exercises in "radical tourism"—Judy Tzu-Chun Wu's evocative term for the excursions, though they also involved liberal and not only radical activists[34]—the visitors met with groups that were affected by the violence, including embattled women who shared their tales of suffering and endurance.

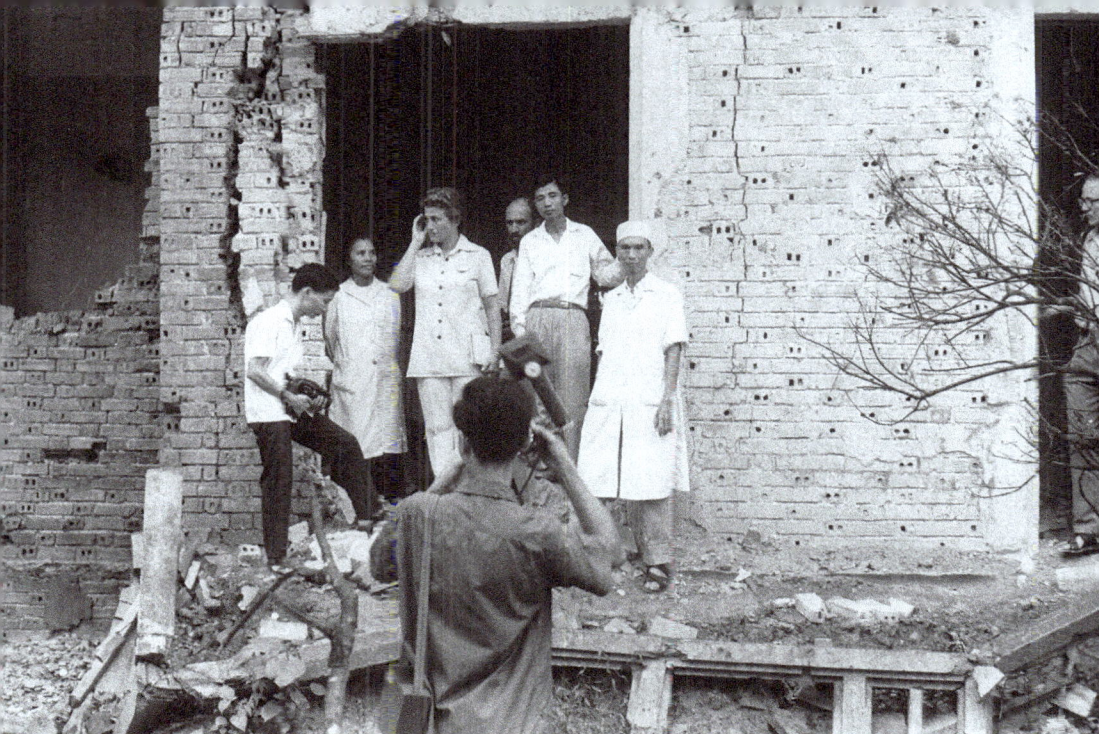

FIGURE 2.9 Antiwar activists being photographed during a visit to North Vietnam. Box 1, Cora Weiss Papers (Collection DG 222), Swarthmore College Peace Collection.

These tours were also photographed. In 1972 displays of the ruins of Hanoi's Bach Mai hospital provided a persuasive rejoinder to the US military's denials that civilian sites were bombed. The presence of Vietnamese photographers implied that it was not enough for visitors to witness; they had to be seen doing so (figure 2.9). Prime Minister Phạm Văn Đồng, who led the DRV, assured activists that he understood that the visitors lacked influence over Washington and the Pentagon.[35]

However, the highly visible nature of these encounters suggests that the DRV hoped that activists could shape public opinion if not sway official policy. Because these northern guides showed sympathetic international visitors sites that revealed the war's brutal impact on the most innocent—particularly on women and children—the tourists came away with the impression of Vietnamese misery in the face of unjust aggression. Vietnamese photographers and their international guests collaborated in producing a picture of women at war by dwelling on their suffering. This overall picture emphasized motherhood and family, themes meant to tug on the heartstrings of visitors, many of whom were also wives and mothers. In this context the Vietnamese hosts drew on a maternal discourse to nurture a sense of sisterhood; women were revolutionary when they mobilized as mothers. A newspaper, published in English by the VWU, marked the occasion of International Children's Day by conveying this emphatic message: "In the name of all Vietnamese mothers, we extend our sincere gratitude to mothers and children-loving people the world over for their support of our just struggle. This support contributes to drawing closer the day when the innocent children of Vietnam will again know peace and happiness."[36] The VNA International Service reinforced this familial appeal, proclaiming that "the Vietnamese women have become a shock brigade of the international movement of women and children."[37]

This appeal to universal experience accords with what Armstrong describes as a solidarity of commonalty, which is based on human rights. Armstrong distinguishes this approach from what she describes as a solidarity of complicity, defined as a stance of resistance to oppression and power imbalances between women, particularly those that arise through colonial violence.[38] Armstrong's framework for solidarity sheds light on the VWU's strategy; the organization sought solidarity of commonality when it emphasized the human rights of mothers to nurture and protect their children from the violence of war. For the VWU, solidarity of commonality offered a promising step toward encouraging North American women to engage in solidarity of complicity, which required a deeper commitment to anticolonial resistance.

When their tours wrapped up, the visitors returned to the United States and Canada, where they participated in speaking tours across North America, occasions that enabled them to show photographs that they had taken or been given and share stories about their journey. For example, issues of *Vietnamese Women Today* are included in the papers of US feminist Charlotte Bunch, a prominent WSP member.[39] Published by the VWU, this illustrated pamphlet includes photographs credited to Mai Nam and other communist photographers, which presented a different side of women's roles during the war than the ones the activists encountered on their tours.

In contrast to images of suffering victims that these visitors saw in Hanoi, the pamphlets featured workers and warriors who exemplified the militarism of Vietnamese women, a reversal of the VNA strategy of appealing to pacifism and a seeming affront to antiwar sensibilities. How did antiwar activists reconcile what they saw—the symbol of the revolutionary Vietnamese woman as a girl with a gun—with what the liberal feminists of this movement believed about the moral rectitude of pacifism? How could solidarity of commonalty, based on human rights, be established in the face of this symbol of violence?

Although the liberal members of the North American women's movement during this period were aware of this martial strand of Vietnamese revolution, they chose to overlook it in favor of a message they found more palatable. Several contradictions were at play here. On the one hand, the martial form of the symbol captivated the popular imagination, no doubt because of taboos about representing *American* women as warriors. (During this time, American women served in the military primarily to provide care as nurses or secretaries and were not permitted to carry or fire weapons.)[40] On the other hand, this martial vision of revolution posed a problem for a prominent liberal wing of the North American women's movement. The fact that Vietnamese women went to war unsettled liberal beliefs about women's ostensibly "natural" pacifism, which members of the radical Left were also starting to unsettle.[41] Sociologist Jennifer Carlson refers to this liberal belief as an ideological "pacifist presumption" that blinds proponents to women's decision to take up arms in defense of "martial maternalism."[42]

Undeterred by these discordances, WSP members sought to bring this message of solidarity with Vietnamese women to North America almost immediately after the first contingent of foreign visitors to Hanoi returned to the United States. Organizers began planning an international conference, with the WSP in collaboration with the WILPF, VoW, and VWU, an official arm of what today is known as the Vietnamese Communist Party.[43] The conference provided a means for Vietnamese women to tell their stories directly, to enrich the secondary accounts provided by North American visitors to Vietnam, at the same time that it offered opportunities to broadcast their image further through carefully orchestrated performances of revolutionary femininity and through the production of images of this performance.

This planning culminated in the 1969 arrival of a delegation of Vietnamese women from the North and the liberated areas of the South, including Madame Nguyễn Ngọc Dung (executive, Student Liberation Movement), Madame Lê Thị Cao (teacher, Catholic Member of National Liberation Party), and Tri Van An (interpreter). This delegation embarked on a whirlwind tour of sites in Canada. Besides, organizers reasoned, the US State Department would almost certainly reject the delegates' visa applications because they hailed from countries with which the United States was at war, albeit undeclared. So although Canada played only a minor role in the global Cold War, its proximity to the United States, seeming innocuousness, and appeal as a haven for American draft dodgers made it an ideal base to broker peace.[44] Organizers accordingly selected sites close to the US border so that American participants could easily join the events, namely North Hatley, Quebec (adjacent to Vermont), Niagara Falls, and Toronto, where a conference on women took place at the University of Toronto. Toronto was an ideal venue because many draft resisters established themselves there at the time, making the city a hotbed of leftist activism.[45]

Niagara Falls was especially important because it enabled the organizers a chance to stage a spectacle meant to dramatize what WSP leader Cora Weiss called a "border incident," with Vietnamese delegates on the Canadian side of the border and busloads of Americans on the US side.[46] However, spectacles require an audience; Weiss and her fellow organizers were disappointed by the limited press coverage of the event and had to settle for stories affirming the ideal of transnational harmony that they placed in movement newsletters.[47] A group of American women marched across the Rainbow Bridge, symbolically overcoming the physical, psychical, and ideological distance between the United States, Canada, and Vietnam. Likewise, photographs of the delegation returned to this theme of motherhood. Significantly, one of the most prominent American participants at the conference, Jane Spock, a passionate antiwar activist who offered an apology to the Vietnamese delegates on behalf of the United States, was continually identified, as was then customary, as the wife of Benjamin Spock, a pediatrician and best-selling author of books on childcare who was also a prominent member of the movement. Indeed, photographs of the tour captured the Vietnamese visitors regarding and embracing the children of participants and exchanging photographs of these encounters (figure 2.10).

Although the WSP deliberately invoked this maternal discourse, it was hardly forced on the delegation. The Vietnamese visitors were not just aware of the terms on which their appeal for solidarity would be most sympathetically heard; they also self-consciously adopted these terms. Significantly, in her plenary address at the 1969 Toronto conference, Madame Dung drew explicitly on maternal rhetoric to connect to her audience, explaining that "our love for our children have [sic] helped us to do the things that seemed to be impossible to do. The whole population in the country have [sic] praised our women because they have done everything that seemed to be impossible. We have come here with some feeling of the Vietnamese wives and mothers' love for children. We think American mothers have the same feeling and that feeling gives the same strength as we have."[48]

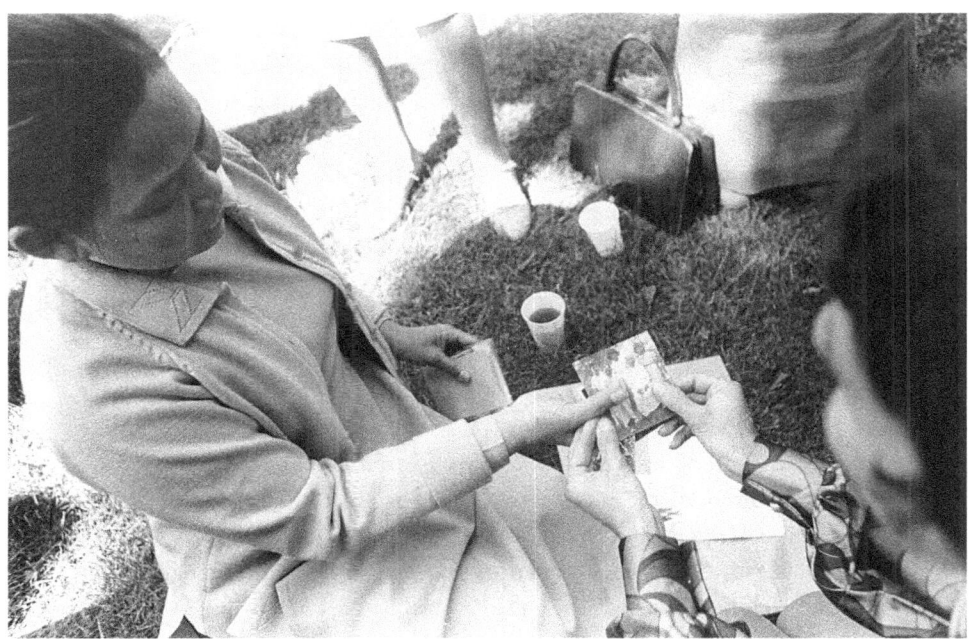

FIGURE 2.10 Voice of Women conference with Vietnamese women in Canada, 1971. Photographer: George deVincent, Box 1, Cora Weiss Papers (Collection DG 222), Swarthmore College Peace Collection.

Following the success of this tour, members of the WSP began planning for a follow-up event consisting of a more ambitious set of back-to-back conferences, raising funds through a collection drive and donations. This second conference took place in 1971, in Vancouver and Toronto, sites that were selected to accommodate participants from both coasts. Unlike the 1969 conference, for the 1971 events the WSP and VoW collaborated with many different women's groups, including Third World, Bread and Roses, Black radicals, and Canadian site volunteers, in organizing the dual events. That this collaboration was less than harmonious attests to the difficulty of achieving solidarity—a problem that the delegates themselves faced.

At this later conference the Vietnamese women were to share the stage with representatives from Laos and Cambodia, a gesture intended to highlight two intersecting forms of solidarity: between Indochinese women and between these women and their North American allies. At the same time, an inter-Asian framework offered insight on the war as a battleground that conscripted more than just American and Vietnamese people. Part of the global

Cold War, this proxy conflict spilled beyond Vietnam's borders and extended into neighboring Laos and Cambodia. By emphasizing Indochinese solidarity in this way, the organizers acknowledged the political groundwork that Southeast Asian women had already laid out independently, even while in so doing they sought allies among North American women.

Ironically, the North American conference participants' eagerness to proclaim alliances with Southeast Asian women obscured the delicate grounds of inter-Asian solidarity. Tellingly, the fact that Cambodian delegates were forced to withdraw from the conference because of logistical problems (the official explanation) that most likely arose from political turmoil in their country further exposed the fragility of their alliance.[49] In 1970, as organizers were putting this event in motion, a coup resulted in the removal of Prince Sihanouk as head of state in Cambodia, an event widely seen as a turning point in the Cambodian Civil War, which ultimately led that same year to the proclamation of the Khmer Republic, led by Lon Nol.[50] The circulation of the symbol of the revolutionary Vietnamese woman cannot be disentangled from the broader global Cold War context. Affected by the global Cold War's geopolitical realignments, the framework for Indochinese women's solidarity was shifting and, at best, unstable (no less than it was for the delicately negotiated alliance between the vwu and North American liberal feminists).[51] Moreover, although the delegates momentarily found common ground, it was not on equal terms; the admission card at the Vancouver conference featured a reproduction of Mai Nam's now-famous photograph of the Vietnamese militiawoman as the emblem of the overall proceedings. This decision reveals a visible hierarchy, with the Vietnamese delegates receiving greater attention than their fellow Laotian participants. Indeed, the spotlight on Vietnamese women overshadowed Laotian and Cambodian perspectives so much that participants hardly seemed to miss the third group when its representatives were forced to drop out.

For their part, numerous groups from within the North American women's movement were drawn to the symbol of the revolutionary woman. These groups included not just the more established VoW and wsp but also organizations that pioneered intersectional approaches to gender, race, class, and sexuality, including such organizations as Third World, the Chicana/o labor group Bread and Roses, and the Black Panther Party. So important was the image of the Vietnamese revolutionary woman for the second conference that she was the very currency on which fund-raising efforts were based: organizers sold copies of a blown-up portrait of the most famous revolutionary leader, Madame Nguyễn Thị Bình, for $2 each (see figure 2.11).

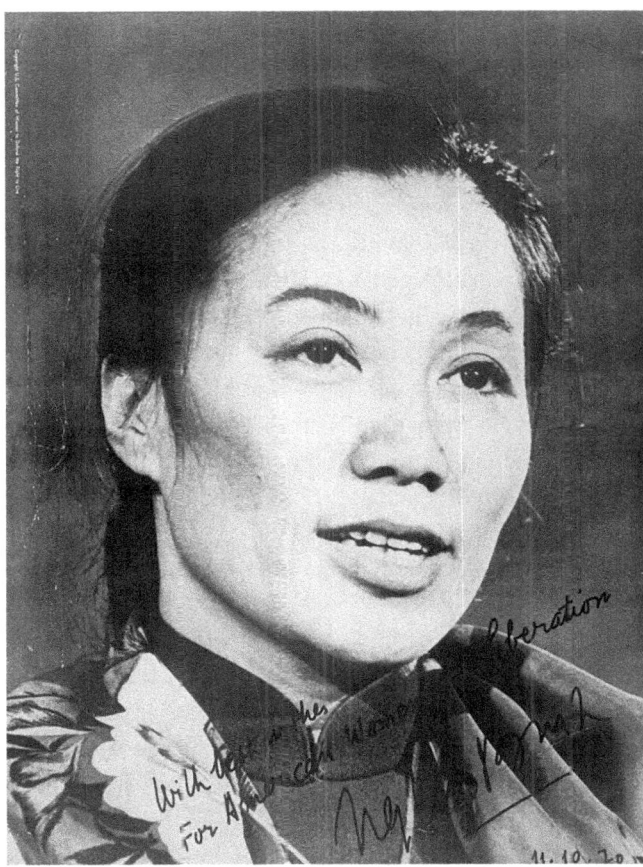

FIGURE 2.11 Poster of Nguyễn Thị Bình. Library of Congress.

In her role as an internationally recognized leader, Madame Bình sought indirectly to avoid tensions by reconciling the Vietnamese women's vision of revolution, which allowed for violence, with the pacifist maternalism emphasized by the liberal wing of the North American women's movement. In a film distributed by the WSP, Madame Bình told her audience to "please take the place of the Vietnamese mothers and wives who are faced by the sight of their homeland devastated each day by thousands of tons of bombs, and who undergo themselves unspeakable suffering and hardships together with their relatives and dear ones."[52] Despite her considerable political power as the foreign minister of the PRG, who negotiated on its behalf at the Paris Peace Talks—a position of leadership that, alongside that of Nguyễn Thị Định, founding member of and general in the National Liberation Front,[53] surpassed any public role that North American women held at the time—she broached the promise of revolution by invoking a now-familiar maternal rhetoric. Just as importantly, the liberal women's organizations that turned to Madame Bình for inspiration *expected* her to voice this maternal rhetoric, as they did when it came to the Vietnamese delegation that visited Canada. In short, Madame Bình's experiences as a mother strengthened her revolutionary resolve, or so she suggested in her carefully pitched message. However, she ended her address to the wsp with a less palatable message to her pacifist audience: "I am sure that you will do just the same as we are doing now." Although she did not explain exactly what it was that Vietnamese women were doing, there is little doubt she alluded to their militarism. For Madame Bình, militarism and motherhood went hand in hand: motherhood, whether its promise or actuality, compelled women to go to war. No one exemplifies this martial maternalism more vividly than Nguyễn Thị Út, the quintessential woman with a gun profiled in communist propaganda documents as an exemplary revolutionary worthy of emulation.[54] In a photograph displayed at the Women's Museum in Ho Chi Minh City, she is portrayed flanked by her children, nursing her child with one arm and brandishing a rifle with the other arm.

Although Madame Bình's own wartime contribution was as a diplomat rather than a soldier, her sacrifices cannot be discounted. Madame Bình's work for the prg took her away from her children, from whom she would be separated for years at a time. However, she asserted that she willingly endured this hardship for the sake of family and nation. Although her nom de guerre of Bình (her real name was Nguyễn Châu Sa) means "peace," underscoring her diplomatic role, she nevertheless did not eschew war as a means toward a revolutionary end. Madame Bình tenderly wrapped the message of military necessity in the soothing folds of maternity, even as she insisted that these conditions were not mutually exclusive, as the pacifists would have it. As historian Helen Anderson puts it, Vietnamese women were "fighting for family."[55]

Yet the coalition of women's movement members organized the 1971 conference for purposes that were significantly allied with yet distinct from those of Madame Bình. And within this coalition, trouble was brewing. wsp historian Arlene Eisen admits that "some of us who participated in the anti-war movement tended to romanticize aspects of the Vietnamese revolution. We created an image to meet our own needs . . . to confirm and legitimize our feminist goals."[56] Meanwhile, the Vietnamese delegates also had their own reasons for participating, which did not harmonize with their hosts' designs. In a memo to her co-organizers, wsp representative Trudi Yung conveyed the concerns of Phan Thị An, the head of the Vietnam Women's Union in Hanoi, as well as the objectives that this organization prioritized. In the memo, Yung noted that Phan Thị An "wanted to make sure we understood that although they were very happy to talk about the struggle of women and their role, they wanted us to keep in mind the framework of ending the war, and that we should be thinking about women's liberation in relation to this goal."[57] This brief note suggests that members of the Vietnam Women's Union understood the significance of women's emancipation for their allies among the North American women's movement and perceived how their own goal of national liberation contrasted with that of their sisters, even as they sought to align these two objectives. Between 1965 and 1971, the liberal wing of the North American women's movement shaped the symbol of the revolutionary Vietnamese woman into a maternal form compatible with its pacifist mission.

At the same time, North American feminists paradoxically found the revolutionary Vietnamese woman to be a compelling symbol because it provided cultural capital for women's emancipation, a cause that was then more reformist than revolutionary, according to Agatha Beins.[58] In her study of US feminist periodicals, Beins shows that at times the symbol of the revolutionary Vietnamese woman illustrated stories as a means of countering New Left and mainstream discourses that trivialized the women's movement. By incorporating this symbol into newspapers such as *Distaff*, *Sister*, and *Ain't I a Woman*, these organizations "appropriated the bodies of radical others, romanticizing and exoticizing women's lives and struggles" to confer substance and edge to the journals' respective concerns. The cause of feminism, dismissed by misogynists in the New Left and by the mainstream media alike as insignificant, became revolutionary by association with the antiwar cause and through solidarity with the symbol of the revolutionary Vietnamese woman. Put simply, Vietnamese women lent a revolutionary luster to the cause of North American women's emancipation. This function helps explain how *textual* explanations of the symbol, which emphasized seemingly universal themes of maternal care, complemented rather than contradicted the *visual* form of this symbol, which militarized motherhood. Textual interpretations of the symbol of revolutionary Vietnamese women helped render the violence palatable and more serviceable to the needs of North American feminist movements.

As radical voices within the women's movement in North America gained prominence, the militaristic thread of revolution would take on greater significance, but for reasons that were, ironically, no more congruent with Vietnamese goals for national liberation. Although radical feminists in North America sought inspiration in the symbol of the revolutionary Vietnamese woman, this did not mean that these Western-based feminists championed the VWU's goals. In any case, they vied for the meaning of the revolutionary Vietnamese woman so that this competition amounted to a warring vision, and these organizations in the United States and North Vietnam managed to establish an uneasy form of solidarity.

Meanwhile, the events meant to solidify solidarity for anti-imperialist struggles ironically exposed rifts within the women's movement, which would widen from the mid- to late 1970s. Radical feminists who expressed gestures of solidarity during 1971-75 broke ranks with the predominantly pacifist women of the liberal wing of the movement, who first advocated on behalf of Vietnamese women's liberation, by embracing the militaristic aspects of revolution. This is not to say that Vietnamese women invented this figure of martial maternalism; in the case of the Black Panthers, African American men and women portrayed themselves with guns as a visually powerful rhetoric of violence, part of a strategy to oppose state violence.[59] At the same time, Black radicals, situating their antiracist activism as more than just local politics, aligned their antiracism with Third World anticolonialism. Illustrations of revolutionary Vietnamese women, drawn by well-known artist Emory Douglas, appeared in the *Black Panther* newsletter. These illustrations attest to the international context with which Black radicals construed their struggles. Indeed, *Vietnam Pictorial* included on its 1973 cover a signed photograph of one of the most famous of these activists, Angela Davis, meeting with a young revolutionary recruit, a decision that suggests that the Vietnamese consumed images as avidly as they produced them (plate 11). Moreover, this cover reveals the North Vietnamese state's sophisticated understanding of the international context of Black radical activism across dispersed sites. Signed by Davis in red, looping cursive, the photograph includes a dedication: "In the spirit of our eternal unity and our determination to bring U.S. imperialism to its knees throughout the world," which she apparently wrote from Berlin, where she was then based—a location that gestures toward other circuits for visual exchange. (In addition to the transpacific route that I trace here, another crucial circuit appears to be the Eastern Bloc.)[60] Intriguingly, the inclusion of the photograph of a meeting between a revolutionary Black woman and a youthful recruit on the cover of the DRV's flagship illustrated magazine signifies intergenerational and interracial solidarity. When it comes to the symbol of the revolutionary woman, Vietnamese editors understood that it was not enough merely to be seen. They also had to look and position how they saw in relation to a "socialist" perspective, which was not necessarily congruent with what I have been describing as socialist ways of seeing Vietnam.

At the Indochinese Women's Conference in 1971, however, a different contest took shape. Feminist historians have documented the grievances that groups committed to lesbian, antiracist, and labor activism launched against the predominantly white organizers, whom they accused of restricting access to the Vietnamese and Laotian delegates.[61] Black Power groups demanded more time with the delegates, Third World groups insisted on a media blackout for fear of state infiltration and surveillance, lesbian collectives laid out many of these charges in their Fourth World Manifesto, the Canadian site committee attacked the American members of the WSP as cultural imperialists, and in Vancouver yet another group staged a piece of guerrilla theater that enacted these critiques.[62] Yet despite their rancor, each of these groups wanted to claim the symbol of the Vietnamese revolutionary woman for its own cause, but not necessarily for the purposes of national liberation that the delegates themselves advocated. Although organizers of the Indochinese Women's Conference strictly limited visual coverage of the event to Third World activists, who raised the alarm about potential state infiltration, an attendee named Jean Hobson managed to get her picture taken with some of the Vietnamese delegates. When she later went on to make an ultimately failed bid for local office in Palo Alto, California, as head of Venceremos, a Chicano political organization, her campaign newsletter featured a photograph of her posing with one of the Vietnamese delegates. Although this delegate does not bear arms in the portrait, Venceremos clearly sought to associate its radicalism with the militarism implicit in the revolutionary women's commitment to people's war and total war. Through her visual association with a Vietnamese revolutionary, Hobson sought to legitimize the militancy of Venceremos. That is, the Vietnamese revolutionary woman became an emblem for radical movements with their own political aims; she helped usher in a Third World sense of solidarity and further nuance the concept of global sisterhood. The Indochinese Women's Conference in 1971 was organized to build transpacific solidar-ties. But as with the conference in 1969, these solidarities were laid, more often than not, on the shifting yet fertile grounds of projection, misinterpretation, and reinvention: a set of productively varied visual exchanges that I describe here as the frictions of "misrecognition." By invoking the concept of misrecognition, I do not mean to suggest that the VWU's version of this symbol offers the true essence of Vietnamese revolutionary women but rather that this version was seen and also not seen by feminist allies in North America, who reinterpreted this symbol for different purposes.

Beyond the United States, the symbol of the revolutionary Vietnamese woman also proved useful in signifying revolution more broadly in accord with local concerns, as evident in the visual connections drawn with allies such as Cuba.[63] Notably, Palestinian resistance groups adapted this symbol to promote their cause, according to Evyn Lê Espiritu Gandhi.[64] Whereas in 1971 the spotlight on Vietnamese delegates at the conference sidelined the Laotian representatives, Palestinian freedom fighters saw in the international fascination with the war in Vietnam an opportunity to attract attention to their then less visible struggles. In the case of the Iranian Revolution, feminists adapted this symbol of the revolutionary Vietnamese woman in the late 1970s and early 1980s, well after the end of the American War in Vietnam, as Donya Ziaee points out, but they ultimately abandoned it after realizing that socialists in Iran paid only lip service to the cause of women's emancipation and in ways that desexualized feminist activists.[65] Socialist ways of seeing, as broached through Vietnamese eyes, only briefly resonated with Iranian socialism before feminists rejected this incarnation of the revolutionary woman as inadequate for representing their political struggles. Although this brief summary provides only a rough sketch of the dispersed routes that this symbol traveled, the two examples from Iran and Palestine gesture toward its influence beyond the immediate cause of national liberation in Vietnam and even beyond the end of the war in Vietnam. The rapprochement among these women's organizations in North and Central America, the Middle East, and doubtless other sites further afield challenges the critical commonplace that insists on recognition as the basis for coalitions and considers misrecognition to spell its end. As these examples show, rather than sabotaging solidarity, misrecognition operates as "friction," in Tsing's sense of the term, as the basis of solidarity, although the exact type of solidarity, commonalty or complicity, was often uncertain. In the hands of activists championing causes that, in some cases, had taken up anticolonial resistance in different ways than in Vietnam, the figure of the revolutionary Vietnamese woman helped bring "local" concerns to public light and international attention, though in contexts where gender and sexuality were defined in ways far removed from the Vietnamese context.

As a symbol with multiple permutations, the revolutionary Vietnamese woman emerged from different parts of Vietnam and circulated beyond Vietnam in the name of solidarity in a manner that sought affiliation yet provoked tension with US models of feminist activism—but also independent from these other models. The story of the revolutionary Vietnamese woman and the transformation of this symbolic figure as she traveled internationally offer salutary lessons about feminism and internationalism. Studies about struggles for women's rights tend to unfold "under Western eyes," according to Chandra Talpade Mohanty, who coined this memorable phrase in her famous critique of the dominant perspective's myopia, which she excoriates for erasing the specificity of local struggles and the agency of Third World women.[66] One might say that Western eyes find what they are looking for; in the case of the liberal North American women's movement, members saw in the revolutionary Vietnamese woman the opportunity to shape this symbol in a way that advanced and legitimized their pacifist platform. However, tracing the transpacific circulation of this figure illuminates the subtle yet substantive ways that Third World women looked back, shaping this figure in full understanding and strategic anticipation of possible misrecognition. A triangulated perspective provides the means to take up Armstrong's call for a new chronotope of women's internationalism, one that takes account of multiple routes of projection and influence.[67] This perspective attends not only to how Western eyes saw but also to how Third World women presented themselves and how they wished to be seen.

NATIONAL LIBERATION AND POSTWAR WOMEN'S EMANCIPATION

The Vietnamese Communist Party was ultimately able to shape the most influential version of this symbol of the revolutionary woman, despite or rather perhaps because its version was flexible enough to absorb and work with the challenges posed by misinterpretation. In Vietnam, through the auspices of the vwu, the state continues to claim the legacy of women's struggles: to render orderly what Leshkowich describes as the "disorderly" category of Vietnamese woman by way of memorials that emphasize the strength and resilience of the militarized mother, a particularly potent version of the revolutionary Vietnamese woman.[68] In 1994 the state began recognizing women's sacrifices by selecting elderly women for distinction as Heroic Mothers. Women who had lost two or more children to the war were honored and awarded modest monthly pensions.

In the Hanoi Women's Museum, display cases feature honorific portraits that, in effect, deify these Heroic Mothers (figure 2.12). In the Southern Women's Museum, in Ho Chi Minh City, a plaster statue repeats the theme of mil-

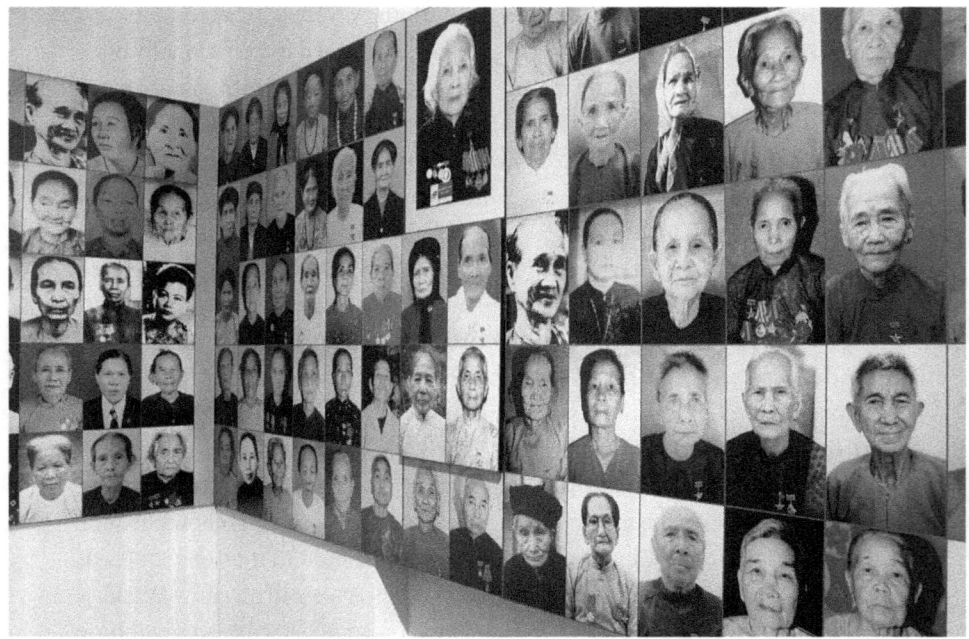

FIGURE 2.12 Heroic Mothers at the Women's Museum in Hanoi. Author photo.

itarized motherhood that photographs taken during the war introduced: an unnamed heroine carries her child while balancing on her rifle, which she has placed firmly on the ground.

The rifle is the base that enables her both to balance herself and bear the weight of her child. Motherhood, the statue suggests, can best be defended through militarism. At the same museum another statue stands at attention with her rifle at her back and children in her arms. In the north, at the Hanoi Women's Museum, a statue in the main entrance further glorifies this theme with a gilded statue of a mother and child, this time rendered in larger-than-life proportions, a magnification of earlier photographic visions. Another major difference is that we see no sign of a rifle. Indeed, the rifle is unnecessary, for the gold statue celebrates women's liberation on the occasion of revolutionary victory. The struggle for women's rights seems to have ended with the successful liberation and reunification of the nation.

During the war the Communist Party rallied women by promising to champion their rights, and the Socialist Republic of Vietnam, the name of the reunified state established in 1976, subsequently boasted the fulfillment of this promise. However this triumphant message is belied by persistent inequalities at all levels: economic, political, educational, and social. In her landmark oral history of the women who fought in the war, Sandra Taylor details the ways that the communist state reneged on its promise of women's rights.[69] These women, who fought for the ideal of family and for their chance to nurture their own families, returned to find themselves unmarriageable and thus deemed of low social status, whether because they were past child-bearing years or because they were physically scarred from the war. Women contributed much and sacrificed even more to the people's war. Yet the problem, according to Taylor, was the very framing of the revolution as a people's war, which absorbed the fight for women's rights so that victory in the former enabled the Vietnamese state to cease and attempt to foreclose further strug-gle in the latter. In 1995 Madame Bình addressed an audience at a three-day workshop on women and stated bluntly, "Equality of women has basically only existed in documents."[70] During the war she was the proud embodi-ment of socialist progress on women's emancipation only to be disappointed by substantial setbacks after the end of the war. Although she was the most prominent PRG leader, the state disregarded her fourteen years of experience in diplomacy, instead granting her the post of minister of education because women presumably have a "natural" aptitude for nurturing young minds.

To this day, according to historian Nhung Tuyet Tran, there is no Viet-namese word for feminism, although there are terms for principles such as gender equality, rights, and so on.[71] Nhung asserts that the state has co-opted women's rights, in effect declaring them as objectives already achieved and not goals to work toward. I would also add that the state has done so by re-producing and "sanctifying" the symbol of the revolutionary woman, at least in her incarnation as maternal symbol of the triumphant merging of socialist revolution and women's liberation. Today the struggle for these rights contin-ues, although there is little sign of that in state-funded museums. If, during the war, the symbol of revolutionary Vietnamese women held out the hope for advancing these rights, now the state has thoroughly absorbed this sym-bol as evidence of progress which has yet to be fully realized in fact. Instead, the state has reshaped the symbol of revolutionary women in the postwar years as part of a rhetoric of progress promised to women during and ostensi-bly achieved because of the war. To judge by the statues that have taken up the visual narrative that war photographs left off, this progress is so great as to ob-viate the need for militancy at all: no longer do girls or women bear arms. The state narrative instead extols their liberation, so these official symbols depict a "post"-revolutionary period as a mother bearing a child in her arms. Having successfully fought for family, as Anderson puts it,[72] the state now represents the fulfillment of Vietnamese women's emancipation as a celebration of family. A socialist way of seeing revolutionary women thus entails overlooking the revolutionary promises made in her name and image.

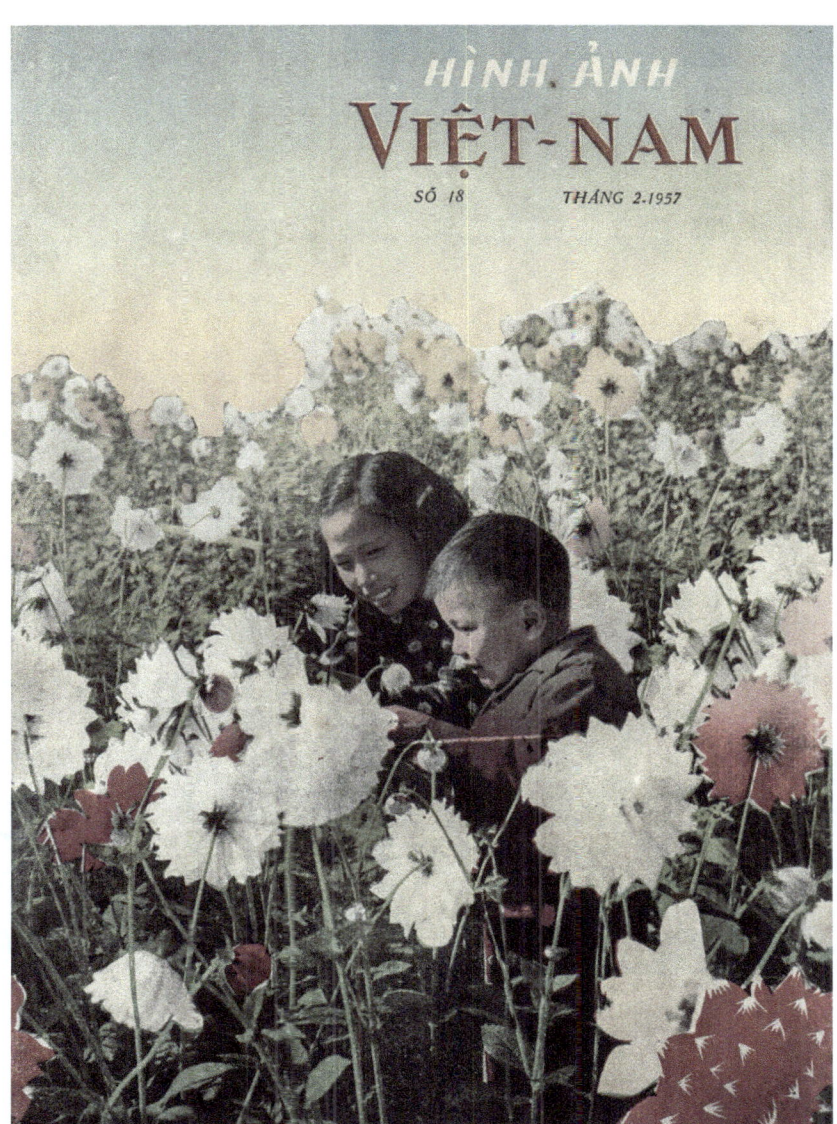

PLATE 1 Cover of *Vietnam Pictorial*, 1957 issue.

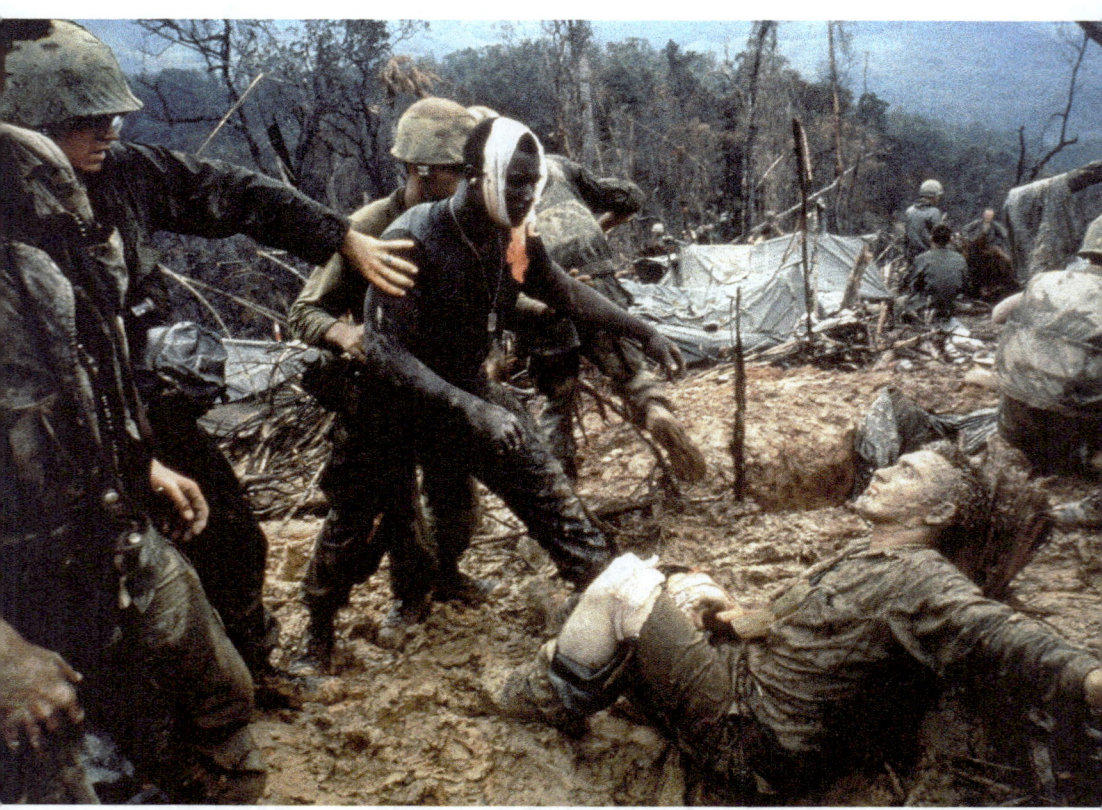

PLATE 2 *Wounded in Vietnam*. Wounded Marine Gunnery Sergeant Jeremiah Purdie (center) is led past stricken comrades after fierce firefight for control of Hill 484, south of DMZ in South Vietnam, 1966. Photographer Larry Burrows. Getty Images.

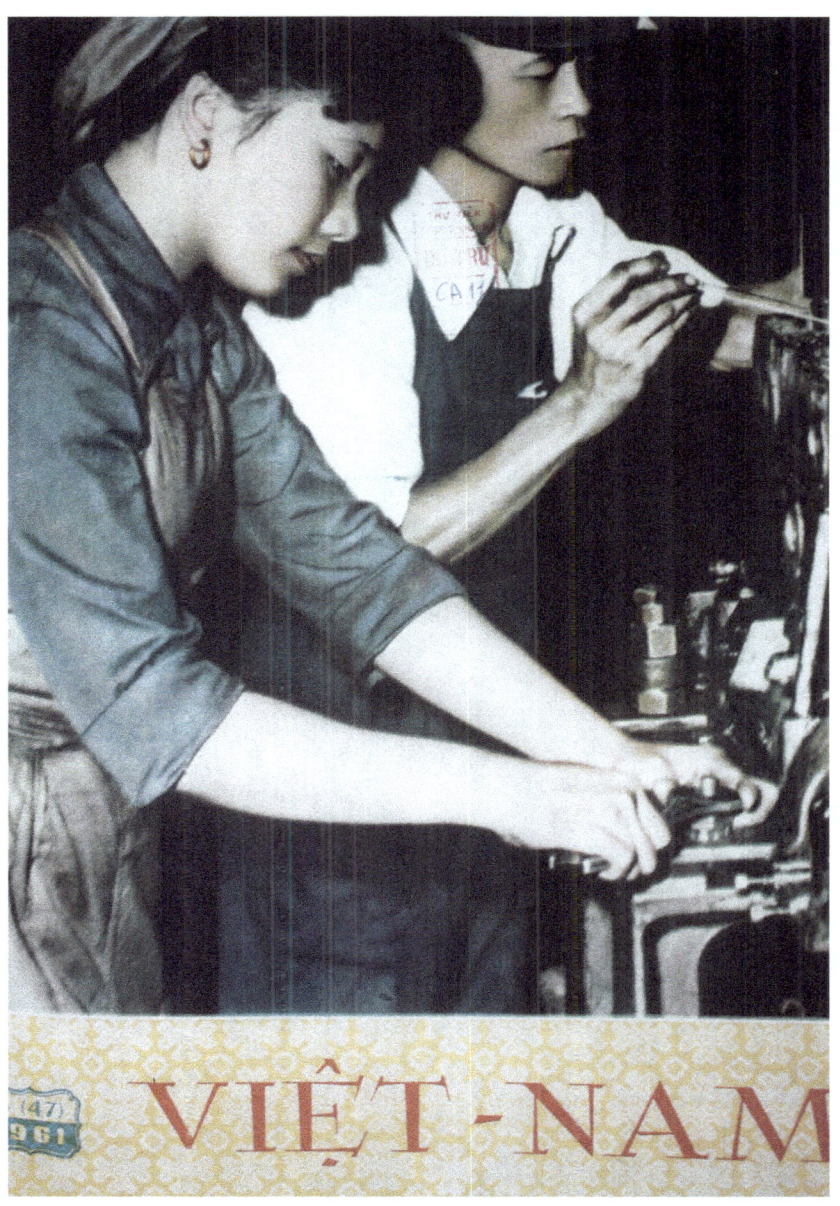

PLATE 3 Cover of *Vietnam Pictorial*, 1961 issue.

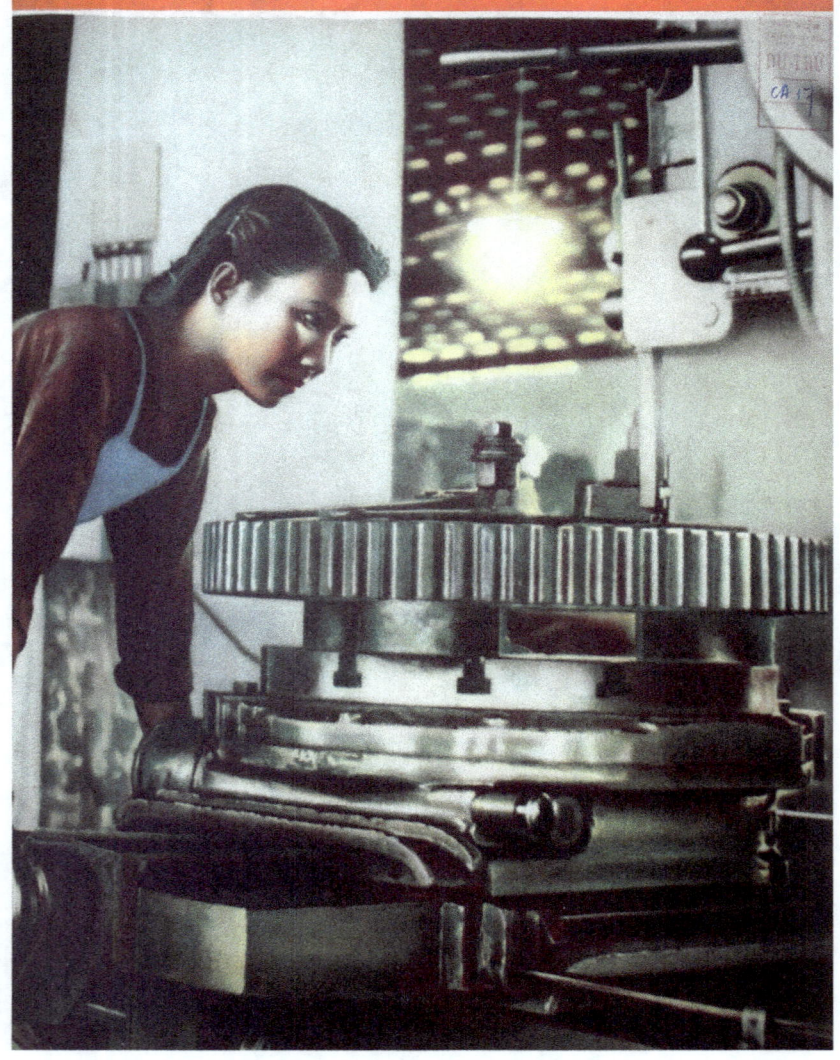

Hình ảnh VIỆT-NAM

SỐ 6 (16) 1958

PLATE 4 Factory workers in *Vietnam Pictorial*, 1958 issue.

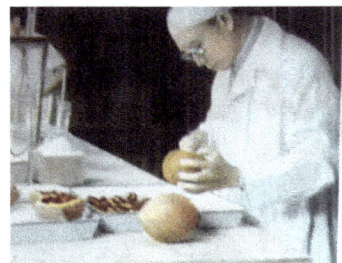

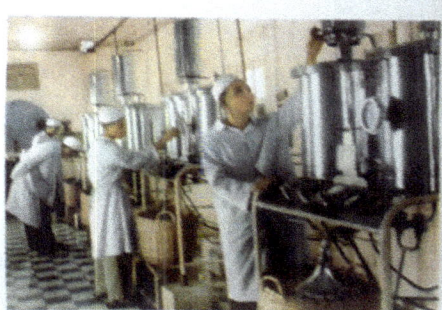

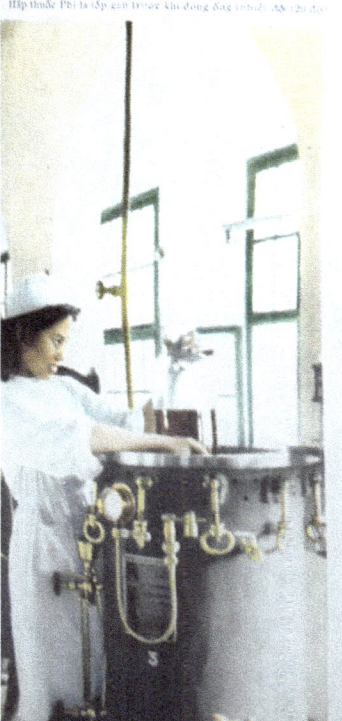

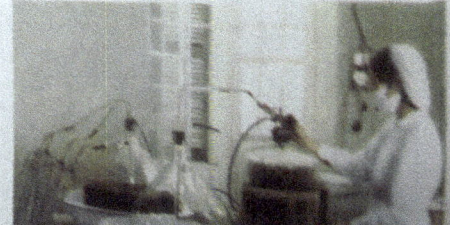

PLATE 5 Colored photographs illustrating a story about science and industry in *Vietnam Pictorial*.

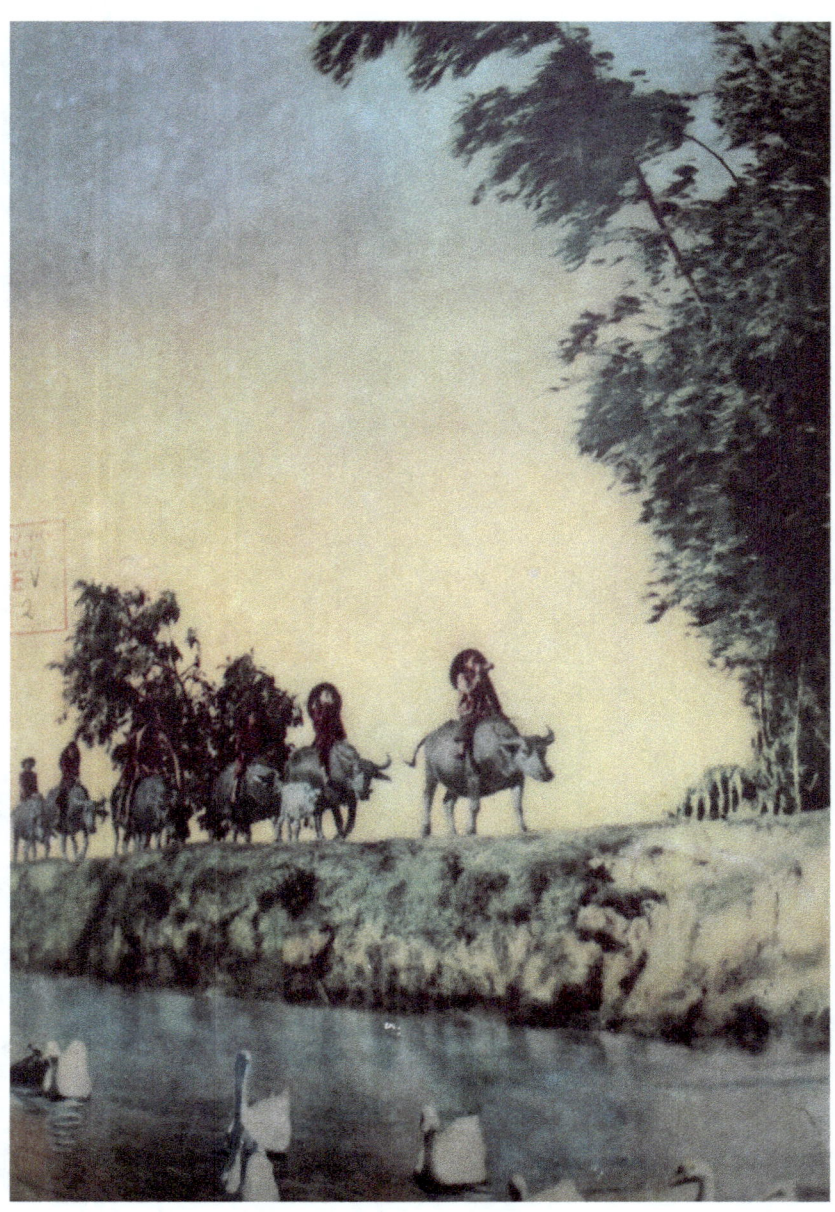

PLATE 6 Farmers riding water buffaloes, *Vietnam Pictorial.*

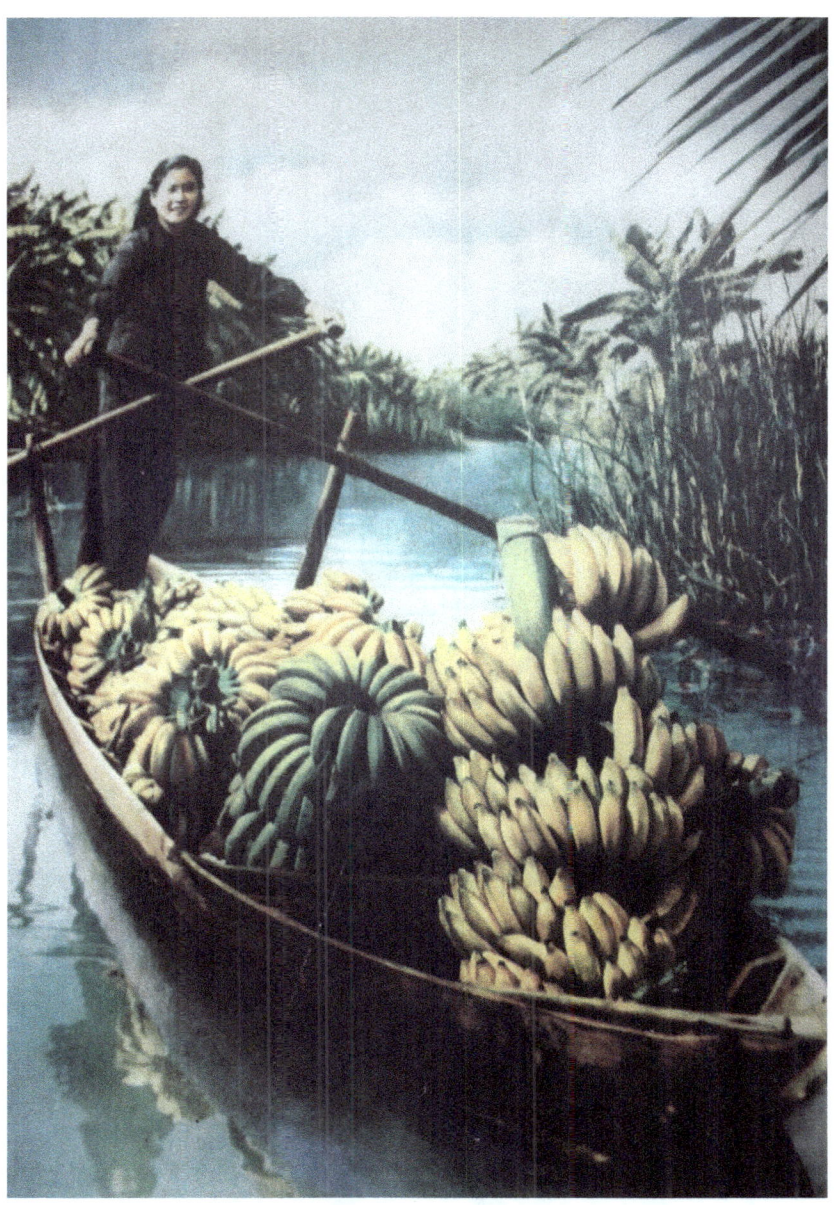

PLATE 7 Bananas on a floating market, *Vietnam Pictorial*.

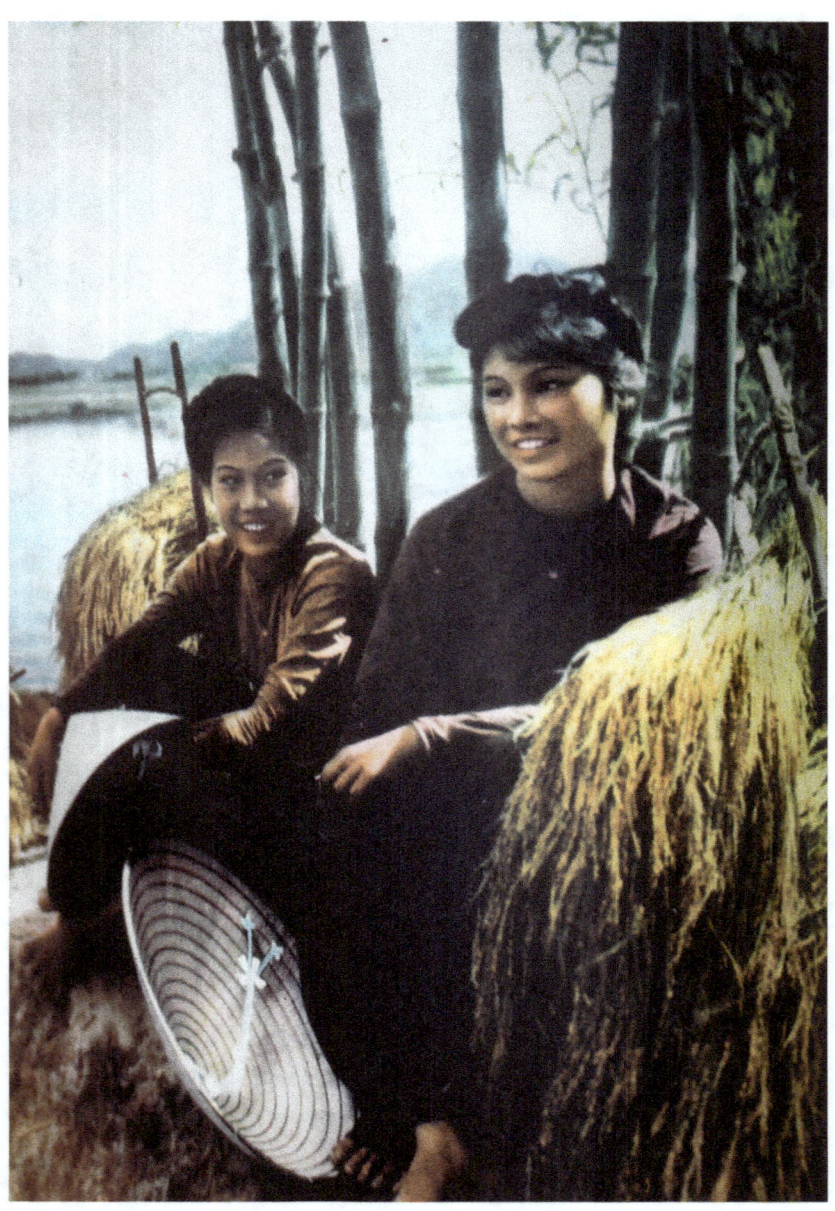

PLATE 8 Peasant women, *Vietnam Pictorial.*

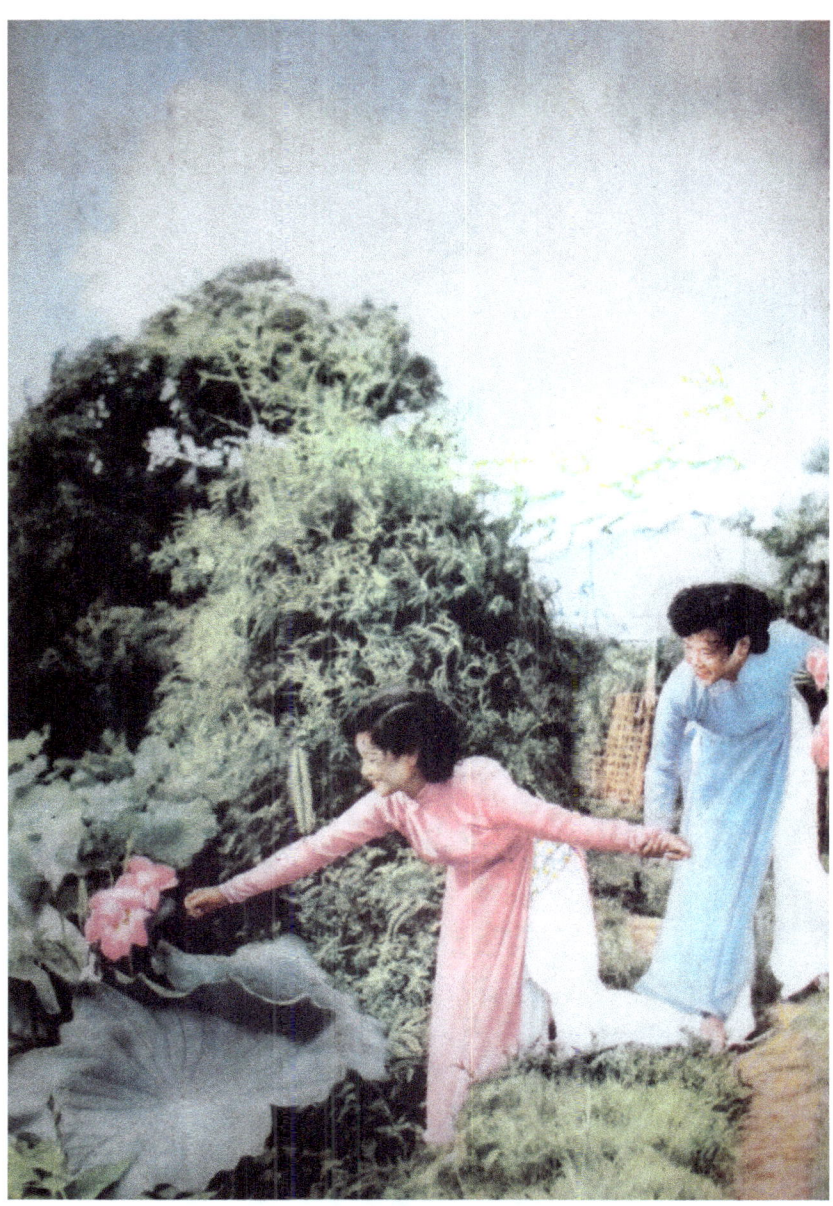

PLATE 9 Women harvesting lotus flowers, *Vietnam Pictorial.*

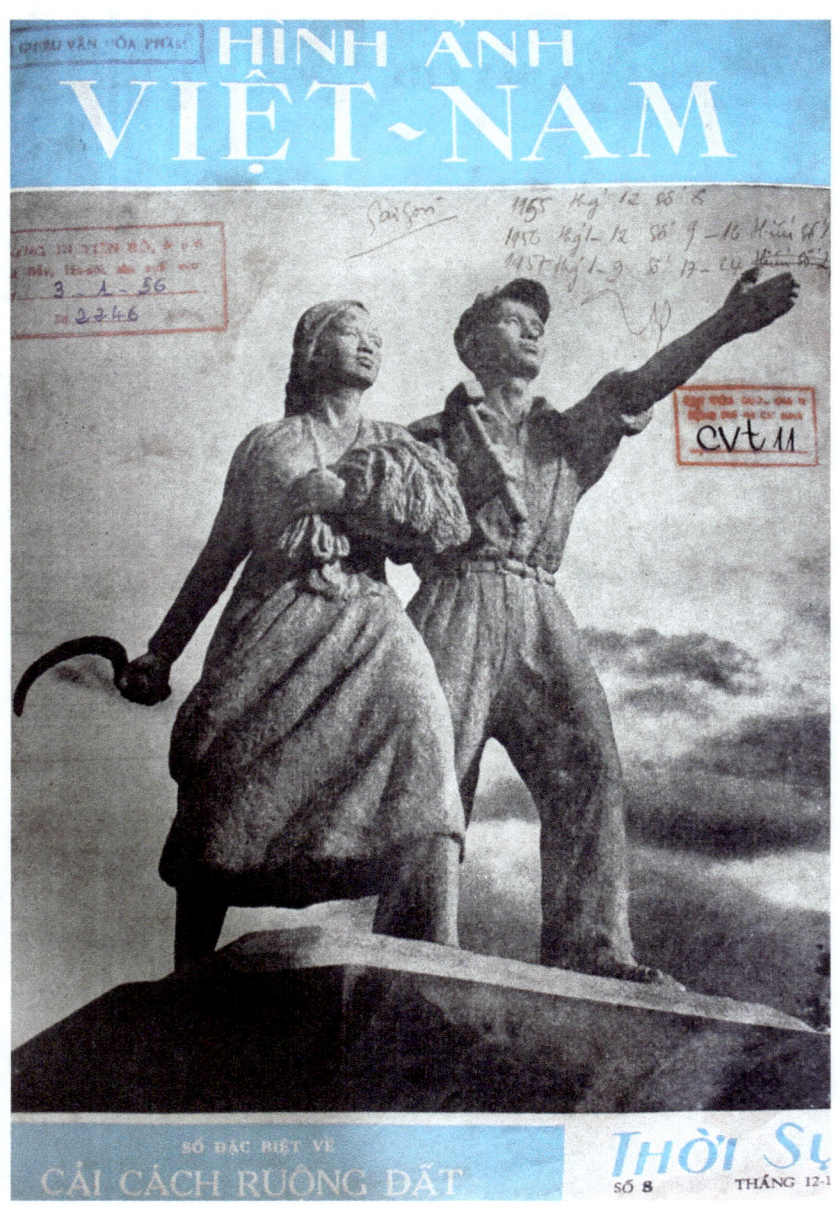

PLATE 10 Cover of *Vietnam Pictorial*.

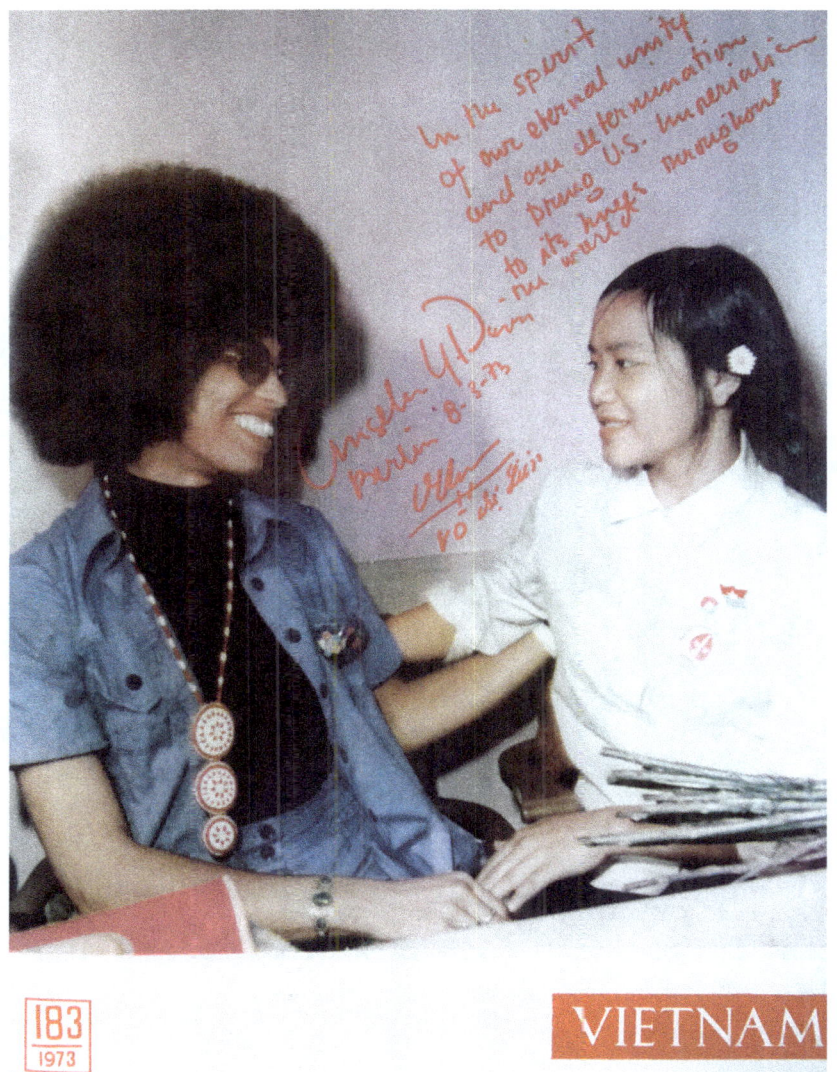

PLATE 11 Angela Davis on the cover of a 1973 issue of *Vietnam Pictorial*.

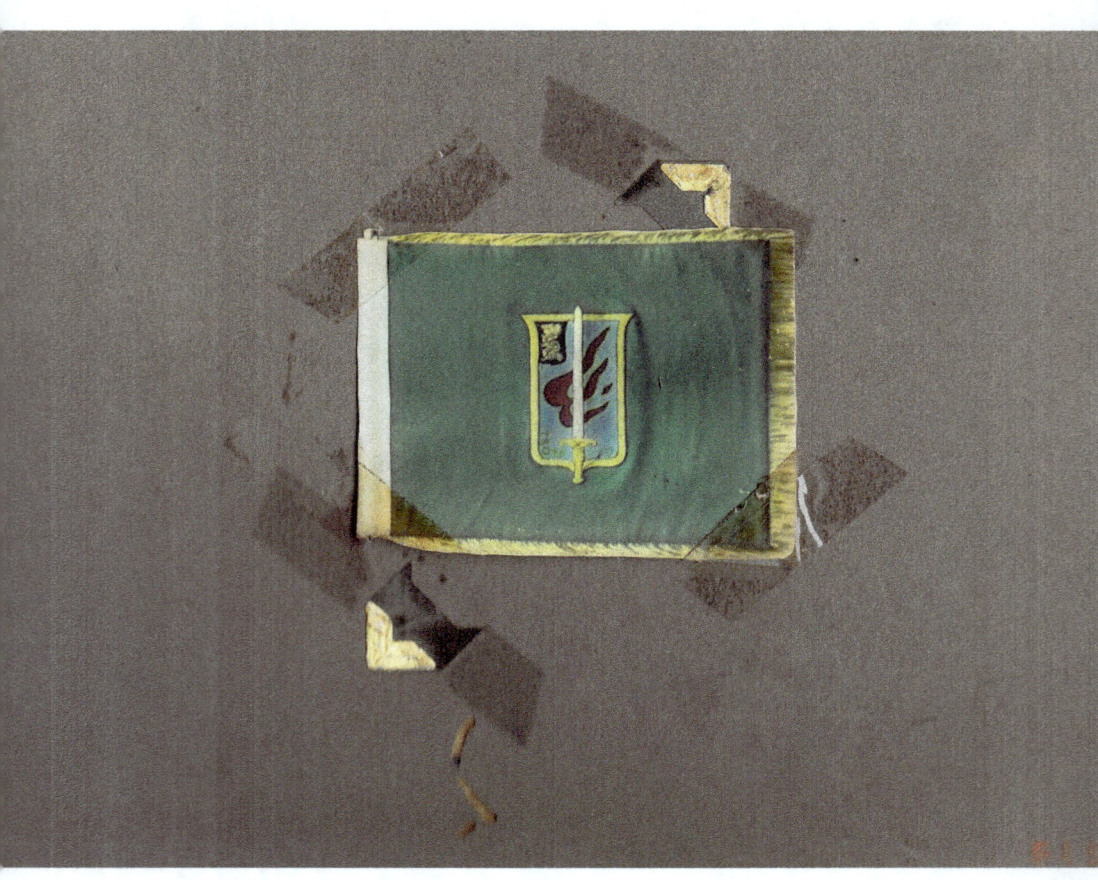

PLATE 12 Thủ Đức Military Academy insignia. Author collection.

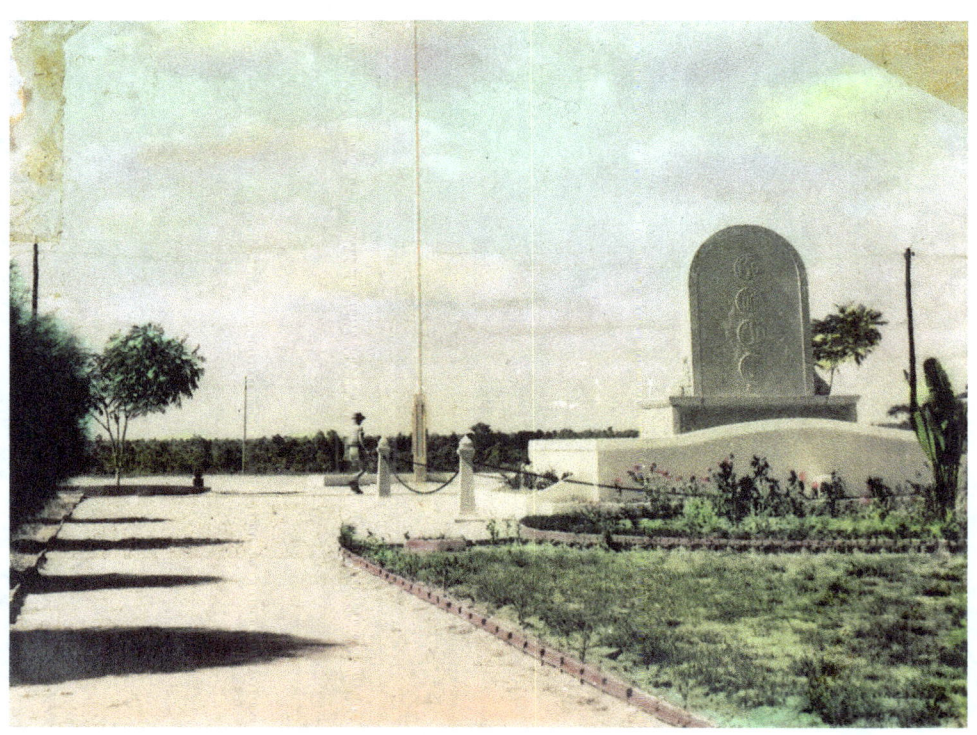

PLATE 13 Flagpole at Thủ Đức Military Academy. Author collection.

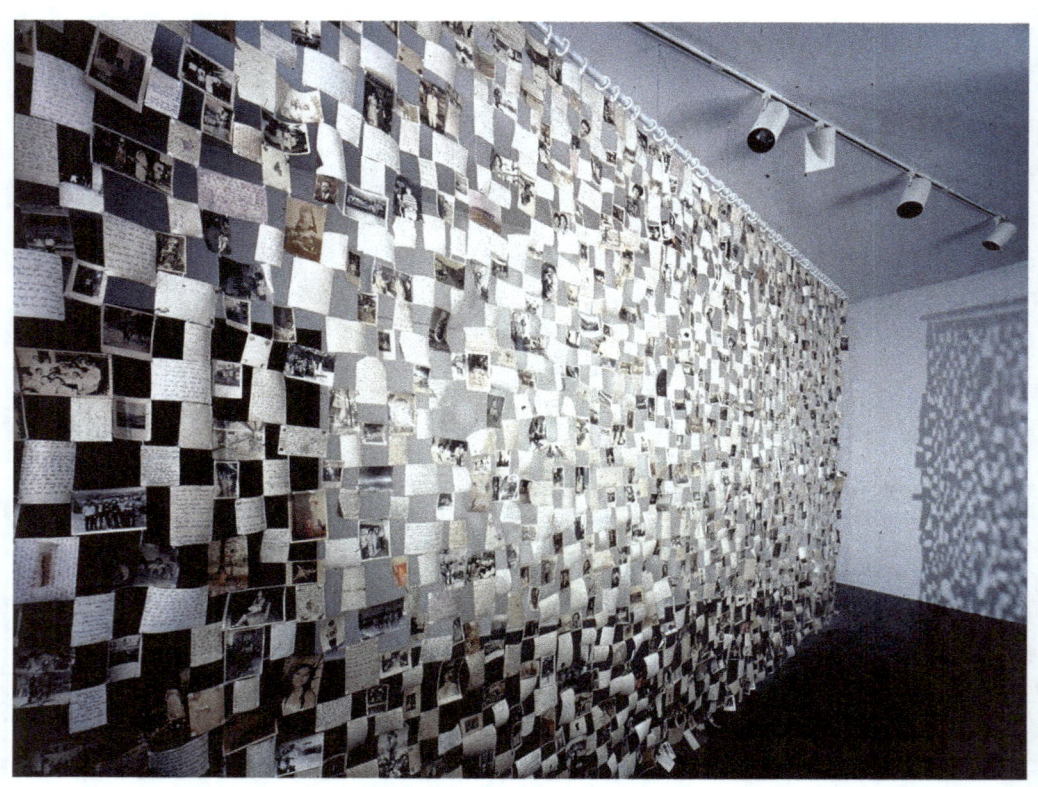

PLATE 14 *Mot Coi Di Ve*, 1998. Dinh Q. Lê.

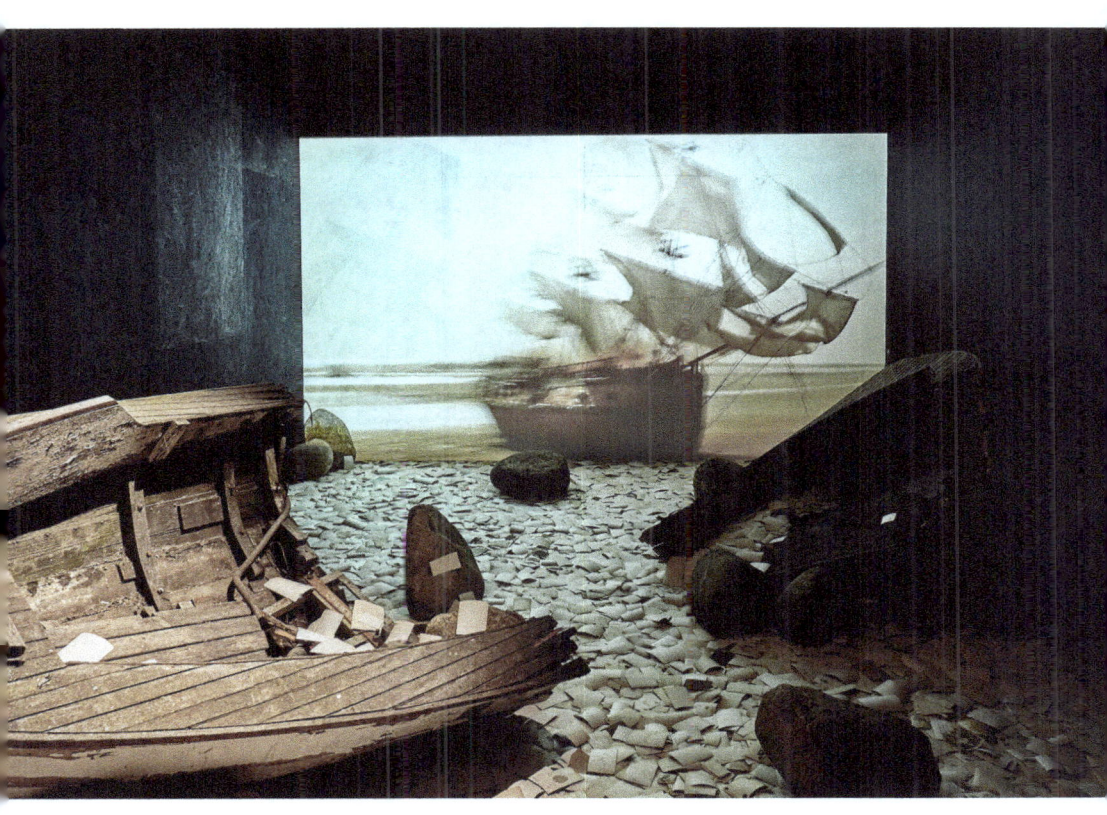

PLATE 15 *Erasure*, 2011. Dinh Q. Lê.

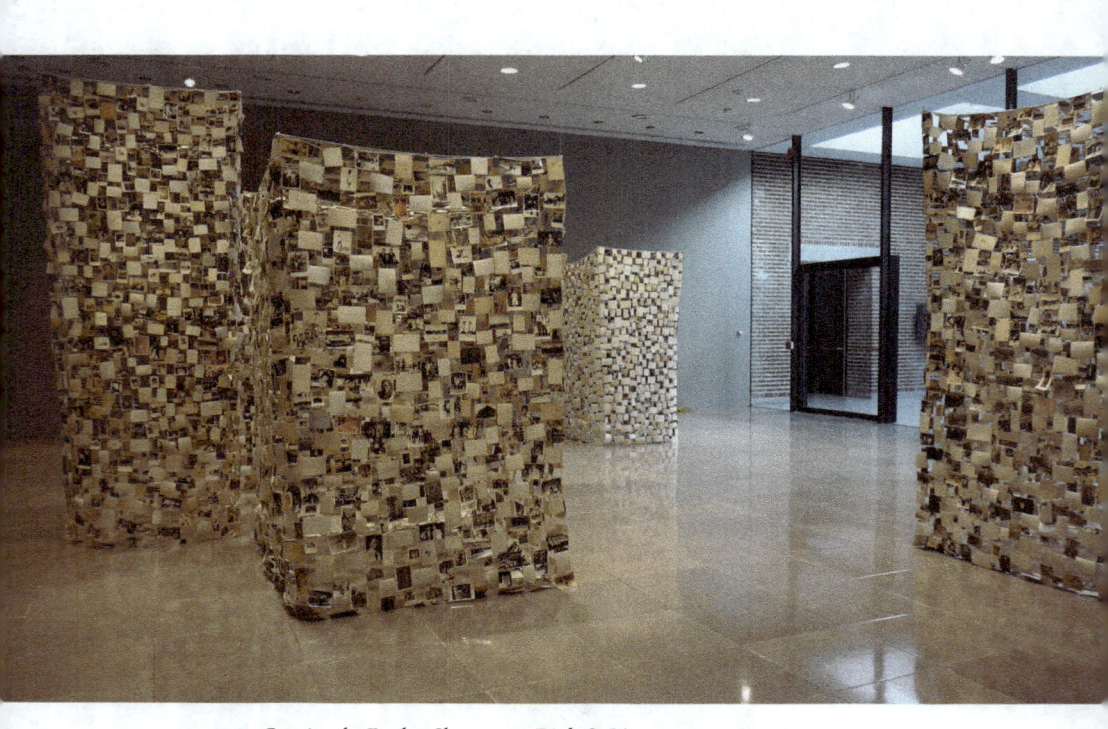

PLATE 16 *Crossing the Farther Shore*, 2014. Dinh Q. Lê.

II

REFRACTIONS

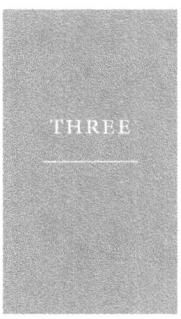

THREE

REENACTMENT AND
REMEMBRANCE

April 30 is a day of liberation, according to the Socialist Republic of Vietnam. For the overseas Vietnamese, however, this is Black April, the anniversary of the day in 1975 when the Republic of Vietnam disappeared. It is a day for commemoration, not celebration. During Black April, some veteran Army of the Republic of Vietnam (ARVN) soldiers from the overseas community unfold and iron old uniforms that, for the rest of the year, are carefully stored. Thus arrayed, they call on old friends and assemble in public squares, where they march in formation with young cadets and elegant women in tailored áo dài. Here the veterans make a solemn entrance; some display their military decorations; most pause to pose for the camera as if to burnish a new image of April 30, one where the Republic of South Vietnam lives again (figure 3.1). The commemorations are rites of remembrance and a form of reenactment.

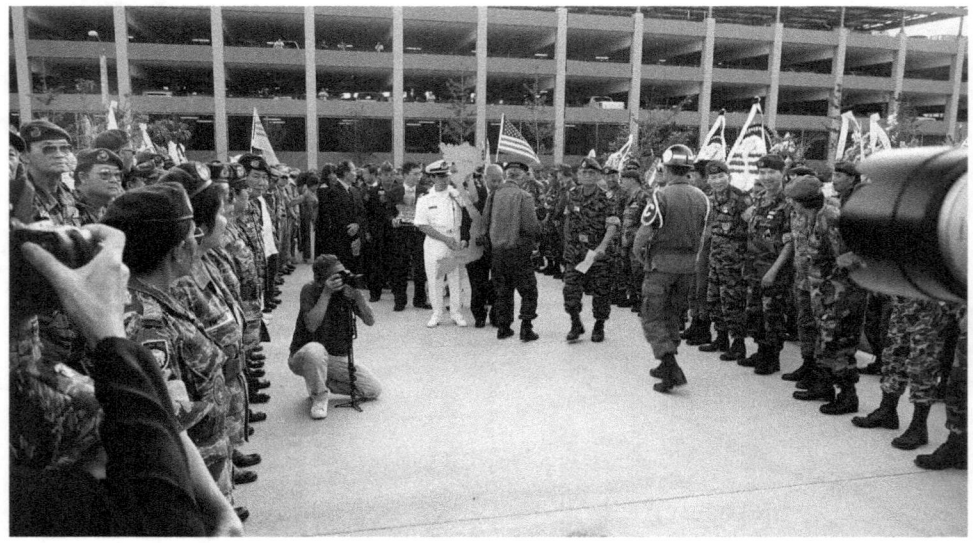

FIGURE 3.1 Black April, Westminster, California, 2015. Photographer: Viet Thanh Nguyen.

Although veterans, cadets, and their onlookers may not always stage actual battles, they conjure the look of war, providing a means of reckoning symbolically with the war's aftermath. In this way, reenactments produce warring visions. As Viet Thanh Nguyen observes, "All wars are fought twice, once on the battlefield and the second time in memory."[1] Reenactments constitute a battle for memory, especially poignant given the dearth of photography for diasporic Vietnamese, many of whom had to destroy or abandon their personal images.

This may not be how one might picture a typical reenactment. The most recognized face of reenactment in the United States is the Civil War hobbyist who restages battles. Since the early twentieth century, when the first groups of American Civil War veterans gathered together to swap stories, thousands of participants have been drawn to this pastime. In the 1950s and 1960s this activity took off in the United States. At a time when the death of Civil War veterans severed direct access to this history and when feminist, antiwar, civil rights, and Black Power movements challenged white patriarchy, reenactments of the national struggle offered the promise of reliving past glory.[2] As a politically charged hobby, reenactments continue to attract predominantly white men, drawn, among other attractions, by the promise of homosocial conviviality and by "period rush," the thrill of immersion aroused at the moment when enthusiasts believe they can touch the past. Curiously, however, women and members of minoritized Black and Asian communities also participate. At the African American Civil War and Memorial Museum, for example, members of the Female Reenactors of Distinction (FREED) don period costumes—a central aspect of reenactments—proudly denoting middle-class status to dispel the myth that in the nineteenth-century Black women were only slaves.[3] Today, reenactments are more than just an American preoccupation; they are an increasingly global and highly mediated phenomenon, with events taking place regularly in the United Kingdom, Poland, Germany, and Australia, and beyond, some of which is documented in photography and or TV and film.[4]

Historian Vanessa Agnew contends that this form of cultural activity is broad in scope.[5] The American Civil War is an abiding preoccupation, but it is by no means the sole focus of reenactments, which increasingly bring to life scenes from some of the twentieth- and twenty-first-century wars in Korea, Vietnam, Afghanistan, and Iraq, to name just a few. Reenactments also span a range of activities: the "living histories" of heritage museums that feature docents in period costumes trying to conjure a past that may not have happened, the staging of battles, and the pageantry of Black April commemoration ceremonies.

Accordingly, I invoke the term *war reenactment* broadly to denote embodied performances.[6] These embodied performances often entail the wearing of period costumes and involve choreographed movement as means of symbolically claiming space. Visual theorist Dora Apel observes that the conduct of modern warfare has become unthinkable apart from its mediatization; for veterans and survivors, the aftermath of war is unfathomable apart from its representation.[7] The depiction of reenactments is one such way that war and its aftermath become visually mediated. After all, some reenactments are created with photographs as their inspiration rather than from personal experience. Moreover, reenactments are, by design, photographic even if an image never emerges, for they are staged for viewers and documented for posterity. That is, they exemplify an "event of photography," Ariella Azoulay's term for photographic encounters that are "subject to a unique form of temporality," which can activate "an infinite series" of further encounters, in contrast to a photographed event, which merely entails the production of a single image frozen in time.[8]

This chapter reconsiders the significance of reenactments as part of—rather than outside—the history of war photography, challenging critical approaches that judge the value of war images on the basis of the authenticity of their depiction of events. Although overseas Vietnamese are unlikely to describe their activities as reenactments, such performances are pivotal to Black April commemorations. Moreover, they are important to consider *as* reenactments precisely because they are a vital way that this community remembers the war. Some members of the overseas Vietnamese community even go so far as to participate in reenactments of the war in Vietnam, as the documentary *In Country* demonstrates.[9] The film follows a group of war reenactors from the Oregon-based First Cavalry Group, a division of the Pacific Northwest Historical Group, including an ARVN vet, Vinh Nguyen. Nguyen puts on army fatigues to replay, again and again, the war in Vietnam, a fantasy he lives out alongside American "soldiers," who are fellow reenactors. Along with the rites and performances on display during Black April and the fantasies invoked through choreographed play battles, photographs of the Vietnamese diaspora also attest to reenactment's role in conjuring and mediating memories of the war. Perhaps most noteworthy of all is the work of Nguyễn Ngọc Hạnh, which has been featured in Black April commemorations but which is also controversial because of its purported status as having been produced as a result of staging: reenacted war scenes. As the introduction explains, Hạnh was an ARVN officer who documented the South Vietnamese perspective of the war in *Vietnam in Flames,* a photo book he produced with Nguyễn Mạnh Đan, which was published under the auspices of the Saigon-based Government of Vietnam. Despite the Vietnam News Agency's disqualification of Hạnh's images as war photographs on the grounds that they are reenactments, the overseas community has drawn inspiration from Hạnh's restaged photographs from the late 1960s and has included them in commemorations that involve other forms of reenactment.

His work stands in contrast to and in parallel with one of the most celebrated examples of reenactment in photography: the series *Small Wars* (1999–2002) by An-My Lê, a Vietnamese American photographer and recipient of the prestigious MacArthur Fellowship. Born and raised in South Vietnam, Lê came to the United States with her family in 1975 after the fall of Saigon. *Small Wars* focuses on the activities of a Vietnam War reenactment group in Virginia and features the photographer herself participating alongside members of this group. Through its invocation of Vietnam by way of Virginia and participation of a Vietnamese body alongside white male bodies, *Small Wars* meditates on the significance of reenactment for activating war memories, suggesting that American experiences of the war in Vietnam must be understood alongside Vietnamese experiences. By focusing on the ways that Hạnh and Lê variously draw on, depict, and invite participation in reenactment, this chapter expands "war photography" to include these embodied

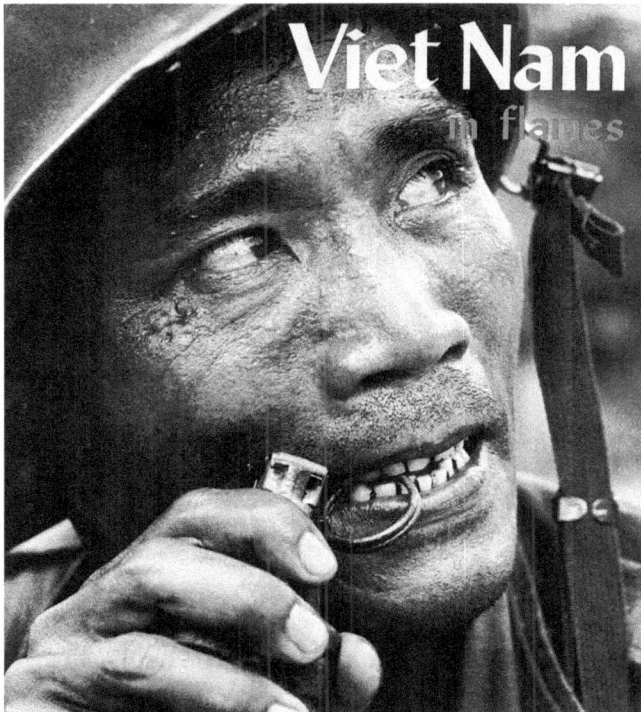

FIGURE 3.2 *Quyết tâm bảo vệ quê hương.* 1968. Photographer: Nguyễn Ngọc Hạnh.

performances as warring visions, projections of dispersed times and places that provide a means of constituting emotional communities in rituals of remembrance. Just as importantly, these rituals of remembrance are connected to, while also misaligned with, American experiences of the war.

STAGING SORROW

Among the Vietnamese diaspora, Hạnh stands out for his documentation of the war as seen from the perspective of South Vietnam. In 1969 Hong Kong publisher Kwok Hing printed hardcover folios of *Vietnam in Flames,* the photo book that Hạnh produced in collaboration with civilian photographer Nguyễn Mạnh Đan (figure 3.2). Clothbound with red cloth and gilt titles, this book, which appeared in English and Vietnamese editions, covered the Tet Offensive and its impact on the heavily hit cities of Huế, Saigon, and Khe Sanh, focusing on the suffering and resilience of South Vietnamese soldiers and civilians alike.

Although the Vietnamese title of the book, *Vietnam Khói Lửa,* emphasizes its principal theme of conflagration, an apt description of many of the book's images of charred destruction, it is also a reminder of photographers' distinctly Vietnamese perspective: *khói lửa* is the Vietnamese idiom for war. (Considering that, to my knowledge, only the English-language version of this rare book is extant, most English-speaking readers would almost certainly miss this nuance.) Taken together, the photographs in the book develop a narrative about a nation under threat. Although this narrative is uninterrupted by chapter breaks, the images can be grouped into sections of sorts. In the first part the photo book focuses on major sites affected by the 1968 Tet Offensive: Khe Sanh, where General Westmoreland mistakenly believed the North Vietnamese Army would strike hardest, and Saigon and Huế, where General Giáp's forces actually advanced, taking South Vietnamese soldiers and their American allies by surprise. Other sections of the book rouse patriotic fervor through a sentimental depiction of pastoral landscapes and feminized representation of the nation's beauty that underscore the stakes of South Vietnam's struggle to survive the conflagration of war.

As an ARVN colonel, Hạnh was imprisoned in a labor and reeducation camp after the war and was only released eight years later, after human rights activists intervened on his behalf. In the 1980s he struggled on his meager earnings as a cyclo driver in Ho Chi Minh City, eventually taking on the role of mentor and teacher at the urging of a group of supporters. Hạnh finally escaped by boat from Vietnam, and after spending nine months in a refugee camp in the Philippines, he immigrated to the United States under the auspices of the Orderly Departure Program. Significantly, Hạnh credited his images with ensuring his escape from the communist state. In an interview included in the documentary about his life and work, Hanh even asserts that his photographs and photo book, which he had brought along the boat journey and kept by his side at the camp, aided his passage to the United States because they confirmed his identity as an ARVN veteran who deserved political asylum.[10]

In terms of genre, this photo book is difficult to place. As noted earlier, the Vietnam News Agency (VNA) thoroughly disparaged the photographs that Hạnh made during the war because of their contrived quality and staged production—because, in other words, they are reenactments. Not surprisingly, the admiration his photographs inspire among the overseas Vietnamese community is in inverse proportion to their disrepute in Vietnam by the VNA, whose hard stance undoubtedly stems from the unapologetic role that *Vietnam in Flames* played in opposing communism. The book offers a potent set of warring visions that compete with socialist ways of seeing. Indeed, to summarily disregard Hạnh's photographs as staged, as the VNA does, is to miss the point. Their staginess is, after all, flagrantly obvious.

Consider one of Hạnh's most notable photographs, *Tiếc Thương* (*Sorrow*), which meditates on melancholy. In this photograph, a lovely young woman, her hair artfully disheveled, weeps into her hands, which cling to her beloved's dog tags (figure 3.3). Shadows edge the back of her head, while warm natural light illuminates her clasped hands and teary face. The photograph's narrative of grief is complicated by the story that Hạnh tells of its making. In an undated interview the photographer recounted that he was moved to take this picture after encountering the gruesome scene of a massacre at Củ Chi, where the famous tunnels were located.[11] He recalled coming upon a woman who searched frantically among a half dozen decapitated bodies for evidence that would confirm her husband's death. After helping this woman comb through the gruesome remains, he tried to photograph her but was unsuccessful because she was too distraught. Ironically, what made this scene photo-worthy—its outpouring of emotion—also rendered it unphotographable. Shortly afterward, Hạnh's daughter found another grieving young woman, Tram, whose lover had been taken prisoner after his plane was shot down. The photographer himself teased out the model's cascading hair, his own daughter read love letters that the woman's beloved had written, and in the background his friend, who was a skilled musician, played the sad songs so often aired on Saigon radio stations. Against this lachrymose backdrop, Tram's tears spilled forth, tears that are a proxy for the other woman, whose paroxysms of grief could not be pictured. Just as important is the fact that of the half dozen perfectly formed tears visible in the portrait, only two of them, on her arm, were ones she actually shed. The two "tears" on her cheek and the two on the dog tags, Hạnh goes on to explain in a documentary about his life and work, were in fact drops of olive oil.[12] Unlike real tears that smudge and dissolve in an instant, olive oil stays put and is more easily photographable. This tale of the making of the photograph underscores the earnest effort that went into these performances to get the historical detail accurate, to make the tone of reenactment just right. Indeed, Hạnh does not even try to hide his contrivances but instead proudly explains how they are solutions to photographic problems.

The idea of reenacting something in order to create a photographic record may seem different from altering what is in the photo, an activity particularly excoriated by photojournalists and other viewers. However, the two approaches form part of a continuum of manipulation.[13] As chapter 1 discusses, manipulation has been a defining characteristic of war photography from the nineteenth century to the present. Indeed, some of the most famous war photographs are restaged or reenacted: Mathew Brady and his assistants

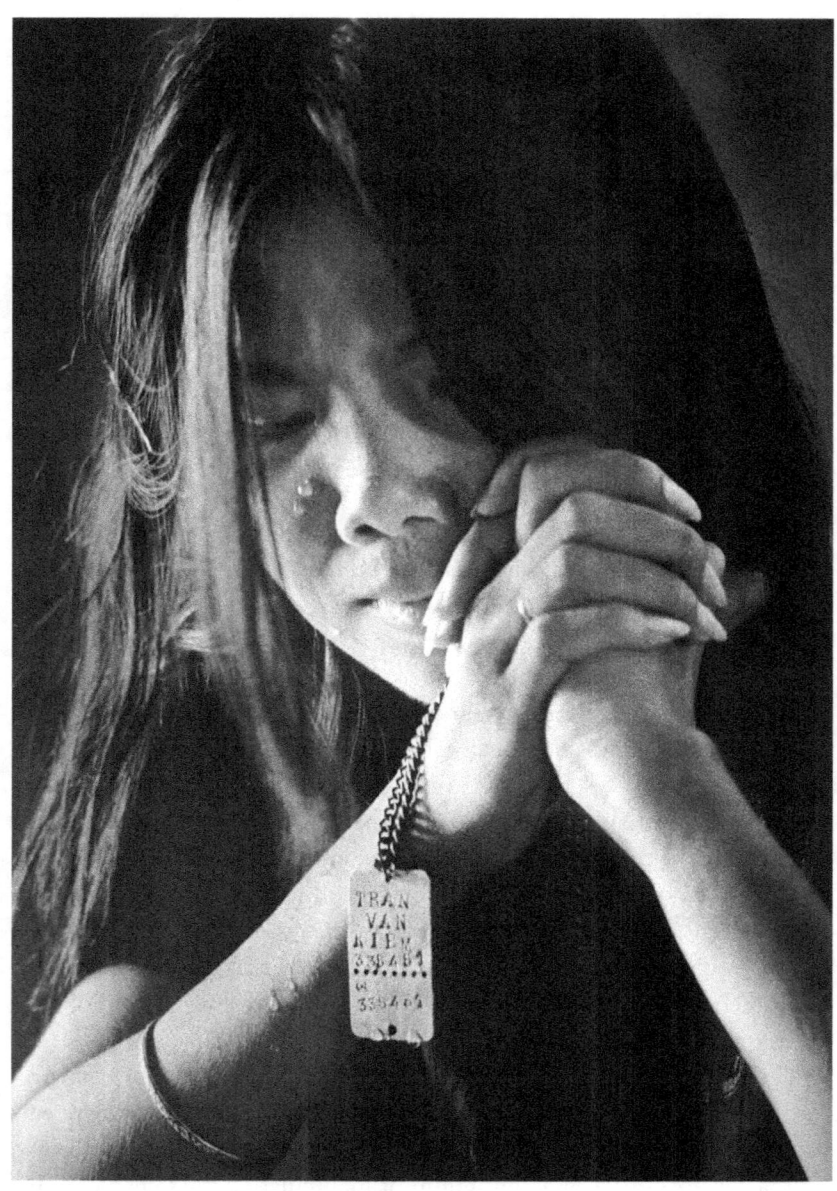

FIGURE 3.3 *Tiếc Thương*. Photographer: Nguyễn Ngọc Hạnh.

moved bodies to produce a more dramatic visual narrative of events, which they were unable to capture because of technical limitations. The most famous photograph of the Spanish Civil War, Robert Capa's *The Falling Soldier*, also sparked controversy when critics pointed out that it was staged.[14] In these instances, photographers set up scenes to produce a more compelling war photograph, particularly in contexts where photography was not possible. These are just two well-known examples that suggest the closeness between reenactment and war photography, a connection that the Socialist Republic of Vietnam (SRV) has disavowed in an echo of pious popular sentiments that have, in recent years, been codified as rules by World Press Photo.[15] Although Hạnh has acknowledged the staged quality of his work in interviews with SBTN, a diasporic Vietnamese news network, he nevertheless insists that his images are authentic documents of the war that register the intensity of the emotions the war engendered.[16]

Tiếc Thương is the most melodramatic of a set of images that are themselves reenactments of the war. In her analysis of post–World War II rhetoric, Elizabeth R. Anker posits that melodrama has emerged in the United States as an increasingly influential form of political discourse that produces shared political emotions and moral resolve for violent wars waged for freedom.[17] Similarly, the melodramatic mood of photographs from *Vietnam in Flames* constitutes a sense of community through collective suffering, sacrifice, and heroism. Considering that *Vietnam in Flames* provides a South Vietnamese approach to looking at the war, it is little wonder that photographs from this photo book should be featured in commemorations of the fallen nation.

This staging is also significant because it reveals the performative function of tears, notwithstanding historian William Reddy's suggestion that they are a spontaneous overflow of emotions, unprompted and unscripted.[18] Instead, tears are a social ritual, according to religious studies scholar Gary L. Ebersole.[19] For this reason, whether they were authentic or inauthentic, induced or spontaneous, matters less than the fact that they are to be seen and recognized. Regardless of their contrivance, tears have a real effect. In this sense the proxy image better captures the nature of weeping than the photograph that Hạnh had originally wanted to take. This image we see is a public engagement with grief, one that requires others to be on hand as active participants, not simply as passive spectators in the ritual of weeping. In this manner the viewers of this photograph might likewise be called upon to observe—and participate in—the act of weeping. This may be why Hạnh preempts his critics when he insists that the young woman's tears were real (*nước mắt thật*), for the sorrow depicted here forms part of a collective ritual that extends beyond

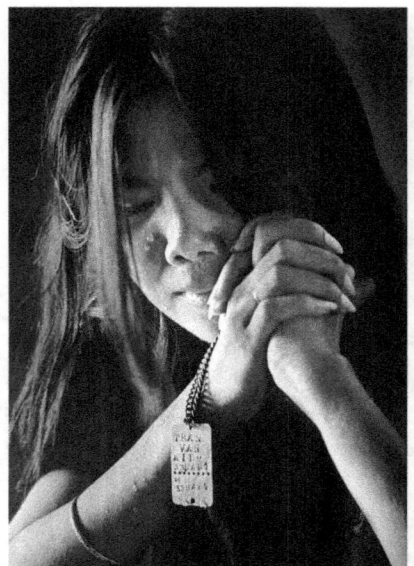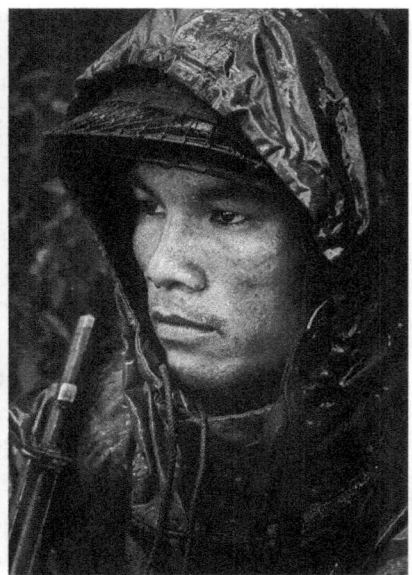

FIGURE 3.4 Adjacent images of weeping woman and stoic soldier in *Vietnam in Flames*. Photographer: Nguyễn Ngọc Hạnh.

the moment of its making. Through its publication and circulation the photograph anticipates and symbolizes the diasporic Vietnamese community's shared lament. This reenactment, in setting the stage for subsequent reenactments, reveals the importance of visual culture in establishing "emotional communities," historian Barbara Rosenwein's term to describe the ways that social groups cohere around shared values and interests.[20] Hạnh's restaged photographs help conjure forth a community of mourners.

To understand the significance of tears for South Vietnamese citizens, who were initially meant to be the primary audience of the photo book (along with Americans stationed in South Vietnam), and for the overseas Vietnamese community, which continues to cherish Hạnh's photographs, we need to consider the adjacent image (figure 3.4). This adjacent image features a soldier—perhaps this weeping woman's beloved or at least a proxy for him—whose face is shown in extreme close-up. Whether his face is clammy with sweat or, more likely, moist with rain is unclear. (The uncertain source of this moistness visually recalls the ambiguous cause of the moistness on the face of the cover photograph of the soldier's intimate grenade-pin "kiss" [see figure 3.2].) However, we might recognize in this pose the now-familiar "thousand-yard stare" of conventional war photography, a trope that emerged in World War II to describe the unfocused gaze of battle-weary and trauma-tized soldiers. Here the unnamed soldier's blank stoicism suggests that when it comes to war, expressionlessness, or what Rebecca Adelman describes, fol-lowing Roland Barthes, as flat affect, is the only form of emotional expression acceptable for men.[21] Yet this is a photograph that evokes weeping through pathetic fallacy. The woman's tears, a proxy for the paroxysm of grief that could not be photographed, are in turn a proxy for those that are shown but withheld on the man's face. By juxtaposing the moistness of a man's stolidly composed features beside that of a tearful woman's face, the photo book gen-ders weeping while also emphasizing grief as its overall mood.

In San Jose, California, where Hạnh eventually moved after his release from a communist reeducation camp in Vietnam, photographs from *Vietnam in Flames* have been exhibited as part of Black April events. Taken many de-cades earlier, these photographs are not just a record of what has been; their melancholic mood seems to presage the devastating loss that was then still to come. In what amounts to a form of nostalgia that Svetlana Boym reminds us is as much prospective as it is retrospective—and which the colored pho-tographs of *Vietnam Pictorial* exemplify[22]—Hạnh recounted this particular scene of ritual weeping with remarkable clarity many years after the photo-graphs were printed, when he had become a prominent member of this dias-poric community. In his remembrance of the scene, the photograph's sorrow becomes a figure for the diaspora's collective lament and provides the basis for a sense of community. The importance that *Vietnam in Flames* places on tears provides unvoiced recognition of proleptic loss.[23] Here tears bring to-gether a community in the absence of a nation. Seen in this way, these tears of sorrow—an embodied performance that unfolds communally—presage the coming loss of nation, the origin story of the Vietnamese diaspora, a commu-nity that for decades has held at its core an attachment to such scenes of lam-entation. Hạnh's photographic reenactments simultaneously help bring this community into being and provide a focus for its shared nostalgia.

SMALL WARS

In contrast to the melodramatic mood of Hạnh's photographs, An-My Lê's work explores the cultural politics of embodied space in a more restrained way. Her series *Small Wars* focuses on a group of Vietnam War reenactors in Virginia. As a condition for photographing this group, An-My Lê was required to participate in their reenactments, namely by wearing the Viet-cong's signature black pajamas and playing the roles of sniper and "kit scout" (figure 3.5). Using a 5×7 large-format-view tripod-mounted film camera, Lê photographed herself, the white male members of this group, and the landscape where these reenactments took place. Although she worked on and produced *Small Wars* in 1999–2002, on the cusp of the digital turn, this series self-consciously references an earlier era of analog photography with its use of film, black-and-white printing, and minimal digital correction.[24] As Richard B. Woodward observes, although Lê had the means to correct for image blur (figure 3.6), that she elects not to do so recalls the imperfections that resulted from the technical constraints of slow shutter speed.[25] Her apparently deliberate and anachronistic invocation of imperfection stands in contrast to the Vietnamese state's visual renovation of images from the socialist archive and historical revision of the war.

Not surprisingly, reviewers and critics of this famous series situate Lê's photographs within a history of American landscape photography that stretches back to the nineteenth-century heyday of western expansion in the United States. These critics remark in particular on the affinities between her work and geologic surveys. Indeed, she deliberately evokes this tradition in her selection of the very camera that the great landscape photographers used. But it is not just any landscape that she depicts, nor is it the sublime American West that has become the signature focus of landscape photographs in this tradition. Instead, *Small Wars* features Virginia, landscape of the American South and key site for American Civil War battles—and preferred playground for reenactors. (Around the same time, Sally Mann used a similar camera for *What Remains* [2003], a series that similarly reflects on the aftermath of the Civil War by exploring life and death in the landscape of the American South, specifically Virginia.)[26] It is perhaps no coincidence, then, that Lê's 5×7 viewfinder camera was also the type likely used during the American Civil War, the first major conflict to be photographed extensively after the Crimean and Mexican-American wars.

On first glance, Lê's self-portrayal opens the series up to "biographical" interpretations, according to Woodward. Significantly, Lê's participation in this series highlights the South Vietnamese body as a racialized figure (arguably what Woodward meant by alluding to the "biographical") whose presence in this landscape prompts questions about memory and migration. Even though this reenactment group in Virginia is concerned with the American experience of the war in Vietnam—a perspective that Lê does not ignore—*Small Wars* nevertheless projects a Vietnamese perspective through the embodied presence of the photographer. The placement of the displaced South Viet-

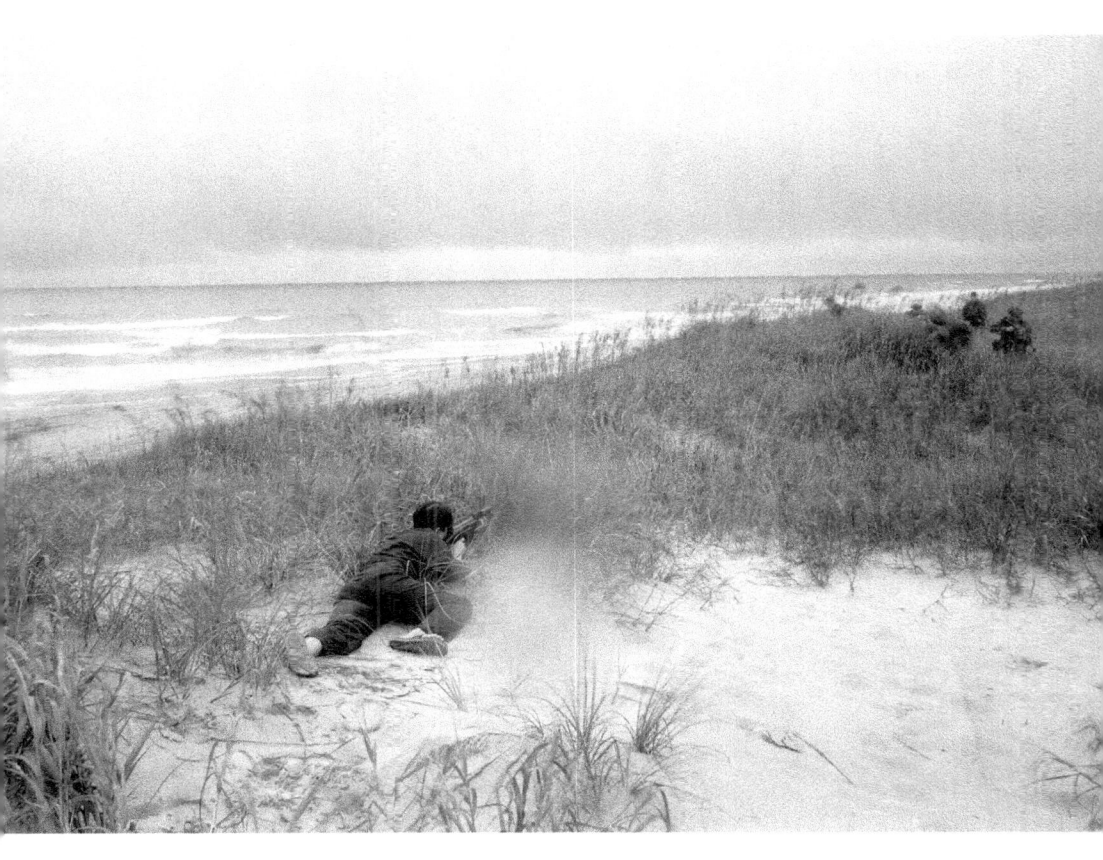

FIGURE 3.5 *Sniper, 1999–2002.*
Photographer: An-My Lê.

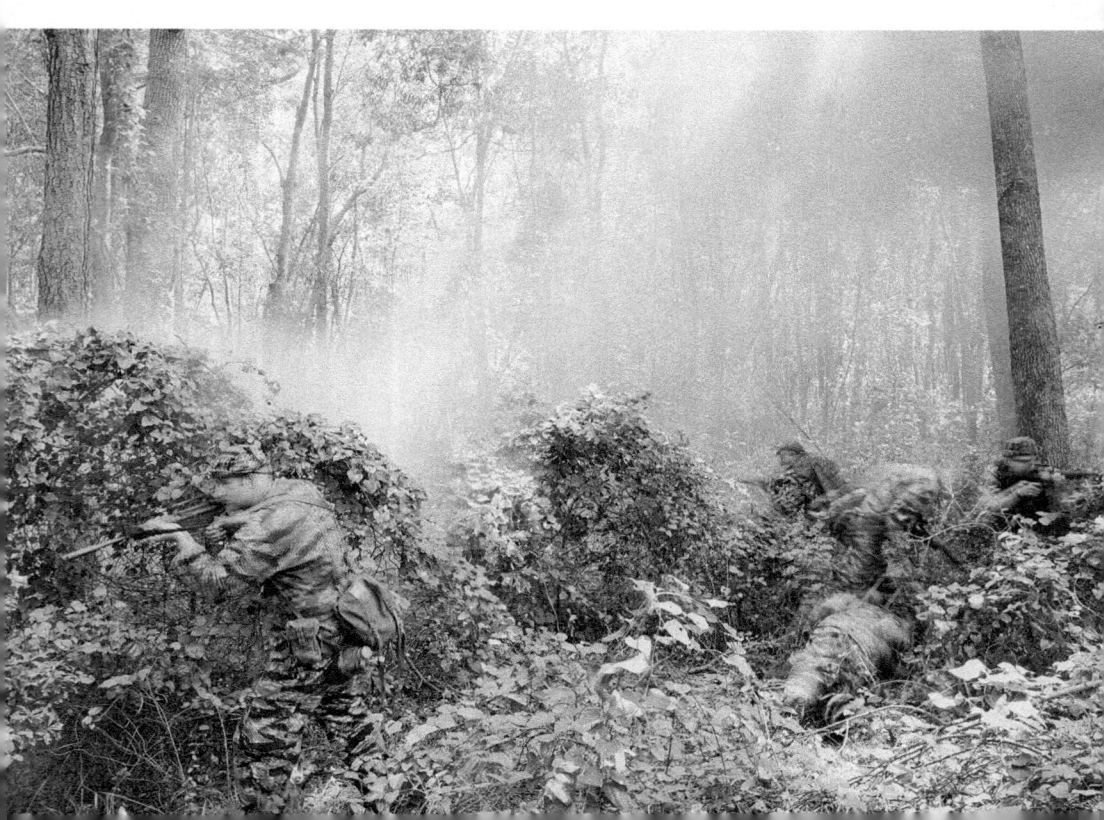

namese body onto this site overlays, however improbably, two southern spaces, the American South and South Vietnam. As Mart A. Stewart observes, the story of Confederate struggle resonates for South Vietnamese communities, who, despite immense differences in histories and experiences with their American counterparts, connect, strangely enough, with tragic themes of division, betrayal, and loss associated with civil wars.[27] Similarly, anthropologist Ann Marie Leshkowich's interviews with *tiểu thương*, female petty traders in Ho Chi Minh City, reveals that these women feel a surprising sympathy with the suffering and sacrifice of Scarlett O'Hara, the famous heroine of Margaret Mitchell's Civil War melodrama.[28] Lê's presence in the photographs and her improbable alignment of two landscapes reveal unexpected parallels, incongruous affinities, between the two Souths and the two periods. Interestingly, Lê's recent work, included in the 2017 Whitney Biennual in New York City, continues to explore the theme of reenactment, this time by focusing on the making of *Free State of Jones*.[29] This thematic return underscores the resonance that this configuration of the South, the racialized terrain of American violence, holds for her as a refugee from the capital of South Vietnam.

At the same time, Lê's *Small Wars* series is unsettling because this parallel can only be partial; the two landscapes are clearly misaligned. Indeed, Lê's photographs are hauntingly out of place: as many viewers have observed, the rolling hills, pine forests, and streams of Virginia hardly come close to resembling the tropical jungles of Vietnam. The landscape of Virginia evokes, without convincingly conjuring, that of Vietnam. In fact, there is only one photograph in which Virginia could perhaps pass for Vietnam (figure 3.7). *Bamboo* is an image that neither links to a specific site nor has a clear relation to people who might inhabit or traverse this site.

Otherwise, *Small Wars* demonstrates that the merging of remote places and discrete times—arguably, reenactment's objective—can only ever be approximations. Moreover, whereas Hạnh's photographs suggest a temporal looping of proleptic loss and a nostalgia that is simultaneously retrospective and prospective, Lê employs an anachronistic method that fuses the two times of the present reality of play and a counterfactual past in a disjointed manner to reveal the spatial misfit between Virginia and Vietnam, and the temporal disjuncture between the present day and an imagined, remote past. In this way Lê's selection of cumbersome equipment for contemporary work expresses this temporal disjunction. Indeed, photographs of reenactments disrupt assumptions about the differences between the fixed quality of an image and the distinctive liveness of performances. Performance theorist Rebecca Schneider notes that although viewers usually perceive photographs

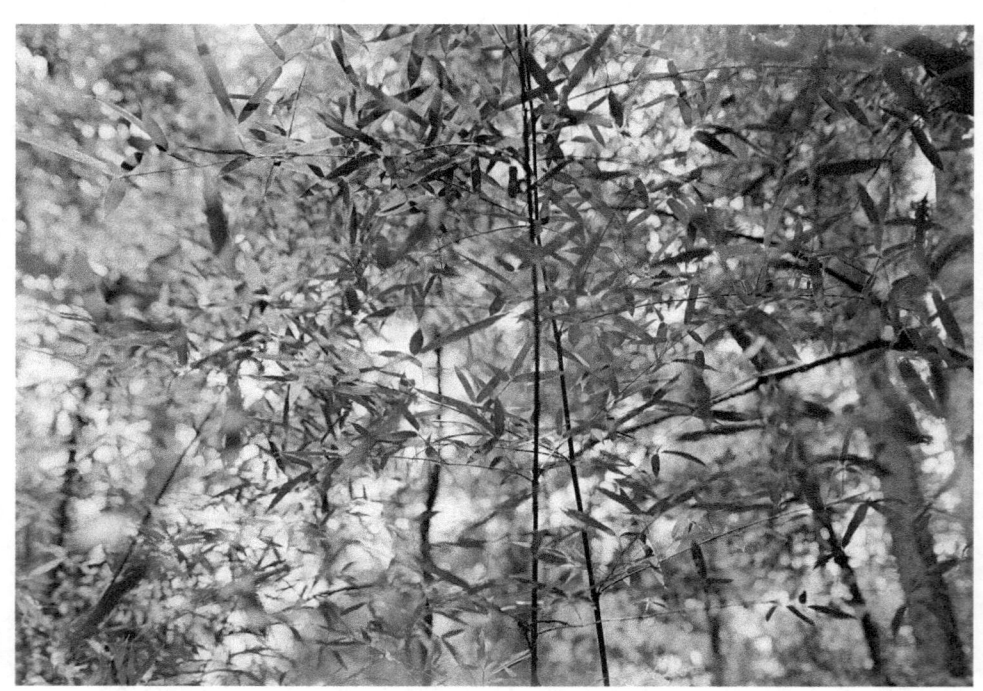

FIGURE 3.7 *Bamboo, 1999–2002*. Photographer: An-My Lê.

as "still," capturing a moment in time, fixed in its frozen pastness, when it comes to reenactments, photographs activate memory—photographs of re-enactments encode multiple temporalities, the past and the present, an imagined past that is experienced as "real"—and map out palimpsestic spaces.[30] Indeed, the imagined past can be experienced as real precisely through invocation of photography's indexicality; the subjunctive mood of reenactment's desire for an alternative history, the dream of otherness, is anchored in the camera's capacity to capture that-which-was.

Contrast Lê's depiction of spatial misfit and temporal disjuncture with the approach of *In Country*, where the directors employ montage to merge a re-enacted ambush smoothly with one that was documented in archival footage. The film's continuity editing provides the effect of seamless action so that the present extends back to—and succeeds in reaching—the past. When Vinh Nguyen participates in reenactments of the war in Vietnam, he hopes to recover time. In the documentary he muses poetically in Vietnamese. The subtitles translate his reflections as follows:

> You know, when you make a tent out of a rain poncho, and the sound of the rain drops falling on the poncho, it made me remember back to when I was a soldier: a time when the communists could attack us at any time; a time when we went out looking for communists to exterminate them; a time when death could come at any time. And our protection was just our little poncho tent, keeping the dew off so we could sleep. All of my memories came back, particularly when I was wearing my military uniform, had a helmet on my head, a knapsack by my side, and an M16 in my arms. I burst out crying because of the sound of raindrops on my poncho tent.

However, Lê's work captures the longing visualized and articulated in the film only to expose the impossibility of this desire to return to the past.

Just as curious is the title of Lê's series, *Small Wars*, which has puzzled viewers. As Woodward observes, there is nothing small about Lê's artistic talent or about the impact of her work. But the title refers not as much to photographic style as it does to military strategy. A literal translation of the Spanish word *guerrilla*, small war is a concept theorized in the nineteenth century by political philosopher Carl Von Clausewitz to analyze conflicts between unevenly matched combatants.[31] In contrast to large or great wars that involve evenly matched state actors (the most emblematic of which are the two world wars), small wars pitch states against nonstate combatants in asymmetric skirmishes, with the technological and financial force of the former overwhelming the resources of the latter. For example, small wars range from nineteenth-century anticolonial resistance struggles to today's broad and intensive "global war on terror." Accordingly, the term *small wars* denotes an approach to warfare rather than the scale of war, or for that matter the scale of photographic representation when it comes to depicting that war or its aftermath.

In 1940 the US Marine Corps prepared a little-known document called *Small Wars Manual*. Emblazoned with the Marine Corps signature eagle, globe, and anchor insignia and motto, "Semper Fidelis" (always faithful), the manual offered prescient guidance for military engagements in this type of conflict. The manual advised that leaders of such conflicts focus not on strategies that rely on overwhelming military force but instead undertake "a wide range of activities, including diplomacy, contacts with the civil population and warfare of the most difficult kind [for] the situation is often uncertain [and] the orders are sometimes indefinite."[32] Yet because this book was published in the World War II era, in the following decades strategists disregarded the handbook's lessons about engaging with insurgent tactics, so profoundly were they shaped by what was perhaps the greatest of the twentieth century's "great wars." By the start of the war in Vietnam, *Small Wars Manual* was all but forgotten, which is why leaders such as General Westmoreland approached battles with big-war strategies in mind, according to journalist and military historian Max Boot.[33] (In taking this approach, Westmoreland was at odds with Edward Lansdale, who was more astute about the nature of the guerrilla conflict in Vietnam.) Misrecognizing the nature of this conflict, strategists projected another type of war onto Vietnam, seeking out big battles and provoking rather than pacifying locals. Somewhat belatedly, Henry Kissinger grasped the consequences of this misperception when, in 1969, he reflected that "we lost sight of one of the cardinal maxims of guerilla warfare: the guerilla wins if he does not lose. The conventional army loses if it does not win."[34]

This context of small-war strategies and the insurgent tactics they are designed to neutralize thus illuminates the quiet quality of Lê's photographs. Her depiction of reenactment is unspectacular in the way that small wars are generally unspectacular. Although critics rightly align her with a longer history of landscape photography, her approach to depicting landscapes is striking for its eschewal of the sublime. Instead of wide-open, expansive spaces evident in her later work on Iraq War training exercises, the *29 Palms* series, Lê's landscapes in *Small Wars* are tight, enclosed, confined.[35] Alongside presumably exciting acts of war, including hiding, running, spying, ambushing, and shooting, Lê's photographs depict the prelude to or aftermath of action: humdrum intervals and restful interludes.

In *Sleeping Soldiers,* for example, Lê portrays a pair of reenactors sprawled across low mats laid out across the floor of a forest clearing (figure 3.8). Another photograph, titled *Cots,* portrays a lone reenactor, his back bare before the camera, in repose amid the messy and mundane accoutrements of war, or rather props to conjure the look of war: equipment and weapons scattered haphazardly, blankets strewn carelessly, laundry laid out on makeshift lines (figure 3.9). The repose of this unnamed "GI" evokes the introspective mood of the overall series, offering a broader commentary on war reenactment as an enterprise founded on fantasy, allohistory realized through counterfactual performance. Although reenactments may often be staged as spectacles, Lê's work emphasizes the quotidian quality of prolonged pauses, by turns restful and boring, which punctuate the business and play of war.

Robert Hariman and others observe that contemporary war photography has increasingly become concerned with the banal.[36] For Franny Nudelman the figure of the sleeping soldier emerges as an exemplary banal figure in works by photographers such as Tim Hetherington. A member of the renowned Magnum cooperative, Hetherington sought, before his untimely death in 2011, to comment on both the banality of war and the banality of conventional war photography through his intimate depictions of sleeping soldiers. In his work, sleeping soldiers challenge the psychoanalytic commonplace that considers fitful sleep—more often than not interrupted by nightmares experienced as flashbacks—as a symptom of trauma, specifically PTSD, according to Nudelman. The 24/7 cycle conscripts all forms of leisure, contends theorist Jonathan Crary.[37] Only sleep resists this conscription. Hetherington's soldiers remind us of sleep's restorative function, Nudelman points out. Sleep, we might add, has the potential to resist neoliberalism's relentless instrumentalization of daily life. Yet according to Nudelman, Heatherington's reference to an earlier tradition of postmortem photography—wherein a maternal gaze peacefully lays to rest the lifeless child—reveals how the trope of sleep does not defuse but instead makes palatable the violence of war.

For Lê the figure of the sleeping soldier directs us to another possibility: the landscape of the American South is a dreamscape, which nudges both reenactors and spectators into a counterfactual dreamwork. We can view the blur as another way to merge these landscapes in an imperfectly dreamy and unrealistic way. Her photographs feature such props as the flash, or rather flare, of light bursting into night's stillness (figure 3.10) and smoke shrouding the carcass of a downed plane (figure 3.11), meant to simulate war's realistic

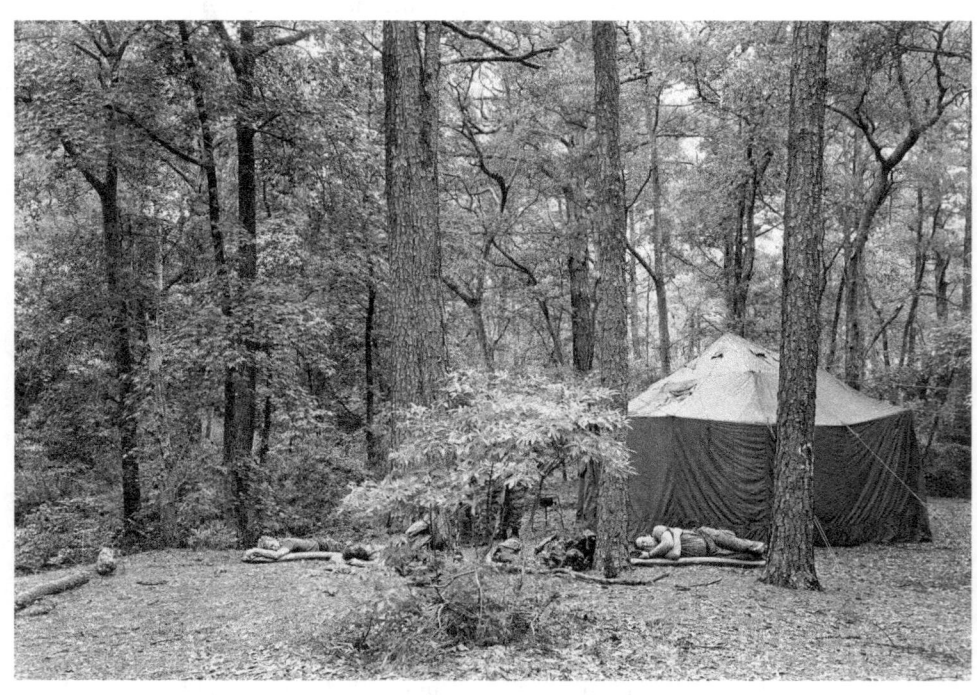

FIGURE 3.8 *Sleeping Soldiers, 1999–2002.* Photographer: An-My Lê.

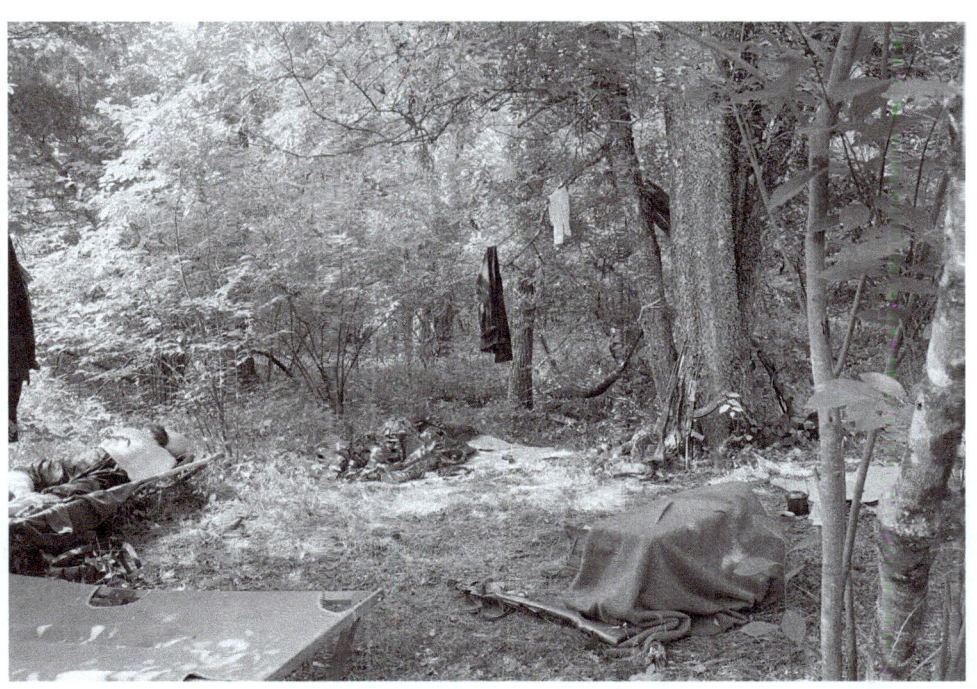

FIGURE 3.9 *Cot*, *1999-2002*. Photographer: An-My Lê.

FIGURE 3.10 *Explosion, 1999-2002.*
Photographer: An-My Lê.

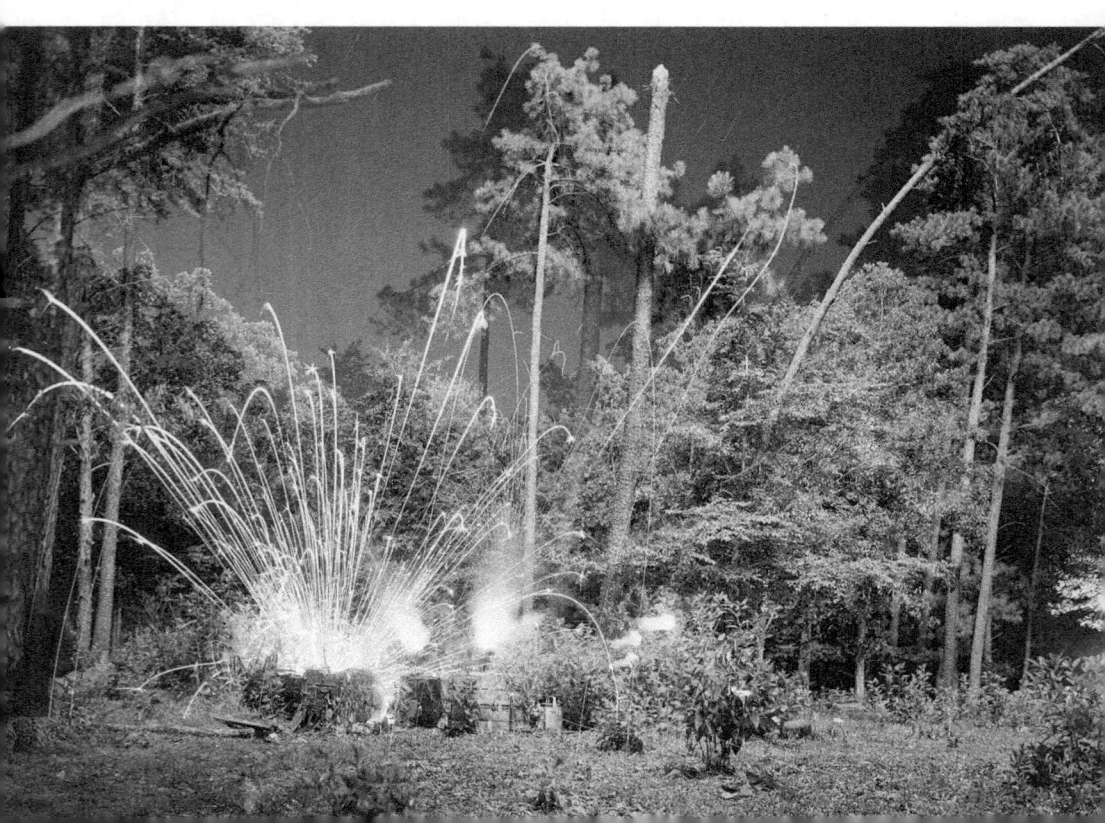

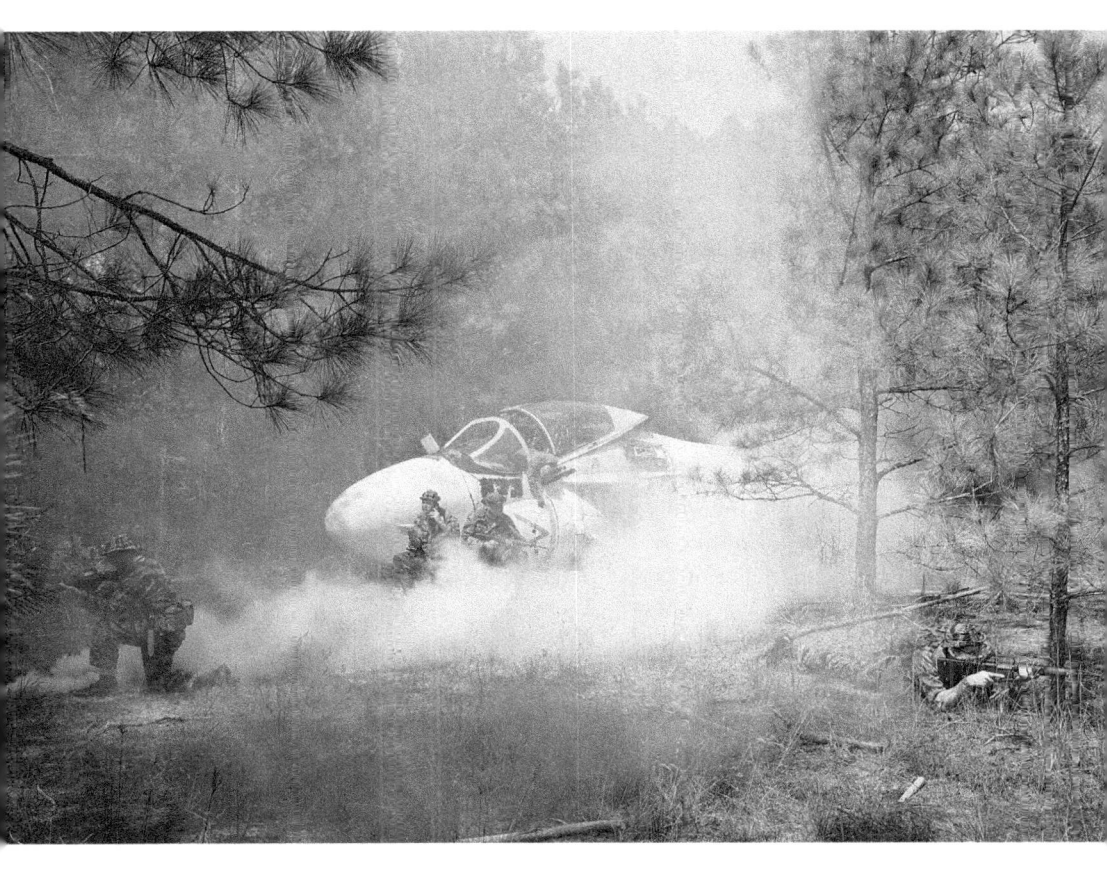

FIGURE 3.11 *Rescue, 1999-2002.*
Photographer: An-My Lê.

effects. However, these props also forge a misty quality, ushering us into an imaginary realm where we might entertain possible proximities between Virginia and Vietnam—despite the misfit and misalignments described above. This dream quality offers the atmosphere for perceiving connections between American and Vietnamese experiences of this war, all the more real because imagined. As Lê puts it in relation to an earlier project, *Viêt Nam* (1996), documenting her bittersweet homecoming during the mid-1990s, "Instead of seeking the real, I began making photographs that use the real to ground the imaginary. The landscape genre or the description of people's activities in the landscape lent itself well to this way of thinking."[38]

In the case of *Small Wars*, Lê plays with the idea of embedded photography, drawing on her close connection to "soldiers"—whose activities she willingly participates in—to develop an ambiguous picture of collaboration. It is not just the white male body that, by putting himself in the picture, seeks to grasp what the war in Vietnam might mean for a generation with no direct experience of its traumatic events. The diasporic Vietnamese body grapples in a similar way for understanding, wrestling with "postmemory"—secondary witnessing on the part of individuals who did not experience trauma directly—in a process that suggests the entanglement of Vietnamese experiences with American experiences of this war.[39] To focus on Vietnamese experiences, as Lê invites us to do by placing her body in the field of vision—at play in reenactment of this war and in drawing on photography as a means of nuancing "warring visions"—is to highlight this bind, one that is based on misperception as much as it is on identification. This misperception stems from wholly different histories of displacement even as it resembles those that move her fellow reenactors to participate in this activity. To collaborate, as Viet Thanh Nguyen puts it in a slightly different context, is to stretch beyond one's own worldview, a capacity that opens up symbolic possibilities for reconciliation.[40] Lê's performance of the enemy, not to mention that of the white reenactors who also take on this role by wearing the VC uniform, suggests an ethical potential in imagining the subject position of others. At the same time, collaboration raises uncomfortable questions about the conditions that conjure this sympathy and the consequences of its conjuring. Collaboration might entail sympathetic cooperation, but it carries the taint of possible betrayal, which, as Lan Duong argues, is a burden borne especially by Vietnamese women.[41] Lê's work invites viewers to ponder this dual nature of collaboration. For all its potential for bringing Vietnamese experiences of the war's aftermath in visual intimacy with American experiences,

Small Wars also provokes questions about what this intimacy entails, not to mention the implications of this intimacy.[42]

Although I have stressed the need to locate Lê's depiction of "small wars" within the frameworks of military history, the history of landscape, and the conventions of war photography, the photographer also invokes small wars metaphorically. This metaphor denotes a different dimension of war: the ways that wars extend beyond their official end, no less diminished for their secondary quality. In this regard Lê's reworking of war photography as a genre amenable to capturing the ambiguities of "small wars" provides a cultural form for the transmission of postmemory in a process that unfolds privately and publicly, with personal and interpersonal resonances.

Lê's presence in the visual field brings to light the dual dimensions of this contest for memory: the ways that misperception might be mutual. Lê's anachronistic use of equipment and photographic style underscores multiplicities of time and space, which reveal themselves on the psychic battleground of reenactment. Her disconcerting presence in scenes of reenactment underscores the sense of misrecognition, as a contentious history replete with attendant misinterpretations (a small war mistaken for a big war) gives way to the imprecise approximations of memory, an imagined projection of a past as it could have happened, replayed without end. *Small Wars* portrays temporal misfits and spatial misalignments to reveal both the appeal of reenactment—the promise that it holds for temporarily "returning" to a place and time where one once was, even, as is the case for Lê herself, who was still a child when the war ended, where one has never been—and its futility and frustration.

If the desire on the part of white male reenactors to relive the war in Vietnam is a perverse compulsion (after all, the outcome of this war was decidedly inglorious for Americans), then surely this desire is even more vexed in the case of diasporic Vietnamese who participate in such activities. Indeed, this group of reenactors usually consists of refugees from what was once South Vietnam. In their case, they lost more than a war; they lost their nation. Although historians usually denigrate reenactments as attempts to whitewash history, the presence of Asian participants complicates the significance of this cultural activity.

For diasporic Vietnamese, reenactments, viewed as events of photography, provide a public and quietly visible means to work through feelings of loss and to momentarily conjure alternative temporalities where they might revive the Republic of South Vietnam once more. These functions prompt further reconsideration of war photography as encompassing not only battles whose outcomes have already been decided and clearly known. War photography can also be seen as documents of events as they could have happened and as retrospective fantasies of what could have been, in the case of Hạnh's images. They are also dynamic events, as Lê's work shows, conjuring communities of mourning even as they bring to light these communities' mutual fantasies and the misalignments between them.

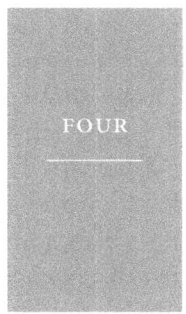

FOUR

UNHOMED: DOMESTIC IMAGES
AND THE DIASPORIC ART OF
RECOLLECTION

Nathalie Huynh Chau Nguyen yearns for a box of photos her family had
shipped to their temporary home in Japan in 1975 that never arrived. Journalist Andrew Lam confesses to the "unforgivable act" of burning his family
photos, which reduced three generations to ashes.[1] During her first journey
back to Vietnam in thirty years, Lan's hired car circles the roads of Bien Hoa,
a town just south of Saigon, in search of the photo studio where dozens of her
portraits were kept, only to learn that the owners have emigrated and that no
one knows what happened to these old photos. She returns to her home in
Markham, Ontario.

   Such stories of yearning are familiar to the Vietnamese diaspora. They are
especially poignant for the first wave of refugees, who fled in 1975 after the
fall of Saigon, as well as for the "boat people" who formed the second wave

of refugees affected by the Indochinese humanitarian crisis of the late 1970s to the early 2000s.[2] For these two groups of refugees, photos are an often fraught, incomplete record of a painful past. As they awaited their chance to flee, some refugees hid, altered, abandoned, buried, or even burned photos that contained incriminating evidence of collaboration with Americans and loyalty to the Republic of Vietnam. Many had to abandon compromising pictures in the name of survival. In other cases, refugees left behind their photos to make room for jewelry to barter with and food to keep them going. Family photographs disappear in numerous ways; they are war's collateral damage. Remarkably, however, thousands of those photos have resurfaced in the marketplace in the form of orphan images and albums separated from their original owners and stories.

Despite these losses, overseas Vietnamese assemble memories through photographs in myriad ways. As we have seen, they produce photos in the course of public gatherings, commemorations, and reenactments. Moreover, many community members collect family photos as best they can, in so doing piecing together the stories hinted at through defaced, discarded, or destroyed images. These images represent a tie to the families left behind, evoked in the form of stories about artifacts that no longer exist or images that somehow survived.

Family photos are probably not what comes to mind when envisioning the Vietnamese diaspora. As a highly conventional and deeply personal genre associated with the shy smiles, chagrined grimaces, and surprised joy that greet such bourgeois rites of passage as birthdays, graduations, weddings, housewarmings, and vacations,[3] family photos seem far removed from the experiences of war that shaped scores of refugees who were directly affected by the war. Given this dominant perspective of war that focuses on spectacular forms of representation for reckoning with the aftermath of proxy battles in Vietnam, documentary or combat photographs would seem more fitting as artifacts for analysis than family photographs, as we saw in earlier chapters. Conversely, critics who approach domestic images—often a synonym for family photos—as a "home mode" of communication may view them as bound solely to the private sphere.[4] However, as Laura Wexler demonstrates in her landmark study of white women photographers and their role in perpetrating "tender violence" within the United States and in imperial missions, particularly in Asia, domestic images are versatile and ideologically portable precisely because they bridge public and private spheres.[5] In other words, domestic images are powerful vehicles for the consolidation of domesticity. However, critics have not yet fully explored the function of family photos produced and circulated across the diaspora in response to US imperialism, even though, as this book shows, the visual representation of war takes numerous forms beyond what critics have acknowledged. Moreover, the ubiquity of violent spectacles as a dominant framework for seeing war may even account for why family photographs have been largely overlooked by both area studies and photography studies scholars.

I turn to family photographs, materials usually considered as ephemera because no official Vietnamese archive of South Vietnam exists. Moreover, the records that do exist in the United States predominantly focus on American experiences. In her influential account of critical refugee studies, Yến Lê Espiritu is obliged to confront the obstacle posed by the public erasure of South Vietnamese history by drawing on unorthodox and highly eclectic materials. She explains that because of the "public erasure" of South Vietnamese history, we need "a different methodology, one deploying personal affect, in order to expose and reclaim 'the something else' that resides at the intersection between private loss and public commemoration."[6] Espiritu begins her inquiry by studying her own family photos. Drawing on a personal dimension for analysis challenges commonplace assumptions about the necessity of objective distance for research rigor. Yet this personal dimension so powerfully evoked through family photography provides a crucial resource for tracing subjects that mainstream archives have marginalized if not wholly erased.[7] As Christina Sharpe shows in her important book on the urgency of "wake work" in the context of the Black diaspora, the personal provides a critically incisive lens into social processes, countering the abstraction of these processes.[8]

Family photos are thus important because of, rather than despite, their quotidian qualities. As a record of the ordinary, family photos shift discussions of war and its aftermath, nudging us even further away from familiar spectacles of violence to consider instead daily struggles to survive. Family photos also matter because of the Vietnamese politicization of family. In his account *The Other Cold War*, anthropologist Heonik Kwon explores how "wartime political bifurcation" fractures the "genealogical unity" of communities in Vietnam well after the war's end.[9] These communities are torn between the familial responsibility to honor their loved ones who died in the war, a predicament that vexes many families because their members fought for both sides, and the political duty to preserve the memories of revolutionary martyrs. Because the latter is a sanctioned, legitimate public rite and the former is not, these communities are forced to reconcile tensions that arise when state obligations overtake familial responsibilities. Kwon's analysis reveals how private ancestral altars, which honor photos of the departed who fought on separate sides, reunify the dead in kinship memory. This practice of kinship memory is a process that tacitly opposes official state history. As practiced by the Vietnamese families featured in Kwon's ethnography, kinship memory sutures treacherous political bifurcations that persist beyond the war's end and despite the nation's reunification.

Whereas Kwon's study focuses on families in postwar Vietnam and their connection to the wartime dead, diasporic Vietnamese families also confront these obstacles; political bifurcations further test often fragile links that families have with one another and with those relatives whom they left behind in Vietnam. In an oral history book on postwar memories, a Vietnamese Australian narrator, Huynh Thuy Ai Lan, movingly recounts the persecution she encountered: "Some policemen concluded I was a CIA agent because they had found a photograph of me with an American. I explained that he had been my English teacher and the photo was taken at his farewell party, but that made no impression at all."[10] This scrutiny of revolutionary credentials may have influenced the very look of families and altered the constitution of these families beyond blood relation. In her ethnographic study of Vietnamese communities in Australia, Nathalie Huynh Chau Nguyen observes that the telltale bars of an Army of the Republic of Vietnam (ARVN) uniform are excised from a family photo that had made its way out of Vietnam.[11] It is not just uniforms that were erased from personal records. Southern Vietnamese families feared that these signs, which betrayed enemy affiliation, would subject them to punishment such as imprisonment at reeducation camps or condemn them to death. In some cases those who wore these uniforms were erased altogether from photos. Families have even destroyed their visual record outright, a phenomenon that Karen Strassler notes also occurred in Indonesia in the wake of the 1965–66 mass killing of communist leaders and supporters.[12] Chi Tan Thai, a Vietnamese Canadian small-business owner who escaped Vietnam in the 1970s, when he was just seventeen, recalls an experience similar to that of Andrew Lam; his father told him to gather all their photos and burn them, worrying that they would provide damaging evidence of his family's American friendships, which helped them build their wartime business of salvaging scrap metal.[13] Even though Tan's family destroyed all their photos, communists confiscated their home, and his father was sent to a reeducation camp. The Thais scattered in the late 1970s, as Tan and his siblings joined hundreds of thousands of ethnic Chinese refugees who braved the high seas. Only in the early 1980s did they reunite with their father, and it was at this point that the family photographed themselves again.

Family photos enable us to trace narratives of migration, not to mention partial stories of images that have been "unhomed": scattered, lost, or left behind. Attending to how personal images are taken up or tossed aside by Vietnamese diasporic communities unsettles entrenched critical perspectives advanced by Pierre Bourdieu, Richard Chalfen, Gillian Rose, and others that family photos serve the ends of the state by reproducing gendered, classist, and heteronormative ideologies.[14] The act of preserving kinship memories by honoring the ancestral rites documented in Kwon's ethnography—and, we might add, by safeguarding family photos to include in these rites or for other purposes—may not necessarily reproduce state ideologies. In some contexts they may even defy these ideologies. Conversely, when families alter or destroy their photos, their actions can be considered attempts to subvert, rather than assent to, state surveillance. Instead of betraying their loved ones, in these cases families preserve their secrets by sacrificing personal archives. Even the most banal of family photos—a genre that, after all, is remarkable for its unremarkable conventionality—acquires layers of complexity, as Strassler has argued.[15] Even when the complete story behind family photos cannot be fully understood, as is the case with orphan images, this gap meaningfully attests to the limits of what can be known and constitutes its own politics of resistance.

Yet for the reasons I have briefly outlined, diasporic Vietnamese family photos are not readily accessible. In some cases they have barely been preserved by family archivists, never mind tidily catalogued and stored within official archives such as libraries or museums, institutions that, as critics Joan Schwartz and Geoffrey Batchen observe, have been slow to recognize the significance of vernacular artifacts.[16] Looking at family photos necessitates looking *for* them. The acts of looking at and looking for family photos are all the more urgent because these objects are powerful artifacts. Family photos can nuance how viewers perceive war, as not just spectacles of violence and suffering but also the quotidian miracle of survival, the quietude of reflection, the aspiration for life to go on.

This chapter explores the meanings of found family photographs as well as considers the significance of images and stories that are irrevocably gone. For South Vietnamese members of the diaspora, the collection of family photographs and the recollection of missing chapters provide a counternarrative of the war, one that is compelling for all that it sometimes refuses complete disclosure.[17] Indeed, when considered closely, family photography can also be seen as war photography. Family photographs constitute an unusual but vital approach to constructing warring visions.

To address the archival challenges outlined above, I turn to three resources. The first consists of orphaned images, presumably left behind by refugees, which can be found in vintage shops in Vietnam, where they are sold as collectibles. The second includes collecting initiatives undertaken by members of the diaspora, namely *Vietnam in the Rearview Mirror*, an exhibition at the Wing Luke Museum in Seattle (2014), and a trio of multimedia works by Dinh Q. Lê, a Vietnamese American artist now based in Ho Chi Minh City, titled *Mot Coi Di Ve* (1998), *Erasure* (2011), and *Crossing the Farther Shore* (2014).[18] The third resource consists of personal photographs included, along with oral histories about these images, within the Family Camera Network, a public archive that I codeveloped with collaborators in partnership with cultural institutions and community organizations.[19] These materials offer diverse perspectives on photography, but they also share a strikingly similar approach. Specifically, they all engage with diasporic communities to gather together and assemble family photos, some of them precious artifacts donated by families but many more of them lost and subsequently "found" orphaned images that have been removed from albums and that disclose little if any information about who they are, not to mention where and to whom they belong. The very existence of these materials discloses a fervent compulsion to collect, one that accords with Jacques Derrida's concept of "archive fever."[20] In turn, this compulsion to collect raises questions about the significance of collecting as a cultural activity, questions that are of ongoing relevance and concern to me, as the primary objective of the Family Camera project is, after all, to produce a public archive. In cases when little, if anything, is known about families, as is the case with thousands of found photos that are included in special collections, orphan images evoke poignant affiliations—and disaffiliations. For the Vietnamese diaspora, family photos, whether in the form of orphan images, preserved in personal collections, or evoked as missing chapters, help shape an alternative perspective on the war and its impact that contests official state discourses.

REFUGEE ID PHOTOS AND LIBERAL HUMANISM

A woman stands against the improvised backdrop of a pale sheet and peers unsmilingly at the camera. She holds her children close while someone's hand—not hers but it's unclear exactly whose it is—clutches a card that identifies by initial and number the boat they arrived on. Refugee ID photos may portray a family, but the somber picture that this portrait draws of dangers barely overcome and adversities still to be endured may not be what one expects of a family photo. Yet this ID document is just one from among the genre of instrumental photography, produced under the auspices of a regulatory official agency, that appears in my own family album—and doubtless in other albums belonging to refugees.

Vietnam in the Rearview Mirror, an exhibition held in 2014 at the Wing Luke Museum in Seattle, Washington, features as its cover image a refugee ID photo donated by a community member (figure 4.1). Given the unhappy themes of destitution and desperation that refugee ID photos conjure, this image seems an unlikely choice. In its presentation of people as numbers—the initials stand for the name of the boat the family arrived in, and the digits indicate the date and the total number of family members—the photo appears far removed from the kind that undertakes what sociologist Pierre Bourdieu calls the characteristic middlebrow familial functions of recording bourgeois rites in recognition and embrace of kinship. They take us far from the ostensible home mode of communication. The concept of home in these documents of uncertain passage is often a site left behind and an uncertain future to which to cling.[21] With the numbers enabling administrators to determine who is at the camp and how many rations are needed, the image instead fulfills an instrumental function—that is, making subjects legible and governable.

Although it is the only ID photo in the exhibition, a close look reveals why this image was selected over others to promote *Vietnam in the Rearview Mirror*: the photograph's surface is as creased as the sheeted backdrop is wrinkled. Such signs of wear disclose the tactile dimensions of feeling when it comes to photography. Indeed, the exhibit director explains that this photo was selected because it was "such a compelling image."[22] These textural signs suggest that the photograph has been thumbed often and handled by many; it was probably passed from photographer to camp administrators and to the family itself, which, after a difficult passage, likely held on to it for decades.

This nexus of exchange, from one hand to many other bodies, from one institution to another, bears out Allan Sekula's insight that instrumental photographs make up the shadow archive of bourgeois portraiture, in which the objectification inherent in the former undermines the humanism of the latter.[23] At the same time, as numerous critics have observed, this genre of family photography is remarkable because of the complexities of the "familial gaze," Marianne Hirsch's term to describe how family photos, usually thought of as artifacts limited to the private sphere, intersect with and move between multiple public spheres and institutional sites.[24] The genre of family photos,

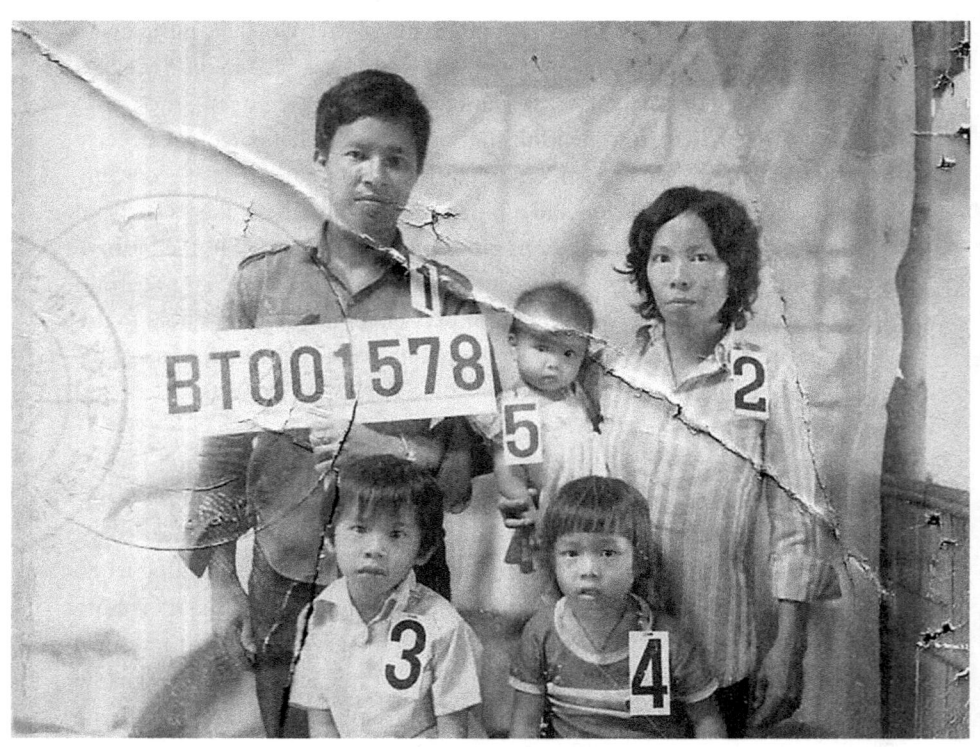

FIGURE 4.1 Refugee ID photo. Courtesy Hanh Pham.

Hirsch points out, comprises not just the usual snapshots and studio portraits that are contained within private albums but may also include less conventional images. In this way ID photos produced by the state for the purposes of surveillance may, on occasion, find their way into family collections.[25]

Yet refugee ID photos are a paradox precisely because they expose the predicament of human rights.[26] As Hannah Arendt explains, the fragile condition of the merely human does not protect subjects but instead renders them vulnerable to abuse.[27] Identification photos are meant to serve humanitarian ends by reducing the humanity of subjects, namely through the numbering of people for bureaucratic purposes. However, the exhibition's prominent display of the refugee ID photo humanizes its subjects, thereby reversing this type of photo's primary purpose of enumeration and objectification.

Although Sekula's analysis of the shadow archive reminds us of how instrumental photographs compromise the humanism of bourgeois portraiture, the inclusion of refugee ID photos as family pictures flips this structure, exposing the discursive complexity of this mode of representation. *Vietnam in the Rearview Mirror* effectively reclaims this instrumental image as a family photo, as my parents did, when they held fast to our refugee ID documents. In fact, my parents were so attached to our refugee images that, to preserve them, they took our albums apart. At some point they must have realized that their inexpensive ringed albums with yellowing adhesive hastened instead of halted the process of degradation. My father opened the album and removed, rephotographed, and scanned our pictures, staving off the threat of loss by saving the images on external drives. He even set them to a soundtrack of covers of sixties rock songs, South Vietnamese lamentations, and soothing French lounge music sung by *Paris by Night* stars, the variety-show performers beloved by overseas Vietnamese. For photographs that have traveled so far, it is ironic but apt that they should be further dispersed in this way, disassembled for the purposes of preservation.

The exhibition reflects on the unsettling, and for me familiar, possibility that refugee ID photos form a haunting part of Vietnamese visual narratives. They also expand the genre of family photography so that the notion of family counters the dehumanizing logic of the refugee ID photos' numbering system and the condition of statelessness that threatens to dissolve refugee subjectivity.[28] The inclusion of this refugee ID photo prompts us to question the constitution of family. Whereas this particular photo featured in the *Vietnam in the Rearview Mirror* exhibition seems to spotlight a nuclear family, oral histories of first- and second-wave diasporic Vietnamese offer accounts of experiences that broaden the concept of family beyond this conventionally limited grouping. In this context, the concept of family includes not just aunts, uncles, cousins, and grandparents but also friends and strangers thrown together in the midst of calamity.[29] By dispensing with mobility and instead embracing the theme of national resettlement, the exhibition reverses the relationship between subjection and humanism.

At the same time, the implicit before/after structure of the refugee-to-immigrant success story in the Wing Luke exhibition upholds self-fashioning as a counter to the violence of subjection. Yet this structure also invokes a controversial form of identity politics, one that has been critiqued by ethnic studies scholars for over a decade. As Espiritu argues, the US commitment to humanitarian intervention in response to the Indochinese refugee crisis marks not a departure from the militarism that gave rise to proxy wars in Southeast Asia, whose violent outcome partially precipitated this crisis, but rather an extension of it. Such humanitarian missions ensured a moral victory for the United States as compensation for the military defeat of the war in Vietnam.[30] Including refugee ID photos as part of diasporic family albums accordingly humanizes subjects in a way that mirrors the logic of liberal humanism. The merging of instrumental photography and family photography lays bare an underlying tension between the surveillance of subjection and identity politics: the latter's gestures of defiance, in response to a history that threatened to erase subjectivity altogether, confronts the seemingly inevitable and deeply ironic compromise of fashioning selfhood in the image crafted by the former. In these cases the shadow archive merges into the bourgeois archive; photos of state surveillance become honorific images.

If Vietnam is in the "rearview mirror," as the exhibition suggests, then the refugee ID photo is a turning point promising visible subjectivity to salve the wounding scrutiny of subjection. The term *rearview mirror* implies that the exhibit reflects on the distance between now and then, drawing on the familiar convention of before-and-after photography and its progressive time line. Shawn Michelle Smith, Laura Wexler, Kate Palmer Albers, and Jordan Bear associate this before-and-after convention with moral reform movements, in particular their emphasis on self-fashioning and social improvement, especially in the contexts of class and race. The Seattle exhibit redefines this instrumental image as a family photo, retrospectively presenting these images as augurs of a new life now realized.[31]

I recognized this symbolic gesture in another photograph from my family's own collection (figure 4.2). Taken from a "before" time, when we still lived in Vietnam, my brother and I pose with our parents outside our grandmother's one-story home; I know this because on the verso someone—we

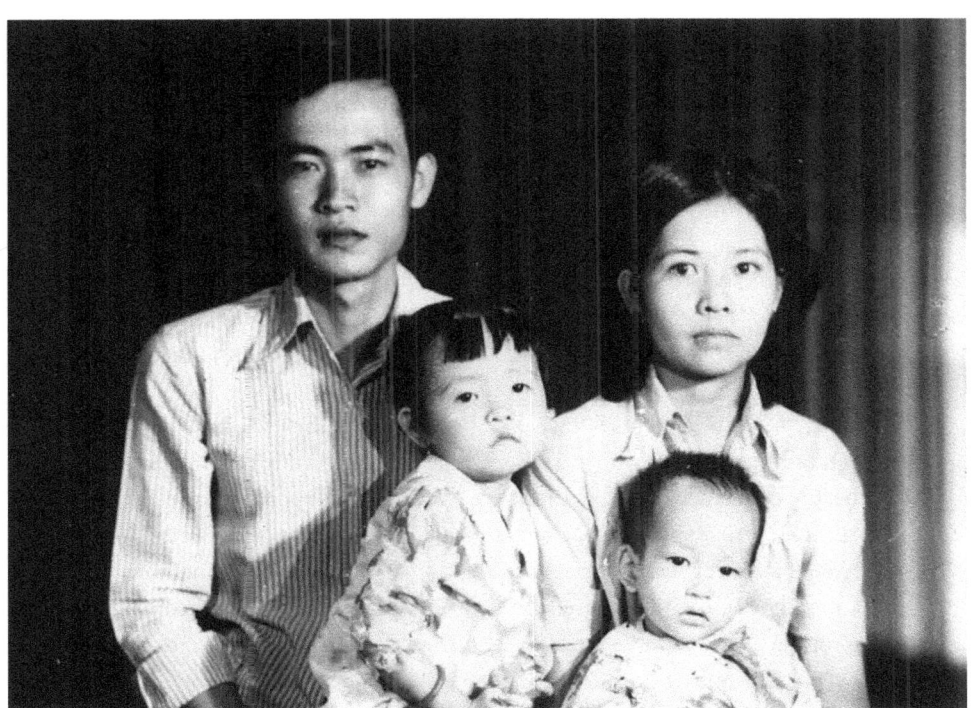

FIGURE 4.2 Family photo, c. 1977. Photographer: unknown. Author collection.

don't know who—has printed our full names. Next to my parents' names are their birth dates. But beside my name and that of my brother, someone has scratched out our birth dates using a thick black marker.

When I asked my parents, who are both in their own way family archivists, for help in deciphering this erasure, they were just as perplexed and could only confirm that this photo was from the "before" period and had actually been left behind in Vietnam. Years after we resettled in Canada, our uncles and aunts, who still lived in Sadec, must have mailed it to our new homes, re-uniting us with our old selves. I pressed further: did the marker erase a truth about our past?

My brother and I learned recently that our official birthdays are not when we were actually born, a discrepancy that is common among refugees. Be-cause my father had forgotten these details, he made up some dates, relat-ing this information to camp administrators who promptly recorded them as facts on our United Nations Refugee Agency (UNHCR) cards. In more ways than one, refugee ID photos marked our rebirth at the camp. As for this fam-ily photo from Vietnam, by the time it caught up to us in Canada an un-known hand—tasked perhaps with the solemn responsibility of family archi-vist—had reset the past to align with the present. Blotting out our birth dates enabled us to start again.

Family albums harbor secrets, as critic Annette Kuhn has shown.[32] In my parents' album two urchins in rags stand awkwardly against a background, the hastily constructed shacks that were their home for three months (figure 4.3). I found this snapshot especially unnerving, smacking of the victim motif that Martha Rosler has excoriated in relation to documentary photography, a frequently exploitative genre.[33] Few would choose to see themselves this way. Yet here, in a family album, my brother and I appear as pitiable waifs. Catherine Zuromskis points out that the desire to be photographed might precede the technology that made self-representation possible.[34] Strange as it may sound, it turns out my waif photograph emerged out of a similar longing for representation: my mother's desire to have a record of our survival.

I later learned that my mother, after happening upon a United Way relief worker carrying a camera, urged this woman to photograph us. This woman, whose name I never learned, promised to develop the negatives and mail the print, evidence of our survival, to a relative's home in Canada. The aid worker kept her word, and when we finally made it to Canada three months later, we discovered that this image, having beaten us to our new home, presaged our arrival. In the refugee photo album, records of a time before occasionally overtake what comes after.

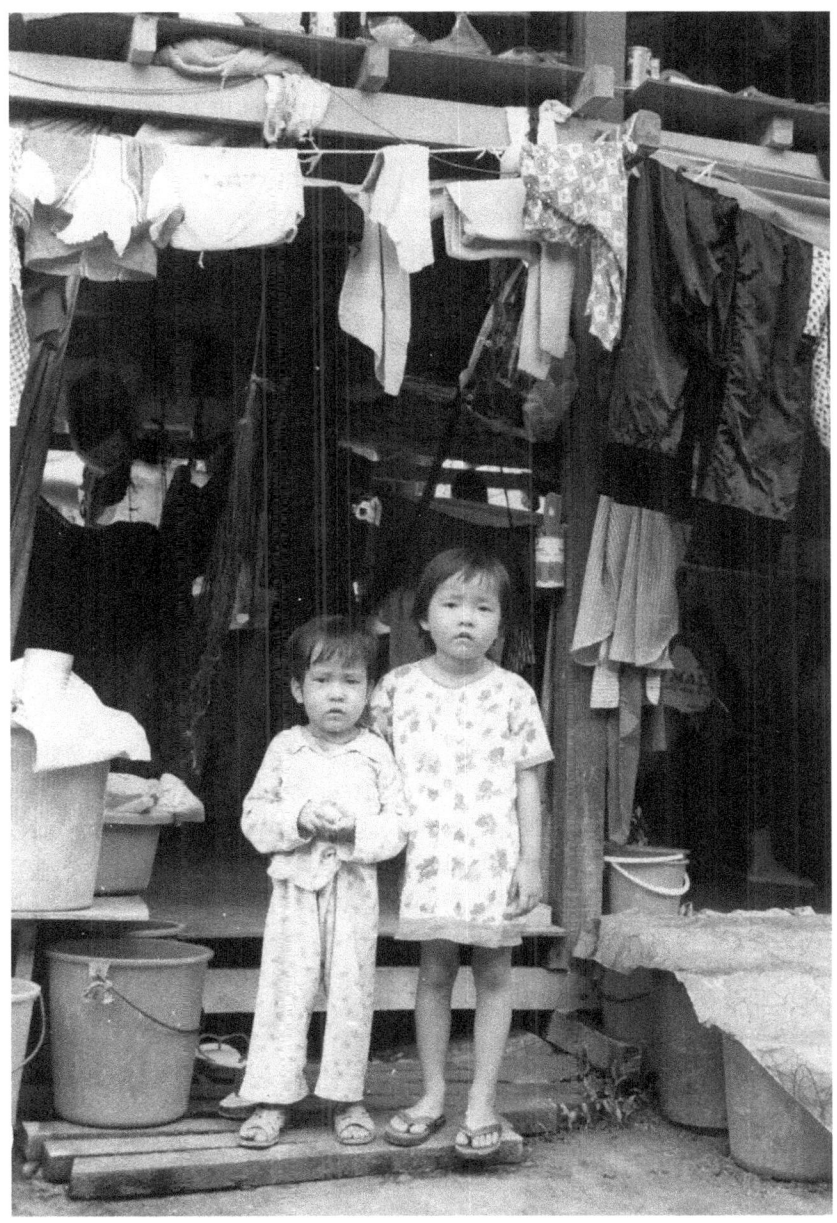

FIGURE 4.3 Refugee camp. Pulau Bidong, Malaysia, circa 1979. Photographer: unknown. Author collection.

Vietnamese family records are seldom complete. Chi Tan Thai's earliest photographs are from 1978, after he arrived in Toronto and was lucky enough to have a friend with a camera document a rare outing at a public park near Lake Ontario. In some cases, however, families retain fragments of their records, making sure to disavow—or disappear—those parts that would endanger them. As noted earlier, this disavowal takes the form of defacing photographs. In other cases it can involve selective destruction.

Although I had looked through my own family photos more often than I can recall, perhaps their familiarity led me to miss what was missing: not one of these images showed my father in uniform. He had been in the South Vietnamese Air Force, and there were enough photos of him from his youth that I had not even noticed this absence of any signs of his life while stationed at an air base in Danang. My mother had to point this out, explaining that she had torn all these photos up after the war ended, fearing communist reprisal. The Lu family shared this fear. In my interview with Hon, Binh, Lucy, and their father, who had formerly served in the ARVN as an officer, the elder Mr. Lu shared his still-unshakable worries that the Socialist Republic of Vietnam would punish him for serving on the losing side.[35] Remarkably, the Lu family preserved one photo of him in uniform. Although he instructed his wife to destroy all such photos, unlike Thai and my mother she disobeyed by leaving intact a single snapshot that reveals their family's allegiance to their lost nation, an image that would have betrayed them had it been discovered. He spoke about, but chose not to show, the photo. Despite having lived in Canada for more than four decades, he remains apprehensive about communist surveillance.

We can glimpse a broader picture of loss from the stories that survivors recall of missing photographs. In this way, I learned, photographs are not just visual artifacts; stories like the ones that the Thai and Lu families shared with me attest to photography as a multisensorial experience and a wide-ranging social practice; the image object is only one element of photography, as numerous cultural critics, including Catherine Zuromskis, Tina Campt, Martha Langford, and Elizabeth Edwards, remind us.[36] Other elements that are just as important include the interpersonal relationships that the experience of photography puts into motion and the performances that this experience entails.[37] Family photographs consist not just of what remains in a collection that one has managed to preserve and carry along from one home to another, along a trail of forced migration and multiple displacements. More than this, family photographs consist of all that no longer remains. They are the photos that one no longer has but still recollects, such as the image of my father in his uniform that my mother is able to describe perfectly (although there's no way to check). They are the photos that one remembers posing for but never saw, as is the case with Thai. He recalls that after his boat was adrift for over a week, everyone on board was rescued just as they were running out of water; when officials moved them to another vessel, they were issued new documents, a process that involved snapping new ID photos. "They gave me a sign with my name and a number," he says, "and then—click!—they took my photo. I don't know what happened later, but I never got that photo. But today I can still see how I looked then."[38] Here the story of photography is the recollection of a photographic event—or as Ariella Azoulay puts it, the event of photography in the absence of a photograph.[39] At times, diasporic Vietnamese such as Thai constitute their visual narratives of the war and its aftermaths in the absence of photographs. The loss of these photographs is integral to rather than separate from these visual narratives.

In these ways, Vietnamese refugees remake and reconstruct images in the absence of photographs and in contexts where records are, for varied reasons, incomplete. The ways that diasporic Vietnamese engage in the process of recollection through their family photographs contest the politicization of family in the state discourses of the United States and socialist Vietnam by symbolically unifying dispersed loved ones. Just as importantly, this process gestures toward multiple temporalities and, in so doing, unsettles the before/after framework that structures conventional refugee narratives.

ORPHAN IMAGES, INTIMATE ESTRANGEMENTS, AND MILITARIZED VISUAL KINSHIPS

A different set of questions arises, however, when it comes to orphaned images.

What can be learned of photographs in the absence of a story, when the memories that bring photographs to life are missing from official records and even personal collections? What stories can be told of photos for which little, if any, context exists? These questions arise with special poignancy in considering the secrets contained in an orphan album depicting life and friendship at a military academy in South Vietnam, which I found at a vintage shop during one of my research trips several years ago. Although some pages are missing photos, on the whole the album, which dates back to the 1950s, is remarkably intact and thus rare in Vietnam, where vintage shops more commonly sell loose photographs.

What makes it even rarer is its subject. Based on the dedications on the verso of some of the portraits included in its pages, I surmised that the album's maker was a man whom I will call Quy, who worked for the Government of Vietnam (GVN) as a member of the secret police: a position that, after the establishment of the communist state, meant that he was targeted for political reeducation (figure 4.4). Even though I was able to establish the first name of the photographer and owner of the album, nevertheless it remains an orphan object. Not only do we not know his full name, the very context in which I found the album, not to mention the information that it discloses about inconvenient loyalties, also attests to its disavowed status. The album's owner, I was fairly certain, did not want to be known, which is why I refer to him by a pseudonym. Understanding the meaning of an orphan album thus entails keeping its secrets instead of divulging them, a task made more urgent given that the Vietnamese state has politicized families during and after the war.[40] Attending to the orphan album's mode of assemblage provides a means of understanding how photography, understood as a social practice rather than simply an image object, defines and politicizes the idea of family in a process that might parallel yet contest state definitions, which reify cultures of memory in ways that are predicated on strategic forgetting.

Quy was a graduate of Thủ Đức Military Academy and eventually went on to serve as a second lieutenant (in some of the photos, he poses with a banded cap that denotes his rank). Located in northeast Saigon, Thủ Đức Military Academy was a school that the French established in 1951. Along with Nam Định, an officer reserve training school located in northern Vietnam, the mandate of the military academy at Thủ Đức was to train a colonial Vietnamese army. Although Nam Định closed after 1952, Thủ Đức continued to operate as an ARVN training school after the Viet Minh defeated the French in 1954 and the Geneva Accords split the nation into North Vietnam and South Vietnam. In the twenty-four years that it operated, the school produced an estimated forty thousand officers for the ARVN.

The album, which is bound by a loose cover of cracked leather emblazoned with a stylized knight astride his steed, memorializes the school and its fraternal community. Indeed, the front inside cover of the album bears the military academy's distinctive insignia of a blazing sword surrounded by a wreath (plate 12). These institutional markers clearly distinguish the album as a collection of school photos. It is no wonder that as an artifact which the Socialist Republic of Vietnam (SRV) would view as betraying enemy allegiance, the album ended up where it did, at a vintage shop in Ho Chi Minh City, presumably discarded and unhomed.

Despite its orphaned status, the album retains a rich amount of information, mainly through verso inscriptions in cursive handwriting that can still

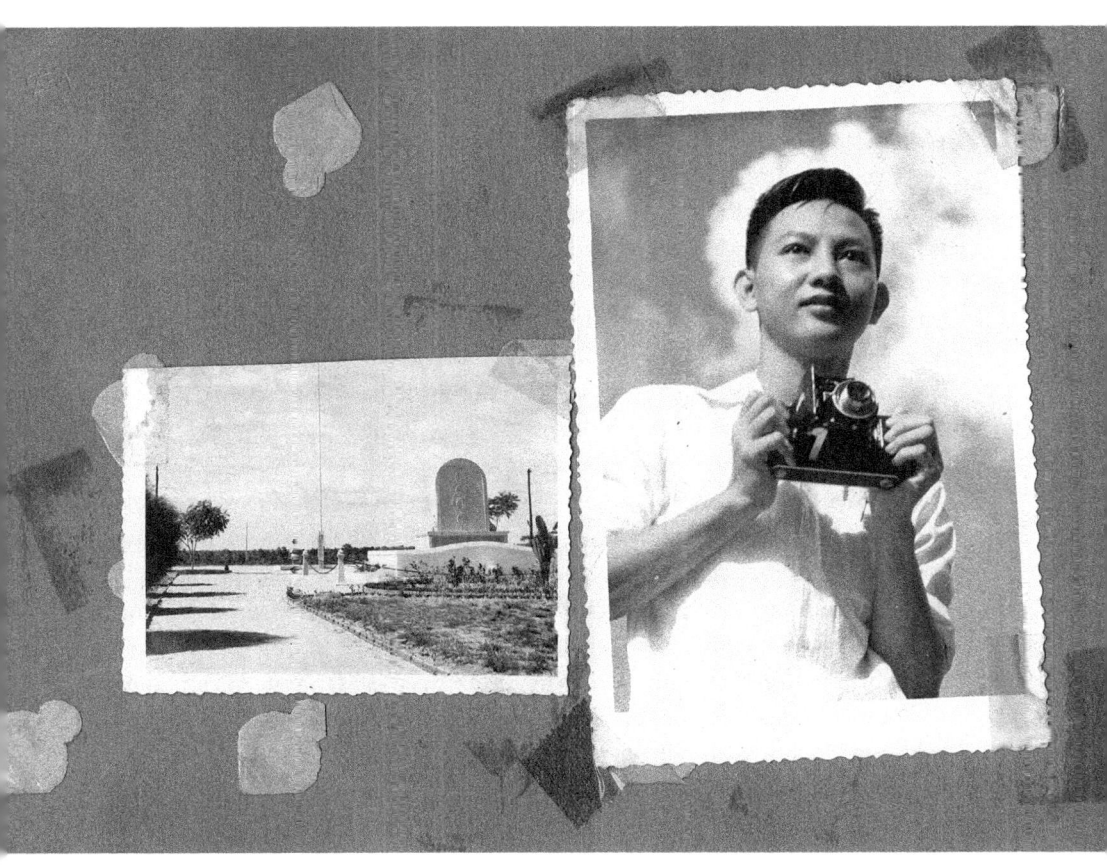

FIGURE 4.4 Creator of the Thủ Đức Military Academy photo album. Author collection.

be read because some photos are inserted between corner holders instead of glued onto cardboard pages. However, many other photos in the album have been fastened onto the pages with glue, so reading them would hasten their deterioration. Viewed thus, the act of preservation inevitably results in destruction, a paradox that Derrida describes as one of the symptoms of "archive fever."[41]

Quy had clearly decided to forgo a chronological arrangement, yet the inscriptions reveal just enough detail to allow for a sketch of this brief moment from his life, from his days as a schoolboy in Saigon; to holidays in his hometown in Bạc Liêu, in the Mekong Delta, where some of his friends sometimes visited him; through to his training in the military academy during critical years when the institution shifted from French to Vietnamese control; and on to his eventual position as department head of the Phòng Nhì, an organization that operated as a kind of secret police in Saigon.[42]

Conventionally, school photos conform to an institutional discourse about the state. They also function pedagogically by producing patriotic citizens. The Thủ Đức Military Academy album can be viewed in this way, but when we consider the broader context, wherein this artifact almost certainly circulated beyond this strictly institutional context, ultimately ending up on the open market and who knows where before that point, it would be reductive to consider this artifact in terms of a strictly defined genre. Moreover, what we assume counts as a family photograph, usually snapshots taken by amateurs and preserved in personal collections, might originate and circulate in other institutional contexts. Notably, school photos are usually produced by professional photographers within a public, institutional setting and may be assembled within this context to form a yearbook, as Marianne Hirsch and Leo Spitzer argue.[43] At the same time, school photos often enter the private sphere of the home, as happens when copies of school portraits are kept in personal albums. Therefore, although this anonymous album details the activities of officers in training and as they undertook their military duties, it may very well have been part of a personal collection, one stored in a private home before appearing once again in public as a vernacular object for sale in a street market. Similarly, viewers often approach family photography with preconceptions about family, assuming it is a fixed structure that lacks a history and is impervious to political influence. But as Kwon reminds us, the socialist reunification of Vietnam was a process that fundamentally politicized family, determining who counts—and who does not count—as part of a national family. A strictly generic approach risks eliding the ideological tensions that consumed the state of South Vietnam, not to mention the politicization of the category of family.

An artifact becomes a family album through its engagement with the idea of family. The care with which Quy assembled his companions' photos displays his closeness to these men. Together, the photos reveal Quy's sense of kinship with them. Regarding any preconceptions about what a family is—when we know that in this case the state has defined this term—and, for that matter, what a family photo looks like, the South Vietnamese military album unsettles these preconceptions. It belongs to the discursive mode that Wexler calls "domestic images." In her analysis of the role of domestic images in securing US imperialism, Wexler theorizes their function. Such images, she argues,

> may be—but need not be—representations of and for a so-called separate sphere of family life. Domestic images may also be configurations of familiar and intimate arrangements intended for the eyes of outsiders, the *heimlich* (private) as a kind of propaganda; or they may be metonymical references to unfamiliar arrangements, the *unheimlich* intended for domestic consumption. What matters is the use of the image to signify the domestic realm. The domestic realm can be figured as well by a battleship as by a nursery if that battleship . . . is known to be on a mission to redraw and then patrol the nation's boundaries, the sina qua non of the homeland.[44]

Whereas Wexler's study draws attention to the ways that white women photographers produce visions of "a peace that keeps the peace,"[45] thereby rendering invisible the violence of US imperial expansion, the South Vietnamese military album offers an intriguing gloss on her concept of domestic visions. Specifically, this album is a male record of domesticity, which through meticulous cutting, pasting, and annotation sought futilely to secure a homeland by representing a peace against the imminence of violence, which nevertheless inscribed itself on the surface of this record. Conventional definitions of family as a bond of biological or adoptive affiliation thus offer just one way of understanding the relationship between loved ones. Therefore, we should not understand this concept simply in terms of biological belonging but also as a photographic practice, one that normalizes and, as this orphan album of homosocial community shows, diverges from a nuclear norm.[46] The album does not signify family in a conventional sense; its sleeves contain only photos of men in training, on drills, and on leave, and omit pictures of bourgeois rites, women, and children. But when viewed closely, the album suggests a sense of militarized domesticity and homosocial kinship, queering notions of family.

The Thủ Đức Military Academy album chronicles five years of fraternal affiliation and homosocial community, with the earliest photo dated 1951, the year that the school opened, and the latest photo dated 1957. The photographs include deckle-edged studio portraits of uniformed officers, snapshots of men at target practice, mid-stride during drills, on furlough at tourist destinations within Vietnam and abroad in Europe and the United States, and at rest, embracing in bed in an expression of physically intimate communion, which is culturally acceptable among Vietnamese men but would be unusual in American contexts (figure 4.5).

In many cases it is hard to tell why certain photographs have been arranged together, only that great care went into these arrangements: some images have been cropped closely to focus on the men in them, others are grouped together in artful patterns, and in still others Qúy has clipped away backgrounds altogether, pasting precisely defined figures of the men themselves onto the cardboard album pages (figure 4.6). However, when we consider that these activities are all organized around their shared military training, the album evinces a form of visual kinship, developed, deepened, and dissolved as part of a story about a war that was then still unfolding. We can discern parts of this broader, patriotic war story by piecing together the album's personal portraits of fraternal affiliation—that is, by looking closely at the background of the photos, in the spaces between these photos, and even in the gaps of lustrous gilded photo corners that once held images that have either fallen out or been removed.

We can nevertheless discern the close connection between the men in the album through the ways they exchanged photos with each other, a practice that Quy honors by saving the images given him. On one object, a postcard produced by a studio in Phan Rang, a friend named Long writes that he sends his portrait "as a memento of those happy days training in Hàm Tân" (figure 4.7). Next to his neat signature, Long inscribes in fine black ink the date, 19/11, 1955. Below Long's inscription, however, someone—perhaps Qúy, although we cannot be sure—has added a note, using brown ink that bleeds slightly, which details the fate of the man in the photo. Only ten days after his photo was taken, we learn that Long "Died on November 29, 1955, at 10am, during a car accident on a business trip from Phan Thiết—Hàm Tân" (*Đã tử nạn ngày 29/11/55 trong khi đi công tác bằng ôtô 4/4 đường Phan Thiết—Hàm Tân lúc 10.00 giờ*). This one photograph thus has an ambiguous double meaning,

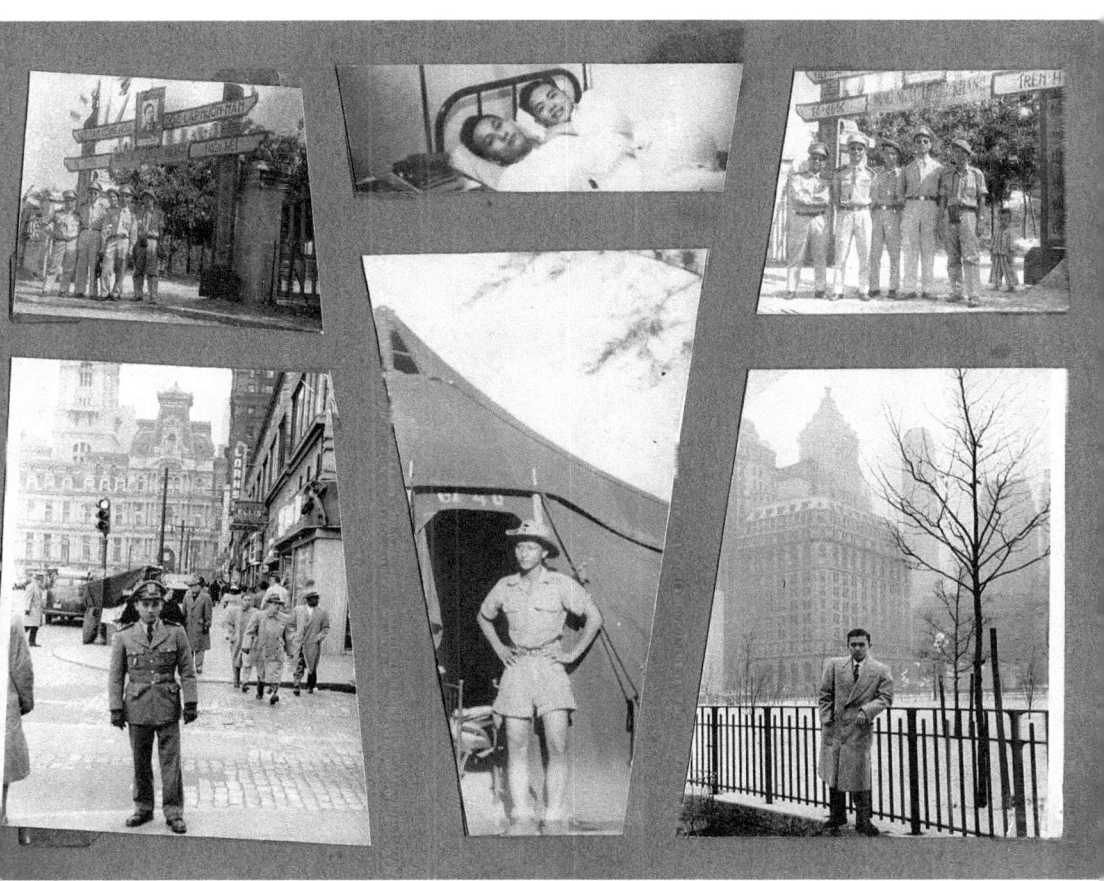

FIGURE 4.5 Fraternal intimacies at Thủ Đức Military Academy. Author collection.

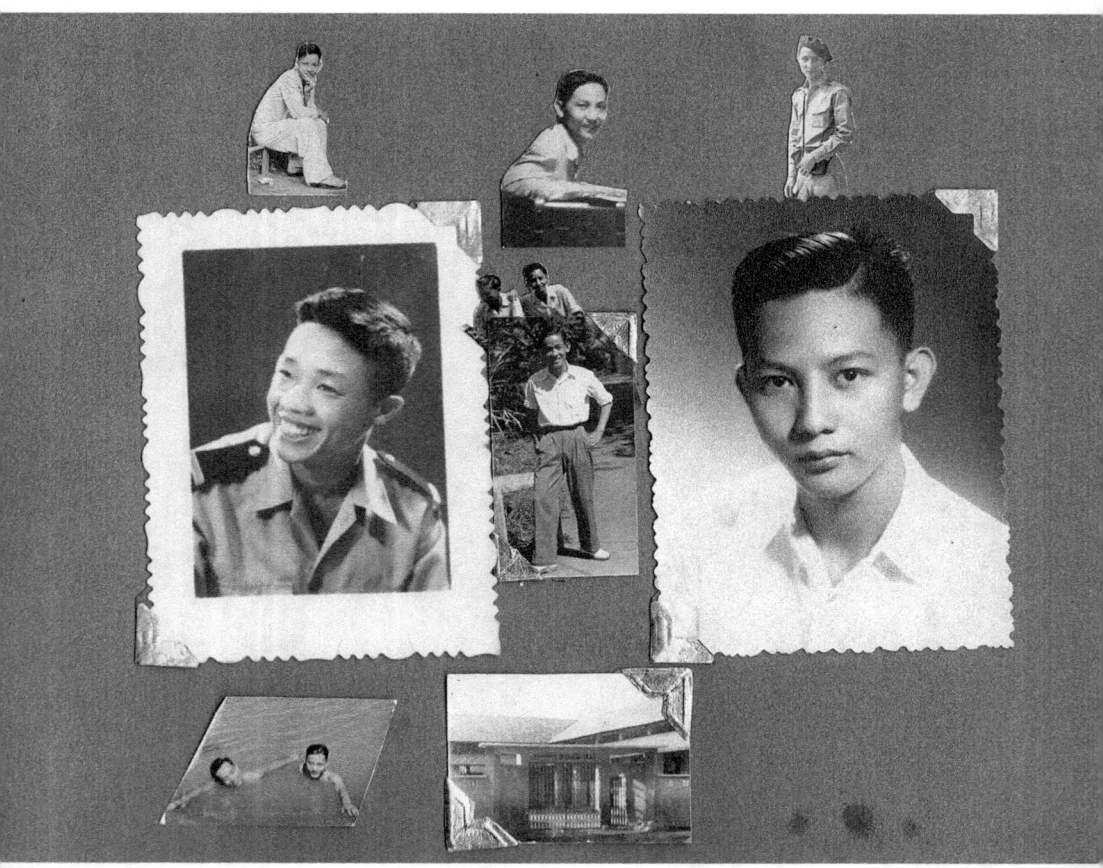

FIGURE 4.6 Page from Thủ Đức Military Academy photo album. Author collection.

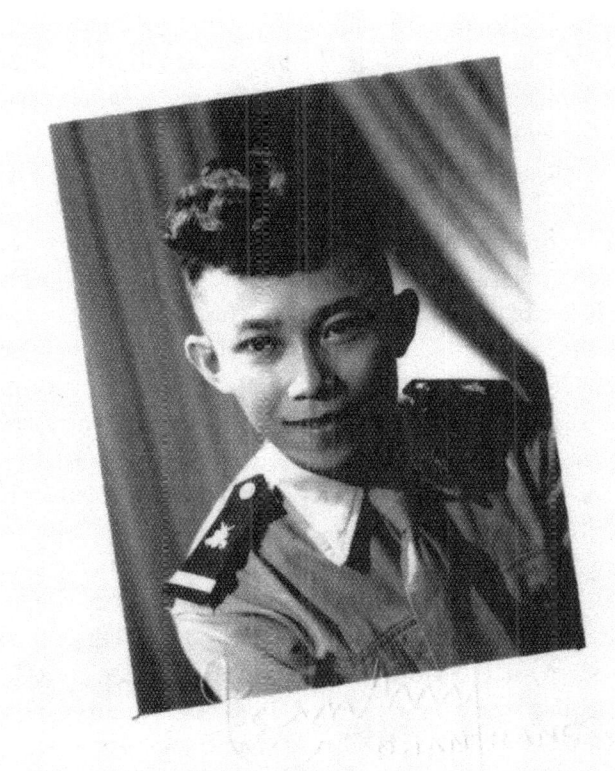

FIGURE 4.7 Mementos of training at Thủ Đức Military Academy, 1955. Author collection.

inscribed as it is by at least two hands, the sender and whomever was the final receiver. This second inscription is even more ambiguous because of its reference to "4/∠." Initially, I thought that this referred to the Peugeot 404, but it turns out this car model was first introduced in 1960. More likely, the numbers meant that all four passengers in the car died. Indeed, there is a third inscription, Hồ Toài 4.424, perhaps the name of the person who informed Qúy of Long's death, although if this is the case, it's strange that he should use a different pen to sign his name than what he used to describe the fate of the passengers in that car.[47] In 1955, according to the inscription, Quy lost at least one other friend, Toan, who died at a battle in Huế. Within the album, then, Quy gathered together his friends, some of whom would travel far and others he would never see again.

Yet the album can also be seen as anticipating disavowal as the ultimate gesture in the face of loss. One photograph from the album seems to eschew memorialization altogether in favor of excision. In a painted photograph of a lone cadet walking in the distance in a public garden on the grounds of the academy, Qúy wrote this inscription: "The Vietnamese flag flutters crisply on a clear day" (*Ngọn cờ VN đang hùng dủng phât phổ, trên nền trời trong sáng của buổi minh đầy hứa hẹn*) (plate 13). Dated March 4, 1954, the photo seems to have been taken less than two months before the French finally surrendered to the Viet Minh at Điện Biên Phủ, on May 7, 1954. Significantly, the photo has been cut in a precise line so that there is no sign of the flag described in the inscription: the cropping of the image, which presumably took place after the defeat of the French, or perhaps even later, after the Fall of Saigon, marks the next chapter in Vietnam's history. The unseen hand that erased the flag of an older colonial order from this photo anticipates a political erasure, visually reinforcing the divided state of the nation, when new flags for North Vietnam and South Vietnam replaced the one removed here. Moreover, this act was done so neatly that viewers glancing only cursorily might easily miss it altogether.

However, the very context in which this object was found, not to mention the information that it discloses about inconvenient loyalties, attests to its repudiated status. The album exemplifies what Eve Tuck and Wayne Yang, in their call for a pedagogy of refusal, evocatively describe as "an objecting object."[48] Reconstructing the ties that bound these men to one another means reckoning with and doing justice to what Martin Manalansan characterizes as the quintessentially queer stuff of archives: its "mess."[49] Discerning the meanings of an album and its mode of assemblage thus means attending to its self-unraveling, its willful obfuscations and disidentification, its disassembly and its dissemblance. Understanding the meaning of this discarded and unclaimed album entails reckoning with mess without seeking to clean it up, protecting—even redacting—its secrets instead of divulging them. The glimpses of fraternal affiliation provided by the album activate the potential for another form of kinship, but one that must confront the limits of its irrevocable estrangements.

By looking closely, we can discern how a fraternal community exchanged and preserved photographs to connect with one another and how, through collecting these materials into an album, one man visually constructed queer kinships with his brothers-at-arms in response to the demise of colonialism and in anticipation of the loss of the nation of South Vietnam. As a whole, the album provides a picture of masculinity that the communist state disavowed.

In its carefully cropped and pieced-together pages, this beautiful album offers a space to linger on male bodies at work, at play, at rest, and in service to a nation long since lost. It would be reductive to label the album as produced solely within such institutions as school or nation. Nor is this just about queer kinship. The album broaches all of these issues; it is more than the sum of its parts. Indeed, it is perhaps fitting that these attachments should come in the form of an orphan album, for the fraternal love glued and removed from its pages has been estranged from the state's metanarrative of family unification. The gaps between photos in the albums, and in the empty spaces where photos were once placed, provide us a glimpse, perhaps just as evocative as the images that remain, of the men who fought for the ARVN and who have been disowned from mainstream histories.

THE ART OF RECOLLECTION

The work of Dinh Q. Lê, a diasporic Vietnamese artist now based in Ho Chi Minh City, further grapples with the epistemological challenges that orphan images pose in reckoning with the aftermath of war.[50] In so doing Lê contributes to an important thread in contemporary art, which meditates on the possibility for transitional justice in the aftermath of mass violence, particularly in work by Christian Boltanski and others. Lê is a renowned queer diasporic Vietnamese contemporary artist born in Hà Tiên in southern Vietnam. When he was ten years old, his family fled Vietnam as refugees by boat and ultimately resettled in the United States.

Lê first made a splash with a series called *From Vietnam to Hollywood* (2003–5), which employs "photo-weaving," a technique that sutures images to create a montage juxtaposing spectacular pop cultural images with iconic documentary photographs of the war in Vietnam. This technique also contrasts a perspective on the war that privileges American experiences against that of Vietnamese survivors who are compelled to live in the shadow of these images but whose experiences are not captured in them.

His work with the less familiar, the unspectacular, and the quotidian provides an even more potent rejoinder to the nuances obscured by the privileging of spectacular representations of war. Since 1998, Lê has been working on a trilogy of installations that feature family photographs, objects that fascinate him because he lost all of his own photographs in the course of his family's forced migration. This is a side of the war and its aftermath that receives short shrift in popular film and mainstream photojournalism. The quiet mood of family photographs sharply contrasts with the sensationalism of these popular images.

When Vietnam opened up to visitors in the early 1990s, Lê eagerly returned. One of the first things he did was scour vintage stores, hoping to find the photos that he had lost. Although he did not unearth his own family's photos, he stumbled on thousands of other family photos, but they were orphaned images that lacked context, having ended up in the open market, he speculates, because they exposed bourgeois indulgence, Western influence, and "disloyalty," inconvenient if not dangerous under the new political regime.

In *Mot Coi Di Ve* (1998), he adapted his method of photo-weaving by stringing them together to form curtains or screens, which visitors see—but also see through—in a negative space that conjures the sense of unfillable absence (plate 14). The title of this installation is taken from the name of a popular Vietnamese song, sometimes translated as "A Place to Leave from and Return To." Lê also translates the song as "Spending One's Life Trying to Find One's Way Home." The varied translations underscore the uncertainty, indeed, impossibility, of locating home, as art historian Kate Palmer Albers points out. From Vietnamese to English—a shift from Vietnam to somewhere else—one stays on a path that inevitably diverges and recedes. This installation establishes links between images as well as their disconnections. Although the found photos suggest that one can still perceive that which was left behind, the gaps, through which only the gallery's blank white wall is visible, reveal that one can never fully return. These gaps are a reminder of the recalcitrance of orphan images. As such, the exhibition forms a fitting vision of the diasporic subject's predicament of displacement, all the more poignant given that Lê has chosen to return to and settle in Vietnam. The installation also provides a concrete form for contemplating loss, a phenomenon compounded by the fact that, as Albers reminds us, the first version of this installation was stolen from its storage space.[51]

Erasure (2011) is the second installation in his trilogy after Lê remade *Mot Coi Di Ve* to replace the lost (stolen) work. A work commissioned by the Sherman Gallery in Sydney, Australia, the installation features a boat wrecked amid a sea of discarded photos, alongside the remains of a hull and the flotsam and jetsam of torn jeans and ragged shirts (plate 15). Visible yet irretrievable, the photos form a broken path that links overseas Vietnamese to dispersed families, the textures of fabrics a complement to the curled edges of the found photos, so that the combination of paper and cloths emphasize tactility: touching that evokes feeling.[52] Removed from their albums and bearing scant if any identifying features, these are orphan images. To whom do these photos belong?

To address these questions, *Erasure* invites visitors to witness what Lê describes as the "liquidation" of personal memory, a term that plays with the dual sense of the waters of oceanic passages, a conduit for survival and a means of destruction. Visitors in the show are invited to make their voyage across this chaotic swirl of images churned up in the course of violent passages. Just as significantly, *Erasure* is an archiving project. The impersonal whir of a digital computer scanner alerts visitors to the storing and ordering of each of these orphan images, unidentified and discarded, a process that also transforms the very objects being preserved, in so doing smoothing out the affective textures of memory. Prints become pixels, the forgotten digitized, memory externalized. They are uploaded to an online database that complements the installation, one that draws on crowd-sourcing from an international community, but most likely comprising the overseas Vietnamese, to identify and claim what was left behind.[53] Through the overlapping parts of the installation—contemplation of found photos and digital compilation of them for the purposes of identification—*Erasure* merges the act of collecting into archiving. The installation begins as a collection, but in the digital form that it continues to take after it has been disassembled, *Erasure* preserves itself as an archive. In this manner these found photos—foundlings or orphan images—are claimed.

As such, for the Vietnamese diaspora the acts of collecting and archiving can be seen as symbolically defiant and reparative gestures, whether in the wake of the Vietnamese state's bifurcation of family loyalties in the postwar period, which makes the very preservation of kinship ties a suspicious and punishable act, or against the conditions of statelessness that would eradicate subjectivity, ironically through the production of ID photos. This process of collecting and archiving attends to the nuances between different archival structures and exposes crucial distinctions between the violence of official history and the erasures of personal memory. These diasporic Vietnamese projects suggest that orphan images should be brought home to a collection, if not an archive in its official sense; at the very least, the collections reveal the conditions that have made the quest to come home impossible. The "orphan" is a figure that not only connotes the literal photographs from family albums that were discarded in desperate haste but also symbolizes the actual family members lost in the course of the journey, either because they could not come along or because they did not survive. In this sense the embrace of the orphan image within collecting projects initiated by members of the Vietnamese diaspora can be seen as a gesture of reparation, if not repatriation, through symbolic acts of reunion.

By encouraging collective participation in this action through a call to identify these orphan images, no matter how haphazardly and impartially this call is answered, Lê stretches the frame of family photos even further. Although family members would presumably be the ones to identify and claim the photos included in his digital archive, this may not always be the case. Apparently, others can claim the photograph too. There is the photographer, who is seldom pictured, not to mention the unrelated person, the stranger, who sometimes appears in the picture. *Erasure* ends up challenging commonplace definitions of family by leaving open the possibility of multiple claims from unexpected sources—by allowing for what Nayan Shah calls, in a different context, "stranger intimacy."[54] Whereas Shah's specific concern is with the intersecting histories of immigration, race, and queer sexuality in the North American West, the concept of stranger intimacy captures the alien and queer affiliations and disaffiliations invoked by this installation.

Indeed, orphan images disclose little about themselves. What we know comes largely by way of legal debates that refer to them as "orphan works," about which the critical problem concerns the challenge that uncertain provenance poses for determining copyright.[55] In response to one of the important questions raised by this installation—to whom do these images belong?—the field of copyright law would likely focus on the identity of rights holders. However, as Campt reminds us, this term connotes something else for the broader field of visual studies, where scholars working with film consider orphan images, those works of unknown provenance, as an epistemological challenge.[56] Following the logic of this second approach, such images belong in the repository of an archive where they can be seen so that what was lost may be found and made known.

Yet when it comes to the visual culture of the Black diaspora, Campt finds this promise of legibility more disquieting than reassuring. That orphan images belong to no one is precisely the point for Campt. She insists on the importance of "fugitivity" for defying knowledge regimes and their associated power, a concept that has special resonance when it comes to scholars of the Black diaspora, who often grapple with the lingering legacy of slavery or, as Sharpe memorably puts it, life in the wake. (For Campt, the concept of fugitivity takes up the figure of the fugitive and her revolt against slavery, a topic also explored in works by Fred Moten and Saidiya Hartman.)[57] Orphan images need not be found in the sense celebrated within film studies, Campt argues, when the condition of loss offers the occasion for contesting the epistemological demands of these regimes. Accordingly, archives can be coercive because they threaten to destroy, or at least neutralize, the waywardness of orphan images.

However, orphan images acquire yet another meaning when it comes to first- and second-wave members of the Vietnamese diaspora. In a context where the state's politicization of families results in their bifurcation, defiance takes the form of collecting and preserving. In short, Campt's concept of fugitivity cannot simply be transposed onto the Vietnamese diaspora, whose transnational experiences as refugees are shaped not by the specter of slavery, as is often the case for the Black diaspora, but rather, as I have shown, by the politicization of family in the aftermath of war. Orphan images provide an intriguing glimpse into this process of politicization.

Who are the families that are pictured in Lê's digital *Erasure* archive? They may be strangers to the artist, but they are the ones he came upon and included when he sought yet could not find his own. They are the ones viewers could claim, although they may not recognize who is pictured in each family photo. Here, where Lê's digital archive opens up to anyone who fulfills the requirement of registering and logging into the website where it is stored, the notion of a stranger intimacy conjured in this way reframes, indeed, queers family. This archiving project experiments with a form of kinship that extends beyond biology, that effectively queers family, in the sense that Shah's concept of stranger intimacy does.

The word *adoption* does not explicitly appear in the *Erasure* installation, but this suggestive metaphor is nevertheless also implied through Lê's handling of orphan images. I would like to pause briefly to discuss the metaphor of adoption, to reflect on its significance in light of debates on transnational and transracial adoptions, a practice that emerged with the end of World War II and accelerated in the aftermath of the Korean War. For critics in adoption studies, this practice generally assigns the burden of reproduction to developing nations in the South and confers moral authority to wealthier nations in the North in their role as benevolent rescuers while obscuring the material histories that have forced impoverished women to relinquish their children.[58] (However, South Korea's central role in the geopolitics of transnational adoptions troubles this bipolar division of global North and South, which nevertheless persists and which I employ advisedly.) Such Cold War structures of feeling, with their politics of pity, have delineated what Alice Toby Volkman calls "new geographies of kinship," in effect, producing, as David Eng points out, a multitude of diasporas that include the orphans and refugees spotlighted in Lê's installation.[59] Although these scholars have focused on power asymmetries between the adopting nations of the North and the "abandoning" nations of the South, few studies have remarked on how Cold War structures of feeling have informed the practice of intranational adoptions. Even fewer have considered the extent to which these new diasporic figures overlap. In the context of the Vietnamese diaspora, for example, the notorious Operation Babylift, which entailed the removal of nearly two thousand Vietnamese babies during the fall of Saigon in 1975, effectively merged two figures: these so-called orphans, many of them still having living parents, are at the same time refugees. How might these entanglements deepen, and how might they unravel, if refugees are the ones who adopt displaced children?

To my knowledge, however, this question has yet to be taken up in a thorough way. In *Erasure* Lê addresses it in an oblique and symbolic manner without providing a resolution. By foregrounding orphan images as the remnants of broken families and inviting viewers, by turns, to grasp the immensity of photos en masse and reflect on the singularity of the faces that peer out from each of these photos contained in the digital archive, the installation provides a means, however messy and uncertain, of visually charting these new geographies of kinship.

Still, Lê's installation offers the clearest expression of a compulsion to collect, a compulsion remarkable precisely because it is manifested in a number of collecting projects initiated by many overseas Vietnamese, projects that aspire to assemble archives. So pronounced is this compulsion to collect that arguably it evinces a desire for visual recollection, a term I invoke deliberately to echo the "burning desire" that Geoffrey Batchen contends lies at the heart of photography's origins.[60] Although Joseph Nicéphore Niépce was the first to voice this sentiment of a burning desire, Batchen shows that because it was shared by many, the origins of photography cannot be attributed solely to a single inventor and original patent registered in that storied year of 1839, as history books continue to avow, but rather marks the fulfillment of a broadly shared longing, the culmination of collective ambitions. Although Batchen's account of the burning desire for photography at its inception in nineteenth-century Europe seems distant from the experiences of the Vietnamese diaspora in the last few decades of the twentieth century, these projects share similar collective impulses. The practice of collecting merges, in the ways I have shown, into archiving to become more than just method; they emerge as vital themes in the works.[61]

This desire to collect matters to the Vietnamese diaspora because family photos have often been overlooked in official institutions. Mainstream institutions in Canada and the United States—two of the nations that, per capita, welcomed the greatest numbers of Vietnamese refugees—have only recently started to collect vernacular artifacts such as family photographs.[62] In Vietnam, where public discussion of the refugee crisis is still discouraged, archives likewise focus on documentary photography and emphasize revolutionary struggles and socialist ways of seeing; they do not, to my knowledge, include family photos. The dearth of vernacular artifacts in institutions is hardly surprising, given the function of national archives as a repository of official state history. Whereas Marita Sturken's case study of US public memory emphasizes the points of contact between personal memories of family photos and institutions of public history, this intersection is the exception rather than the rule.[63] For the Vietnamese diasporic family, such personal images seldom turn up in the public record. Accordingly, the differences between personal memory and national history can be critical, especially when considered in light of Kwon's reminder of the importance of the former in posing a direct, if subtle, challenge to the latter. The dearth of vernacular artifacts in national archives, coupled with the destruction and abandonment of family photos, intensifies the Vietnamese diaspora's archival desire. Even when other institutions are open to the inclusion of family photos, the two should not merely be merged without attending to their differences. On the one hand, by collecting family photos these diasporic initiatives compensate for the limits of state archives; on the other hand, the projects offer a critique of the politics of erasure associated with official archives.

This context helps explain the urgency behind digital projects by diasporic artists. Lê's *Erasure* promises to supply these missing pictures but in a paradoxical format: as the title suggests, the preservation of these photographs implies an inevitable disappearance and destruction, especially with respect to their tactile dimensions and the affective resonances of this sense of touch. Significantly, the title of Lê's installation emphasizes how, in the face of loss, a sense of community is established through a collective act of seeking and finding its own images, however difficult they are to recognize, however impossible they are to claim fully. These projects supplement—even as they are shaped in tension with—state archives, which have been averse, for one reason or another, to collecting family photos.

In his third installation made from family photographs, *Crossing the Farther Shore* (2014, 2017), Lê returns to the techniques of his earlier work, in particular *Mot Coi Di Ve*, with its screens woven out of thousands of family photos. In *Crossing the Farther Shore*, however, Lê weaves the screens formed from these individual artifacts together into sculptural pieces (plate 16). The physical footprint of the installation reminds us of the spaces of absence. Suspended from the ceiling, these pieces form cubes that resemble refugee camp enclosures. Visitors can also look closely upon the pieces as individual photographs in addition to sculptures. These are sculptures that are hollow: between their enclosures there is space, occasionally strewn with snapshots, just out of the visitor's reach and impossible to see clearly. Just as the space within the cubes is empty—except for the family photos that form them and that, in a sense, fill them—the spaces *between* the cubes are empty and await being filled by the wandering visitor.

Visitors who make their way among these structures are struck as much by what is invisible as they are by the installation's almost luminous display. A close look at the individual photographs shows that some of them are turned backward. Unless viewers touch such a photograph, in violation of a cardinal precept of galleries and museums, they cannot actually see it. One of the cubes is even woven entirely out of prints that have only the blank verso visible.

Crossing the Farther Shore hinges on the tension between disclosure and refusal: it shows us the presence of photographs only to prevent us from seeing them fully. The family photographs also hint at stories that are told only as fragments when they are told at all. The backs of many of these images are inscribed with cursive writing, some of it unreadable, which reveals dates and names, enigmatic messages to long-lost loved ones. If viewers listen to family photos, they might hear this as the pre-1975 past speaking to the dispersed Vietnamese diaspora in the present. In Lê's hands the diasporic community speaks back to this past as well. With the help of his assistants, he inscribed on the surface of some of these family photographs excerpts from oral history interviews with Vietnamese refugees who have resettled in the United States as well as passages from the *Tale of Kieu*, a nineteenth-century epic poem about the travails of a woman whose story of suffering and survival is widely seen as a national allegory, which has acquired heightened meaning for the diasporic community brought together by their grief over a nation that no longer exists.

The installation imparts a partial vision of the past, a pre-1975 period before the fall of Saigon. One need not be familiar with this past to be affected by the poignancy of the plight of displaced families; *Crossing the Farther Shore* resonates with most visitors, regardless of their personal histories. Who among us has not had pages torn from our own family albums, family members curiously absent from album pages, or strangers appearing far too often for it to be a coincidence? These experiences are arguably transcultural. Yet the installation resonates in particular ways for the Vietnamese diaspora.

Walking through the show with my own family, for example, I was struck with how my parents viewed the photographs. We paused together to point out details, such as the uniform of unknown soldiers, evidence that they fought for the wrong side and reason enough for the photograph to be tossed away. My parents saw in the photographs signs of a life that no longer exists, the nation of South Vietnam, which crumbled in 1975, and they recog-

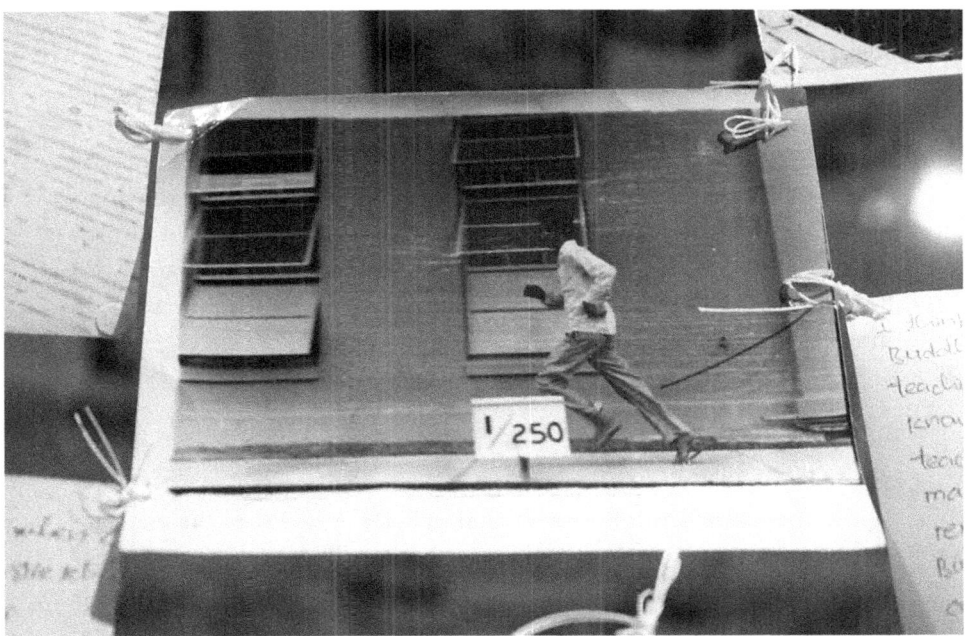

FIGURE 4.8 Detail from *Crossing the Farther Shore*, 2014. Dinh Q. Lê.

nized landmarks, school uniforms, details meaningless to me and, I suspect, to scores of other visitors. In a way, they saw themselves in these photographs. More than this, they felt a kinship with the strangers whose portraits they looked upon with wonder and wistfulness, strangers whom they will never know but might have once known.

I linger in particular on one photo, which Lê stitched to others to form one of his sculptural cubes and which I had overlooked on numerous occasions (figure 4.8).[64] The photo is unremarkable: a number, a figure. It certainly doesn't look like a typical family photograph, but it somehow ended up in the stacks that he used for his installation, suggesting that it had been pulled from a family collection, although its origins may never be known. Within the context of the show this ordinary image—a shot testing for shutter speed—provides an intriguing self-reflection about photography itself. I marvel at this mundane photo of movement suspended in time and space (four milliseconds to be precise) because it seems to me to reach back from the past. When stitched to a structure where the present speaks back to an estranged past, this photograph seems to attest, in an understated way, to the power and poignancy of photography and its capacity to thread together, as Lê does in this installation, the gaps between time, to evoke a sense of relationality as well as to reflect on the impossibility of ever fully filling in these gaps.

Crossing the Farther Shore is a compelling installation that elicits intense emotional attachments between far-flung communities that may never meet; it provides a form of affiliation to navigate the treacherous divide of time and space. In this way the installation also disrupts the "straight" or "chromonormative" temporalities critiqued by Elizabeth Freeman.[65] Perhaps not surprisingly, Lê considers these orphaned images as a surrogate family, a family that he finds and that he creates, through a weaving of impossible connections, an intimacy among strangers.

THE FAMILY CAMERA NETWORK

When I started exploring the role of family photos in mediating the Vietnamese diaspora, these collecting projects seemed to offer intriguing resolutions to the limits imposed by the narrow ideological interests of national and state archives; my subsequent work on the Family Camera Network, a collaborative research project, provided further insights. This project undertakes the work of collecting family photographs and the stories about them, recognizing that community archives often do not have the resources to ensure long-term preservation and that mainstream institutions are only beginning to consider seriously the significance of vernacular materials. Our methodology was simple: we wanted to preserve what, for us, was an integral part of family photography—the stories behind them, although we respect the fact that sometimes these stories cannot be told. This is why we combined the methodologies of oral history with visual analysis, understanding that each of them had their strengths but also their limitations. For example, oral historians draw on family photos as aide-mémoire and illustrations of life stories for the ends of photo elicitation, and seldom as integral aspects of the stories themselves.[66] Conversely, art historians and critics in photography studies have acknowledged the oral roots of family photos and are starting to reflect on the sonic dimensions of visual culture, but most critics appear to focus on privately held collections, as I have done in a limited way here, no doubt because these are the most readily available images that provide any sort of context. The stray domestic images that surface in existing archives often lack this crucial context, or they are orphan images that keep their secrets close, even if these images found themselves in the open market, whether on eBay, where a large number of personal items end up for sale to the highest bidder, or gathering dust in cluttered vintage shops. So, for us, collecting required from the outset the tasks of collecting family photos along with the stories behind them. These oral histories may not tell us everything there is to know about the photos, but they offered more than we had to start with.[67]

Although the Family Camera Network is concerned with how family photographs mediate experiences of migration in a broad sense, stories from Vietnamese diasporic communities form a key part of the archive. Family photos shared by members of these communities shed new light on major themes in these stories and prompt us to further rethink our very assumptions about family photos.

Dana Tran, for example, began the story of her family's passage from Vietnam with a printed copy that, she admitted, was not actually her photo. As her grown daughter, Anne, asked, "Is it all right if we use photos that don't belong to us to tell our story?" When I replied that I was interested in their relationship to images, they explained why they started here, with what turned out to be an iconic image of a chaotic group of people clamoring to board a helicopter in Saigon, the very image that this book started with. Mrs. Tran said she found the photo on the internet around April 2015, roughly the fortieth anniversary of the end of the war in Vietnam, and asked her daughter to print it out for her. "No, we aren't in this picture, but we were on one of those helicopters," she explained.[68] She had a premonition then that the end was coming and urged her extended family to head to Saigon, where her wealthy in-laws bribed one of the attendants, who helped them jump the queue. She had rushed out without wearing proper shoes and with her young daughter in her arms, and she had barely remembered to bring along a pillow to comfort the toddler. For decades, the image of that day remained seared in her mind. It is a historical photo, but when she laid out selections from her personal album across her daughter's dining table, it is clear that she has claimed it as her own family photo.

When the extended Lu family left Vietnam in 1977, they boarded different boats at different times; they reasoned this strategy would ensure the survival of the family line, for surely not all of the boats would sink. The two young sons, Binh and Hon, went with their parents, who packed rations of food and water and some gold bars, which they hid among their clothes. Everything else was left behind, including one of the family's priceless treasures, their personal photographs. Mrs. Luong Lu-Thai was an avid amateur photographer who, during the war, extensively documented her family life in Nha

Trang. So devoted was she to her hobby of capturing images of her family that one of her treasured wedding gifts was a Super 8 camera. Her husband, a machinist who sold and repaired scooters and cars, had numerous US military contacts and access to coveted foreign supplies sold in the PX, which enabled him to keep his wife well stocked with film. He was even able to acquire color film, a rarity in the early 1960s, and arranged for his military acquaintances to develop her color film during their furloughs in Thailand because it could not be easily developed in Vietnam. Given how much her photographs meant to her, it must have pained Luong to part with them, so it was not surprising that shortly after she arrived safely in Hong Kong and started settling with her husband and sons into the refugee hotel they shared with about two hundred other families, she wrote to her parents, who were preparing to leave Vietnam themselves. In this letter she implored them to arrange for safe passage for her albums also. In response, her father replied in a letter to Hong Kong, written in Chinese and highly coded so as to evade state surveillance, warning his daughter against writing again, for they would, in his guarded language, see each other again shortly. With his letter, he enclosed copies of his identity photos for her to safeguard in anticipation of the day when he would need to prove his refugee claim. In keeping with the family's strategy of survival through separation, her parents boarded a boat while the nearly dozen albums dispersed on just as many different boats.

The photos survived the journey, but her parents did not. In a bitter twist, Mrs. Thai-Lu was reunited with her precious photos at around the same time she realized that she had become orphaned. The Lus are unusual: unlike many Vietnamese refugees, they have an extensive family record. In the following years, as the family unsettled and resettled, the photos journeyed with them. Mrs. Thai-Lu pored over her growing collection—and growing and dispersing extended family—singling out the images that her children describe as "mythical photos," the special ones where they appear as a single unit. These mythical photos she reprinted and laminated, taking care as she did so to write the year of the original print, the year of reprinting, and the number of copies she made. Then, her task done, she sent these mythical photos out into the world, mailing them, one by one, to her family members in Canada and the United States, calling, indeed conjuring them, together through this act of visual recollection.

The relationship between losing photos and finding them may not be as simple as it might seem in the collecting projects surveyed here. I began to grasp just how vexed these layers of complexity were during research visits to Vietnam, inspired in part by Dinh Q. Lê's work. In the course of these visits, I eagerly traced not the trail of visual artifacts churned up in this installation but Lê's very steps through Ho Chi Minh City to one of the sources of this work. It led to a street well-known for junk and antique shops filled with sundry bric-a-brac: lacquerware, communist kitsch, and photographs. This is where Lê found the snaps and studio portraits for his installation.

This was where I found both less and more than I looked for, in the form of stacks of photos ripped from family albums. The prospect of flipping through thousands of them, portraits of men, women, and children of a bygone era, coiffed, preening, smiling—in search of what and to what end?—was too overwhelming to contemplate. A cursory review confirmed what I suspected: few had any writing or dates. Nonetheless, a portion of them, despite this frustrating lack of context, hinted at the reasons for their abandonment: men and women wearing the wrong uniform, posing with white friends who were likely American, or having indulged in bourgeois amusements, such as travel to a foreign country. In a nation where public discussion of the flag of the defeated South Vietnam is forbidden, it is little wonder that those stained with such signs of misalliance should have surrendered them.

Despite the fascinating secrets hinted at in each of these single photos, as a critic of visual culture I share the preference of galleries and museums for family albums over single photos because of the former's potential to disclose more historical information, even as I am mindful of the power wielded by these national institutions. A family album is like a personal micro-archive. A collection of albums promises to hold a wealth of historical information. Removed from their albums, photographs lose much of their value, or so I thought.

I wanted to know: what happened to the albums? The shopkeepers explained that no albums existed and that the images were already "orphaned"— already torn from their albums and, to follow this metaphor fully, disowned by their families They insisted that no one sold intact albums.

On my last day in the city, however, I stumbled on a treasure trove: a shop that stored, in its dark display cases, several albums. After I flipped through some of them, the owner said she had heaps more at her house on the outskirts of the city, if I was willing to brave a scooter ride through the snarl of rush-hour traffic. She read my excitement in my trembling hands. At her house, my host, whom I will call Mai, led me up narrow stairs to her covered rooftop where they were indeed piled amid rusted lamp bases, dusty scrapbooks of American pinups, and junked math exercise books. There were dozens of them, some sticky, a few falling apart, others well preserved.

Many of the albums were empty, however. It turns out Mai and her husband also plundered the albums in response to customers' demands. Anticipating that someone like me would come along, they leave some untouched. But they take most of them apart. These customers are, apparently, researchers who are keen to look at evolving hairstyles, dress styles, and body shapes. They use the photos for histories, expositions, and exhibitions. The photos were valuable for the information they provided to these researchers. They meant something else for the shopkeepers. In a savvy response to this demand, they had determined that the photos were more valuable by the piece than when collected within albums.[69]

Still, I could not help wondering what value that photos of anonymous people—someone else's family and not one's own—could have to anyone? When I began my research, I believed that the value of photos lay in the connections between them; torn from the context of their albums, the prospect of deciphering the photos' meanings is daunting, a problem that Lê's work seeks to overcome. Then again, perhaps all who are on the hunt, whether to satisfy intellectual curiosity, to sate a visual longing, or to collect for its own acquisitive sake, are struck by archive fever. My training directs me to archives. Yet my brief adventure suggests that sometimes one produces the archives one looks for.

I close with an anecdote that reveals the other side of this search. Although the diaspora's desires are decipherable, I was surprised, but should not have been, that those who had been left behind, so to speak, also had their own desires. On this trip to Vietnam I was told that a famous artist paid around $50 USD per kilogram for the photos he used in his installation. Was it Lê, I wondered? I have yet to ask him. But what I do know is that this is a reasonable price when compared to the current market value of American GI photo albums on eBay, which is close to $300 each. The business of war memorabilia is thriving. By contrast, whereas fewer people want Vietnamese albums, demand has nevertheless been strong enough to keep Mai and her fellow shopkeepers busy. For such bulk orders, Mai and her husband spent hours ripping and tearing. Archival desire, Derrida reminds us, is a paradox: reckoning with the losses of the past, this desire is propelled by a sense of futurity;

keen to preserve, it inevitably destroys.[70] Yet the seeming "triumph" of capitalism represented in the market for memorabilia can also be seen as a rejoinder to the Vietnamese state's earnest attempts to construct a unified national history, one that disregards the partial visual narratives on display in vintage shops for those who wish to look and are willing to pay.[71] In the late-socialist marketplace, everything is for sale, even, perhaps especially, artifacts of a side all but extinguished from history. Ironically, the state's shift to late socialism has commodified war images, even as it makes newly visible images that align with the state's official history. The shaping of an archive through the collecting of family photographs also entails the shaping of communities—of diasporic Vietnamese and those entrepreneurs who, it turns out, are not quite left behind but are rather keen to forge ahead.

In a forward-looking Vietnam where locals tend to favor the new over the old, entrepreneurs such as Mai make a living feeding the diaspora's hunger for the discarded, disassembling and reassembling the archives it desires. These savvy entrepreneurs thus fully embrace Đổi Mới by providing the images that the Vietnamese diaspora—me included—want to see.

Yet this entrepreneurial spirit of late socialism quickly exhausts itself. In my last trip to Vietnam I ventured again to this shop but found myself circling the block, sure that it existed but uncertain where it stood exactly, only to be told by a neighboring shopkeeper that its owners had quit; Mai was nowhere to be found. The rents were too high; the price fetched by these artifacts was too low. These are communities entangled around the photographs that they by turns take apart, conjure up, and resignify for each other. The challenge, from beginning to end, is knowing where and how to look.

On my first trip to Vietnam, in 2005, we reunited with relatives whom we'd left behind. They said it was as though we'd never left. But before this trip, I could not picture these faraway aunts, uncles, and cousins, even though over the years they'd sent letters and, occasionally, photographs to my parents. So when at last I visited with my parents, it was unsurprising that after paying respects at the ancestral altar and my grandparents' graves, my relatives should pull out their family albums.

In the albums kept in Sadec, my mother's hometown, I didn't glimpse much of the war. Such an omission was understandable given the state's politicization of family. My grandfather, who went missing in 1961, appears in some of the pages, smiling and handsome, but with no visible sign of his military service. My grandmother, who worked at a women's prison in Bien Hoa, about an hour's drive southwest of Ho Chi Minh City, poses elegantly, her hair coiffed perfectly, her dress tailored beautifully. Made in wartime, the album dreams of peace. It's only fitting that through this shared act of looking and during peaceful times we should participate in a rite of reclamation for an experience that can't be discerned on the surface of the images. Since the end of the war, our extended family has grown, and photos of weddings—unions of brides and grooms from families loyal to opposing sides—offer one way of understanding reconciliation: no hint of differences here.

At the same time that I lingered on the laminated pages of the Sadec albums, which conjured forth the intimate estrangements of a world I did not know but which claimed me, I realized that my perspective provided just one view of "visual reunion." In what other ways, I wondered, might photography conjure not just warring visions but also reconciliation?

Warring visions of anticolonial resistance and national liberation were registered, as this book has shown, in photographs that widened the scope of how war came to be seen, felt, and known. Warring visions include thunderous explosions muted by the lull between skirmishes and battles; the camaraderie of brothers- and sisters-in-arms united by a common cause; the repose of soldiers; landscapes pristine and ruined, the latter no less sublime; the mundane routines of everyday life; and beyond. More than seeing, feeling, and knowing, warring visions of Vietnam attest to how photography actively *waged* war, staking claims for a community's loyalty and, not least, its memories. Nor has this process of waging war ended. Warring visions persist even when the war has ended and do so alongside attempts at reconciliation, whether quotidian or spectacular.

Shortly after the liberation of Saigon in 1975, for example, Võ An Khánh invoked the trope of family to symbolize the fulfillment of the dream of national reunification (figure E.1). In this carefully composed photograph, two Vietnamese matriarchs joyfully embrace. Formerly divided by their competing allegiances, they have now overcome the tribulations that have been etched on their careworn faces. In his depiction of family reunion, Khánh composed an allegory of gendered national reunification. Here divisions are reconciled now that the older generation's dreams of peace have been realized.

Whereas Khánh's photograph of visual reunion adopts a Vietnamese-centered prism—as a reunion of North and South—other projects approach the question of reconciliation through a broader, more explicitly transnational framework. Most notably, *Requiem: By the Photographers Who Died in Vietnam and Indochina*, a collaborative project by Tim Page and Horst Faas, honors photographers from around the world who fought and died while covering the war both in Vietnam and as it spread into Laos and Cambodia. First appearing as a book in 1997, *Requiem* subsequently traveled as an exhibition. At its initial launch in Japan, a group of Kentucky-based war veterans bought the show and reorganized it under the auspices of "Requiem—The Vietnam Collection Project." Under the Kentucky committee's oversight, the show then traveled to the Newseum in Washington, DC, and onward to London, Lausanne, and farther afield.[1] It was eventually brought to Vietnam, first in Hanoi and then Ho Chi Minh City, at the War Remnants Museum, where it remains on permanent display.

Requiem is remarkable for its attempt to transcend an American framework for seeing. The project strives to represent the eyes of the world by including photographers from Japan, France, Australia, Vietnam, South Vietnam, and more, uniting them through their shared commitment to documenting the

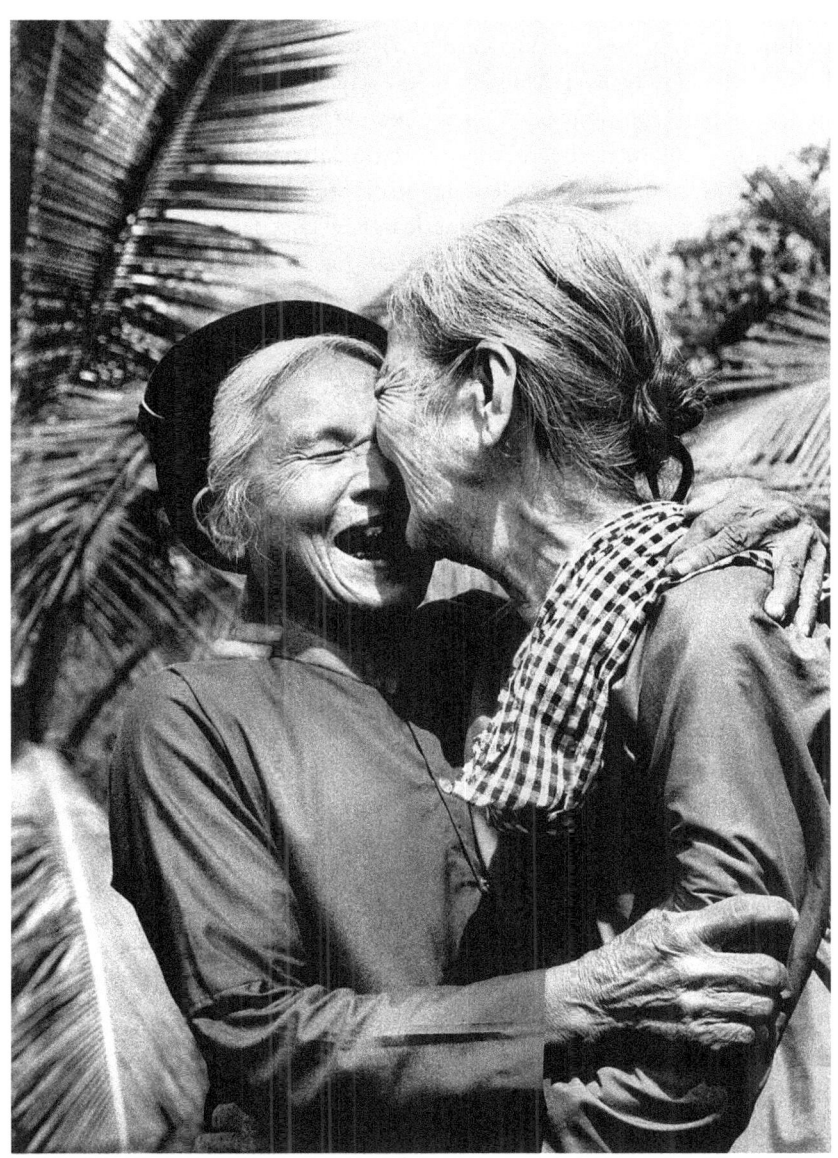

FIGURE E.1 Women embrace at news that the war has ended, 1975. Photo: Võ An Khánh.

war and through the poignancy of their fate. No matter their differences in nationality, ideology, and life experiences, photographers are joined in their struggle to make photographs, one that resulted in the ultimate sacrifice of death. At its core, *Requiem* pays earnest tribute to universal humanism, a sentiment echoed in Nguyen Khuyen's brief essay in the book, which affirms the photographers' common experiences. Despite this, *Requiem* retains the very American framework it so earnestly strives to overcome. Indeed, the reliance on this framework is evident in journalist David Halberstam's foreword to the book, which laments the American negligence of its own history and praises the project for relieving this malaise. According to Christina Schwenkel, the collaboration, which broadened to include Vietnamese museum organizers and which culminated in the Hanoi and Ho Chi Minh City exhibitions, evokes not so much a uniform understanding of reconciliation but rather contradictory ideas of visual reunion. As Schwenkel further observes, Faas's speech at the opening of the exhibition at the War Remnants Museum reverted to the language of "us" and "them," "communism" and "anticommunism," thus invoking division yet all the while seeking reconciliation.[2] Moreover, because panel texts in Vietnamese were translated from the English text included in the photo book, they advanced an American understanding of the war, most notably by underscoring anticommunism instead of anticolonial resistance as motivation. Indeed, as Schwenkel comments, the fact that four photojournalists in the show from South Vietnam were separated from a group simply described as "Vietnam" underscores just how partial reconciliation was at the time. At the initial opening in Ho Chi Minh City, reconciliation thus served as another means of projecting warring visions. That the four South Vietnamese men have since been included in the "Vietnam" group suggests that notions of nationhood have expanded in accordance with a shift in what reconciliation can accommodate.

Requiem is not the only project seeking visual reunion. In 2017 PBS aired *Vietnam: A History*, a ten-part, eighteen-hour documentary directed by Ken Burns and Lynn Novick, an occasion that attracted much attention. Critics praised the documentary's inclusion of Vietnamese voices and stories, which for them signaled a refreshing departure from mainstream media representations of the war. This shift in approach can be seen in publicity posters, which feature a "reflection": an image of a GI on patrol "mirrored" by a Vietnamese peasant bearing a shoulder pole presumably weighted by newly harvested crops.[3] The war, this promotional image suggests, affected both sides, so the documentary begins by "rewinding," reversing footage in order to understand how we—both Americans and Vietnamese—arrived here.

Visually, the rewind technique is a conceit associated with film. Yet documentaries by Burns and Novick are also, at their core, photographic. Indeed, the distinctive "Ken Burns effect" pulls viewers into and outside an image by means of panning and zooming, directing us to discern which details of an image to linger on closely and when to survey the bigger picture. First introduced in the landmark documentary *The Civil War* (1990), the so-called Burns effect was meant to address the problem of filmic treatment of a topic that predates film. Because there was no footage to draw from, animating photographs in this way helped achieve dynamic movement. Since then, the effect has become a signature style of Burns and Novick projects, employed so often that, as one critic wryly puts it, these documentaries are "restless," with the directors determined to coach viewers on how to look at photographs. So well-known is this effect that it has become part of the popular lexicon and is included as a technique in video editing programs such as iMovie and Final Cut Pro. As a complement, then, to the rewind opening, which launches viewers into a revision of history focused on absorbing firsthand accounts of the seemingly ordinary people who experienced it, the Burns effect encourages viewers to linger on the youthful vulnerability of the faces who appear in the documentary's selection of photos, to ponder the brashness, hope, and torment expressed in these faces. By means of panning out, the effect also encourages viewers to contemplate the larger landscape and greater forces that direct the faces of the everyday men and women who are featured in the documentary. That is, the effect strives to achieve reconciliation by zooming in on individuals and then panning out to ponder the tragedy that befalls humanity as a consequence of war.

Juxtaposition helps reinforce the humanist thrust of the documentary. For example, when interviewer Duong Van Mai Elliot recollects her earlier prejudice against communist soldiers and revises it with the admission that the enemy was human after all, Burns and Novick pair these impressions with images of National Liberation Front (NLF) recruits. These photographs serve as rejoinders to Elliott's harsh initial impressions (episode 4, 1: 12.30). The same episode introduces the theme of universalism through a montage that parallels American and North Vietnamese mutual recognition of the enemy's humanity (episode 4, 58: 00). The documentary establishes further parallels, most notably between Tim O'Brien and Bao Ninh, both of whom were lowly foot soldiers (grunts and bộ đội), albeit on opposing sides, who went on to become acclaimed writers whose novels deplored the waste of youth, lives, and dreams.

Despite these gestures, the documentary remains primarily concerned with American experiences. Indeed, *The Vietnam War* is the latest in a number of documentaries that attest to the directors' abiding preoccupation with what critic Ian Parker describes as Burns's "American canon."[4] Consider, for example, the implications of a stirring moment in the documentary. One of the North Vietnamese veterans, Ho Van Luu, having just spoken movingly of the massacre of civilians in Huế in the wake of the Tet Offensive, a sensitive political subject, addresses the directors. "Please be careful making your film," he cautions, "because I could get into trouble" (episode 6, 25: 53). Although his account of the atrocity is powerful, it's surprising that his narration of it should be included in the documentary at all, given the fear he expressed for sharing the story. Perhaps Burns and Novick exercised caution in their final edits, but because how or even if they did so isn't explained, viewers are left to wonder whether Burns and Novick prioritized telling the story of reconciliation instead of being fully committed to this principle. Or rather, the kind of reconciliation that Burns and Novick actually commit to has less to do with Vietnam and everything to do with "the notion of a unified [American] monoculture," as TV critic Alex Shephard points out.[5] The Vietnam War's imperative to tell Luu's story despite the danger posed by doing so undermines the documentary's express wish to aid reconciliation between American and Vietnamese experiences. Put simply, this moment exposes a contradiction between what the documentary says and what it does: the inclusion of Vietnamese experiences in a manner that imperils its teller serves the filmmakers' ends more than it does justice to Ho Van Luu's story. In this way, the Burns effect reinstates, even as it aspires to enlarge, the American framework for viewing.[6]

In *Warring Visions* I too have zoomed in on select images while panning out to contemplate larger views. But despite superficial similarities to the Burns effect, I like to think my aims differ markedly from those of Burns and Novick. Rather than seeking to get the story right, to capture the story no matter the cost, or for that matter to find just the right image, this book sought to bring to light the distinctiveness of Vietnamese experiences while also attending to unexpected alignments between American frameworks and Vietnamese experiences and to ongoing misalignments between them.

Unlike other projects that have aspired to be comprehensive in coverage, this book's perspective is modest. Here, ways of seeing are partial and can only be so. They are partial because of the incomplete state of mainstream archives, a condition that sent me off in search of disparate sources and that resulted in an eclectic, perhaps even chaotic, range of materials including vernacular images, personal collections, and artwork. They are also partial, I realize, because of my deeply personal attachment to the images and the stories behind them. After all, my training in the visual began well before my academic training, back to those days long ago when my brother and I watched that first, dreary documentary about the war. I began studying photography and visual culture in part because I wanted to understand how to make sense of images that didn't accord with my family's experiences—and to understand the images that we treasured but that remain outside the dominant story of the war—only to realize that my perspective didn't fit into the models I learned from the critics I most admired. Although I resist the temptation to generalize from the personal, this partial way of seeing provides a means of critically situating and grappling with my role in perpetuating and reconciling warring visions. Perhaps the partial perspective will enable readers to situate themselves as well.

UNSETTLED PLOTS

On my last trip to Vietnam, I decided to visit the Army of the Republic of Vietnam (ARVN) cemetery, Nghĩa Trang Nhan dan Bình An, which is located about an hour away from Ho Chi Minh City. Commonly known as Bien Hoa cemetery, this is where martyrs from South Vietnam are buried. Because of the sensitive political nature of the site, after 1975 and the emergence of the Socialist Republic of Vietnam, it was placed under the management of the Ministry of Defense, and no visitors were permitted to enter. Although this prohibition was lifted in 2006, few visitors ventured out. Who manages the cemetery and how—and whether it is cared for—are crucial issues when it comes to the project of national reunification.

To get there, my friend, who lives in Vietnam, hired a car and driver, and for over an hour we traversed increasingly bumpy roads in a dusty, cigarette-stained sedan, hobbling through back alleys and bumping over potholes, before arriving at one of the entrances. We had our story ready before we set out early in the morning. The cemetery was unlikely to be on any tourist itinerary and, long after officials opened its gates to visitors, still wasn't a place that locals sought out.

Sure enough, at the entrance a guard stopped us and asked why we had come. "To visit our uncle," my friend replied. "We were told he might be buried here." Americans had made the search for and repatriation of MIA soldiers a contentious political issue throughout the 1980s and into the 1990s, with negotiations over the lifting of sanctions and the normalization of relations with the United States pivoting, in part, on the full accounting of missing servicemen. Meanwhile, an estimated 300,000 communist soldiers were missing in action, and thousands more ARVN had disappeared, so our explanation of how *we*, who were obviously Viet Kieu, came to be there was plausible. Who hasn't lost a loved one in this war?

Above a set of stairs and a simple shrine established at its base, an obelisk rises high into the cloudless sky. The obelisk was worn, spotted with rust and moss, but also protected by a heavy concrete ring that encircled it. My friend, who collects antiquities, likened the circular enclosure and the phallic structure to *linga* and *yoni*, Hindu symbols of fertility, except that this was a monument to death, not to life. When we stepped out into the circle, it seemed the weight of an airless void descended upon us. Though small, the space was empty, still, and quiet.

The soldiers were buried below in plots, a few with small vases of dried flowers and cans of Saigon beer, offerings to the dead. Signs of care from the living. Some of the tombstones have even been rebuilt. Etched onto their surfaces are photographs of soldiers, forever young. But most of these plots are unmarked and untended. Who were they, and who did they leave behind?

We stepped carefully through leaf-strewn rows, pausing on the unknown soldiers and then at gravestones where family members had obviously taken pains to tend and restore their chipped or broken surfaces. We peered at carved memorials, hoping to answer these questions or at least glimpse some clues.

We did not get far, for by then the midday sun was unrelenting in the cloudless sky. It was another unusually hot December day. And the more we waded in the uncut grass, among the overgrown trees and between untended rows of tombstones, the more the mosquitoes swarmed upon us, feasting on sticky limbs. We had forgotten our sprays. We chafed in the heat, scratching at bites, swatting at bugs, before hastily retreating to our car and driver, chased by mosquitoes whose angry buzzing served as a reminder of just how unsettled these plots remain.

Even as the Vietnamese diaspora has put pressure on the state to improve the cemetery and despite efforts to tame the jungle, the tasks of making peace with the dead, of reconciling memories of the war, are ongoing. I left the cemetery wishing that I had seen more, knowing that what I'd wished to see and understand—visual reunion—has yet to be fully realized. The vision that this book tries to resolve, then, is my own. In the end, I am in the picture too.

1   Chong, *The Oriental Obscene*, 76. For a fascinating overview of the varied cultural forms taken up in remembering this war, see Chong and Schlund-Vials, *(Re)Collecting the Vietnam War*.
2   Maclear worked for the Canadian Broadcasting Corporation and freelanced briefly for the *New York Times*. See Maclear, dir., *Vietnam: The Ten Thousand Day War*.
3   Lewinsky, *The Camera at War*, 197.
4   For landmark histories of the two wars involving the French and the Americans, see, for example, Young, *The Vietnam Wars, 1945–1990*; and Logevall's Pulitzer Prize–winning *Embers of War*.
5   Bonier, Champlain, and Kolly, *The Vietnam Veteran*.
6   Arlen, *Living-Room War*. See also Hoskins, *Televising War*; Small, *Covering Dissent*; and Mandelbaum, "Vietnam: The Television War."
7   Moeller, *Shooting War*, 358.
8   On the role of the US media in covering Vietnam, see Hammond, *Reporting Vietnam*; Hallin, *The Uncensored War*; and Hagopian, "Vietnam War Photography as a Locus of Memory."
9   On the significance of icons, see Hariman and Lucaites, *No Caption Needed*; Kroes, *Photographic Memories*; and Andermann and Rowe, eds., *Images of Power*.
10 Gendy Alimurung, "Nick Ut's *Napalm Girl* Helped End the Vietnam War. Today in L.A., He's Still Shooting," *LA Weekly*, July 17, 2014, accessed March 13, 2017, www.laweekly.com/news/nick-uts-napalm-girl-helped-end-the-vietnam-war-today-in-la-hes-still-shooting-4861747.
11 For studies of the political and social influence of images, see Zelizer, *About to Die*; Kennedy, *Afterimages*; and Perlmutter, *Photojournalism and Foreign Policy*.
12 Quoted in Hallin, *The Uncensored War*, 3.
13 As Hariman points out in the context of the Syrian conflict, it is difficult to prove whether images can influence policy: the truth, media historians have demonstrated, lies somewhere between these extreme positions, with images functioning equivocally rather than decisively. See Hariman, "Why Photographs Don't Stop the War."

14 Sontag, *On Photography*, 11.

15 Nudelman, "Against Photography."

16 Sontag, *Trip to Hanoi*.

17 Burgin, ed., *Thinking Photography*; Tagg, *The Burden of Representation*.

18 Sekula, "The Body and the Archive," 10.

19 Linfield, *The Cruel Radiance*, 7.

20 The concept of the global Cold War broadens scholarship to consider arenas of conflict beyond the dominant US–USSR binary. See Kwon, *The Other Cold War*; Gaddis, *We Now Know*; and Westad, *The Global Cold War*. Regarding outside players, see Man, *Soldiering through Empire*; and Blackburn, *Mercenaries and Lyndon Johnson's More Flags*.

21 See Dang, "The Cultural Work of Anticommunism in the San Diego Vietnamese American Community."

22 See Adelman and Kozol, "Unremarkable Suffering."

23 Moeller, *Shooting War*, 3.

24 Important historical studies that draw attention to Vietnamese perspectives include Duiker, *The Communist Road to Power in Vietnam*; Bradley, *Vietnam at War*; Ninh, *A World Transformed*; Schwenkel, *The American War in Contemporary Vietnam*; and Lien-Hang T. Nguyen, *Hanoi's War*. For an official account from the "other" side, see Military History Institute of Vietnam, *Victory in Vietnam*.

25 Poole, *Vision, Race and Modernity: A Visual Economy of the Andean World Image*.

26 Kennedy introduces the term *American worldview* to underscore the ways that the political economy of photojournalism overwhelmingly favors the interests of US foreign policy. See Kennedy, *Afterimages*, 3–4.

27 "Horst Faas interview with Sarit Hand," Oral History Archivist, Associated Press Oral History Program, New York, September 29, 1997, Associated Press Corporate Archives.

28 According to Malcolm Browne, the Associated Press paid stringers $5 per photograph (or the equivalent in Vietnamese piastres). See *A Short Guide to News Coverage in Viet Nam*. Photographer Jorge Lewinsky alleges that Horst Faas was one of the editors who used Vietnamese stringers "quite ruthlessly," adding that the AP Saigon bureau chief "would buy their pictures, which they had frequently taken at great personal risk, for paltry amounts; the pictures were not even credited to the individual photographers on publication." See Lewinksy, *The Camera at War*, 208.

29 Sam Roberts, "Nguyen Ngoc Luong, *Times* Guide in Vietnam, Dies at 79," *New York Times*, December 7, 2016, accessed January 19, 2017, www.nytimes.com/2016/12/07/world/asia/luong -interpreter-vietnam-new-york-times.html.

30 Shipler, "In Vietnam, a Patriot without a Place."

31 Hess, "The 'Cheaper Solution'"; Smyth, "Out on a Limb"; and Seo, "Marginal Majority at the Postcolonial News Agency."

32 To this day I see this skewed perspective play out at conferences when presenters shift from slide after slide of atrocity images, often culminating in *Trang Bang 1972*, the anguish of a racialized child as backdrop to arguments that don't center on the child.

33 On the figure of the American soldier and the antiwar movement, see Kreusch, "Violent Representation."

34 Dudziak, *Cold War Civil Rights*.

35 Nguyễn Thắng, interview with author, Hanoi, May 10, 2013.

36 Phu, *Picturing Model Citizens*. See also Mimi Thi Nguyen, *The Gift of Freedom*.

37 Viet Thanh Nguyen, *Nothing Ever Dies*. See also Tai, *The Country of Memory*; and Schwenkel, *The American War in Contemporary Vietnam*.

38 On critical refugee studies and Vietnamese subjectivity, see Viet Thanh Nguyen, *Nothing Ever Dies*; Vinh Nguyen, *Our Hearts and Minds*; Espiritu, *Body Counts*; and Mimi Thi Nguyen, *The Gift of Freedom*.

39 Since the late 1990s, a handful of exhibitions, photo books, and documentary films have examined Vietnamese photography but are primarily configured as works from the "other" side. These include Emering, *Viet Cong*; Faas and Page, *Requiem*; Page, Niven, and Riley, *Another Vietnam*; Guenette, dir., *Vietnam's Unseen War*; and Chauvel, *Ceux du Nord*. Vietnamese photographers have also published books that feature their works from the war. See Tính, *Khoảnh Khắc*; and Nam, *Một Thời Hào Hùng*. The few scholarly studies of Vietnamese photography include Schwenkel's brilliant analysis of the *Requiem* exhibition and museum as sites where memory is negotiated transnationally and Hien's research on photography in late-socialist Vietnam. See Schwenkel, "Exhibiting War, Reconciling Pasts"; and Hien, *Reanimating Vietnam*. In addition to exhibitions on photography, scholars have examined propaganda posters from the other side, including Heather, *Vietnam Posters*.

40 Zhuang, *Photography in Southeast Asia*.

41 Takata, "Photography in Vietnam from the End of the Nineteenth Century to the Start of the Twentieth Century, by Nguyễn Đức Hiệp."

42 Although Minh's history of Vietnamese photography was unpublished at his death, it circulates widely online for overseas Vietnamese readers. See, for example, Minh, "Lịch Sử Nhiếp Ảnh Việt Nam."

43 A statue was unveiled to commemorate Đặng Huy Trứ. See "Tưởng Nhớ Ông Tổ Nghệ Nhiếp Ảnh Đặng Huy Trứ," *Nhân Dân*, March 14, 2016, accessed June 13, 2016, www.nhandan .com.vn/vanhoa/dong-chay/item/29009102-tuong-nho-ong-to-nghe-nhiep-anh-dang-huy -tru.html.

44 Strassler, *Refracted Visions*.

45 "The Pursuit of Beauty."

46 Quoted in "The Pursuit of Beauty."

47 Nguyễn Mạnh Đan, interview with author, Ho Chi Minh City, May 6, 2013.

48 It is unclear why the Government of Vietnam opted to print the book in Hong Kong, but considering the scarcity of supplies during the war, it is possible that outsourcing was the expedient option.

49 Benjamin, "The Work of Art in the Age of Mechanical Reproduction."

50 Đức Chính Nguyễn, *Văn Hóa Nhiếp Ảnh*.

51 See Phu, *Picturing Model Citizens*.

52 Hariman and Lucaites, *No Caption Needed*.

53 Noble, "The Politics of Emotion in the Mexican Revolution."

54 On war in photography, see Griffin, "Media Images of War"; Brasheeth, "Projecting Trauma"; Butler, *Frames of War*; Baker and Mavlian, eds., *Conflict, Time, Photography*; Moeller, *Shooting War*; Kennedy and Patrick, *The Violence of the Image*; Kozol, *Distant Wars Made Visible*; Zarzycka, *Gendered Tropes in War Photography*; and Stallabrass, *Memory of Fire*.

55 Kwon, *Ghosts of War in Vietnam*.

56 See, for example, Thanh Tan's contribution to the opinion section of the *New York Times*, "What Do Vietnamese-Americans Think about 'The Vietnam War?,'" October 3, 2017, accessed October 7, 2017, www.nytimes.com/2017/10/03/opinion/what-do-vietnamese -americans-think-of-the-vietnam-war.html?rref=collection%2Fcolumn%2Fvietnam-67 &action=click&contentCollection=opinion&region=stream&module=stream_unit&version =latest&contentPlacement=2&pgtype=collection.

57 Tsing, *Friction*.

ONE. AESTHETIC FORM, POLITICAL CONTENT

1   In Vietnam the vna is also known as ttxvn, which stands for Thông tấn xã Việt Nam.

2   Morozov and Lloyd, eds., *Soviet Photography*, 7.

3   In "Camera Obscura," Dickerman persuasively shows that photographers wrestled with the issue of revolutionary form long after this issue seemed officially resolved with the implementation of socialist realism.

4   Leslie, *Walter Benjamin*, 138.

5   Benjamin, "A Little History of Photography."

6   Smith and Sliwinski, eds., *Photography and the Optical Unconscious*, 4.

7   Benjamin, "The Work of Art," 222.

8   Benjamin, "The Work of Art," 240, 238.

9   Jameson, *The Political Unconscious*.

10 In one camp we find modernists such as John Szarkowski and Edward Steichen, who disseminated their interest in aesthetics in reviews, books, and exhibitions. Notably, Steichen's 1955 *Family of Man* circulated within and responded to a Cold War context. Through its circulation, this exhibition contributed its immensely popular vision of humanism to the era's cultural politics. By famously closing the exhibition with a photograph of the sublime mushroom cloud, the *Family of Man* resolved a problem that vexed Cold War ideologues: how to make visible and manageable invisible phenomena such as the emotions. Photographs conferred color and form to the most chilling of Cold War fears, nuclear annihilation. According to Joseph Masco in *The Theatre of Operations*, visual culture not only produced but also discursively salved these fears.

11 See, for example, Arlen, *Living-Room War*; Kennedy, "Securing Vision"; and Small, *Covering Dissent*.

12 For more on Cold War visuality, see the special issue of *Visual Studies*, edited by Bassnett, Noble, and Phu, on "Cold War Visual Alliances."

13 Sontag, *Trip to Hanoi*, 16.

14 Debord, *The Society of the Spectacle*.

15 King persuasively documents the visual violence in the USSR, which was pivotal to establishing the Stalinist cult. See his landmark book, *The Commissar Vanishes*. See also Plamper, *The Stalin Cult*; Leese, *Mao Cult*; and Dror, "Establishing Ho Chi Minh's Cult."

16 See Barthes, *Image Music Text* and *Mythologies*. See also Sontag, *On Photography*; Tagg, *The Burden of Representation*; and Sekula, *Photography against the Grain*.

17 Although Vietnam might have been on the minds of many of these visual theorists, critics

writing outside Hanoi and Saigon were most likely more familiar with images produced by the Western press (Sontag seems to have been unusual in this regard). The few photo books published in the United States, Europe, and Australia that consider Vietnamese photography of this war include Faas and Page, eds., *Requiem*; Page, Niven, and Riley, *Another Vietnam*; and Chauvel, *Ceux du Nord*. For a compelling analysis of the ways that the Vietnamese state draws on revolutionary photography for postwar memorialization practices, see Schwenkel, *The American War in Contemporary Vietnam* and "Exhibiting War, Reconciling Pasts." This closing of distance moved many to antiwar activism in order to end this suffering and prompted others to reject such images as themselves dehumanizing. Even the Vietnamese insist on the enduring influence of the war in establishing a visual vocabulary for coverage of subsequent conflicts.

18 Xiaobing Tang, *Visual Culture in Contemporary China*, 11.

19 This characterization about visual culture as "the transcultural experience of the visual in daily life" can be found in Mirzoeff, *An Introduction to Visual Culture*, 26.

20 In *Faking It*, Fineman convincingly demonstrates the persistence of manipulation throughout the history of photography.

21 Hien, "The Good, the Bad, and the Not Beautiful."

22 Kwon, *The Other Cold War*. See also Kwon, "Cold War in a Vietnamese Community."

23 Mai Nam, interview with author in Hanoi, May 7, 2013.

24 Nam interview.

25 See, for example, Reid, *Style and Socialism*.

26 Kim Đằng, interview with author, Hanoi, May 12, 2013.

27 At least one woman worked as a retoucher during the war, however; Lê Thị Năng. Năng was a photo retoucher born in 1949 in Thuận Mỹ, An Giang province. She died in 1972 in Kampong Cham province, Cambodia.

28 Books and exhibitions refer to several female photojournalists who were an exception to this overwhelming rule, such as Nguyễn Thị Thế, Lê Thị Nang, and Ngọc Hương. However, they do not provide extensive information. See Faas and Page, eds., *Requiem*; and Đức Chính Nguyễn, *Văn Hóa Nhiếp Ảnh*.

29 Văn Sắc, interview with author, Hanoi, May 10, 2013.

30 Nguyễn, *Văn Hóa Nhiếp Ảnh*, 58.

31 Võ An Khánh, interview with author, Bac Lieu, Vietnam, May 18, 2013.

32 Landsberger explains that propaganda posters were "cheaply and easily produced," which explains their popularity for giving "concrete expression to many different policies." Although his observations focus on the subject of Chinese art after the establishment of the People's Republic in 1949, they provide useful insight into favored forms of visual communication, which were subsequently taken up in other sites. See Landsberger, "The Rise and Fall of the Chinese Propaganda Poster," 16.

33 A reenactment of this clever technique can be seen in Guenette, dir., *Vietnam's Unseen War*.

34 Tzu-Chun Wu, *Radicals on the Road*.

35 In *Even the Women Must Fight*, Turner adds that the planting of the broken frame on the firmness of the soil reorients viewers' perspectives on war, from the abstract heights of aerial supremacy to the ground where innocent civilians are targeted. This museum thus offers a grounded perspective on the war.

36 Meekosha observes that as a field, disability studies has developed in a way that foregrounds the concerns of the global North but has yet to take full account of the concerns of postcolonial nations, which have to grapple with enablement amid the wreckage caused by colonial and imperial violence. See Meekosha, "Decolonising Disability"; and Grech, "Decolonising Eurocentric Disability Studies."

37 Kriebel, "Photomontage in the Year 1932."

38 Indeed, to observe that Vietnamese revolutionary photography was produced as propaganda is news to no one. Photography lay under the purview of the Ministry of Information, not the Ministry of Art and Culture; training was explicitly designed to educate practitioners in methods of producing propaganda; and a directive of ten points distributed by the NLF photography division listed, as its primary and most important point, photography as a "sharp weapon" of information and propaganda (*nhiếp ảnh là võ khí thông tin, tuyên truyền sắc bén*). See Đức Chính Nguyễn, *Văn Hóa Nhiếp Ảnh*, 55.

39 Phạm Tiến Dũng, interview with author, Hanoi, May 9, 2013.

40 Đức Chính Nguyễn, *Văn Hóa Nhiếp Ảnh*, 55.

41 The DRV considered propaganda (*tuyên truyền*) to be an integral part of its cultural mission of promoting socialism. Notably, when Hồ Chí Minh founded the Socialist State Enterprise for Photography and Motion Pictures in 1953, he underscored that the two functions of these materials were to build socialism and to struggle for the liberation of the South and for national reunification. See Duong, *Treacherous Subjects*. See also Charlot, "Vietnamese Cinema"; Ninh, *A World Transformed*; Pham, "Vietnam: A Brief History of Vietnamese Films"; and Trinh, *30 Years of Vietnam's Cinema Art*.

42 Đức Chính Nguyễn, *Văn Hóa Nhiếp Ảnh*, 56, 65.

43 The function of a pictorial is distinct from the concerns of pictorialism, an aesthetic movement. Although some of the photographs in *Vietnam Pictorial* suggest the influence of pictorialism, particularly in its stylization, the overarching concern of the magazine, as evident in the fact that it was also published under the title *Vietnam Images,* was not to promote this movement but rather to advance nationalism, a project that drew on other styles as well.

44 Blaszczyk, *The Color Revolution.*

45 Stein, "Mainstream Difference."

46 Moeller, *Shooting War.*

47 Hunt, "Editor's Note," 5.

48 Moeller, *Shooting War*; Kennedy, *Afterimages.*

49 Quoted in Marien, *Photography*, 422.

50 I am told that archival documents of any kind relating to *Vietnam Pictorial*, never mind those disclosing the editorial process, do not exist.

51 Batchelor, *Chromophobia.*

52 Bajorek, "On Color Photography in an Extra-moral Sense."

53 In her book on Indian painted photography, Dewan explores the transcultural significance of this genre, emphasizing its significance in "embellishing" reality. See Dewan, *Embellished Reality.*

54 In his ruminations on the significance of Chinese propaganda posters, Landsberger asserts that the images rendered on these objects "were often figurative and realistic, almost as if photographs had been directly copied. Their aim was to portray the future in the present, not

only showing 'life as it really is,' but also 'life as it ought to be.' They were painted in a naïve style, with all forms outlined in black, filled in with bright pinks, reds, yellows, greens and blues. These works created a kind of 'faction,' a hybrid of 'fact' and 'fiction,' stressing the positive and papering over anything negative." See Landsberger, *Chinese Propaganda Posters*, 16.

55 Zelizer, *About to Die.*

56 My thanks to Sally Stein for this observation.

57 Mackerras, McMillen, and Watson, eds., *Dictionary of the Politics of the People's Republic of China.*

58 Crowly, *Posters of the Cold War.*

59 Boym, *The Future of Nostalgia*, xvi.

60 Leshkowich, *Essential Trade.*

61 My thanks to Susan Reid for pointing out this parallel to me.

62 Although the reasons for the disregard of photomontage in *Vietnam Pictorial* may never be known, it stands out when contrasted with other contemporaneous practices, whether socialist or not. After all, art historians associate photomontage with the socialist avant-garde, especially the work of John Heartfield and Alexander Rodchenko, whose bold style influenced generations of artists on the Left from regions well beyond Germany, where they were based.

63 Đức Chính Nguyễn, *Văn Hóa Nhiếp Ảnh.*

64 See Schwenkel and Leshkowich, eds., special issue, "Neoliberalism in Vietnam."

65 The work of socialist photographers provides glimpses of the limits of vision, in the sense that Smith describes in *At the Edge of Sight*, her counterintuitive book that expands critical commonplaces about the camera as an instrument that makes subjects by attending to the ways that it discloses invisibility.

66 Đoàn Công Tính, interview with author, Ho Chi Minh City, May 16, 2013.

67 However, recent publications are starting to feature disabled bodies that previously had been censored.

68 Đằng interview.

69 See Hien, "Ho Chi Minh City's Beauty Regime." See also Hien, "The Good, the Bad, and the Not Beautiful" and "Photo Resurrections before and after Images."

70 This discourse of ableism has in recent years begun to evolve, to take up more directly the issue of Agent Orange and its ongoing impact on Vietnamese civilians as part of the state's larger concern with reparation. Although the issue of Agent Orange as exemplifying war's slow violence, to invoke Robert Nixon's helpful phrase, is urgent, it is beyond the scope of this chapter, which focuses on the ways that the state envisioned socialism.

71 The exhibit *Faking It: Manipulated Photography before Photoshop*, MOMA, October 11, 2012–January 27, 2013, provides a comprehensive and convincing overview of manipulation as a quintessential feature of photography.

72 Chauvel, *Ceux du Nord.*

73 Helle Maj and Jørn Stjerneklar, "Aber Warum," *May Day Press*, last modified June 2, 2015, www.maydaypress.com/blog/files/Opinions%20from%20Africa.html. A follow-up article argues that even the "original" image appears to have been Photoshopped. See "Excuse My French!," *May Day Press*, last modified June 10, 2015, www.maydaypress.com/blog/files /2ce9a7cd940027138ec55075ed76716b-25.html.

74 Quoted in Haski, "Une 'affaire Photoshop' dans le temple photojournalisme."

75 Campbell has written extensively, on behalf of World Press Photo, on the topic of manipulation and journalistic ethics. See, for example, "Photo Manipulation and Verification."

76 Schwenkel, "Exhibiting War," 46.

77 Robert F. Turner Collection, 74040-10. A–V, Hoover Institute, Stanford University. However, I am not aware of the fate of this defector after April 30, 1975.

78 Turner Collection, 74040-10.

79 Historians have documented manipulation in the coverage of conflicts in the nineteenth century, including the Mexican-American War, the Crimean War, and the American Civil War. In the twentieth century, manipulation persists as part of the practice of war photography, perhaps most notably in the case of Robert Capa's *Falling Soldier*. See, for example, Debroise, *Mexican Suite*; Collins, "Living Skeletons"; and Panzer, *Mathew Brady and the Image of History*.

80 For a fascinating account of memorialization practices in Vietnam, see Schwenkel, *The American War in Contemporary Vietnam*.

TWO. REVOLUTIONARY VIETNAMESE WOMEN, SYMBOLS OF SOLIDARITY

1 See Mirzoeff, *An Introduction to Visual Culture*. For critiques of this claim about visual culture's transhistorical qualities, see Xiaobing Tang, *Visual Culture in Contemporary China*; and Noble, "Visual Culture and Latin American Studies."

2 See, for example, Kampwirth, *Women and Guerilla Movements*; Chinchilla, "Revolutionary Popular Feminism in Nicaragua"; and Shayne, *The Revolution Question*.

3 On the role of women in the Vietnamese Revolution, see Turner and Ho, *Even the Women Must Fight*; Taylor, *Vietnamese Women at War*; and *Vietnamese Women, Vietnam Studies*, 10.

4 Taylor surmises that the term was first used to describe Madam Nguyễn Thị Định. See "The Long-Haired Warriors," fn 22, 187, 182. Another reference to the origin of the term can be found in Định's memoir, *No Other Road to Take*. However, Tétreault writes that the Diem regime coined the term *the long-haired Army*. See Tétreault, "Women and Revolution in Vietnam," 121.

5 Nail, *The Figure of the Migrant*.

6 Armstrong and Prashad, "Solidarity," 222.

7 Tétreault, ed., *Women and Revolution in Africa, Asia, and the New World*.

8 Tsing, *Friction*.

9 Cumings, *Parallax Visions*.

10 Nguyễn Thị Bình, *Family, Friends, and Country*.

11 Honig, "Maoist Mappings of Gender"; Salaff and Merkle, "Women in Revolution," 182.

12 Fall, ed., *Ho Chi Minh on Revolution*, 336.

13 Transcript of Ho Chi Minh's address to the VWU meeting, October 1966.

14 Nguyễn Thị Định, *No Other Road to Take*, 150.

15 Võ Nguyên Giáp, *People's War, People's Army*, 79.

16 Madame Ngô Đinh Nhu, "Law and Harmony."

17 See, for example, a well-known *Life* magazine cover featuring Madame Nhu: http://content.time.com/time/covers/0,16641,19630809,00.html, accessed May 30, 2018.

18 Lieu, "Remembering 'The Nation' through Pageantry"; Ann Marie Leshkowich, "The Ao Dai Goes Global."

19 Madame Ngô Đình Nhu, "In the Face of Hate," *Vietnam Courier*, March 21, 1963. The cadres were to receive a pay of 1,800 piastres per month, which American intelligence officers considered high in contrast to the 900 piastres that self-defense corpsmen received but which Madame Nhu thought to be a modest amount in defense of the republic. Given widespread perception that corruption was rampant during the Diem regime, Madame Nhu's bean counting was meant to allay suspicions about how her pet project was to be funded and to legitimize this project as a fully autonomous yet cost-effective national defense strategy.

20 Department of State dispatch, July 15, 1960. A Department of State representative later commented that "by nature Madame Nhu does not mix easily with the common people. For example, in the afternoon of March 22, she distributed prizes to a number of women and girls, but her manner was rather cool and aloof and unlikely to win political support for herself or the Ngô family." Dispatch no 437, March 22, 1961, 3.

21 According to John J. Heible, "At any rate, the short 76 hour training course and the lack of weapons for the new group seem to foreshadow a record of ineffectiveness for the women in the face of any Viet Cong threat. It would probably be more useful to spend the time and money in orienting them on some subject as first aid." John J. Heible, American consul, August 6, 1962.

22 "First Lady Leading Movement in Defiance of Viet Cong Terrorism," Hoover International Archives.

23 In this regard Madame Nhu was progressive on women's rights though in an inconsistent way that lagged behind the Vietnamese Communist Party. When she banned nightclubs, the press mocked her Catholic prudery. But shortly after the Diem regime fell (with the CIA-backed assassination of her husband and brother-in-law), her fears about the moral costs of US support seemed to be realized. By 1963, Saigon had plunged into militarized decadence with flourishing bars, nightclubs, red-light districts, and a thriving sex industry that exploited the desperation of impoverished women. Transcript of Madame Nhu address to WSM, August 3, 1963, Department of State telegram.

24 In comparison, the practice of paid maternity leave did not become enforced in US federal law until 1993, with states presiding over cases. By contrast, in Canada the federal government amended the Canada Labour Code in 1971 to protect maternity-leave benefits.

25 Open Letter from Central Committee of the Vietnam Women's Paramilitary Training Center, August 21, 1962.

26 See Jacobs's work on the intricacies of this alliance: *Cold War Mandarin* and *America's Miracle Man in Vietnam*. See also Miller, *Ngo Dinh Diem, the United States, and the Fate of South Vietnam*; and Chapman, *Cauldron of Resistance*. Quotations are from Department of State outgoing telegram, June 9, 1962.

27 Department of State telegram no. 214, August 29, 1962.

28 Nhu, "In the Face of Hate."

29 Madame Nhu to WSM, August 3, 1963, *The Times of Vietnam* 5, no. 31; "Holiness without Culture Is Blind. Culture Without Holiness Is Bookish," August 4, 1963, 16.

30 Thi Tuyet Mai Nguyen, *The Rubber Tree*.

31 There is no question that this number is inflated. Ambassador Joseph A. Mendenhall noted

that "while there is . . . a theoretical possibility of a Woman's Paramilitary Force of 216,000, practical difficulties will probably prevent there being more than a few thousand in existence by the end of 1962." Department of State, foreign dispatch no. 346, February 23, 1962. In "Stimulated Apostles of Peace," Madame Nhu (Thị Định) claimed that there were 1,127,000 active members "in addition to an infinite number of associate members."

32 Leshkowich, "Wandering Ghosts of Late Socialism."

33 Nguyễn Thị Định, "Stimulated Apostles of Peace."

34 Tzu-Chun Wu, *Radicals on the Road.*

35 Hershberger, *Traveling to Vietnam.* On Vietnam as a travel destination during the war, see Laderman, *Tours of Vietnam.*

36 "A Letter from Vietnamese Mothers to Mothers and Children-Loving People in the World."

37 VNA International Service, October 1966, Vietnam Archives, Lubbock, Texas.

38 Armstrong, "Before Bandung," 305.

39 *Papers of Charlotte Bunch*, 1967-1985, Arthur and Elizabeth Schlesinger Library on the History of Women in America, Radcliffe Institute for Advanced Study, Harvard University.

40 See, for example, Enloe, *Bananas, Beaches and Bases.*

41 At the same time, on the radical Left images of women as warriors would have been somewhat familiar, given, for example, the vaunted status of women in the Cuban Revolution, the fame of militant activist Angela Davis, and the notorious activities of the Weathermen, which suggests they would not have found the Vietnamese symbol of the revolutionary woman to be as discordant as the peace activists did.

42 Although Carlson's study of the reasons that conservative Caucasian women embrace guns focuses on the current context of so-called postfeminism in the United States, this fundamental tension between pacifist presumption and martial maternalism resonates with the earlier Vietnam War period. See Carlson, *Citizen-Protectors.* On women and militarism, see Enloe, *Maneuvers.*

43 The Vietnam Women's Union took several different forms in the course of the twentieth century. The organization traces its origins to the Anti-imperialist Women's Association, which emerged in 1930 and became the Democratic Women's Association in 1936, the Liberation Women's Association in 1939, and the National Salvation Women's League in 1941 before merging with other groups to become what today is known as the Vietnam Women's Union in 1946, after the Viet Minh won independence for North Vietnam from France. See Steinman, *Women in Vietnam: The Oral History.*

44 See, for example, Teigrob, *Warming Up to the Cold War;* and Whitaker and Hewitt, *Canada and the Cold War.*

45 Churchill has written widely on the topic of draft dodgers and their influence on leftist politics in Toronto. See, for example, "American Expatriates and the Building of Alternative Social Space in Toronto, 1965-1977," and "Draft Resisters, Left Nationalism, and the Politics of Anti-imperialism."

46 Cora Weiss, "Letter to NCC on Behalf of the NY Steering Committee," May 6, 1969, Swarthmore College Peace Collection.

47 An unidentified member of the WSP lamented the paucity of press coverage: "We were quite distressed about the press . . . why would AP be picked up by the Mt. Vernon Argus and no one of consequence?" See the Swarthmore College Peace Collection. *The New American*

Movement newsletter drew inspiration from the struggles of Vietnamese women. See the Charlotte Bunch collection at the Schlesinger Library. The few newspaper articles that covered this conference include Elizabeth Shelton, "Women and the War," *Washington Post*, July 16, 1969; *Globe and Mail*, July 16, 1969; and *Toronto Star*, July 7, 1969. Renee Blackan reported on the 1971 conference in "Women Meet Indochinese in Canada," *Guardian*, April 17, 1971, 5.

48 A transcript of Madame Dũng's speech can be found in the Swarthmore College Peace Collection.

49 However, American organizers who offered this explanation for the absence of Cambodian delegates did not elaborate on the nature of these problems.

50 Although the Cambodian delegates did not appear to provide a clear explanation for their withdrawal from the conference, the organizers' delicately worded notes suggest that this context was the likely cause.

51 By the mid-1970s, the Communist bloc had started to unravel, with border skirmishes between Vietnam and Cambodia intensifying into outright war that would culminate in the Vietnamese invasion of Phnom Penh and overthrow of the Khmer Rouge in December 1978.

52 Excerpted transcript of Madame Nguyễn Thị Bình speaking to American women from an October 1970 film made available through Women Strike for Peace, Swarthmore College Peace Collection.

53 Nguyễn Thị Định recounts her story in her memoir, *No Other Road to Take.*

54 "Nguyen Thi Ut: Heroine of South Vietnam Liberation Army," *Vietnam Courier*, March 10, 1966, Douglas Pike Collection (Unit 08), Texas Tech University Vietnam Archive, item # 2361209106. See also *Heroes and Heroines of the Liberation Armed Forces of South Vietnam.*

55 Anderson, "Fighting for Family," 297–316.

56 Eisen, *Women and Revolution in Vietnam*, 5.

57 See Swarthmore College Peace Collection.

58 Beins, "Radical Others."

59 Black Panther militarism was a defiant response to the Mulford Act, a 1967 California law that repealed the law allowing the public carrying of loaded firearms. Widely seen as a racially targeted law—in the United States, legislators seem passionate about limiting the Second Amendment right to bear arms when Black citizens would exercise this right while invoking this amendment when it comes to white citizens—the Mulford Act moved the Black Panthers to take up guns as a symbolic means of challenging racism. See Pal Singh, "The Black Panthers and the 'Underdeveloped Country' of the Left"; Raiford, *Imprisoned in a Luminous Glare*; Pau, "Shooting the Movement"; Austin, *Up against the Wall*; and Spencer, *The Revolution Has Come.*

60 James, *Common Ground.*

61 See, for example, Tétreault, "Women and Revolution in Vietnam." For a comprehensive history of maternalism as a discourse among female antiwar activists, see Swerdlow, "'Not My Son, Not Your Son, Not Their Sons.'" On the question of solidarity, see Armstrong and Prishad, "Solidarity."

62 Arguably, the harshest indictment of the conference can be found in a document titled "The Fourth World Manifesto." In this document, the unnamed author, who aligned herself with a group called the Autonomous Women's Liberation Movement, insisted, "We do not feel that we have to concede to these women [the organizers] the title of anti-imperialist since we

strongly feel that they themselves are acting as colonial-native (female) administrators for the male-defined Left in relationship to other women—in this case especially to Women's Liberation women." "Fourth World Manifesto," 1.

63 Susan Martin, ed., *Decade of Protest*.

64 Phu, Gandhi, and Ziaee, "Vietnamese Revolutionary Women and Global Solidarity," in *Cold War Camera* (forthcoming from Duke University Press).

65 Phu, Gandhi, and Ziaee., "Vietnamese Revolutionary Women."

66 Mohanty, "Under Western Eyes."

67 Armstrong, "Before Bandung."

68 Leshkowich, *Essential Trade*.

69 Taylor, *Vietnamese Women at War*.

70 "Vietnam 'Needs Ministry for Women.'"

71 Nhung Tuyet Tran, "Woman as Nation."

72 Anderson, "Fighting for Family."

THREE. REENACTMENT AND REMEMBRANCE

1 Viet Thanh Nguyen, *Nothing Ever Dies*, 4.

2 Horwitz, *Confederates in the Attic*; Bigley, "Living History and Battle Reenactment"; Handler and Saxton, "Dyssimulation: Reflexivity, Narrative, and the Quest for Authenticity in 'Living History.'"

3 Davis, "The Other Southern Belles." Every year in Walton County, Georgia, African Americans reenact the 1946 lynching of two Black couples, George W. and Mae Murray and Roger and Dorothy Malcolm, a crime for which the white supremacist perpetrators were acquitted. Even though participants are often overcome with grief in the course of their performance, they consider it a necessary though agonizing reminder that past injustices remain unresolved and demand reckoning.

4 McCalman and Pickering, eds., *Historical Reenactment*; Kaye, "Challenging Certainty"; Rosenfeld, "Why Do We Ask 'What If?'"; Magelssen, "Making History in the Second Person"; Auslander, "Touching the Past."

5 See Vanessa Agnew's work on historical reenactment in *Rethinking History*, 2007, and, in *Criticism*, 2004, coedited with Jonathan Lamb.

6 However, I do not stretch this term so capaciously that it includes all forms of commemoration. For example, the parades that the Socialist Republic of Vietnam presently organizes each year for Reunification Day, to mark the communist victory in the American War, are not reenactments: the pomp and ceremony on display in this context distinguish between past and present. The purpose is to reify metanarratives about the war and revolutionary heroism. Reunification Day affirms the present ideological order of things rather than projecting fantasies about the past and alternative futures, which is the key function of reenactments.

7 Apel, *War Culture and the Contest of Images*.

8 Azoulay, *Civil Imagination*, 26.

9 Attie and O'Hara, dirs., *In Country*.

10 See Destiny Nguyen, *Nhiếp Ảnh Gia NGUYỄN NGỌC HẠNH: Cuộc Đời và Tác Phẩm*, SBTN,

April 2, 2015, accessed October 18, 2017, www.youtube.com/watch?v=1iL86PP5Nmw. Hạnh explained his work to online overseas Vietnamese communities in "Photography Gia."

11 Dan Huynh, "Nhiếp ảnh gia Nguyễn Ngọc Hạnh và những tác phẩm một thời vang bóng," *Người Việt*, January 1, 2011, accessed April 27, 2016, http://saigonecho.info/main/doisong /danhnhan/23694-nhip-nh-gia-nguyn-ngc-hnh-va-nhng-tac-phm-mt-thi-vang-bong.html.

12 Destiny Nguyen, *Nhiếp Ảnh Gia NGUYỄN NGỌC HẠNH: Cuộc Đời và Tác Phẩm.*

13 Griffin, "The Great War Photographs."

14 Capa's *The Falling Soldier* can be viewed here: www.metmuseum.org/art/collection/search /283315, accessed March 26, 2019.

15 See "What Counts as Manipulation."

16 Destiny Nguyen, *Nhiếp Ảnh Gia NGUYỄN NGỌC HẠNH: Cuộc Đời và Tác Phẩm.*

17 Anker, *Orgies of Feeling*; Williams, *Playing the Race Card.*

18 Reddy, *The Navigation of Feeling.*

19 Ebersole, "The Function of Ritual Weeping Revisited."

20 Rosenwein, *Emotional Communities in the Middle Ages.*

21 Adelman, *Beyond the Checkpoint*, chapter XX.

22 Boym, *The Future of Nostalgia.*

23 Cho, "Future Perfect Loss."

24 Somerstein, "War Photography."

25 Richard B. Woodward, "Essay," in *Small Wars: An-My Lê.*

26 My thanks to Sarah Parsons for alerting me to this connection in work by An-My Lê and Sally Mann. See Smith, *Photographic Remains.*

27 Stewart also notes the unlikely popularity of *Gone with the Wind* in Vietnam. See Stewart, "Teaching *Gone with the Wind* in the Socialist Republic of Vietnam." On the enduring nostalgia for antebellum America, see Horwitz, *Confederates in the Attic.*

28 Leshkowich, *Essential Trade.*

29 See Ross, dir., *Free State of Jones.* This is a feel-good Hollywood film about a disillusioned white Confederate soldier, played by Matthew McConaughey, who leads a militia of women and fellow deserters against the corrupt Confederate government. For all its liberal guilt the film's reenactment of the American Civil War once again centers whiteness by entrenching the white savior myth.

30 Schneider, *Performing Remains.*

31 Daase and Davis, eds., *Clausewitz on Small Wars.*

32 *Small Wars Manual*, 32.

33 Boot, *The Savage Wars of Peace.*

34 Quoted in Ibrahim, "Conceptualization of Guerilla Warfare."

35 My thanks to Kelly Wood for this observation.

36 Adelman and Kozol, "Unremarkable Suffering." On the proliferation of images, see Hariman and Lucaites, *The Public Image.*

37 Nudelman, "Sleeping Soldiers" and *Fighting Sleep*; Crary, *24/7.*

38 Interview with Hilton Als in An-My Lê, *Small Wars: Photographs by An-My Lê*, 119.

39 Marianne Hirsch, *Family Frames* and "The Generation of Postmemory."

40 Viet Thanh Nguyen, *Nothing Ever Dies.*

41 Duong, *Treacherous Subjects.*

42　Notably, Lê's work with the Weekend Warriors, the Virginia-based Vietnam War reenactors, prefigures her deepening collaboration with the military, first evident in *29 Palms* (2003–4), a series in which she documented military training exercises in California's Mojave Desert. Lê's relationship with the military continued with the publication of *Events Ashore* (2014), a series in which she first ventured into color photography. Lê undertook *Events Ashore*, completed over the course of a decade, after she was invited by the US Navy to document the course of its ships as they traversed a span of global missions, both military and humanitarian. In none of these cases can Lê be considered an officially embedded photographer, a category conferred to applicants only at the discretion of the Department of Defense's Foreign Press Center or of the command in charge of a particular conflict. In fact, during the Iraq war, Lê's petition to "embed" with the military was denied. Instead of serving as embedded photographer with deployed soldiers on a battlefield, in *29 Palms* Lê was granted permission to document these soldiers as they prepared for deployment in Afghanistan and Iraq. In short, although she had access to soldiers, she was denied direct access to the war zone; Lê negotiated her proximity within the constraints of spatial distance. This paradoxical condition of distanced proximity threads together Lê's three projects: *Small Wars*, *29 Palms*, and *Events Ashore*. Distanced proximity is a stance that enables Lê to observe varied acts of war, whether real or simulated, and with the military's permission, but without judgment and at such a remove as to suggest a self-conscious questioning of conventions of objectivity. Distanced proximity provides Lê with an ambivalent visual form.

FOUR. UNHOMED

1　Nathalie Huynh Chau Nguyen, *Memory Is Another Country*; Lam, *Perfume Dreams*.
2　Although the first and second waves of the Vietnamese diaspora have been the primary focus of scholars working in Asian American studies and area studies, recently critics have begun to consider the significance of other aspects of the diaspora, particularly its resettlement in the former Eastern bloc. See, for example, Schwenkel, "Rethinking Asian Mobilities"; and Dao, "Writing Exile."
3　Critics often consider family photos as instruments of ideology that entrench class structures and normalize conventions about race, gender, and sexuality. See Bourdieu, *Photography*; Chalfen, *Snapshot Versions of Family Life*; and Coe and Gates, *The Snapshot Photograph: The Rise of Popular Photography*. Although other critics acknowledge the complex function of family photos as materials that intersect with other visual genres, debates tend to emphasize how these images reproduce domestic ideology. See Julia Hirsch, *Family Photographs*; Marianne Hirsch, *Family Frames*; Rose, *Doing Family Photography*; and Zuromskis, *Snapshot Photography*.
4　Chalfen, *Snapshot Versions of Family Life*.
5　Wexler, *Tender Violence*.
6　Espiritu, *Body Counts*, 124.
7　Scholarly works on the colonial archive include Stoler, *Along the Archival Grain*; and Arondekar, *For the Record*. For an analysis of the power of archives in a settler-colonial context, see Wakeham, "Unreconciled Archives," forthcoming.

8   Sharpe, *In the Wake*, 8.

9   Kwon, *The Other Cold War*, 39; "Cold War in a Vietnamese Community."

10 Quoted in Nathalie Huynh Chau Nguyen, *Memory Is Another Country*, 20.

11 Nguyen, *Memory Is Another Country*.

12 Strassler, *Refracted Visions*.

13 Chi Tan Thai, interview with author, Toronto, August 24, 2016.

14 See especially Bourdieu, *Photography*; Julia Hirsch, *Family Photographs*; Marianne Hirsch, *Family Frames*; Spence, *Putting Myself in the Picture*; Spence and Holland, eds., *Family Snaps*; and Rose, *Doing Family Photography*. However, as Marianne Hirsch is careful to point out in her contrast between the ideological "gaze" and the individual "look," the discursive ends of family institutions are contestable. Roland Barthes provides the most influential analysis of the highly personal and intense emotional resonances of family photographs in *Camera Lucida*.

15 Strassler, *Refracted Visions*. The paradox of family snaps, as art historian Catherine Zuromskis explains, stems from the fact that they elicit intense emotional attachments even though their repetitive visual conventions make them banal. See Zuromskis, *Snapshot Photography*.

16 Schwartz, "The Album, the Art Market, and the Archives." Batchen also makes this argument in his essay "Dreams of Ordinary Life."

17 Found Vietnamese family photographs are a prominent theme taken up in *The Family Camera: Missing Chapters*, an exhibit that I cocurated with Deepali Dewan, Jennifer Orpana, Julie Crooks, and Sarah Bassnett, which was on view at the Art Gallery of Mississauga, May 6 to August 27, 2017.

18 Although as of this writing, I have not had the occasion to visit these installations personally, I have copies of exhibition catalogs and have discussed the works with the artist in a meeting in Ho Chi Minh City in January 2012 and through a series of emails.

19 Phu, Brown, and Dewan, "The Family Camera Network."

20 Derrida, *Archive Fever*.

21 Bourdieu, *Photography*.

22 Email exchange between author and Michelle Kumata, exhibit director, Wing Luke Museum, June 26, 2014.

23 Sekula, *Photography against the Grain*.

24 Marianne Hirsch, ed., *The Familial Gaze*.

25 In *Listening to Images*, Campt further nuances the ways that instrumental photography can become family photography through listening to images and attending to the affective resonances of images.

26 Phu, "Proximate Spectatorship in the Time of Cold War Human Rights."

27 Arendt, *The Origins of Totalitarianism*.

28 Phu, "Refugee Photography and the Subject of Human Interest."

29 For example, the oral histories collected by Hoang include accounts of orphans who found surrogate siblings and parents in refugee camps. See Hoang, *The Boat People*.

30 Espiritu, *Body Counts*.

31 See Smith, *American Archives*; Wexler, *Tender Violence*; and Bear and Albers, *Before-and-After Photography*.

32 Kuhn, *Family Secrets*.

33 Rosler, "In, Around, and Afterthoughts (on Documentary Photography)."

34 Zuromskis, *Snapshot Photography*.

35 Hon, Binh, Lucy, and Mr. Lu, interview with author, Toronto, October 11, 2016.

36 Zuromskis, *Snapshot Photography*; Campt, *Image Matters*; Langford, *Suspended Conversations*; Edwards, "Photographs and the Sound of History."

37 Zuromskis, *Snapshot Photography*.

38 Thai interview.

39 Azoulay, *Civil Imagination*.

40 See Kwon, *Ghosts of War in Vietnam*; and Duong, *Treacherous Subjects*.

41 Derrida, *Archive Fever*.

42 Spector, *Advice and Support*. North Vietnamese domestic intelligence was similarly structured. See Goscha, "Intelligence in a Time of Decolonization."

43 Marianne Hirsch and Leo Spitzer, *School Photos in Liquid Time*.

44 Wexler, *Tender Violence*, 21.

45 Wexler, *Tender Violence*, 33.

46 My thanks to LiLi Johnson for this insight.

47 I have not been able to discover what the additional number 4.424 might mean, although perhaps it denotes the military number of the officer who glossed the photo. Still, it is striking that so many fours—considered unlucky numbers in Vietnamese culture—should appear in such a short space.

48 Tuck and Yang, "Unbecoming Claims: Pedagogies of Refusal in Qualitative Research," 814.

49 Manalansan, "The 'Stuff' of Archives."

50 See Việt Lê, "The Art of War."

51 Albers, *Uncertain Histories*.

52 Sedgwick emphasizes the tactile dimensions of affect in *Touching Feeling*. For a discussion of tactility and affect in relation to photography, see Brown and Phu, eds., *Feeling Photography*.

53 Dinh Q. Lê, *Erasure*.

54 Shah, *Stranger Intimacy*.

55 See, for example, Hoang, "US Copyright Office Orphan Works Inquiry."

56 Campt, *Image Matters*.

57 Sharpe, *In the Wake*. See also Best and Hartman, "Fugitive Justice"; Hartman, *Lose Your Mother*; Harney and Moten, *The Undercommons*; and Moten, *Stolen Life*.

58 For discussions of adoption as a Cold War process of subject formation, see, for example, Eng, *The Feeling of Kinship*; Jodi Kim, *Ends of Empire*; and Briggs, *Somebody's Children*.

59 Volkman, ed., "Introduction: New Geographies of Kinship," in *Cultures of Transnational Adoption*; Eng, *The Feeling of Kinship*.

60 Batchen, *Burning with Desire: The Conception of Photography*.

61 Albers, *Uncertain Histories*.

62 In Toronto the Art Gallery of Ontario, a publicly funded institution, features the Max Dean Collection, a collection of family albums, the bulk of which are orphaned.

63 In her study of the ways that American culture grapples with memories of the Vietnam War, Sturken considers how family photographs enter the public sphere. See Sturken, *Tangled Memories*.

64 My thanks to Celio Barreto for pointing this photograph out to me.

65 Freeman, *Time Blinds*.

66 In the Family Camera Network we combine the methods of oral history and visual studies—fields that seldom converge in substantive ways (with the notable exception of the work of Freund and Thomson). Oral historians most often consider visual artifacts as aide-mémoire, the backdrop or illustration of life stories. They employ photo elicitation as a means to prompt recollection. Conversely, in photography studies, despite the work of scholars who posit the integral connection between orality and photography, this insight has yet to be fully explored. See Freund and Thomson, *Photography and Oral History*; Fobear, "Nesting Bodies"; and Collier and Collier, *Visual Anthropology*.

67 For more on the project's methodology, see Phu, Brown, and Dewan, "The Family Camera Network."

68 Anne Tran Fazzalari and Dana Tran, interview with author, Toronto, November 24, 2016.

69 For a discussion of the currency of photographs, see Holmes, "The Stereoscope and the Stereograph."

70 Derrida, *Archive Fever*.

71 Schwenkel, *The American War in Contemporary Vietnam*.

EPILOGUE. **VISUAL REUNION**

————

1 Tim Page, email correspondence with author, February 2019.

2 Schwenkel, *The American War in Contemporary Vietnam*.

3 The promotional image for *The Vietnam War* documentary can be seen here: www.pbs.org /kenburns/the-vietnam-war/home/?utm_source=promourl&utm_campaign=vietnamwar _2017&utm_medium=direct, accessed March 18, 2019.

4 Parker, "Ken Burns's American Canon."

5 Shephard, "The Insidious Ideology of Ken Burns's *The Vietnam War*."

6 Breitbart discusses how the Burns effect in turn reinforces a Burns brand, so the history to which the documentaries ultimately contribute is characterized by celebrity. See Breitbart, "The Burns Effect."

Adelman, Rebecca A. *Beyond the Checkpoint: Visual Practices in America's Global War on Terror.* Amherst: University of Massachusetts Press, 2014.

Adelman, Rebecca A., and Wendy Kozol. "Unremarkable Suffering: Banality, Spectatorship, and War's In/visibilities." In *In/Visible War: America's 21st Century Armed Conflicts,* edited by Jon Simon and John Lucaites, 89–108. Brunswick, NJ: Rutgers University Press, 2017.

Agnew, Vanessa. "History's Affective Turn: Historical Reenactment and Its Work in the Present." *Rethinking History* 11, no. 3 (2007): 299–312.

Agnew, Vanessa, and Jonathan Lamb, eds. "Extreme and Sentimental History." Special issue, *Criticism* 46, no. 4 (2004).

Albers, Kate Palmer. *Uncertain Histories: Accumulation, Inaccessibility, and Doubt in Contemporary Photography.* Berkeley: University of California Press, 2015.

Alonso, Harriet Hyman. *Peace as a Women's Issue: A History of the U.S. Movement for World Peace and Women's Rights.* Syracuse, NY: Syracuse University Press, 1993.

Andermann, Jens, and William Rowe, eds. *Images of Power: Iconography, Culture and the State in Latin America.* New York: Berghahn, 2006.

Anderson, Helen E. "Fighting for Family: Vietnamese Women and the American War." In *The Columbia History of the Vietnam War,* edited by David L. Anderson, 297–316. New York: Columbia University Press, 2010

Anker, Elizabeth R. *Orgies of Feeling: Melodrama and the Politics of Feeling.* Durham, NC: Duke University Press, 2014.

Apel, Dora. *War Culture and the Contest of Images.* New York: Rutgers, 2012.

Arendt, Hannah. *The Origins of Totalitarianism.* 1951. New York: Houghton Mifflin Harcourt, 2001.

Arlen, Michael J. *Living-Room War.* 1969. Syracuse, NY: Syracuse University Press, 2003.

Armstrong, Elizabeth. "Before Bandung: The Anti-imperialist Women's Movement in Asia and the Women's International Federation." *Signs: Journal of Women in Culture and Society* 41, no. 2 (2016): 305–31.

Armstrong, Elisabeth B., and Vijay Prashad. "Solidarity: War Rites and Women's Rights." *CR: The New Centennial Review* 5, no. 1 (2005): 213–53.

Arondekar, Anjali. *For the Record: On Sexuality and the Colonial Archive in India*. Durham, NC: Duke University Press, 2009.

Attie, Mike, and Meghan O'Hara, dirs. *In Country*. Oregon: Naked Edge Films, 2014.

Auslander, Mark. "Touching the Past: Materializing Time in Traumatic 'Living History' Reenactments." *Signs and Society* 1, no. 1 (spring 2013): 161–83.

Austin, Curtis J. *Up against the Wall: Violence in the Making and Unmaking of the Black Panther Party*. Fayetteville: University of Arkansas Press, 2006.

Azoulay, Ariella. *Civil Imagination: A Political Ontology of Photography*. Translated by Louise Bethlehem. London: Verso, 2015.

Bajorek, Jennifer. "On Color Photography in an Extra-moral Sense." *Third Text* 29, no. 3 (2015): 221–35. Accessed September 16, 2017. doi:10.1080/09528822.2015.1106136.

Baker, Simon, and Shoair Mavlian, eds. *Conflict, Time, Photography*. London: Tate, 2014.

Barthes, Roland. *Camera Lucida: Reflections on Photography*. 1981. Translated by Richard Howard. New York: Hill and Wang, 2010.

Barthes, Roland. *Image Music Text*. Translated by Stephen Heath. New York: Hill and Wang, 1977.

Barthes, Roland. *Mythologies*. Translated by Annette Lavers. New York: Hill and Wang, 1972.

Bassnett, Sarah, Andrea Noble, and Thy Phu. "Cold War Visual Alliances." *Visual Studies* 30, no. 2 (2015): 119–22. Accessed September 16, 2017. doi:10.1080/1472586X.2015.1024976.

Batchelor, David. *Chromophobia*. London: Reaktion, 2000.

Batchen, Geoffrey. *Burning with Desire: The Conception of Photography*. Cambridge, MA: MIT Press, 1999.

Batchen, Geoffrey. "Dreams of Ordinary Life: Cartes-de-visite and the Bourgeois Imagination." In *Photography: Theoretical Snapshots*, edited by J. J. Long, Andrea Noble, and Edward Welch, 80–97. Oxon, UK: Routledge, 2009.

Bear, Jordan, and Kate Palmer Albers. *Before-and-After Photography: Histories and Contexts*. London: Bloomsbury, 2017.

Beins, Agatha. "Radical Others: Women of Color and Revolutionary Feminism." *Feminist Studies* 41, no. 1 (2015): 150–83.

Benjamin, Walter. "A Little History of Photography." In *Walter Benjamin: Selected Writings*. Vol. 2, *1927–1934*, edited by Michael W. Jennings, Howard Eiland, and Gary Smith, translated by Rodney Livingstone et al., 507–30. Cambridge, MA: Belknap, 2005.

Benjamin, Walter. "The Work of Art in the Age of Mechanical Reproduction." In *Illuminations*, edited by Hannah Arendt, translated by Harry Zohn, 219–52. New York: Harcourt, 1968.

Best, Stephen, and Saidiya Hartman. "Fugitive Justice." *Representations* 92, no. 1 (2005): 1–14.

Bigley, James D. "Living History and Battle Reenactment: The Dilemma of Selective Interpretation." *History News* 46, no. 6 (1991): 12–18.

Blackburn, Robert M. *Mercenaries and Lyndon Johnson's More Flags: The Hiring of Korean, Filipino, and Thai Soldiers in the Vietnam War*. Jefferson, NC: McFarland, 1994.

Blaszczyk, Regina Lee. *The Color Revolution*. Cambridge, MA: MIT Press, 2012.

Bonier, David E., Steven M. Champlain, and Timothy S. Kolly. *The Vietnam Veteran: A History of Neglect*. New York: Praeger, 1984.

Boot, Max. *The Savage Wars of Peace: Small Wars and the Rise of American Power*. New York: Basic, 2014.

Bourdieu, Pierre. *Photography: A Middle-Brow Art*. 1965. Translated by Shaun Whiteside. Stanford, CA: Stanford University Press, 1999.

Boym, Svetlana. *The Future of Nostalgia*. New York: Basic, 2001.

Bradley, Mark Philip. *Vietnam at War*. Oxford: Oxford University Press, 2009.

Brasheeth, Haim. "Projecting Trauma: War Photography and the Public Sphere." *Third Text* 20, no. 1 (2006): 57–71.

Breitbart, Eric. "The Burns Effect: Documentary as Celebrity Advertisement." *New England Review* 28, no. 1 (2007): 168–78.

Briggs, Laura. *Somebody's Children: The Politics of Transracial and Transnational Adoption*. Durham, NC: Duke University Press, 2012.

Brown, Elspeth, and Thy Phu, eds. *Feeling Photography*. Durham, NC: Duke University Press, 2014.

Burgin, Victor, ed. *Thinking Photography*. London: Palgrave Macmillan, 1982.

Burrows, Larry. "South Viet Nam's Madame Nhu." *Time*, August 9, 1963. http://content.time.com/time/covers/0,16641,19630809,00.html.

Butler, Judith. *Frames of War: When Is Life Grievable?* London: Verso, 2010.

Campbell, David. "Photo Manipulation and Verification." Accessed August 13, 2015. www.david-campbell.org/topics/photo-manipulation-verification.

Campt, Tina. *Image Matters: Archive, Photography, and the Making of the African Diaspora in Europe*. Durham, NC: Duke University Press, 2012.

Campt, Tina. *Listening to Images*. Durham, NC: Duke University Press, 2017.

Carlson, Jennifer. *Citizen-Protectors: The Everyday Politics of Guns in an Age of Decline*. Oxford: Oxford University Press, 2015.

Chalfen, Richard. *Snapshot Versions of Family Life*. Bowling Green, OH: Bowling Green University Press, 1987.

Chapman, Jessica M. *Cauldron of Resistance: Ngo Dinh Diem, the United States and 1950s Southern Vietnam*. Ithaca, NY: Cornell University Press, 2013.

Charlot, John. "Vietnamese Cinema: First Views." *Journal of Southeast Asian Studies* 22, no. 1 (1991): 33–62.

Chauvel, Patrick. *Ceux du Nord*. Paris: Aranesh, 2014.

Chinchilla, Norma Stoltz. "Revolutionary Popular Feminism in Nicaragua: Articulating Class, Gender, and National Sovereignty." *Gender and Society* 4, no. 3 (1990): 370–97. www.jstor.org/stable/189649.

Cho, Lily. "Future Perfect Loss: Richard Fung's *Sea in the Blood*." *Screen* 49, no. 4 (2008): 426–39.

Chong, Sylvia Shin Huey. *The Oriental Obscene: Violence and Racial Fantasies in the Vietnam Era*. Durham, NC: Duke University Press, 2011.

Chong, Sylvia Shin Huey, and Cathy Schlund-Vials, eds. "(Re)Collecting the Vietnam War." Special issue, *Asian American Literary Review* 6, no. 2 (2015).

Churchill, David. "American Expatriates and the Building of Alternative Social Space in Toronto, 1965–1977." *Urban History Review* 39, no. 1 (2010): 31–44.

Churchill, David. "Draft Resisters, Left Nationalism, and the Politics of Anti-imperialism." *Canadian Historical Review* 93, no. 2 (2012): 227–60.

Coe, Brian, and Paul Gates. *The Snapshot Photograph: The Rise of Popular Photography*. London: Ash and Grant, 1977.

Collier, John, and Malcolm Collier. *Visual Anthropology: Photography as a Research Method.* Albuquerque: University of New Mexico Press, 1986.

Collins, Kathleen. "Living Skeletons: Carte-de-visite Propaganda in the American Civil War." *History of Photography* 22, no. 2 (1988): 103–20.

Crary, Jonathan. *24/7: Late Capitalism and the Ends of Sleep.* London: Verso, 2014.

Crowly, David. *Posters of the Cold War.* London: V&A, 2008.

Cumings, Bruce. *Parallax Visions: Making Sense of American–East Asian Relations at the End of the Century.* Durham, NC: Duke University Press, 2002.

Daase, Christopher, and James W. Davis, eds. *Clausewitz on Small Wars.* London: Oxford University Press, 2015.

Dang, Thuy Vo. "The Cultural Work of Anticommunism in the San Diego Vietnamese American Community." *Amerasia Journal* 31, no. 2 (2005): 64–86.

Dao, Thang. "Writing Exile: Vietnamese Literature in the Diaspora." PhD diss., University of Southern California, 2012.

Davis, Patricia G. "The Other Southern Belles: Civil War Reenactment, African American Women, and the Performance of Idealized Femininity." *Text and Performance Quarterly* 32, no. 4 (2012): 308–31.

Debord, Guy. *The Society of the Spectacle.* 1967. New York: Zone, 1995.

Debroise, Olivier. *Mexican Suite: A History of Photography in Mexico.* Austin: University of Texas Press, 2001.

Derrida, Jacques. *Archive Fever: A Freudian Impression.* Translated by Eric Prenowitz. Chicago: University of Chicago Press, 1998.

Dewan, Deepali. *Embellished Reality: Indian Painted Photographs.* Toronto: ROM, 2012.

Dickerman, Leah. "Camera Obscura: Socialist Realism in the Shadow of Photography." *October* 93 (2000): 139–53. Accessed September 16, 2017. doi:10.2307/779160.

Đoàn Công Tính. *Khoảnh Khắc.* Ho Chi Minh City: Nhà xuất bản Tổng hợp, n.d.

Dror, Olga. "Establishing Ho Chi Minh's Cult: Vietnamese Traditions and Their Transformations." *Journal of Asian Studies* 75, no. 2 (2016): 433–66.

Dudziak, Mary. *Cold War Civil Rights: Race and the Image of American Democracy.* Princeton, NJ: Princeton University Press, 2000.

Duiker, William J. *The Communist Road to Power in Vietnam.* Boulder, CO: Westview, 1981.

Duong, Lan P. *Treacherous Subjects: Gender, Culture, and Trans-Vietnamese Feminisms.* Philadelphia: Temple University Press, 2012.

Ebersole, Gary L. "The Function of Ritual Weeping Revisited: Affective Discourse and Moral Discourse." *History of Religions* 39, no. 3 (2000): 211–46.

Echols, Alice. *Daring to Be Bad: Radical Feminism in America, 1967–1975.* Minneapolis: University of Minnesota Press, 1989.

Edwards, Elizabeth. "Photographs and the Sound of History." *Visual Anthropology Review* 21, no. 1 (2005): 27–46.

Eisen, Arlene. *Women and Revolution in Viet Nam.* London: Zed, 1984.

Emering, Edward J. *Viet Cong: A Photographic Portrait.* Atglen, PA: Schiffler Military History, 1999.

Eng, David. *The Feeling of Kinship: Queer Liberalism and the Racialization of Intimacy.* Durham, NC: Duke University Press, 2010.

Enloe, Cynthia. *Bananas, Beaches and Bases: Making Feminist Sense of International Politics.* Berkeley: University of California Press, 2000.

Enloe, Cynthia. *Maneuvers: The International Politics of Militarizing Women's Lives.* Berkeley: University of California Press, 2000.

Espiritu, Yen Le. *Body Counts: The Vietnam War and Militarized Refugees.* Oakland: University of California Press, 2014.

Faas, Horst, and Timothy Page, eds. *Requiem: By the Photographers Who Died in Vietnam and Indochina.* New York: Random House, 1997.

Fall, Bernard B., ed. *Ho Chi Minh on Revolution: Selected Writings, 1920–66.* London: Praeger, 1967.

Fineman, Mia. *Faking It: Manipulated Photography before Photoshop.* New York: Metropolitan Museum of Art, 2012.

Fobear, Katherine. "Nesting Bodies: Exploration of the Body and Embodiment in LGBT Refugee Oral History and Participatory Photography." *Social Alternatives* 35, no. 3 (2016): 33–43.

"The Fourth World Manifesto." Paper presented at the Indochinese Women's Conference, 1971.

Freeman, Elizabeth. *Time Binds: Queer Temporalities, Queer Histories.* Durham, NC: Duke University Press, 2010.

Freund, Alexander, and Alistair Thomson. *Photography and Oral History.* London: Palgrave Macmillan, 2011.

Gaddis, John Lewis. *We Now Know: Rethinking Cold War History.* New York: Oxford University Press, 1998.

Goscha, Christopher. "Intelligence in a Time of Decolonization: The Case of the Democratic Republic of Vietnam at War (1945–50)." *Intelligence and National Security* 22, no. 1 (2007): 100–138.

Grech, Shaun. "Decolonising Eurocentric Disability Studies: Why Colonialism Matters in the Disability and Global South Debate." *Social Identities: Journal for the Study of Race, Nation, and Culture* 2 21, no. 1 (2015) 6–21.

Griffin, Michael. "The Great War Photographs: Constructing Myths of History and Photojournalism." In *Picturing the Past: Media, History, and Photography,* edited by Bonnie Brennan and Hannah Hardt, 122–53. Champaign: University of Illinois Press, 1999.

Griffin, Michael. "Media Images of War." *Media, War, and Conflict* 3, no. 1 (2010): 7–41.

Guenette, Robert, dir. *Vietnam's Unseen War: Pictures from the Other Side.* 20th Century Fox, 2002.

Hagopian, Patrick. "Vietnam War Photography as a Locus of Memory." In *Locating Memory: Photographic Acts,* edited by Annette Kuhn and Kirsten Emiko McAllister, 201–22. New York: Berghahn, 2006.

Hallin, Daniel C. *The Uncensored War: The Media and Vietnam.* New York: Oxford University Press, 1986.

Hammond, William M. *Reporting Vietnam: Media and Military at War.* Lawrence: University Press of Kansas, 1998.

Handler, Richard, and William Saxton. "Dyssimulation: Reflexivity, Narrative, and the Quest for Authenticity in 'Living History.'" *Cultural Anthropology* 3, no. 3 (1988): 242–60.

Hariman, Robert. "Why Photographs Don't Stop the War." December 19, 2016. www.reading thepictures.org/2016/12/why-photos-dont-stop-the-war.

Hariman, Robert, and John Lucaites. *No Caption Needed: Iconic Photographs, Public Culture, and Liberal Democracy*. Chicago: University of Chicago Press, 2007.

Hariman, Robert, and John Louis Lucaites. *The Public Image: Photography and Civic Spectatorship*. Chicago: University of Chicago Press, 2016.

Harney, Stefano, and Fred Moten. *The Undercommons: Fugitive Planning and Black Study*. London: Minor Compositions, 2013.

Hartman, Saidiya. *Lose Your Mother: A Journey along the Atlantic Slave Route*. New York: Farrar, Straus and Giroux, 2007.

Haski, Pierre. "Une 'affaire Photoshop' dans le temple photojournalisme." Rue 89. Last modified November 21, 2016. www.nouvelobs.com/rue89/rue89-rue89-culture/20150609.RUE9409/une-affaire-photoshop-dans-le-temple-du-photojournalisme.html.

Heather, David. *Vietnam Posters: The David Heather Collection*. Munich: Prestel, 2009.

Heroes and Heroines of the Liberation Armed Forces of South Vietnam. Saigon: Liberation Editions, 1965.

Hershberger, Mary. *Traveling to Vietnam: American Peace Activists and the War*. Syracuse, NY: Syracuse University Press, 1998.

Hess, Stephen. "The 'Cheaper Solution.'" *American Journalism Review* 16, no. 3 (1994): 27–29.

Hien, Nina. "The Good, the Bad, and the Not Beautiful: In the Street and on the Ground in Vietnam." *Trans Asia Photography Review* 3, no. 2 (2013). Accessed September 16, 2017. http://hdl.handle.net/2027/spo.7977573.0003.202.

Hien, Nina. "Ho Chi Minh City's Beauty Regime: Haptic Technologies of the Self in the New Millenium." *positions: east asia critique* 20, no. 2 (2012): 473–93. Accessed September 16, 2017. muse.jhu.edu/article/478971.

Hien, Nina. "Photo Resurrections before and after Images: An Ancestor Story." *Trans Asia Photography Review* 1, no. 1 (2010). Accessed September 16, 2017. http://hdl.handle.net/2027/spo.7977573.0001.104.

Hien, Nina. "Reanimating Vietnam: Icons, Photography and Image Making in Ho Chi Minh City." PhD diss., Cornell University, 2007.

Hirsch, Julia. *Family Photographs: Content, Meaning, and Effect*. New York: Oxford University Press, 1981.

Hirsch, Marianne, ed. *The Familial Gaze*. Hanover, NH: University Press of New England, 1999.

Hirsch, Marianne. *Family Frames: Photography, Narrative, Postmemory*. Cambridge, MA: Harvard University Press, 1997.

Hirsch, Marianne. "The Generation of Postmemory." *Poetics Today* 29, no. 1 (2008): 101–28.

Hirsch, Marianne, and Leo Spitzer. *School Photos in Liquid Time: Reframing Difference*. Seattle: University of Washington Press, 2020.

Hoang, Carina. *The Boat People: Personal Stories from the Vietnamese Exodus, 1975–1996*. New York: Beaufort, 2013.

Hoang, Olive. "US Copyright Office Orphan Works Inquiry: Finding Homes for the Orphans." *Berkeley Technology Law Journal* 21, no. 1 (2014): 265–88.

Holmes, Oliver Wendell. "The Stereoscope and the Stereograph." *Atlantic*, June 1859.

Honig, Emily. "Maoist Mappings of Gender: Reassessing the Red Guards." In *Chinese Femininities, Chinese Masculinities: A Reader*, edited by Susan Brownell and Jeffrey N. Wasserstrom, 255–68. Berkeley: University of California Press, 2002.

Horwitz, Tony. *Confederates in the Attic: Dispatches from the Unfinished Civil War*. New York: Pantheon, 1998.

Hoskins, Andrew. *Televising War: From Vietnam to Iraq*. London: Continuum, 2004.

Hunt, George P. "Editor's Note." *Life*, January 25, 1963, 5.

Ibrahim, Azeem. "Conceptualization of Guerilla Warfare." *Small Wars and Insurgencies* 15, no. 3 (2004): 112–24.

Jacobs, Seth. *America's Miracle Man in Vietnam: Ngo Dinh Diem, Religion, Race, and U.S. Intervention in Southeast Asia*. Durham, NC: Duke University Press, 2004.

Jacobs, Seth. *Cold War Mandarin: Ngo Dinh Diem and the Origins of America's Cold War in Vietnam, 1950–1963*. Lanham, MD: Rowman and Littlefield, 2006.

James, Sarah E. *Common Ground: German Photographic Culture across the Iron Curtain*. New Haven, CT: Yale University Press, 2013.

Jameson, Fredric. *The Political Unconscious: Narrative as a Socially Symbolic Act*. Ithaca, NY: Cornell University Press, 1981.

Kampwirth, Karen. *Women and Guerilla Movements: Nicaragua, El Salvador, Chiapas, Cuba*. University Park Pennsylvania State University Press, 2002.

Kaye, Simon T. "Challenging Certainty: The Utility and History of Counterfactualism." *History and Theory* 49 (2010): 38–57.

Kennedy, Liam. *Afterimages: Photography and U.S. Foreign Policy*. Chicago: University of Chicago Press, 2016.

Kennedy, Liam. "Securing Vision: Photography and US Foreign Policy." *Media, Culture and Society* 30, no. 3 (2008): 279–94. Accessed September 16, 2017. doi:10.1177/0163443708088788.

Kennedy, Liam, and Caitlin Patrick. *The Violence of the Image: Photography and International Conflict*. London: I. B. Tauris, 2014.

Kim, Jodi. *Ends of Empire: Asian American Critique and the Cold War*. Minneapolis: University of Minnesota Press, 2010.

King, David. *The Commissar Vanishes: The Falsification of Photographs and Art in Stalin's Russia*. London: Tate, 2014.

Kozol, Wendy. *Distant Wars Made Visible: The Ambivalence of Witnessing*. Minneapolis: University of Minnesota Press, 2014.

Kreusch, Jeremy. "Violent Representation: Photographs, Soldiers and an Ideological War." In *Mythologizing the Vietnam War: Visual Culture and Mediated Memory*, edited by Jennifer Good, Paul Lowe, Brigitte Lardinois, and Val Williams, 3–21. London: Cambridge Scholars Publishing, 2014.

Kriebel, Sabine. "Photomontage in the Year 1932: John Heartfield and the National Socialists." *Oxford Art Journal* 31, no. 1 (2008): 92–127. Accessed September 16, 2017. doi:10.1093/oxartj /kcn007.

Kroes, Rob. *Photographic Memories: Private Pictures, Public Images, and American History*. Hanover, NH: Dartmouth College Press, 2007.

Kuhn, Annette. *Family Secrets: Acts of Memory and Imagination* London: Verso, 1995.

Kwon, Heonik. "Cold War in a Vietnamese Community." In *Four Decades On: Vietnam, the United States, and the Legacies of the Second Indochina War*, edited by Scott Laderman and Edwin A. Martin, 84–102. Durham, NC: Duke University Press, 2013.

Kwon, Heonik. *Ghosts of War in Vietnam*. Cambridge: Cambridge University Press, 2008.

Kwon, Heonik. *The Other Cold War.* New York: Columbia University Press, 2010.

Laderman, Scott. *Tours of Vietnam: War, Travel Guides, and Memory.* Durham, NC: Duke University Press, 2008.

Lam, Andrew. *Perfume Dreams: Reflections on the Vietnamese Diaspora.* Berkeley, CA: Heyday, 2005.

Landsberger, Stefan R. "The Rise and Fall of the Chinese Propaganda Poster." In *Chinese Propaganda Posters,* edited by Min Anchee, Duo Duo, and Stefan R. Landsberger, 16–17. London: Taschen, 2003.

Langford, Martha. *Suspended Conversations: The Afterlife of Memory in Photographic Albums.* Kingston, ON: McGill-Queens University Press, 2008.

Lê, An-My. *Events Ashore: Photographs by An-My Lê.* 2014.

Lê, An-My. *Small Wars: Photographs by An-My Lê.* New York: Aperture, 2015.

Lê, An-My. *29 Palms: Photographs by An-My Lê.* 2003–4.

Le, C. N. "'Better Red Than Dead': Anti-communist Politics among Vietnamese Americans." In *Anti-communist Minorities in the U.S.,* edited by Ieva Zake, 189–209. London: Springer, 2009.

Lê, Dinh Q. *Erasure.* Accessed June 2, 2014. www.erasurearchive.net/index.php?option=com _content&view=article&id=1&Itmid=2.

Lê, Việt. "The Art of War: Vietnamese American Visual Artists Đình Q. Lê, Ann Phông and Nguyễn Tân Hoàng." *Amerasia Journal* 31, no. 2 (2005): 21–35.

Leese, Daniel. *Mao Cult: Rhetoric and Ritual in China's Cultural Revolution.* Cambridge: Cambridge University Press, 2011.

Leshkowich, Ann Marie. "The Ao Dai Goes Global: How International Influences and Female Entrepreneurs Have Shaped Vietnam's 'National Costume.'" In *Re-orienting Fashion: The Globalization of Asian Dress,* edited by Sandra Niessen, Ann Marie Leshkowich, and Carla Jones, 79–115. Oxford: Berg, 2003.

Leshkowich, Ann Marie. *Essential Trade: Vietnamese Women in a Changing Marketplace.* Cambridge: Cambridge University Press, 2011.

Leshkowich, Ann Marie. "Wandering Ghosts of Late Socialism: Conflict, Metaphor, and Memory in a Southern Vietnamese Marketplace." *Journal of Asian Studies* 67, no. 1 (2008): 5–41.

Leslie, Esther. *Walter Benjamin: Overpowering Conformism.* London: Pluto, 2000.

"A Letter from Vietnamese Mothers to Mothers and Children-Loving People in the World." *Women of Vietnam,* no. 2 (1967): 3.

Lewinsky, Jorge L. *The Camera at War: War Photography from 1848 to the Present Day.* London: W & J MacKay, 1978.

Lieu, Nhi T. "Remembering 'the Nation' through Pageantry: Femininity and the Politics of Vietnamese Womanhood in the Hoa Hau Ao Dai Contest." *Frontiers* 21, no. 1–2 (2000): 127–51.

Linfield, Susie. *The Cruel Radiance: Photography and Political Violence.* Chicago: University of Chicago Press, 2010.

Logevall, Fredrik. *Embers of War: The Fall of an Empire and the Making of America's Vietnam.* New York: Random House, 2012.

Mackerras, Colin, Donald H. McMillen, and Andrew Watson, eds. *Dictionary of the Politics of the People's Republic of China.* London: Routledge, 1998.

Maclear, Michael, dir. *Vietnam: The Ten Thousand Day War.* Directed by Michael Maclear. CBC, 1980.

Magelssen, Scott. "Making History in the Second Person: Post-touristic Considerations for Living Historical Interpretation." *Theatre Journal* 58, no. 2 (2006): 291–312.

Maj, Helle, and Jørn Stjerneklar. "Aber Warum." *May Day Press.* Last modified June 2, 2015. www.maydaypress.com/blog/files/Opinions%20from%20Africa.html.

Maj, Helle, and Jørn Stjerneklar. "Excuse My French!" *May Day Press.* Last modified June 10, 2015. www.maydaypress.com/blog/files/2ce9a7cd940027138ec550756d76716b-25.html.

Man, Simeon. *Soldiering through Empire: Race and the Making of the Decolonizing Pacific.* Berkeley: University of California Press, 2018.

Manalansan, Martin. "The 'Stuff' of Archives: Mess, Migration, and Queer Lives." *Radical History Review* 120 (2014): 94–107.

Mandelbaum, Michael. "Vietnam: The Television War." *Daedalus* 111, no. 4 (1982): 157–69.

Marien, Mary Warner. *Photography: A Cultural History*, 4th ed. New York: Pearson: 2015.

Martin, Susan, ed. *Decade of Protest: Political Posters from the United States, Viet Nam, and Cuba, 1965–1975.* Berkeley: Small Art, 1996.

Masco, Joseph. *The Theatre of Operations: National Security Affect from the Cold War to the War on Terror.* Durham, NC: Duke University Press, 2014.

McCalman, Iain, and Paul A. Pickering, eds. *Historical Reenactment: From Realism to the Affective Turn.* Basingstoke, UK: Palgrave Macmillan, 2010.

Meekosha, Helen. "Decolonising Disability: Thinking and Acting Globally." *Disability and Society* 26, no. 6 (2011) 667–82. Accessed September 16, 2017. doi:10.1080/09687599.2011.602860.

Military History Institute of Vietnam. *Victory in Vietnam: The Official History of the People's Army of Vietnam, 1954–1975.* Translated by Merle L. Pribbenow. Lawrence: University Press of Kansas, 2002.

Miller, Edward Harvey. *Ngo Dinh Diem, the United States, and the Fate of South Vietnam.* Cambridge, MA: Harvard University Press, 2013.

Minh, Lê Ngọc. "Lịch Sử Nhiếp Ảnh Việt Nam." Accessed March 12, 2017. http://www.vccottawa .com/am-nhac-nghe-thuat/lichsunhiepanhvietnam.

Mirzoeff, Nicholas. *An Introduction to Visual Culture.* London: Routledge, 1999.

Moeller, Susan D. *Shooting War: Photography and the American Experience of Combat.* New York: Basic, 1989.

Mohanty, Chandra Talpade. "Under Western Eyes: Feminist Scholarship and Colonial Discourses." *boundary 2* 12/13, no. 3 (1984): 333–58.

Morozov, Sergei, and Valerie Lloyd, eds. *Soviet Photography: An Age of Realism.* New York: Greenwich House, 1984.

Moten, Fred. *Stolen Life.* Durham, NC: Duke University Press, 2018.

Nail, Thomas. *The Figure of the Migrant.* Stanford, CA: Stanford University Press, 2015.

Nam, Mai. *Một Thời Hào Hùng.* Hanoi: Nhà xuất bản Thanh niên, n.d.

Nguyen, Destiny. *Nhiếp Ảnh Gia NGUYỄN NGỌC HẠNH: Cuộc Đời và Tác Phẩm.* SBTN Video. April 2, 2015. www.youtube.com/watch?v=1iL86PP5Nmw.

Nguyễn, Đức Chính. *Văn Hóa Nhiếp Ảnh.* Hanoi: Nhà Xuất Bản Thông Tấn, 2008.

Nguyen, Lien-Hang T. *Hanoi's War: An International History of the War for Peace in Vietnam.* Chapel Hill: University of North Carolina Press, 2012.

Nguyen, Mimi Thi. *The Gift of Freedom: War, Debt, and Other Refugee Passages*. Durham, NC: Duke University Press, 2012.

Nguyen, Nathalie Huynh Chau. *Memory Is Another Country: Women of the Vietnamese Diaspora*. Santa Barbara, CA: Praeger, 2009.

Nguyen, Thi Tuyet Mai. *The Rubber Tree: A Memoir of a Vietnamese Woman Who Was an Anti-French Guerilla, a Publisher, and Peace Activist*. Edited by Monique Senderowicz. Jefferson, NC: McFarland, 1994.

Nguyen, Viet Thanh. *Nothing Ever Dies: Vietnam and the Memory of War*. Cambridge, MA: Harvard University Press, 2016.

Nguyen, Viet Thanh. *Race and Resistance: Literature and Politics in Asian America*. London: Oxford University Press, 2002.

Nguyen, Vinh. "Our Hearts and Minds: (Post) Refugee Affect and the War in Viet Nam." PhD diss., McMaster University, 2015.

Nguyễn Ngọc Hạnh. "Photography Gia." March 17, 2012. www.aihuubienhoa.com/a1647/nhiep-anh-gia-nguyen-ngoc-hanh.

Nguyễn Ngoc Hanh and Nguyễn Manh Dan. *Viet Nam in Flames*. English ed.: Hong Kong: Kwoc Hing, 1969.

Nguyễn Thị Bình. *Family, Friends, and Country*. Ho Chi Minh City: Trí Thức, 2012.

Nguyễn Thị Bình. *No Other Road to Take: The Memoirs of Mrs. Nguyen Thi Dinh*. Translated by Mai Elliott. Ithaca, NY: Southeast Asia Program, Cornell University Press, 1976.

Nhu, Madame. "Holiness without Culture Is Blind. Culture without Holiness Is Bookish." *The Times of Vietnam*, August 4, 1963, 16.

Ninh, Kim N. B. *A World Transformed: The Politics of Culture in Revolutionary Vietnam, 1945–1965*. Ann Arbor: University of Michigan Press, 2002.

Noble, Andrea. "The Politics of Emotion in the Mexican Revolution: The Tears of Pancho Villa." In *Latin American Visual Culture: Politics, Media, Affect*, edited by Geoffrey Kantaris and Rory O'Bryen, 249–70. Woodbridge, UK: Tamesis, 2013.

Noble, Andrea. "Visual Culture and Latin American Studies." *New Centennial Review* 4 (2004): 219–38.

Nudelman, Franny. "Against Photography: Susan Sontag's Vietnam." *Photography and Culture* 7, no. 1 (2014): 7–20.

Nudelman, Franny. *Fighting Sleep: The War for the Mind and the US Military*. London: Verso, 2019.

Nudelman, Franny. "Sleeping Soldiers: Tim Hetherington RIP." Paper presented at the American Studies Association, Toronto, September 2015.

Page, Timothy, Douglas Niven, and Riley Christopher. *Another Vietnam: Pictures of the War from the Other Side*. New York: National Geographic Society, 2002.

Pal Singh, Nikhil. "The Black Panthers and the 'Underdeveloped Country' of the Left." In *The Black Panther Party Reconsidered: Reflections and Scholarship*, edited by Charles E. Jones, 57–105. Baltimore: Black Classic, 1998.

Panzer, Mary. *Mathew Brady and the Image of History*. Washington, DC: Smithsonian Institute, 1997.

Parker, Ian. "Ken Burns's American Canon." *New Yorker*, September 4, 2017. www.newyorker.com/magazine/2017/09/04/ken-burns-american-canon.

Perlmutter, David D. *Photojournalism and Foreign Policy: Icons of Outrage in International Crises.* Westport, CT: Praeger, 1998.

Pham, Ngọc Trưởng. "Vietnam: A Brief History of Vietnamese Films." In *Films in South East Asia: Views from the Region,* edited by David Hanan, 59–82. Hanoi: SEAPAVVA, the Vietnam Film Institute, the National Screen and Sound Archive in Australia, 2001.

Phu, Thy. *Picturing Model Citizens: Civility in Asian American Visual Culture.* Philadelphia: Temple University Press, 2012.

Phu, Thy. "Proximate Spectatorship in the Time of Cold War Human Rights." Paper presented at the Doing Photography conference, Durham, UK, January 2013.

Phu, Thy. "Refugee Photography and the Subject of Human Interest." In *Photography and Migration,* edited by Tanya Sheehan, 135–49. London: Routledge, 2018.

Phu, Thy. "Shooting the Movement: Black Panther Party Photography and the Traditions of Protest." *Canadian Review of American Studies* 38, no. 1 (2008): 165–89.

Phu, Thy, Elspeth Brown, and Deepali Dewan. "The Family Camera Network." *Photography and Culture* 10, no. 2 (2017): 1–17.

Phu, Thy, Evyn Lê Espiritu, and Donya Ziaee. "Vietnamese Revolutionary Women and Global Solidarity." In *Cold War Camera.* Forthcoming.

Plamper, Jan. *The Stalin Cult: A Study in the Alchemy of Power.* New Haven, CT: Yale University Press, 2012.

Poole, Deborah. *Vision, Race and Modernity: A Visual Economy of the Andean Image World.* Princeton, NJ: Princeton University Press, 1997.

"The Pursuit of Beauty." *Vietnam Heritage Magazine* 7, no. 4 (2014). www.vietnamheritage.com .vn/pages/en/208143542o515-The-pursuit-of-beauty.html.

Raiford, Leigh. *Imprisoned in a Luminous Glare: Photography and the African American Freedom Struggle.* Chapel Hill: University of North Carolina Press, 2011.

Reddy, William. *The Navigation of Feeling: A Framework for the History of Emotions.* Cambridge: Cambridge University Press, 2001.

Reid, Susan E. *Style and Socialism: Modernity and Material Culture in Post-war Eastern Europe.* Oxford: Berg, 2000.

Rose, Gillian. *Doing Family Photography: The Domestic, the Public and the Politics of Sentiment.* London: Routledge, 2010.

Rosenfeld, Gavriel. "Why Do We Ask 'What If?' Reflections on the Function of Alternate History." *History and Theory* 41, no. 4 (2002): 90–103.

Rosenwein, Barbara *Emotional Communities in the Middle Ages.* Ithaca, NY: Cornell University Press, 2006.

Rosler, Martha. "In, Around, and Afterthoughts (on Documentary Photography)." In *Martha Rosler: 3 Works, 1. The Restoration of High Culture in Chile; 2. The Bowery in Two Inadequate Descriptive Systems; 3. In, Around, and Afterthoughts (On Documentary Photography).* 1981. Halifax: Nova Scotia College of Art and Design, 2006.

Ross, Gary, dir. *Free State of Jones.* Burbank, CA: STX Entertainment.

Salaff, Janet, and Judith Merkle. "Women in Revolution: The Lessons of the Soviet Union and China." *Berkeley Journal of Sociology* 15 (1970): 182.

Schneider, Rebecca. *Performing Remains: Art and War in Times of Theatrical Reenactment.* Abingdon, UK: Routledge, 2011.

Schwartz, Joan. "The Album, the Art Market, and the Archives." Paper delivered at the Collecting and Curating Photographs: Between Private and Public Collections colloquium, Ryerson Image Centre, Toronto, Canada, May 3, 2014.

Schwenkel, Christina. *The American War in Contemporary Vietnam: Transnational Remembrance and Representation.* Indianapolis: Indiana University Press, 2009.

Schwenkel, Christina. "Exhibiting War, Reconciling Pasts: Photographic Representation and Transnational Commemoration in Contemporary Vietnam." *Journal of Vietnamese Studies* 3, no. 1 (winter 2008): 36–77. Accessed September 16, 2017. doi:10.1525/vs.2008.3.1.36.

Schwenkel, Christina. "Rethinking Asian Mobilities: Socialist Migration and Postsocialist Repatriation of Vietnamese Contract Workers in East Germany." *Critical Asian Studies* 46, no. 2 (2014): 235–48.

Schwenkel, Christina, and Ann Marie Leshkowich, eds. "Neoliberalism in Vietnam." Special issue, *positions: east asia critique* 20, no. 2 (2012). Accessed September 16, 2017. doi:10.1215 /106798471538461.

Sedgwick, Eve Kosofsky. *Touching Feeling.* Durham, NC: Duke University Press, 2003.

Sekula, Allan. "The Body and the Archive." *October* 39 (1986): 3–64.

Sekula, Allan. *Photography against the Grain: Essays and Photo Works, 1973–1983.* Halifax, NS: Press of the Nova Scotia College of Art and Design, 1984.

Seo, Seomin. "Marginal Majority at the Postcolonial News Agency: Foreign Journalistic Hires at the Associated Press." *Journalism Studies* 17, no. 1 (2016): 39–46.

Shah, Nayan. *Stranger Intimacy: Contesting Race, Sexuality, and the Law in the North American West.* Berkeley: University of California Press, 2011.

Sharpe, Christina. *In the Wake: On Blackness and Being.* Durham, NC: Duke University Press, 2016.

Shayne, Julie D. *The Revolution Question: Feminisms in El Salvador, Chile, and Cuba.* New Brunswick, NJ: Rutgers University Press, 2004.

Shephard, Alex. "The Insidious Ideology of Ken Burns's *The Vietnam War.*" *New Republic,* September 19, 2017. https://newrepublic.com/article/144864/insidious-ideology-ken-burnss -vietnam-war.

Shipler, David K. "In Vietnam, a Patriot without a Place." *Shipler Report,* December 2, 2016. Accessed January 19, 2017. http://shiplerreport.blogspot.com.

A Short Guide to News Coverage in Viet Nam. Saigon AP Bureau Handbook, 1963. Accessed October 19, 2017. www.pbs.org/weta/reportingamericaatwar/reporters/browne/ap_01.html.

Small, Melvin. *Covering Dissent: The Media and the Anti-Vietnam War Movement.* New Brunswick, NJ: Rutgers University Press, 1994.

Small Wars Manual. 1940. Washington, DC: U.S. Marine Corps, 2009.

Smith, Shawn Michelle. *American Archives: Gender, Race, and Class in Visual Culture.* Durham, NC: Duke University Press, 1999.

Smith, Shawn Michelle. *At the Edge of Sight: Photography and the Unseen.* Durham, NC: Duke University Press, 2013.

Smith, Shawn Michelle. *Photographic Remains.* Duke University Press. Forthcoming.

Smith, Shawn Michelle, and Sharon Sliwinski, eds. *Photography and the Optical Unconscious.* Durham, NC: Duke University Press, 2017.

Smyth, Frank. "Out on a Limb: The Use and Abuse of Stringers in the Combat Zone." *Columbia Journalism Review* 31, no. 6 (1992): 43–45.

Somerstein, Rachel. "War Photography." *Afterimage* 41, no. 3 (2013): 36.

Sontag, Susan. *On Photography*. New York: Farrar, Straus and Giroux, 1977.

Sontag, Susan. *Trip to Hanoi*. New York: Farrar, Straus and Giroux, 1969.

Spector, Ronald H. *Advice and Support: The Early Years, 1941–1960*. Washington, DC: Government Printing Office, 1988.

Spence, Jo. *Putting Myself in the Picture*. Seattle: Cornet, 1998.

Spence, Jo, and Patricia Holland, eds. *Family Snaps: The Meanings of Domestic Photography*. London: Virago, 1991.

Spencer, Robyn. *The Revolution Has Come: Black Power, Gender, and the Black Panther Party in Oakland*. Durham, NC: Duke University Press, 2016.

Stallabrass, Julian. *Memory of Fire: Images of War and the War of Images*. Brighton, UK: Photoworks, 2013.

Stein, Sally. "Mainstream Difference: The Distinctive Looks of *Life* and *Look* in US Media Culture." Paper presented at the Print Matters Workshop, New York Public Library, April 10–11, 2016.

Steinman, Ron. *Women in Vietnam: The Oral History*. Westport, CT: Hutton Electronic, 2005.

Stewart, Mart A. "Teaching *Gone with the Wind* in the Socialist Republic of Vietnam." *Southern Cultures* 11, no. 3 (2005): 9–34.

Stoler, Ann Laura. *Along the Archival Grain: Epistemic Anxieties and Colonial Common Sense*. Princeton, NJ: Princeton University Press, 2010.

Strassler, Karen. *Refracted Visions: Popular Photography and National Modernity in Java*. Durham, NC: Duke University Press, 2010.

Sturken, Marita. *Tangled Memories: The Vietnam War, the AIDS Epidemic, and the Politics of Remembering*. Berkeley: University of California Press, 1997.

Swerdlow, Amy. "'Not My Son, Not Your Son, Not Their Sons': Mothers against the Vietnam Draft." In *Give Peace a Chance: Exploring the Vietnam Antiwar Movement*, edited by Melvin Small and William D. Hoover, 159–70. Syracuse, NY: Syracuse University Press, 1991.

Tagg, John. *The Burden of Representation: Essays on Photographies and Histories*. Minneapolis: University of Minnesota Press, 1988.

Tai, Hue-Tam Ho. *The Country of Memory: Remaking the Past in Late Socialist Vietnam*. Berkeley, CA: University of California Press, 2001.

Takata, Ellen. "Photography in Vietnam from the End of the Nineteenth Century to the Start of the Twentieth Century, by Nguyễn Đức Hiệp." *Trans Asia Photography Review* 4, no. 2 (2014). Accessed October 7, 2017. https://quod.lib.umich.edu/t/tap/7977573.0004.204/photography-in-vietnam-from-the-end-of-the-nineteenth?rgn=main, view=fulltext.

Tang, Xiaobing. *Visual Culture in Contemporary China: Paradigms and Shifts*. Cambridge: Cambridge University Press, 2015.

Taylor, Sandra C. *Vietnamese Women at War: Fighting for Ho Chi Minh and the Revolution*. Lawrence: University of Kansas Press, 1999.

Teigrob, Robert. *Warming Up to the Cold War: Canada and United States' Coalition of the Willing, from Hiroshima to Korea*. Toronto: University of Toronto Press, 2009.

Tétreault, Mary Ann ed. *Women and Revolution in Africa, Asia, and the New World*. Columbia: University of South Carolina Press, 1994.

Tétreault, Mary Ann. "Women and Revolution in Vietnam." In *Women and Revolution in Af-

rica, Asia, and the New World, edited by Mary Ann Tétreault, 111–36. Columbia: University of South Carolina Press, 1994.

Tran, Nhung Tuyet. "Woman as Nation: Tradition and Modernity Narratives in Vietnamese Histories." *Gender and History* 24, no. 2 (2012): 411–30.

Trinh, Mai Diễm. *30 Years of Vietnam's Cinema Art*. Hanoi: Vietnam Film Archives, 1983.

Tsing, Anna Lowenhaupt. *Friction: An Ethnography of Global Connection*. Princeton, NJ: Princeton University Press, 2005.

Tuck, Eve, and K. Wayne Yang. "Unbecoming Claims: Pedagogies of Refusal in Qualitative Research." *Qualitative Inquiry* 20, no. 6 (2014): 811–18.

Turner, Karen Gottschang, and Phan Thanh Ho. *Even the Women Must Fight: Memories of War from North Vietnam*. New York: Wiley, 1998.

"Vietnam 'Needs Ministry for Women.'" *Vietnam Investment Review*, March 6–12, 1995.

The Vietnam War. PBS. Accessed March 18, 2019. www.pbs.org/kenburns/the-vietnam-war /home/?utm_source=promourl&utm_campaign=vietnamwar_2017&utm_medium=direct.

Vietnamese Women, Vietnam Studies 10. Hanoi: Xunhasaba, 1966.

Võ Nguyễn Giáp. *People's War, People's Army*. Honolulu: University Press of the Pacific, 2001.

Volkman, Alice Toby, ed. *Cultures of Transnational Adoption*. Durham, NC: Duke University Press, 2005.

Wakeham, Pauline. "Unreconciled Archives: The Truth and Reconciliation Commission of Canada, the Struggle for Settler State Records, and the Future of History." Forthcoming.

Westad, Odd Arne. *The Global Cold War: Third World Interventions and the Making of Our Times*. Cambridge: Cambridge University Press, 2007.

Wexler, Laura. *Tender Violence: Domestic Visions in an Age of U.S. Imperialism*. Chapel Hill: University of North Carolina Press, 2000.

"What Counts as Manipulation." *World Press Photo*. Accessed September 8, 2017. www.world pressphoto.org/activities/photo-contest/verification-process/what-counts-as-manipulation.

Whitaker, Reginald, and Steve Hewitt. *Canada and the Cold War*. Toronto: Lorimer, 2003.

Williams, Linda. *Playing the Race Card: Melodramas of Black and White from Uncle Tom to O. J. Simpson*. Princeton, NJ: Princeton University Press, 2002.

Wu, Tzu-Chun Judy. *Radicals on the Road: Internationalism, Orientalism, and Feminism during the Vietnam Era*. Ithaca, NY: Cornell University Press, 2013.

Young, Marilyn B. *The Vietnam Wars, 1945–1990*. New York: HarperCollins, 1991.

Zarzycka, Marta. *Gendered Tropes in War Photography: Mothers, Mourners, Soldiers*. New York: Routledge, 2017.

Zelizer, Barbie. *About to Die: How News Images Move the Public*. Oxford: Oxford University Press, 2010.

Zhuang, Wubin. *Photography in Southeast Asia: A Survey*. Singapore: National University of Singapore Press, 2017.

Zuromskis, Catherine. *Snapshot Photography: The Lives of Images*. Cambridge, MA: MIT Press, 2013.

www.ingramcontent.com/pod-product-compliance
Lightning Source LLC
Chambersburg PA
CBHW051211170526
45166CB00005B/1847